Britain's rural Muslims

MANCHESTER
1824

Manchester University Press

Britain's rural Muslims

Rethinking integration

Sarah Hackett

Manchester University Press

Published by Manchester University Press
Altrincham Street, Manchester M1 7JA
www.manchesteruniversitypress.co.uk

British Library Cataloguing-in-Publication Data
A catalogue record for this book is available from the British Library

ISBN 978 1 5261 1014 5 hardback
ISBN 978 1 5261 1015 2 paperback

First published 2020

Typeset by Newgen Publishing UK

Contents

Preface and acknowledgements

This book is the first comprehensive study of Muslim migrant integration in rural Britain across the post-1960s period. It stems from an interest in both migration policies and the everyday lives of ethnic minority communities at the local level, as well as a sense that there is a need to shift the focus on British Muslims away from urban conurbations of settlement towards more non-metropolitan and peripheral settings. It uses Wiltshire as a case study, a county in the south-west of England whose local authority and Muslim migrant populations have long recognised the inherent rurality of their local surroundings. The book draws upon both a range of previously unexplored archival material and oral histories carried out with members of the Muslim communities, and reveals what is a clear, and often complex, relationship between rurality and integration. In doing so, it challenges the long-held presumption that local authorities in more rural areas have been inactive, and even disinterested, in devising and implementing migration, integration and diversity policies, and sheds light on small and dispersed Muslim communities that have traditionally been written out of Britain's immigration history.

The study of Muslim integration in Britain in historical perspective across the post-1960s period is not without its challenges and difficulties. Indeed, much of the local authority documentation drawn upon throughout this book is framed within discussions on ethnicity and race, not religion, due to religious affiliation not being considered a significant marker of identity until more recently, and since the 1990s especially. Furthermore, whilst the inherent diversity of Wiltshire's Muslim communities' experiences and identities is central to the book's arguments, its focus on Muslims undoubtedly leads to the prioritisation of religion over what are other equally important components of identity, such as class, ethnicity and gender. Some challenges emerged as a result of studying Muslim populations in a more rural setting at the county level. Wiltshire's local authority did not have one specific committee or unit that monopolised issues of migration, integration and local Muslim populations' needs and demands. To the contrary, debates, policies and strategies permeated numerous levels of local government and a wide range of committees and sub-committees, meaning that finding the necessary documentation required extensive and detailed archival research. Similarly, Wiltshire's Muslim communities are small and dispersed across what is a large county divided by Salisbury Plain. Thus, it was necessary to build up trust and engage with multiple scattered, and at times 'hidden', Muslim communities across a wide geography.

More often than not, historical research is a solitary task, but I have been fortunate to receive advice and support from a wide range of people throughout the completion of this book. The challenges and difficulties that such a study is prone to were mitigated by the great deal of help and support this project received in Wiltshire from the beginning. I am incredibly thankful to the staff at the Wiltshire and Swindon History Centre in Chippenham for their assistance and patience, and for going out of their way to make suggestions and allow me to access uncatalogued material. I am extremely grateful to Lance Allan at Trowbridge Town Council, Simon Fisher at Devizes Town Council and Steve Jones at Swindon Borough Council for granting me access to minute books and providing me with spaces in which to consult them, and to Darryl Moody at Swindon Central Library whose knowledge and generous help proved invaluable. I owe special thanks to Farzana Saker and Wali Rahman for doing so much to offer me an insight into Wiltshire's Muslim communities, and for inviting me to community events and always making me feel welcome.

At Bath Spa University, I am grateful to both fellow historians and colleagues from across the institution for their encouragement and support, and in particular to Dr David Coast, Dr Alison Hems, Prof. Iftikhar Malik, Prof. Alan Marshall, Dr Helen Moore, Dr Andrew Smart, Prof. Astrid Swenson and Dr Heather Winlow. I am thankful to the university for the financial support I received, which allowed me to have the oral history interviews transcribed and attend numerous conferences where I was able to present and develop my arguments and ideas. Many thanks also to my students who have shown such an interest in migration history and have challenged me to think in new ways. I have also continued to benefit from the academic camaraderie, encouragement and guidance of many colleagues, both within and beyond the field of migration history, and I am particularly grateful to Prof. Lawrence Black, Dr Ranji Devadason, Prof. Christhard Hoffmann, Dr Samantha Knapton, Prof. Panikos Panayi, Prof. Philippe Rygiel, Prof. Gavin Schaffer, Prof. Marlou Schrover and Dr Brian Shaev. I would also like to thank the anonymous reviewers who provided very useful and encouraging comments on both the book proposal and the manuscript draft, and Manchester University Press for their patience and work getting this book ready for publication. Any remaining mistakes and shortcomings are, of course, my own.

My family and friends have supported this book project from the beginning, especially my dad who read drafts of all chapters. I am thankful for their love, patience and words of encouragement. Above all, this book was made possible by my husband, Matthew, who has been unfailingly supportive, offered advice, and helped with the editorial process. Finally, my greatest debt of gratitude is to the people I interviewed as part of this project. They showed me incredible warmth and hospitality, gave me access to their lives and shared their stories. I am fully aware that nothing I write could ever do justice to their rich and vibrant experiences of migration, but I hope this book is a start. Their personal testimonies are evidence of the need to move beyond both the rhetoric of confrontation, incompatibility and suspicion, and the study of major conurbations of Muslim settlement. Therefore, it is with great appreciation, admiration and respect for Wiltshire's Muslim communities that I dedicate this book to them.

Introduction: Muslim integration in Britain – a theoretical and analytical framework

The history of Muslim communities in Britain is widely documented. A small number of Ottoman Muslims were already present during the late sixteenth century and, as a result of vast imperial connections and its reputation as a place of opportunity, Muslims migrated from the Indian subcontinent, the Middle East and North Africa during the late eighteenth and nineteenth centuries. Furthermore, it was the Indian, Somali and Yemeni seamen who began arriving particularly after the opening of the Suez Canal in 1869, and settled in port cities and towns like Cardiff, Liverpool and South Shields, who are often perceived to have comprised Britain's first Muslim communities.[1] Yet despite this rich historical context, the vast majority of Muslims in Britain today have their roots in the nation's post-1945 immigration history. A mass influx of Muslim immigrants from the Indian subcontinent took place during the 1950s and 1960s as a result of both a need for workers to help with Britain's post-war economic reconstruction and the process of decolonisation, and was followed by large-scale family reunification. Other Muslim communities who arrived and settled across the post-war years consisted of economic migrants, students, skilled professionals and refugees from a range of countries in the West Indies, the Middle East, the Balkans, and North and East Africa, including Bosnia, Egypt, Guyana, Iraq, Morocco, Saudi Arabia, Somalia, Tunisia and Turkey.[2]

There is an increasingly multidisciplinary, sizeable and vibrant academic literature on Islam and Muslims in post-war Britain, much of which has been dominated by the larger, and thus more visible, Muslim communities from the Indian subcontinent, and especially those of Bangladeshi and Pakistani origin.[3] This body of research is widely cited and well known, and addresses a plethora of topics and themes, including geographical distribution, residential and employment patterns, educational attainment, multiculturalism, assimilation, social cohesion, segregation, belonging, and religious practices and identities.[4] It portrays British Muslims as having a young age profile, as being overwhelmingly rural in origin and religious, as having strong family values, and as largely marrying within their communities. Furthermore, it documents a prevalence of socio-economic marginalisation and exclusion, discrimination and disadvantage, and struggles regarding identity, recognition and equality of opportunity. More specifically, it has long argued that Muslims in Britain suffer from higher rates of unemployment, have become concentrated in poor-quality housing, experience educational underachievement, endure persistent mis-representation, and suffer ever-increasing levels of racism and Islamophobia.[5] Yet simultaneously, it reminds us that Muslims in Britain have long enjoyed entrepreneurial, political, organisational and leadership success; that they are catching up educationally, especially when it comes to university credentials; and that there is ample evidence that points towards a successful integration into British society.[6] Furthermore, despite these bold and definitive findings and conclusions regarding British Muslims, we are correctly reminded that by no means do they constitute one homogenous community.[7] To the contrary, Muslims in Britain originate from a range of ethnic, social, cultural and lin-guistic backgrounds, belong to various religious denominations, and represent numerous migration experiences, levels of education, religious practices, and generational and gender differences. Some are religiously active, whilst others have inherited their religion, but do not practise it, and their experiences of migration and integration have naturally been varied and multifaceted.

It is a common assumption that this history of post-war Muslim minority populations in Britain is a history of urban communities. Indeed, the historiog-raphy largely depicts first-generation Muslim settlers as rural–urban migrants who originated from rural areas like Anatolia, Azad Kashmir and Sylhet in Turkey, Pakistan and Bangladesh, respectively, and became concentrated in a handful of British cities.[8] This is not surprising as it is primarily cities with sizeable migrant populations that have long provided the geographical frameworks within which a significant share of post-war migration has taken place. Whether accounts of inner-city racial tension and discrimination during the 1960s and 1970s,[9] studies of individual minority communities of the 1980s and 1990s,[10] or the increased focus on cities amongst scholars of migration and diaspora during the 2000s,[11] immigration has long been associated with the urban landscape. With regard to Muslim communities specifically across the post-war period, they quickly became concentrated in a small number of large urban areas: Greater London, the East Midlands, Greater Manchester, the West Midlands and West Yorkshire.[12] As a consequence, it has overwhelmingly been the likes of Birmingham, Bradford, Leicester, London and Manchester that have come to represent Britain's story of Muslim migration and settlement.[13]

Conversely, an assessment of smaller Muslim migrant communities in more rural and semi-rural areas remains overwhelmingly absent from the academic literature, and it is this historiographical gap that has acted as inspiration for this book. It examines the previously unexplored relationship between Muslim migrant integration and rural Britain by using the county of Wiltshire in the south-west of England as a case study. It adopts a historical approach across the post-1960s period, and assesses both local authority policies and strategies, and Muslim communities' personal experiences of migration and integration in the county. The book offers an insight into a range of areas, sectors and topics in relation to Muslims from various ethnic backgrounds, including Bangladeshi, Indian, Moroccan, Pakistani and Turkish. It charts how Wiltshire's local authority has responded to, and provided for, the arrival and settlement of Muslim communities, as well as how the county's Muslims' migration and integration experiences have been shaped by their rural surroundings.[14] In doing so, it suggests that there has long existed a clear rural dimension to Muslim integration in Britain.

The rural context

With immigration, integration and diversity traditionally being perceived as urban phenomena, issues of migration and race have rarely been associated with rural Britain.[15] Instead, in the words of Sarah Neal, 'pastoral images of England – rolling green fields, winding lanes, cream teas, chocolate box villages – have, historically and contemporarily, provided the corner-stones of a specific national identity'.[16] Despite calls to recognise the fact that the historical correlation between British rurality and 'ethnic purity' is being challenged by the presence of 'people of colour',[17] rural Britain continues to be seen as being white, pure, safe, stable, peaceful and still untouched by immigration. As Neil Chakraborti and Jon Garland argue, 'the rhetoric of rural living has the capacity to evoke powerful feelings of patriotism and nationalism, characterized, for example, by images of "England's green and pleasant land"... such imagery conjures up notions of a homogenous, quintessentially English haven to which the more problem-ridden urban world can aspire'.[18] The consequence of this has been twofold. Firstly, the academic research that exists on immigration, race and minority communities in rural Britain is fairly limited compared to that which has been carried out at the city level. Secondly, the available research has shown that the prevalence of overwhelmingly small ethnic minority communities in more rural settings has often led to both increased racial harassment and a tendency amongst local authorities to maintain that migration and integration are not pressing policy concerns. Thus, despite enduring racism and discrimination, minority communities living in more rural areas have often been ignored from both an academic and political perspective.

Nevertheless, there was a surge in scholarly attention regarding rural racism and intolerance from the 1990s to the mid-2000s. Much of this research was local in focus, and went some way towards highlighting the frequency of racist prejudice and racial exclusion, and the need for adequate policy responses, in more rural contexts across Britain. The turning point and inspiration for this focus on rural racism is often perceived to have at least partially been the publication of a series of reports during the early to mid-1990s, most notably *Keep Them in Birmingham* in 1992, which was commissioned by the Commission for Racial Equality (CRE) and examined both the prevalence of racism and local authority responses in Cornwall, Devon, Dorset and Somerset.[19] It found that not only was racism extensive in the south-west, but also that there was 'widespread complacency' and a perception that 'there is no problem here'.[20] Sarah Neal has maintained that it was the publication of this research that helped advance an awareness that policy intervention in the areas of rural race and racism was needed.[21]

This notion that racism and discrimination were common in rural Britain, yet simultaneously 'invisible', was a theme that dominated subsequent studies. From Norfolk to Lincolnshire and from Shropshire to rural Scotland, not only was it argued that small rural ethnic minority populations also experienced racism, were often more isolated and vulnerable than their urban counterparts, and that they lacked a community support network, but it was maintained that they continued to be overlooked from a policy perspective and that context-specific responses were lacking.[22] These works considered a range of rural and semi-rural areas and explored experiences of racism amongst small ethnic minority communities, and stressed that there was a pressing need to further develop an understanding of the attributes and profiles of rural minority populations. Writing at the turn of the twenty-first century, Mohammed Dhalech contended that, compared to what was the case in urban areas, work on issues of race equality in rural Britain had 'just begun'.[23] Philomena de Lima went as far as to argue that, during the early 2000s, the rural policy context still continued to largely ignore ethnic minority communities, and that there was no clear strategy on how to address rural racism and race issues.[24] Moreover, these findings and pleas of the 1990s and early 2000s emerged alongside a belief that rural Britain's ethnic minority communities were likely to grow in size in subsequent years due to a number of factors, including increased mobility and job opportunities.[25]

Yet contrary to what one might expect, there has since been something of a lull in academic research on immigration, race and minority communities in rural Britain. In fact, since the mid-2000s, studies addressing the relationship between rurality and ethnicity have been sporadic at best. Key works from the last decade or so include those of Katharine Tyler on Leicestershire, which uncover majority white racialised urban and rural discourses, as well as perceptions and portrayals of British Asians amongst white middle-class villagers.[26] Further examples are the studies by Kye Askins and Caroline Bressey on how ethnic minorities perceive and make use of rural space, and on the extent to which the black presence has been excluded from white imaginaries of the English countryside, respectively.[27] Some research, inspired by the migration flows that followed the 2004 enlargement of the European Union, has addressed Eastern European migrants working in the agricultural and horticultural sectors in rural Britain.[28] Other studies, although not focusing on the rural context specifically, have also gone some way towards shifting the attention away from inner cities and urban areas. These include the study by Anoop Nayak on race and racism in white English suburbs, and that of Daniel Burdsey on racism and marginalisation at the English seaside.[29]

Thus, there is an awareness that further investigation into migration and diversity in more rural and peripheral areas with small ethnic minority populations is needed, and that more needs to be done to frame this scholarship within wider debates on race and multiculturalism in Britain. Yet as Charlotte Williams argued in 2007 in relation to her work on the Welsh countryside, 'the race/racism and the countryside debate has, with few exceptions, progressed... arguably as something of a sideshow to the "real stuff" of British race relations'; this argument still holds true today.[30] This is especially the case regarding the arrival, settlement and integration of Muslim communities, a topic covered by only a handful of studies. Most notably is Rhys Dafydd Jones' work, which exposes the challenges and experiences encountered by Muslims in West Wales.[31] Similarly, Larry Ray and Kate Reed and Tom Villis and Mireille Hebing's research on East Kent and Cambridge, respectively, reveals how smaller Muslim communities that reside outside of the main conurbations of Muslim settlement frequently encounter barriers when trying to practise their religion and constitute fragmented communities.[32] Beyond these studies, whilst the wider historiography on ethnic minority communities in rural Britain periodically mentions Muslims, and the literature on Muslims in Britain occasionally acknowledges the rural context, neither deals with more rural Muslim communities in great detail or depth.[33] Instead, Muslims in Britain continue to largely be portrayed exclusively as having transitioned from a rural, and often South Asian, background to British cities with significant Muslim and ethnic minority populations.[34] Whilst this book acknowledges that residents of more rural areas are more likely to be white and of a Christian religious affiliation, it also recognises that there are smaller and scattered Muslim migrant populations, and ethnic minorities more generally, who live outside the urban centres associated with migration about whom we still lack an understanding.

Aims of the book

This study shifts the focus away from the traditional British hubs of migration towards comparatively smaller, and previously unexplored, Muslim communities. In doing so, it aims to challenge the notion that migration is purely an urban phenomenon, as well as the practice of reducing the study of locality in migration studies to the study of cities, and global or gateway cities in particular.[35] It also responds to calls for both a need to increase our understanding of migration at a local level in more peripheral and non-metropolitan settings, and for research on Muslims in Britain to recognise that geography and locality matter in shaping British Muslims' experiences and identities, and that there is a need to move beyond the main areas of Muslim settlement.[36] Therefore, the study aims to build upon works that have invoked varying definitions and interpretations of 'rurality', and gone some way towards shedding light on the experiences of smaller and more 'hidden' Muslim communities in Cambridge, semi-rural East Kent, and in and around the market towns of West Wales.[37]

Indeed, the notion of 'the rural' runs throughout this study, a concept whose definition and meaning have been widely contested and debated. 'Rurality' has been used to describe more peripheral communities with small migrant populations that are perceived to be largely static and homogenous. There have been varying definitions according to population size and transport links, as well as levels of deprivation, poverty and social issues. The concept has been applied to localities whose wider geographical contexts are considered to be sparsely populated, as well as to settings that are associated with a romanticised image of national identity and idyllic environments. Furthermore, it is increasingly being recognised that there is no one definition of 'the rural', and that how rurality is identified changes across both time and locality.[38] This book engages with all of these definitions at different points and to varying degrees. Moreover, this study is also rooted in the fact that both Wiltshire's local authority and its Muslim minority communities have conventionally stressed the rurality of their policies and experiences, respectively.

The notion of integration also sits at the very centre of this study. Although like 'rurality', it also remains a debated and contested term, 'integration' continues to be widely used in research on migration across disciplines and is recognised as a key analytical tool for the study of migrant communities.[39] Following the frameworks established by a range of scholars, both historians and non-historians alike, this study adopts a broad definition of integration, taking it to refer to what Leo Lucassen terms 'the general sociological mechanism that describes the way in which all people, migrants as well as non-migrants, find their place in society'.[40] Rather than perceiving integration to mean assimilation, it interprets it as a long-term and evolving process, and recognises significant differences according to ethnicity, class, gender, generation, religious identities and migration backgrounds. Furthermore, it understands that integration is not a one-way process, but that receiving societies adapt in a number of ways in order to accommodate migrant populations, and that successful integration should not necessarily be seen as the natural conclusion to any migratory experience. Whilst there are many works that have studied integration at a fixed moment in time, in relation to one migrant community, and from the perspective of either the receiving society or the migrant community in question, they tend to only partially capture what constitutes the integration process.[41] This book proposes an examination of how integration has been approached and interpreted by both members of local Muslim populations and a local authority, the extent to which this has or has not changed across time and ethnic groups, and the degree to which there has existed a clear rural sphere to the integration process.

Framed around this notion of integration are five key arguments and themes that run throughout this book and through which it makes a contribution to academic scholarship. Firstly, in assessing integration from the perspectives of both local government and the Muslim communities themselves, this study reveals that Wiltshire's rural nature and identity have long played a part in influencing the integration process in a range of different ways. In doing so, it builds upon the aforementioned literature that recognises that there is a clear rural dimension to local-level migration and integration policymaking and the experiences of ethnic minorities in Britain, whilst also both championing the need to extend the academic focus beyond the more traditional emphasis on rural racism and offering an unprecedented insight into Muslim communities specifically. Secondly, this study examines the manner in which Wiltshire's local authority has negotiated and approached immigration, integration and diversity across the post-1960s period, as well as the relationship between local- and national-level migration policy and mandate. Thereby, it uncovers the extent to which Britain's post-war immigration history and political framework have filtered down and influenced the county's policies and practices. Whilst some attention has been awarded to how urban authorities with sizeable migrant populations have adopted national policy directives and legislation,[42] we still lack an understanding of the extent to which more rural areas with smaller ethnic minority communities have adhered to a national mandate. Contrary to a large proportion of the academic literature that asserts that local authorities in more rural areas have often failed to devise adequate policy responses,[43] this work argues that Wiltshire's local authority has long acknowledged, and actively responded to, its Muslim migrant populations as well as its ethnic minority communities more broadly.

Thirdly, this book supports and furthers the increasingly sizeable body of academic literature that moves beyond the study of the traditional 'national model of integration', and recognises the importance of studying both migration policy-making and migrant communities' experiences and integration at the local level.[44] In doing so, it argues that offering a historical insight into a more rural locality increases our understanding of the local dimension of migration that has largely been shaped by the study of the urban context.[45] Fourthly, this book champions the need to both study Muslim migrant populations at a grassroots level and to pursue a more interdisciplinary and cross-sector approach to migration history in doing so. It purposefully shifts the focus away from the heated political and popular accusations and debates regarding conflict and incompatibility that British Muslim communities have found themselves at the centre of, especially since the turn of the twenty-first century. Indeed, the Rushdie Affair, Islamist extremism and terrorism, and fears and suspicions regarding Shari'a law, the treatment of women and cultural segregation have firmly categorised Muslims as 'them' in the 'them and us' dichotomy. They have become the main protagonists in allegations of parallel lives, the retreat from political multiculturalism and the perceived need for greater community cohesion. To the contrary, this book's local-level approach offers a much more positive assessment of the integration of British Muslims in a more rural and peripheral setting. It does so by bridging a range of different indicators of integration and topics, from education, housing and entrepreneur-ship to multiculturalism, social cohesion and religious identity and practice. These themes feed into the fifth point, and what is the book's central argument, which is that the integration of Muslim migrant communities in Wiltshire has long been pursued and achieved in a number of ways. Indeed, despite the fact that there were often a series of limitations to the county's local authority's measures, policies and practices, and that its Muslim populations by no means avoided experiences of constraint, discrimination and prejudice, there was nevertheless a clear and con-sistent commitment to pursuing integration on both sides.

In charting and assessing Wiltshire's local authority's immigrant, integration and diversity policies and strategies and its Muslim communities' experiences of migration and integration in the county across the post-1960s period, this study both draws and builds upon concepts, findings and theories from a range of different bodies of scholarship beyond those that have already been mentioned. These include historical works on the topics of immigration to, and migrant communities and Muslims in, Britain;[46] and studies addressing the migrant and Muslim experience in Britain's employment, housing and educa-tion sectors,[47] Muslim practice, recognition and representation,[48] and racism, victimisation and Islamophobia;[49] as well as those that have examined Muslim communities of particular ethnic backgrounds, and considered the place of Islam in wider debates on migrant integration.[50] In doing so, this book aims to complement these various historiographies through its unique combined historical and rural approach.

Sources and chapter overview

This book attempts to move beyond the traditional study of migration that draws upon either government documentation or oral history interviews.[51] Instead, it pursues the study of integration from the perspectives of both local government and the Muslim communities themselves. As such, the aim is to re-examine, and develop a more dynamic understanding of, Muslim integration in Britain in a more rural setting. It charts local government policy through major turning points across the post-war period, including the introduction of race relations legislation, the resettlement of Ugandan Asians, the emergence of a multicultural ideology and subsequent community cohesion agenda, and the persistent shift in the construction of difference from a focus on 'race' to 'ethnicity' to 'faith'. In an attempt to capture the complete picture, this study adopts a lenient and flexible definition of 'local policy', taking it to include not just adopted policy, but also local authority correspondence, reports and suggested measures and practices that also offer an insight into Wiltshire's local authority's attitudes towards its Muslim migrant populations. Furthermore, it considers inaction, and thus 'non-policy', as well as local institutions, such as Community Relations Councils, as crucial parts of the local policymaking process.[52]

It is important to recognise that it proves difficult to research and assess local-level policymaking with regard to post-war Muslim migrant communities in Britain. For much of the period, and as was also the case at the national level, local authority documents identified minority communities according to their race and ethnicity rather than their religion, and those pertaining to Wiltshire were no exception. Thus, this book aims to study the county's local authority's political response to Muslim minority populations before religious identities and affiliations were officially considered and recorded.[53] This means that whilst there are some references to Muslim communities specifically amongst the documentation employed, minority populations are predominantly discussed along ethnic lines. An additional challenge is that, due to Wiltshire's rural nature and it being home to small Muslim communities, there was no specific unit or committee that was entirely responsible for issues of migration.[54] This resulted in its local authority's response permeating various levels and aspects of local government, from county, district and town councils to a wide range of committees and sub-committees, including those relating to community development and services, education and schools, environment, finance, health, housing, policy and resources, race relations, social services, the resettlement of Ugandan Asians, and youth. More specifically, the local government documentation that this book draws upon, the vast majority of which is held at the Wiltshire and Swindon History Centre, consists largely of agenda papers, correspondence, minutes and reports from a series of councils and committees, which include the Education Committee, the Executive Committee, the Religious Education Standing Advisory Council, the Housing Committee, the North and West Wiltshire, Kennet, Salisbury Racial Equality Council, the County Local Government Joint Committee, and the Environmental Committee, to name but a few.

These government records are used alongside oral history interviews carried out with members of Wiltshire's Muslim communities. An assessment of both the practice of oral history within the field of migration studies and the oral history research carried out for this study specifically will be provided in more detail in Chapter 5.[55] For now, it is important to stress that the interviews uncover the 'human' side of the migration and integration process, and allow for individual and unique histories and voices regarding past and ongoing experiences as Muslims in a more rural and peripheral setting. The interviewees were first-generation, 1.5-generation and second-generation migrants who shared their experiences, perceptions and circumstances across a range of areas, including employment and entrepreneurship, housing and the neighbourhood, the formation of multi-ethnic Muslim communities, racism and prejudice, and religious identity and practice.[56] Thus, the two very different types of sources that sit at the centre of this book provide both an insight into the established narrative of the state and uncover invaluable first-hand Muslim migrant stories and experiences. To a much lesser extent, census data, the press and a number of research reports are also drawn upon. Crucially, rather than limiting the scope to certain dimensions or indicators of integration, this study is shaped around those areas and themes that emerged from the source material, and from the local government documents and oral history testimonies especially.

The next chapter, Chapter 1, introduces Wiltshire and the rationale for choosing this county as a case study. It offers an insight into its towns, economy, landscape, history of immigration and its post-war Muslim communities. Chapters 2 to 4 address local government policy from the early 1960s to the early twenty-first century. They chart policies and political strategies from the arrival of the first waves of post-war Muslim immigration to the passing of the Race Relations Act 1976, the pursuit of multicultural policies during the 1980s, and the subsequent importance awarded to equal opportunities, community cohesion and religious identity. The chapters show that despite persistent claims that more rural areas in Britain have long shied away from devising policies due to their numerically small immigrant communities, a range of measures were introduced in Wiltshire, albeit often at a slower pace, and with less frequency and different priorities than those implemented in cities with larger migrant populations. Chapter 5 draws upon the oral history interviews, which give a voice to what are often visible and long-settled, yet under-researched and 'hidden', Muslim migrant communities whose experiences of integration are simply not captured in the official archival narrative. Chapter 6 places the Wiltshire case study and findings within the context of rural Britain, and considers the extent to which it can be argued that there exists a rural dimension to the integration process. Finally, the conclusion moves beyond the novelty of the Wiltshire case study, and frames the study's key findings and conclusions within a range of debates pertaining to local, national and international contexts.

Notes

1 For an insight into the historical Muslim presence in Britain, see Colin Holmes, *John Bull's Island: Immigration and British Society, 1871–1971* (Basingstoke: Macmillan, 1988); Rozina Visram, *Asians in Britain: 400 Years of History* (London: Pluto Press, 2002); Humayun Ansari, *'The Infidel Within': Muslims in Britain since 1800* (London: Hurst, 2004); and Sophie Gilliat-Ray, *Muslims in Britain: An Introduction* (Cambridge: Cambridge University Press, 2010).

2 See Serena Hussain, *Muslims on the Map: A National Survey of Social Trends in Britain* (London: I.B. Tauris, 2008), pp. 23–37; and Gilliat-Ray, *Muslims in Britain*, pp. 44–52.

3 See Badr Dahya, 'Pakistanis in Britain: transients or settlers?', *Race*, 14:3 (1973), 241–77; Philip Lewis, *Islamic Britain: Religion, Politics and Identity among British Muslims* (London: I.B. Tauris, 1994); and Pnina Werbner, *Imagined Diasporas among Manchester Muslims: The Public Performance of Pakistani Transnational Identity Politics* (Oxford: James Currey, 2002).

4 For some other key works on Muslims and Islam in Britain, see Ansari, *'The Infidel Within'*; Tahir Abbas (ed.), *Muslim Britain: Communities under Pressure* (London: Zed Books, 2005); Tariq Modood, *Multicultural Politics: Racism, Ethnicity and Muslims in Britain* (Edinburgh: Edinburgh University Press, 2005); Peter Hopkins and Richard Gale (eds), *Muslims in Britain: Race, Place and Identities* (Edinburgh: Edinburgh University Press, 2009); Gilliat-Ray, *Muslims in Britain*; John Bowen, *On British Islam: Religion, Law, and Everyday Practice in Shari'a Councils* (Princeton, NJ: Princeton University Press, 2016); and Philip Lewis and Sadek Hamid, *British Muslims: New Directions in Islamic Thought, Creativity and Activism* (Edinburgh: Edinburgh University Press, 2018).

5 See Humayun Ansari, *Muslims in Britain* (London: Minority Rights Group International, 2002); Elizabeth Poole, *Reporting Islam: Media Representations of British Muslims* (London: I.B. Tauris, 2002); Abbas (ed.), *Muslim Britain*; Gilliat-Ray, *Muslims in Britain*; and Waqar Ahmad and Ziauddin Sardar (eds), *Muslims in Britain: Making Social and Political Space* (Abingdon: Routledge, 2012).

6 See Pnina Werbner, 'From rags to riches: Manchester Pakistanis in the textile trade', *New Community*, 8:1–2 (1980), 84–95; Nahid Afrose Kabir, *Young British Muslims: Identity, Culture, Politics and the Media* (Edinburgh: Edinburgh University Press, 2010); Sarah Hackett, *Foreigners, Minorities and Integration: The Muslim Immigrant Experience in Britain and Germany* (Manchester: Manchester University Press, 2013); Mario Peucker and Shahram Akbarzadeh, *Muslim Active Citizenship in the West* (Abingdon: Routledge, 2014), pp. 33–4; and Richard Alba and Nancy Foner, *Strangers No More: Immigration and the Challenges of Integration in North America and Western Europe* (Princeton, NJ: Princeton University Press, 2015).

7 For example, see Ansari, *'The Infidel Within'*, pp. 145–65.

8   See Ceri Peach, 'South Asian migration and settlement in Great Britain, 1951–2001', *Contemporary South Asia*, 15:2 (2006), 133–46; and Olgu Karan, *Economic Survival Strategies of Turkish Migrants in London* (London: Transnational Press, 2017).

9   For example, see John Rex and Robert Moore, *Race, Community and Conflict: A Study of Sparkbrook* (London: Oxford University Press, 1967); and John Rex and Sally Tomlinson, *Colonial Immigrants in a British City: A Class Analysis* (London: Routledge and Keegan Paul, 1979).

10 For example, see Werbner, 'From rags to riches'; and John Eade, 'Identity, nation and religion: educated young Bangladeshi Muslims in London's "East End"', *International Sociology*, 9:3 (1994), 377–94.

11 For example, see Joanna Herbert, *Negotiating Boundaries in the City: Migration, Ethnicity, and Gender in Britain* (Aldershot: Ashgate, 2008); and Seán McLoughlin, William Gould, Ananya Jahanara Kabir and Emma Tomalin (eds), *Writing the City in British Asian Diasporas* (Abingdon: Routledge, 2014).

12 See Tufyal Choudhury, *Muslims in the UK: Policies for Engaged Citizens* (New York and Budapest: Open Society Institute, 2005), p. 204.

13 See Lewis, *Islamic Britain*; Steven Vertovec, 'Multiculturalism, culturalism and public incorporation', *Ethnic and Racial Studies*, 19:1 (1996), 49–69; Werbner, *Imagined Diasporas among Manchester Muslims*; Richard Gale, 'The multicultural city and the politics of religious architecture: urban planning, mosques and meaning-making in Birmingham, UK', *Built Environment*, 30:1 (2004), 30–44; McLoughlin, Gould, Kabir and Tomalin (eds), *Writing the City in British Asian Diasporas*; and Sarah Glynn, *Class, Ethnicity and Religion in the Bengali East End: A Political History* (Manchester: Manchester University Press, 2014).

14 Although this study employs the term 'local authority', it charts policies and strategies implemented at various levels of local government, including county, district, town and parish.

15 Whilst some research has been carried out in Scotland and Wales, much of the literature on migrant communities and racism in rural Britain has focused on England.

16 Sarah Neal, 'Rural landscapes, representations and racism: examining multicultural citizenship and policy-making in the English countryside', *Ethnic and Racial Studies*, 25:3 (2002), 443.

17 For example, see Julian Agyeman and Rachel Spooner, 'Ethnicity and the rural environment', in Paul Cloke and Jo Little (eds), *Contested Countryside Cultures: Otherness, Marginalisation and Rurality* (London: Routledge, 1997), pp. 197–217; Jon Garland and Neil Chakraborti, 'Racist victimisation, community safety and the rural: issues and challenges', *British Journal of Community Justice*, 2:3 (2004), 21–32; and Larry Ray and Kate Reed, 'Community, mobility and racism in a semi-rural area: comparing minority experience in East Kent', *Ethnic and Racial Studies*, 28: 2 (2005), 212–34.

18 Neil Chakraborti and Jon Garland, 'England's green and pleasant land? Examining racist prejudice in a rural context', *Patterns of Prejudice*, 38:4 (2004), 384–5.

19 Eric Jay, *'Keep Them in Birmingham'*: *Challenging Racism in South-West England* (London: Commission for Racial Equality, 1992). Two years later, the CRE sponsored a second landmark report on ethnicity and the country-side. See Helen Derbyshire, *Not in Norfolk: Tackling the Invisibility of Racism* (Norwich: Norwich and Norfolk Racial Equality Council, 1994).

20 Jay, *'Keep Them in Birmingham'*, p. 3.

21 Neal, 'Rural landscapes, representations and racism', 453.

22 See Derbyshire, *Not in Norfolk*; Parveen Nizhar, *No Problem? Race Issues in Shropshire* (Telford: Race Equality Forum for Telford and Shropshire, 1995); Satnam Virdee, 'Racial harassment', in Tariq Modood, Richard Berthoud, Jane Lakey, James Nazroo, Patten Smith, Satnam Virdee and Sharon Beishon (eds), *Ethnic Minorities in Britain: Diversity and Disadvantage* (London: Policy Studies Institute, 1997), p. 271; Paul Henderson and Ranjit Kaur (eds), *Rural Racism in the UK: Examples of Community-based Responses* (London: Community Development Foundation, 1999); Philomena de Lima, *Needs Not Numbers: An Exploration of Minority Ethnic Communities in Rural Scotland* (London: Commission for Racial Equality/Community Development Foundation, 2001); Neil Chakraborti and Jon Garland, 'An "invisible" problem? Uncovering the nature of racist victimisation in rural Suffolk', *International Review of Victimology*, 10:1 (2003), 1–17; and Philomena de Lima, ' "Let's keep our heads down and maybe the problem will go away": experiences of rural minority ethnic households in Scotland', in Sarah Neal and Julian Agyeman (eds), *The New Countryside? Ethnicity, Nation and Exclusion in Contemporary Rural Britain* (Bristol: The Policy Press, 2006), pp. 73–97.

23 Mohammed Dhalech, *Challenging Racism in the Rural Idyll* (Exeter: National Association of Citizens Advice Bureaux, 1999), p. 28.

24 Philomena de Lima, 'John O'Groats to Land's End: racial equality in rural Britain?', in Neil Chakraborti and Jon Garland (eds), *Rural Racism* (Cullompton: Willan Publishing, 2004), p. 42.

25 See Neal, 'Rural landscapes, representations and racism', 448.

26 Katharine Tyler, 'Debating the rural and the urban: majority white racialized discourses on the countryside and the city', in Bo Petersson and Katharine Tyler (eds), *Majority Cultures and the Everyday Politics of Ethnic Difference: Whose House is This?* (Basingstoke: Palgrave Macmillan, 2008), pp. 75–93; and Katharine Tyler, 'The English village, whiteness, coloniality and social class', *Ethnicities*, 12:4 (2012), 427–44.

27 Kye Askins, 'Crossing divides: ethnicity and rurality', *Journal of Rural Studies*, 25:4 (2009), 365–75; and Caroline Bressey, 'Cultural archaeology and historical geographies of the black presence in rural England', *Journal of Rural Studies*, 25:4 (2009), 386–95.

28 For example, see Helen Moore, 'Shades of whiteness? English villagers, Eastern European migrants and the intersection of race and class in rural England', *Critical Race and Whiteness Studies*, 9:1 (2013), 1–19; and Allan Findlay and David McCollum, 'Recruitment and employment regimes: migrant labour

channels in the UK's rural agribusiness sector, from accession to recession', *Journal of Rural Studies*, 30 (2013), 10–19.

29   Anoop Nayak, 'Race, affect, and emotion: young people, racism, and graffiti in the postcolonial English suburbs', *Environment and Planning A: Economy and Space*, 42:10 (2010), 2370–92; and Daniel Burdsey, ' "The foreignness is still quite visible in this town": multiculture, marginality and prejudice at the English seaside', *Patterns of Prejudice*, 47:2 (2013), 95–116.

30   Charlotte Williams, 'Revisiting the rural/race debates: a view from the Welsh countryside', *Ethnic and Racial Studies*, 30:5 (2007), 742.

31   Rhys Dafydd Jones, 'Islam and the rural landscape: discourses of absence in West Wales', *Social & Cultural Geography*, 11:8 (2010), 751–68; and Rhys Dafydd Jones, 'Negotiating absence and presence: rural Muslims and "subterranean" sacred spaces', *Space and Polity*, 16:3 (2012), 335–50.

32   Ray and Reed, 'Community, mobility and racism in a semi-rural area'; and Tom Villis and Mireille Hebing, 'Islam and Englishness: issues of culture and identity in the debates over mosque building in Cambridge', *Nationalism and Ethnic Politics*, 20:4 (2014), 415–37.

33   For example, see Sarah Neal and Julian Agyeman (eds), *The New Countryside? Ethnicity, Nation and Exclusion in Contemporary Rural Britain* (Bristol: The Policy Press, 2006); and Hopkins and Gale (eds), *Muslims in Britain*.

34   For example, see Gilliat-Ray, *Muslims in Britain*, p. 210; and Glynn, *Class, Ethnicity and Religion in the Bengali East End*.

35   For a critique of the way in which the study of migration has been restricted to global cities, see Nina Glick Schiller and Ayşe Çağlar, 'Towards a comparative theory of locality in migration studies: migrant incorporation and city scale', *Journal of Ethnic and Migration Studies*, 35:2 (2009), 177–202.

36   See Richard Gale and Peter Hopkins, 'Introduction: Muslims in Britain – race, place and the spatiality of identities', in Peter Hopkins and Richard Gale (eds), *Muslims in Britain: Race, Place and Identities* (Edinburgh: Edinburgh University Press, 2009), p. 15. These arguments and calls have also extended to Northern Ireland. See Paul Hainsworth (ed.), *Divided Society: Ethnic Minorities and Racism in Northern Ireland* (London: Pluto Press, 1998); and Ruth McAreavey, *New Immigration Destinations: Migrating to Rural and Peripheral Areas* (Abingdon: Routledge, 2017).

37   See Ray and Reed, 'Community, mobility and racism in a semi-rural area'; Jones, 'Islam and the rural landscape'; Jones, 'Negotiating absence and presence'; and Villis and Hebing, 'Islam and Englishness'.

38   For an insight into some of these definitions, see Chakraborti and Garland, 'England's green and pleasant land?'; Perminder Dhillon, 'Rethinking rural race equality: early interventions, continuities and changes', in Sarah Neal and Julian Agyeman (eds), *The New Countryside? Ethnicity, Nation and Exclusion in Contemporary Rural Britain* (Bristol: The Policy Press, 2006), pp. 232–3; Jones, 'Islam and the rural landscape'; and McAreavey, *New Immigration Destinations*, pp. 6–7.

39   See Rinus Penninx, Karen Kraal, Marco Martiniello and Steven Vertovec (eds), *Citizenship in European Cities: Immigrants, Local Politics and*

Integration Policies (Aldershot: Ashgate, 2004); Jonathan Laurence, *The Emancipation of Europe's Muslims: The State's Role in Minority Integration* (Princeton, NJ: Princeton University Press, 2012); Marlou Schrover and Willem Schinkel (eds), *The Language of Inclusion and Exclusion in Immigration and Integration* (Abingdon: Routledge, 2014); and Alba and Foner, *Strangers No More.*

40 Leo Lucassen, *The Immigrant Threat: The Integration of Old and New Migrants in Western Europe since 1850* (Urbana, IL: University of Illinois Press, 2005), p. 18. See also Ibrahim Sirkeci, Betül Dilara Şeker and Ali Çağlar (eds), *Turkish Migration, Identity and Integration* (London: Transnational Press, 2015); and Blanca Garcés-Mascareñas and Rinus Penninx (eds), *Integration Processes and Policies in Europe: Contexts, Levels and Actors* (Dordrecht: Springer, 2016).

41 For a few exceptions, see Lucassen, *The Immigrant Threat*; and Leo Lucassen, David Feldman and Jochen Oltmer (eds), *Paths of Integration: Migrants in Western Europe (1880–2004)* (Amsterdam: Amsterdam University Press, 2006).

42 For example, see Wendy Ball and John Solomos (eds), *Race and Local Politics* (Basingstoke: Macmillan, 1990); Romain Garbaye, *Getting into Local Power: The Politics of Ethnic Minorities in British and French Cities* (Oxford: Blackwell Publishing, 2005); and Sarah Hackett, 'The "local turn" in historical perspective: two city case studies in Britain and Germany', *International Review of Administrative Sciences*, 83:2 (2017), 340–57.

43 Much of this literature has already been cited, but in particular see Jay, '*Keep Them in Birmingham*'; Derbyshire, *Not in Norfolk*; and de Lima, 'John O'Groats to Land's End'.

44 For a few key works that have addressed the British national model of integration, often from a comparative perspective, see Adrian Favell, *Philosophies of Integration: Immigration and the Idea of Citizenship in France and Britain* (Basingstoke: Macmillan Press, 1998); Christian Joppke, *Immigration and the Nation-State: The United States, Germany, and Great Britain* (Oxford: Oxford University Press, 1999); Randall Hansen, *Citizenship and Immigration in Post-war Britain: The Institutional Origins of a Multicultural Nation* (Oxford: Oxford University Press, 2000); and Martin Schain, *The Politics of Immigration in France, Britain, and the United States: A Comparative Study* (Basingstoke: Palgrave Macmillan, 2008).

45 For an insight into some of the literature that has exposed the importance of studying migration at the local level, see Patrick Ireland, *Becoming Europe: Immigration, Integration, and the Welfare State* (Pittsburgh, PA: University of Pittsburgh Press, 2004); Tiziana Caponio and Maren Borkert (eds), *The Local Dimension of Migration Policymaking* (Amsterdam: Amsterdam University Press, 2010); Nina Glick Schiller and Ayşe Çağlar (eds), *Locating Migration: Rescaling Cities and Migrants* (Ithaca, NY: Cornell University Press, 2011); and Tiziana Caponio, Peter Scholten and Ricard Zapata-Barrero (eds), *The Routledge Handbook of the Governance of Migration and Diversity in Cities* (Abingdon: Routledge, 2019).

46   See, for example, Ansari, *'The Infidel Within'*; Gilliat-Ray, *Muslims in Britain*; and Panikos Panayi, *An Immigration History of Britain: Multicultural Racism since 1800* (Harlow: Longman, 2010).

47   For example, see Sally Tomlinson, *Race and Education: Policy and Politics in Britain* (Maidenhead: McGraw-Hill Open University Press, 2008); Ken Clark and Stephen Drinkwater, 'Recent trends in minority ethnic entrepreneurship in Britain', *International Small Business Journal*, 28:2 (2010), 136–46; and Deborah Phillips, 'Claiming spaces: British Muslim negotiations of urban citizenship in an era of new migration', *Transactions of the Institute of British Geographers*, 40:1 (2015), 62–74.

48   See Joel S. Fetzer and J. Christopher Soper, *Muslims and the State in Britain, France, and Germany* (Cambridge: Cambridge University Press, 2005); and Parveen Akhtar, *British Muslim Politics: Examining Pakistani Biraderi Networks* (Basingstoke: Palgrave Macmillan, 2013).

49   See Chris Allen, *Islamophobia* (Farnham: Ashgate, 2010); and John L. Esposito and Ibrahim Kalin (eds), *Islamophobia: The Challenge of Pluralism in the 21st Century* (Oxford: Oxford University Press, 2011).

50   For example, see Alison Shaw, *Kinship and Continuity: Pakistani Families in Britain* (Amsterdam: Harwood Academic, 2000); Ceri Peach, 'Muslims in the 2001 Census of England and Wales: gender and economic disadvantage', *Ethnic and Racial Studies*, 29:4 (2006), 629–55; Myriam Cherti, *Paradoxes of Social Capital: A Multi-Generational Study of Moroccans in London* (Amsterdam: Amsterdam University Press, 2008); Laurence, *The Emancipation of Europe's Muslims*; Bowen, *On British Islam*; and Jed Fazakarley, *Muslim Communities in England 1962–90: Multiculturalism and Political Identity* (Cham: Palgrave Macmillan, 2017).

51   For a few key works that have drawn upon oral history, see Kathy Burrell, *Moving Lives: Narratives of Nation and Migration among Europeans in Post-war Britain* (Aldershot: Ashgate, 2006); and Herbert, *Negotiating Boundaries in the City*. For examples of studies that have made use of government documentation, see Hansen, *Citizenship and Immigration in Post-war Britain*; and Gurharpal Singh, 'Multiculturalism in contemporary Britain: reflections on the "Leicester model"', *International Journal on Multicultural Societies*, 5:1 (2003), 40–54.

52   For an insight into works that have approached and defined local migration policy in this way, see John Solomos, *Race and Racism in Britain* (Basingstoke: Palgrave Macmillan, 2003), pp. 97–8; and Michael Alexander, *Cities and Labour Immigration: Comparing Policy Responses in Amsterdam, Paris, Rome and Tel Aviv* (Aldershot: Ashgate, 2007), p. 38.

53   The Census, for example, did not include a question on religious affiliation until 2001. As a result, attempts to calculate the number of Muslims in Britain, or the size of a specific Muslim community, were mere approximations. For example, see Ceri Peach, 'The Muslim population of Great Britain', *Ethnic and Racial Studies*, 13:3 (1990), 414–19.

54   This was frequently the case in cities. For example, see Mano Candappa and Danièle Joly, *Local Authorities, Ethnic Minorities and 'Pluralist Integration': A*

Study in Five Local Authority Areas (University of Warwick: Monograph Series in Ethnic Relations No. 7, 1994).

55 For an insight into the importance of oral history for the study of migration, see Alistair Thomson, 'Moving stories: oral history and migration studies', *Oral History*, 27:1 (1999), 24–37; Cynthia Brown, 'Moving on: reflections on oral history and migrant communities in Britain', *Oral History*, 34:1 (2006), 69–80; and Herbert, *Negotiating Boundaries in the City*.

56 First-generation migrants were born abroad and arrived in Britain as adults (after the age of 16). 1.5-generation migrants were born abroad and arrived in Britain during childhood (before the age of 16). Second-generation migrants were born in Britain and had parents who had been born abroad. See Anthony Heath, Stephen Fisher, Gemma Rosenblatt, David Sanders and Maria Sobolewska, *The Political Integration of Ethnic Minorities in Britain* (Oxford: Oxford University Press, 2013), pp. 33–4. The 1.5-generation is also referred to as the 'one-and-a-half generation'. See Cherti, *Paradoxes of Social Capital*.

1

Wiltshire: diverse Muslims, unexplored communities

Wiltshire is by no means the first area that comes to mind when discussing migrant communities in Britain. Acting as a gateway to the West Country, it is a county comprised of historic market towns, picturesque villages and Areas of Outstanding Natural Beauty. It is renowned for the Stonehenge and Avebury World Heritage Site, Salisbury Plain and Cathedral, the Kennet and Avon Canal, Silbury Hill and the Marlborough Downs. Its rolling green hills are pebble-dashed with crop circles, Neolithic long barrows, a plethora of historic houses and gardens, walking trails and the famous white horse chalk hillside carvings. Its romantic, mystical and 'quintessentially English' feel has made its landmarks and villages the ideal settings for a range of Jane Austen film and television adaptations and historical period dramas. Daniel Defoe's early eighteenth-century encounter with 'a vast continued body of high chalky hills, whose tops spread themselves into fruitful and pleasant downs and plains, upon which great flocks of sheep are fed', 'divers pleasant and profitable rivers', and 'a chain of fruitful meadows, and rich pastures... interspersed with innumerable pleasant towns, villages, and houses', still rings true today. Indeed, one could be forgiven for thinking that Wiltshire really does boast 'the most pleasant and fertile country in England'.[1]

In economic terms, Wiltshire has long been renowned for its history of farming, its wool trade, and its cloth, paper-making and iron-working industries. The nineteenth century witnessed a growth in light industry, including bacon-curing, tanning and glove-making. It was without a doubt the town of Swindon that experienced the most direct and visible change as a result of the Industrial Revolution. Being chosen in 1840 as the location for the Great Western Railway's railway works transformed it from what Michael Harloe called 'a small, possibly declining town on top of a hill in rural Wiltshire' to one that began to enjoy economic growth.[2] Other Wiltshire towns also experienced economic development as was seen through the Bowyers meat company in Trowbridge, the Harris bacon factory in Calne and Ware Bros. Ltd., a tanning firm in Salisbury, which all have their roots in the nineteenth century.[3] Today, Wiltshire's economy is grounded in design and technology, advanced manufacturing, and farming and agriculture. It has been home to a number of global companies, including Dyson and Honda, it has a significant military presence, and its rural economy is comprised of a range of heritage and visitor attractions.[4]

At the time of the 2011 Census, Wiltshire had a population of 680,137, of which 209,156 lived in Swindon. Major areas of settlement include Chippenham (45,337), Trowbridge (41,715), which is the county town, and Salisbury (41,682), Wiltshire's only city. Other key towns are Devizes (36,326), Amesbury (32,874), Warminster (24,454), Melksham (24,079), Royal Wootton Bassett and Cricklade (23,755), Calne (23,196) and Marlborough (22,935).[5] Wiltshire is a county with a large retired and ageing population, a low crime rate, a strong economy, a flourishing arts and heritage scene, and children who reach national levels of educational attainment. Yet it also suffers from problems and challenges typically associated with rural areas, including a high cost of living, poor transport networks, pockets of rural deprivation and isolation, and scarce private, public and voluntary sector services.[6] Since 2009, local government in Wiltshire consists of two unitary authorities: Wiltshire Council and Swindon Borough Council.

In general, Wiltshire is a county for which there does not exist a bountiful historiography. Perhaps because it lacks its own university, and thus an academic centre for local history, or due to the popularity enjoyed by its fellow south-western counties, it has long been overshadowed by the likes of Cornwall, Devon and Somerset. Furthermore, the abundance of historical coaching inns and milestones, and the number of major roads and railway lines that dissect the county's rural landscape, are evidence that Wiltshire has long held the role of thoroughfare between London, Bath, Bristol and Exeter, and thus has often been a place of passage rather than a destination in its own right.

There are nevertheless several reasons why Wiltshire is a pertinent case study for an assessment of Muslim migrant integration in rural Britain. Firstly, it is home to a range of settled Muslim minority communities who are rarely recognised as being part of the county's post-war history and remain under-researched. These include Moroccans in Trowbridge, a Moroccan community frequently referred to as being Britain's largest outside of London, as well as Bangladeshis, Indians, Pakistanis and Turks in Chippenham, Devizes and Melksham. Secondly, local government in Wiltshire has long been active in devising and implementing immigrant, integration and diversity policies; thus there is an abundance of unexplored archival material that will be drawn upon in subsequent chapters. Thirdly, despite their relatively small numbers, Wiltshire's Muslims constitute proactive and vocal communities, and have long displayed both a clear sense of agency and self-determination, as well as a commitment to community cohesion and integration. Fourthly, both local government and the Muslim minority communities themselves have frequently stressed the rurality of their policies and experiences, respectively, thus making Wiltshire a valuable case study through which to explore the extent to which there exists a rural dimension to Muslim integration in Britain.

Wiltshire's migration history and Muslim communities

Behind what is a somewhat romanticised image of a pure, static and unchanging rural county lies a history of migration and diversity that exists, but is rarely recognised. For example, research has shown that the black presence in Wiltshire dates back to at least the sixteenth century.[7] During the seventeenth century, a small number of Germans and Poles arrived in Trowbridge to work in the town's cloth industry, and Flemish weavers fleeing religious persecution settled in the town of Corsham. Furthermore, the county experienced Irish immigration during the nineteenth century. During the First World War, POW and work camps across Wiltshire, including in Chippenham, Chiseldon, Codford, Lark Hill and Wootton Bassett, held Austrian, German and Turkish prisoners, and Swindon offered refuge to Belgian refugees. During the Second World War, German prisoners worked on the Kennet and Avon Canal, and Polish airmen served at Yatesbury aerodrome.[8] This history of migration and diversity continued into the post-war period and stretches beyond the Muslim communities that this book addresses. Archival material held at the Wiltshire and Swindon History Centre, for example, shows that Wiltshire was home to substantial Italian and Polish communities during the 1960s, and received and supported Vietnamese refugees during the late 1970s.[9]

During the 2000s, Wiltshire has witnessed the arrival of a significant number of people from EU accession countries, especially Poland, and other ethnic minorities include the Black/African/Caribbean/Black British, the Filipino and the Nepalese communities. Yet despite the presence of these minority groups, like much of rural Britain, Wiltshire is predominantly white. In the 2011 Census, for example, 96.6% of the county's population recorded its ethnic group as White, with much smaller groups identifying themselves as Asian/Asian British (1.3%), Mixed (1.2%) and Black/African/Caribbean/ Black British (0.7%). The extent to which diversity in Wiltshire increased between the 2001 Census and that of 2011 can be seen in the fact that the White UK population went from constituting 96.2% to 93.4% of the total population in this decade.[10] As might be expected, the situation in Swindon is different. At the time of the 2001 Census, 91.5% of people in Swindon's unitary authority described themselves as White British. By the time of the 2011 Census, this figure had fallen to 84.6%. During this same period, the proportion of ethnic minorities increased from 8.5% to 15.4%, and the proportion of people belonging to the Asian/Asian British ethnic group almost tripled in size from 2.1% to 5.9%.[11]

There are a number of diverse and well-settled ethnic minorities who constitute the core of Wiltshire's Muslim population, yet their histories have never been documented. The migration of Indians, Pakistanis and Bangladeshis to the county, like elsewhere in Britain, is linked to Britain's imperial past.[12] As a result of both Britain's post-war economic boom and their rights as Commonwealth subjects, South Asians, and often single males, settled in Wiltshire from the 1950s and 1960s, and were soon joined by a chain migration of other male workers, wives and families, and eventually the emergence of a British-born generation. The 2011 Census recorded 1,547 Indians, 215 Pakistanis and 595 Bangladeshis in the county. A large proportion of the Indian community can be found in Chippenham, Salisbury and Trowbridge, and there are smaller concentrations in Marlborough and Tidworth.[13] The Pakistani and Bangladeshi populations live in towns across the county, including in Bradford-on-Avon, Calne, Devizes, Melksham and Salisbury.[14] Regarding Swindon unitary authority, the population figures for the Indian, Pakistani and Bangladeshi communities at the time of the 2011 Census stood at 6,901, 1,292 and 936, respectively.[15]

Moroccan Muslims began migrating to Trowbridge during the 1960s and consisted largely of unskilled males and females from Oujda in north-eastern Morocco. They formed part of a wider wave of Moroccan migration to Britain, which saw communities emerge in London as well as in nearby towns, such as Crawley, Slough and St. Albans. Compared to South Asian Muslims, the Moroccan Muslim population in Britain is small and has received scant academic attention.[16] The same holds true for the community in Trowbridge. They largely migrated to this Wiltshire town during the 1960s and 1970s to work in factories, with two of the main ones being the Bowyers meat factory and the Airsprung bed and mattress manufacturer.[17] They have since become a little more residentially scattered, but remain concentrated in the Trowbridge community area.[18] They have repeatedly been referred to in council documents, official reports and the press as being the largest Moroccan community in Britain outside of London,[19] a claim that was perhaps most publically endorsed in a 2015 episode of *Nigel Slater: Eating Together* in which he travelled to Trowbridge to cook with one of the town's Moroccan families.[20] Yet as has long been the case regarding other British Moroccan communities, it proves difficult to capture its exact size.[21] A report issued by the South West Trades Union Congress estimated that Trowbridge has around 700 Moroccans.[22] Recent newspaper articles have frequently referred to there being around eighty Moroccan families in the town.[23]

Other smaller groups of Muslims have also long been present in Wiltshire, including Arabs, Turks and Tunisians. Respondents of the 2011 Census declared both that they spoke Turkish as their main language (218) and that Turkish was their national identity (160). Furthermore, 288 respondents identified

Arab as their ethnic group and 14 chose Iranian as their national identity.[24] In Swindon unitary authority, ethnic groups identified by respondents included Turkish (308), Arab (200), Iranian (125), Afghan (107), Kurdish (37) and North African (15), and 310 and 101 respondents declared that Turkish and Arabic were their main languages, respectively.[25] Regarding religion specifically, the 2011 Census recorded 2,074 Muslims in Wiltshire unitary authority who made up 0.4% of the population, and showed that they were spread quite unevenly across the county's community areas. Trowbridge had the largest Muslim population (459), followed by Salisbury (318), Chippenham (179) and Royal Wootton Bassett and Cricklade (162). Smaller Muslim communities included those of Devizes (111), Melksham (104), Calne (73), Amesbury (72) and Bradford-on-Avon (33). In Swindon unitary authority, 3,538 respondents identified as Muslim at the time of the 2011 Census.[26]

This study recognises from the outset that the county of Wiltshire can by no means be perceived to be homogenous when discussing both ethnic minorities and Muslim communities specifically. In fact, as well as comparing and contrasting Muslim integration in the county across the post-1960s period with developments in other rural areas, as well as in cities and Britain as a whole, one of the themes running throughout subsequent chapters is the extent to which diversity also exists within Wiltshire. The brief introduction to Wiltshire's Muslim communities above has already exposed various migration histories, areas of settlement and community sizes. Whilst discrepancies exist between locations across Wiltshire, the town that perhaps sits most at odds with the rest of the rural county is Swindon. Indeed, in many ways, Swindon's profile is markedly different from that of the rest of Wiltshire: it is the largest town in the county, both its railway heritage and its industrial success during the post-war period give the town a distinct economic character, and it has experienced comparatively greater levels of ethnic and religious diversity, especially by the turn of the twenty-first century.

There are, however, a number of reasons why Swindon has been included in this study. Firstly, Swindon did not become a unitary authority area until 1997 at which point it became administratively independent of Wiltshire County Council.[27] This means that, for much of the post-1960s period, Swindon was frequently considered alongside other areas of Wiltshire in government correspondence, policies and reports on migration and diversity, including those of the Wiltshire County Council Education Committee, Wiltshire Anti-Racism Network and Wiltshire Racial Equality Council.[28] Secondly, although greater than those of other towns and areas across Wiltshire, Swindon has traditionally been home to far smaller Muslim communities than other British towns and cities typically associated with Muslim migration during the post-war period. The 3,538 Muslims recorded in the unitary authority in the 2011 Census, which constituted 1.7% of the population,[29] cannot begin to compare with London's Tower Hamlets (34.5%) and Newham (32%) or with cities like Bradford (24.7%) and Birmingham (21.8%). Furthermore, it falls well below the overall figure for England and Wales of 4.8%.[30] As such, the inclusion of Swindon helps shift the academic focus to some of Britain's smaller and under-researched Muslim communities, an aim that sits at the very core of this study. Thirdly, not only does the Borough of Swindon include rural areas,[31] but as will be discussed in later chapters, the town's Muslims and local authority have often seen their experiences and policies as having a rural and peripheral dimension, as forming part of a wider Wiltshire paradigm, and as comprising an alternative to those in British cities with larger Muslim populations.

Existing research

Despite the fact that Wiltshire has long experienced migration and diversity, this aspect of the county's history has never been comprehensively documented. Even the Moroccan community in Trowbridge has attracted no more than a few fleeting mentions in general studies on Moroccans in Britain.[32] Furthermore, local council and official reports have rarely gone beyond offering statistical profiles, which are overwhelmingly based on the Census. Nevertheless, some further details about the county's migrant communities can be obtained from a variety of sources. A 1967 study, for example, estimated that there were around 600–650 Indians and 150 Pakistanis in Swindon who largely lived in the older areas of the town and were employed in a range of jobs, including in factories, and as labourers, builders and restaurateurs.[33] In 1978, Thamesdown and District Community Relations Council published three reports on Swindon's ethnic minority communities. These explored the difficulties they encountered when trying to secure mortgages, their experiences in relation to apprenticeships, and the extent to which firms in the Thamesdown area had implemented equal opportunity policies following the Race Relations Act of 1976.[34] Overall, they found that there was a general lack of understanding with regard to the discrimination faced by minorities, and that much more needed to be done to raise awareness and combat this.

Furthermore, the 1982–83 Thamesdown and District Council for Racial Equality annual report acknowledged that a significant proportion of the area's ethnic minority communities were unable to pursue their religious and cultural needs due to a lack of adequate community facilities, and that integration would thus be difficult to achieve.[35] Reports during the 1990s discussed the isolation experienced by Bangladeshi women, as well as low participation in leisure and recreational activities amongst Muslim populations.[36] Additionally, local newspaper articles from across the post-war decades covered a range of relevant stories and developments, including working men's clubs and factories operating a colour bar; the difficulties encountered when trying to establish mosques and community centres, as well as eventual successes; examples of cross-community activities and engagement; racist incidents and harassment; opposition to ritual slaughter and plans for an Islamic school; and the honouring of Muslim leaders for their positive role in the local community.[37] Overall, many of these discussions and findings were framed against the backdrop that these Muslim communities were both small and located in a more peripheral and non-metropolitan setting.

Wiltshire's rural context was increasingly acknowledged in official reports addressing the county's migrant populations. In 2002, Wiltshire County Council and Wiltshire Racial Equality Council published a report, which used focus groups and interviews in order to uncover the 'hidden voices' of the county's ethnic minority residents.[38] Arguing against the widely held belief that racism was not a problem in rural areas, it found that not only was racism prevalent in Wiltshire, but that it had a particular rural dimension in that it consisted largely of 'prejudice and negative stereotyping, borne out of the lack of presence of people of different ethnic cultures and backgrounds'.[39] In general, the report exposed the extent to which migrants' experiences living in Wiltshire were shaped by its status as a rural county with small ethnic minority communities across a range of areas, including religious practice and recognition, employment and education, and feelings of isolation and loneliness.

In 2008 and 2013, two further studies sought to gain an insight into the lives of the county's migrant populations with regard to service access and delivery in particular.[40] Both furthered the notion that Wiltshire's Muslims' experiences and levels of integration have long been influenced by living in a rural environment with small ethnic minority and Muslim communities more broadly, whether considering levels of racism and prejudice, a local understanding of Islam or available provisions for religious practice. All three reports will be further explored in Chapter 5. This increasing interest in the lives of Wiltshire's ethnic minorities ran parallel to the growing confidence, proactivity and visibility of the county's Muslim migrant communities in their more rural surroundings as they strove to promote cross-community engagement, community cohesion and integration. By capturing both the local authority's approach to the arrival and settlement of ethnic minority communities and diverse Muslim voices, this study builds upon this existing research and further develops the relationship between integration and rurality in the county in historical perspective across the post-1960s period.

Notes

1   Daniel Defoe, *A Tour through the Whole Island of Great Britain* (London: Penguin Books, 1986), p. 196. Defoe appears to offer this description with regard to the wider chalk downlands, though it is frequently attributed to Wiltshire specifically.

2   Michael Harloe, *Swindon: A Town in Transition. A Study in Urban Development and Overspill Policy* (London: Heinemann, 1975), p. 15.

3   For an insight into Wiltshire's economic history, see Elizabeth Crittall (ed.), 'Economic history', in *A History of the County of Wiltshire: Volume 4* (London, 1959), pp. 1–6. *British History Online* www.british-history.ac.uk/vch/wilts/vol4/pp1-6 (accessed 18 July 2017); and Elizabeth Crittall (ed.), 'Other industries', in *A History of the County of Wiltshire: Volume 4* (London, 1959), pp. 220–53. *British History Online* www.british-history.ac.uk/vch/wilts/vol4/pp220-253 (accessed 18 July 2017).

4   See Swindon Wiltshire Local Enterprise Partnership, *Swindon and Wiltshire Economic Assessment 2016. Chapter 1: Executive Summary* (May 2016).

5   These figures represent Area Board areas, which have regularly been used in Wiltshire following the creation of Wiltshire's unitary authority in 2009. Each area tends to include a market town and surrounding villages.

6   See Wiltshire Community Foundation, *Wiltshire Uncovered Report 2014* (Devizes, 2014).

7   Some research into the history of immigrant and diverse populations in Wiltshire was carried out by SEEME Wiltshire, a Heritage Lottery-funded community project that ran between 2010 and 2013. Information about the project can be found on the Wiltshire and Swindon History Centre website.

8   See W.D. Bavin, *Swindon's War Record* (Swindon: John Drew Ltd, 1922); R.P. Beckinsale, *The Trowbridge Woollen Industry as Illustrated by the Stock Books of John and Thomas Clark 1804–1824* (Devizes: Wiltshire Archaeological and Natural History Society, 1951); Panayi, *An Immigration History of Britain*, p. 90; T.S. Crawford, *Wiltshire and the Great War: Training the Empire's Soldiers* (Ramsbury: The Crowood Press Ltd, 2012); Steve Wallis, *Wiltshire through Time* (Stroud: Amberley Publishing, 2013); and Stanley C. Jenkins and Angela Long, *Marlborough & Around through Time* (Stroud: Amberley Publishing, 2015).

9   Wiltshire and Swindon History Centre (WSHC), F8/933/E.B.26, Swindon Borough Education Committee, Elementary Education Correspondence Files, Basic Subjects – Immigrant Pupils, 1953–1973, 'Progress Report on the Teaching of Immigrants, first half of autumn term, 1968'; and WSHC, F1/201/10/3, Wiltshire County Council Schools Subcommittee of Education Committee Agenda Papers, 1973–1996, 'Education of Vietnamese Refugees in Wiltshire', 17 December 1979.

10   See Wiltshire Council, *Wiltshire's Diverse Communities: Results from the 2011 Census* (undated report).

11   See Swindon Joint Strategic Needs Assessment, *Census 2011 Profile Number One. Population Overview of Swindon* (July 2014).

12   For an excellent insight into the migration and settlement of South Asians in Britain, see N. Ali, V.S. Kalra and S. Sayyid (eds), *A Postcolonial People: South Asians in Britain* (London: Hurst, 2006).

13   See Wiltshire Council, *Wiltshire's Diverse Communities*.

14   This is based on my own knowledge of, and familiarity with, Wiltshire's Bangladeshi and Pakistani communities.

15   These figures were obtained from the 2011 Census for England and Wales.

16   For a few exceptions, see Cherti, *Paradoxes of Social Capital*; Hein de Haas, Oliver Bakewell and Agnieszka Kubal, *The Evolution of Moroccan Migration to the UK* (THEMIS Scoping Study Report, International Migration Institute, University of Oxford, January 2011); and Moha Ennaji, *Muslim Moroccan Migrants in Europe: Transnational Migration in its Multiplicity* (New York: Palgrave Macmillan, 2014).

17   See Stina Backer, 'Pork Pies Help Build Civic Links with Muslim Town', *Independent* (28 March 2009).

18   See Wiltshire Council, *Wiltshire's Diverse Communities*.

19   For example, see Morwenna Blake, 'Moroccan Town Link Bid Takes Big Step Forward', *Wiltshire Times* (22 March 2006); 'Trowbridge in Wiltshire First in Britain to be Twinned with Muslim Arab Town', *Telegraph* (27 March 2009); Wiltshire Assembly, *People, Places and Promises: The Wiltshire Community Plan 2011–2026* (2011); and Wiltshire Racial Equality Council, *Placement Report in Human Rights* (2012).

20   See Tanya Yilmaz, 'Trowbridge Family to Serve up Moroccan Flavours on BBC Food Show', *Wiltshire Times* (27 June 2015). The episode in question is episode five of *Nigel Slater: Eating Together*, which aired on 29 June 2015.

21   See Myriam Cherti, *British Moroccans – Citizenship in Action* (London: Runnymede Trust, 2009). It has traditionally been impossible to establish the exact size of the Moroccan community in Britain. The 1991 and 2001 Census tied ethnicity to racial and national identities. The 2011 Census included 'Arab' as an ethnic category for the first time. Yet although some Moroccans identify as Arabs, some do not. Whilst respondents had the option of ticking the 'Other' box and writing in their ethnicity, gaining an accurate figure of the community depends on all respondents specifying 'Moroccan'.

22   South West Trades Union Congress, *Who Makes Up the South West? The Facts Around the Region's Population and Migration* (Bristol, undated report).

23   For example, see Benjamin Parkes, 'Moroccan Centre Plan Falls Flat', *Wiltshire Times* (20 September 2007); and Backer, 'Pork Pies Help Build Civic Links with Muslim Town'. A 1977 local newspaper article stated that there were around 36 Moroccan families in Trowbridge at the time. See 'Muslims' Ritual Slaughter Raises Outcry', *Wiltshire Times and News* (28 January 1977).

24   See Wiltshire Council, *Wiltshire's Diverse Communities*.

25   These figures were obtained from the 2011 Census for England and Wales.

26 These figures were obtained from the 2011 Census for England and Wales and summary reports created for Wiltshire's community areas produced by Wiltshire Intelligence.

27 Swindon Borough Council was formed in 1997.

28 For example, see WSHC, F1/101/10/2, Wiltshire County Council Education Committee Minutes, 1982–1990; WSHC, 3231/24, Wiltshire Racial Equality Council, Papers of Anti-Discriminatory Working Group, later the Wiltshire Anti-Racial Network, 1994–1995; and WSHC, 3231/3, Wiltshire Racial Equality Council, Council Minutes, 1991–1997.

29 See Swindon Joint Strategic Needs Assessment, *Census 2011 Profile Number One*. The 2001 Census recorded 1,850 Muslims in Swindon who constituted 1.03% of the total population.

30 See Office for National Statistics, *Religion in England and Wales* (11 December 2012); and Muslim Council of Britain, *British Muslims in Numbers: A Demographic, Socio-economic and Health Profile of Muslims in Britain Drawing on the 2011 Census* (London, 2015).

31 See Wiltshire Community Foundation, *Wiltshire Uncovered Report 2014*.

32 For example, see Cherti, *British Moroccans – Citizenship in Action*; and de Haas, Bakewell and Kubal, *The Evolution of Moroccan Migration to the UK*.

33 Kenneth Hudson, *An Awkward Size for a Town: A Study of Swindon at the 100,000 Mark* (Newton Abbot: David & Charles, 1967), pp. 171–2.

34 Thamesdown and District Community Relations Council, *Mortgage Bar in Swindon* (March 1978); Thamesdown and District Community Relations Council, *Black Apprentices in Thamesdown* (April 1978); and Thamesdown and District Community Relations Council, *Equal Opportunity – A Survey of Local Firms* (May 1978).

35 Thamesdown and District Council for Racial Equality, *Annual Report: 1982–83* (Swindon, 1983).

36 WSHC, 3371/121, Voluntary Action Swindon, Management Information, Reports on day care provision for elderly mentally dependent people and the Community Care Plans, growth provision and Bangladeshi women, 1979–1993, 'Bangladeshi Women: A Forgotten Minority. A Study of the Needs of Bangladeshi Women in Swindon', 1990/91; and WSHC, G30/924, Swindon Borough Council, Publications and Reports, Corporate Policy and Research Unit Report, Borough of Thamesdown, 'A Review of Leisure Provision for the Minority Ethnic Population in Thamesdown', 1992.

37 A few examples of local newspaper articles include: 'A Touch of the Taj Mahals', *Wiltshire Times and News* (17 January 1964); '£40 Fine for Assault on Pakistani', *Wiltshire Times and News* (24 November 1967); Anne Tomkinson, 'Swindon's Town Hall Becomes Community's "Mosque"', *Evening Advertiser* (5 February 1970); 'Muslims' Ritual Slaughter Raises Outcry'; 'Investigation of Colour Bar Claim at Bradford', *Wiltshire Times* (6 May 1977); Paul Wilenius, 'Club Sparks Racist Row', *Evening Advertiser* (14 September 1977); 'Bid to Beat Racism', *Evening Advertiser* (15 October 1983); Robert Buckland, 'Anger at Mosque Go-ahead', *Evening Advertiser* (8 October 1993); David Vallis,

'Meeting Room Battle is Over', *Salisbury Times* (2 March 1999); and Ben Fitzgerald, 'So Proud to be Swindonian!', *Evening Advertiser* (1 October 2001).

38   Wiltshire County Council and Wiltshire Racial Equality Council, *Hidden Voices: A Study of Wiltshire's Minority Ethnic Residents* (April 2002).

39   *Ibid.*, p. 67.

40   See Wiltshire Council, *Qualitative Consultation with Wiltshire's Minority Ethnic Residents* (2008); and Wiltshire and Swindon Users' Network, *Diverse Communities: A Study of Diverse Communities Living in Wiltshire and their Experiences with Health, Public and Social Care Services* (2013).

2

Local government policy:
the early years, 1960s to 1976

British immigration policy during the immediate post-war decades has been widely documented. Initially pursuing an 'open door' policy on immigration from the Commonwealth during the late 1940s and throughout the 1950s, the British government began to implement migration controls during the early 1960s. This was at least partially driven by an increase in Indian and Pakistani arrivals in particular, as well as by progressively prevalent social concerns and public hostility regarding immigration. This turning point in government policy was marked by the Commonwealth Immigrants Act 1962, and was followed by the Commonwealth Immigrants Act 1968 and the Immigration Act 1971. All three pieces of legislation sought to control and restrict the settlement of non-white immigrants from the Commonwealth and colonies. Indeed, the years covered in this chapter, often remembered for the racist campaign of the Conservative candidate in Smethwick, Peter Griffiths, Enoch Powell's 'Rivers of Blood' speech, and the response to the Kenyan and Ugandan Asian Crises, witnessed a transition from, in Randall Hansen's words, 'one of the most liberal migration regimes in the world, granting citizenship to hundreds of millions of colonial subjects across the globe' to one characterised by 'post-1960s restrictiveness'.[1] Alongside immigration controls, a further aspect of Britain's national government's approach to migration during this period consisted of integration legislation and policies implemented with ethnic minorities already settled in Britain in mind. The first stage was its race relations legislation, which consisted of the Race Relations Acts of 1965, 1968 and 1976, all of which were devised to tackle discrimination and promote integration. Whether they were genuine well-meaning attempts to counter racial discrimination, or simply seen as a means to combat the social problems that black immigration was often linked to, they were central to Britain's distinct race relations framework that prevailed well into the 1980s.[2]

This chapter discusses local government policy in Wiltshire between the early 1960s and the implementation of the Race Relations Act 1976, which marked a key turning point in the county's immigrant, integration and diversity policies and strategies. It charts local policy through to the arrival of the first waves of post-war Muslim immigration to the county, and offers an insight into how policymakers in Wiltshire perceived and addressed the integration, accommodation and experiences of Muslim migrants. In general, immigration and integration policy during this period at the local level in Britain has not been thoroughly explored. Although studies examining the local level are nothing new, it has not been until the twenty-first century that the importance of locality in devising and implementing migration, integration and diversity policies has been fully recognised within the migration studies scholarship. Furthermore, the academic literature addressing city case studies in Britain, as well as those in Europe more widely, has overwhelmingly focused on more recent late twentieth and twenty-first-century settings.[3] Yet recognising that migration has largely been an urban phenomenon and that it has often been cities that have provided the geographical frameworks within which experiences of migration unfold, a number of scholars have gone some way towards investigating city-level policies in Britain during the 1960s and early 1970s.

For example, it has been established that Newcastle upon Tyne's local authority began to develop a series of progressive immigrant policies from the 1960s, especially in the areas of entrepreneurship, housing and education.[4] It has been widely claimed that, during the 1960s and 1970s, Leicester was renowned for racism, discrimination and ethnic segregation, a local outlook perhaps best encapsulated in the infamous 1972 advert taken out by Leicester City Council in an attempt to discourage Ugandan Asians from moving to the city.[5] Regarding Birmingham, Romain Garbaye has argued that this West Midlands city showed real indifference, and even hostility, towards its immigrant populations from the 1950s to the 1970s, and that it was not until the early 1980s that it committed itself politically to equal opportunities and race relations.[6] Thus, whilst it might be assumed that local authorities that have operated within Britain's highly centralised unitary state would have drawn up and implemented political measures and strategies with similar, and even overlapping, aims, focuses and scopes, we know that this has not always been the case.[7] Instead, British cities have long been home to clear local variation and particularism when it comes to migration and integration policies.

In comparison, there is scarce information available about local government policy in non-city contexts during this period for which there are a number of reasons, some of which have already been addressed. Firstly, rural Britain has tended to be overlooked by migration scholars, with the majority having traditionally focused on the national and city contexts. Secondly, those that have addressed rural areas have frequently emphasised the absence of policies, lamenting that migration and integration are not pressing policy concerns, and stressing the need for appropriate policy responses. Policymakers in more rural areas have long been accused of assuming that immigration and the long-term settlement of migrant communities, and by extension the prevalence of racism and notions of integration and racial equality, are urban phenomena that are of no relevance to rural Britain. Thirdly, studies that have exposed instances in which more peripheral and non-metropolitan local authorities in Britain have concerned themselves with minority ethnic populations have largely maintained that this is a trend that did not emerge until more recently and, in some cases, not until the 2000s.[8] Whilst in no way seeking to refute or discount this existing academic research, this chapter initiates the alternative account of local government policy that runs throughout this study. Despite persistent claims that rural areas have long shied away from devising coherent and well-thought-out policies due to their small migrant communities, a range of measures were introduced in Wiltshire. Although these policies of the 1960s and the first half of the 1970s were by no means aimed specifically at Muslims, but rather at the county's minority populations as a whole, it was this period that witnessed the early stages of the arrival, settlement and development of what are today Wiltshire's diverse and well-established Muslim communities.

The local immigration context

There is no doubt that Wiltshire's story of immigration during the 1960s and early 1970s unfolded somewhat differently to the British urban post-war immigration narrative. In Devizes, for example, leaflets produced for newcomers were largely issued with army families in mind and, in and around Swindon, much of the political debate focused on the local Italian and Polish communities rather than on colonial or New Commonwealth migration.[9] Furthermore, concerns and discussions about the latter's expansion during the 1960s were framed within the context of an influx of Londoners rather than immigrants from abroad.[10] This was undoubtedly due to the fact that the number of residents from Commonwealth countries, colonies and protectorates was low during this period. At the time of the 1961 Census, for example, 2,172, 437, 155 and 115 of Wiltshire's residents had been born in India, Jamaica, Pakistan and Kenya, respectively. Of those people born in India and Jamaica, 864 and 132, respectively, lived in Swindon Municipal Borough.[11] By the time of the 1971 Census, Wiltshire was home to 8,290 residents who had been born in New Commonwealth countries, including in India (2,610), Jamaica (805), Kenya (355), Pakistan (320) and Uganda (55). There were also residents who had been born in non-Commonwealth Muslim countries, such as Iran (60) and Turkey (25).[12] Of those people in Wiltshire who had been born in New Commonwealth countries, 1,897 were in Swindon Municipal Borough and included those born in India (1,125) and Pakistan (129).[13] Overall, immigrants born in New Commonwealth countries constituted 1.7% and 2.1% of Wiltshire and Swindon's populations, respectively, in 1971. These figures stood in stark contrast to those of the traditional British urban centres of migration, including Birmingham (6.73%) and London (6.4%).[14]

Nevertheless, despite these comparatively lower numbers, Wiltshire's experience of immigration progressively began to resemble that of Britain more widely during this period. It acted as a safe haven for Kenyan and Ugandan Asian refugees, it witnessed the arrival of Indian and Pakistani immigrants, and it gradually initiated a political debate on how best to cater for, and integrate, minority populations of diverse backgrounds, ethnicities, languages, cultures and religions. Furthermore, whilst the Race Relations Act 1976 did prompt an enhanced local authority focus on ethnic minorities in the county, as was the case across Britain, the pre-1976 era was by no means marked by an absence of attention and policy in this area. It should be noted, however, that Swindon was more politically proactive than the rest of Wiltshire during, and even prior to, this period. Indeed, it is during this chapter's chronology that differences between towns within Wiltshire were at their most acute, and the available archival material, and thus also this chapter's focus, display a clear bias towards Swindon and the town's surrounding district. The Swindon and District Council for Community Relations 1972–1973 annual report, for example, made reference to Swindon having a history of welcoming newcomers from across Britain, Europe and the Commonwealth, and pointed out how already during the 1950s much had been done 'to create understanding and confidence between the host community and these newcomers'.[15] Nevertheless, despite the fact that some level of diversity existed within Wiltshire, immigration and corresponding political measures and strategies were in fact often county-wide phenomena. This chapter will now offer an insight into the three areas to which Wiltshire's local authority awarded the most attention during the 1960s and the first half of the 1970s: education, the resettlement of Ugandan Asians and community relations. Whilst its political approach to its migrant communities during this period was implemented through a 'race relations' or 'ethnic' lens, many of the targets and recipients of these measures and practices were in fact Muslim. Furthermore, the policies outlined in this chapter also constitute the foundation of how Wiltshire's local authority negotiated and addressed immigration, integration and diversity across the post-1960s period, as well as of the relationship between local and national policy and mandate in the county.

Education

During the 1960s and 1970s, the education of ethnic minority children became a serious policy concern in Britain. The arrival of Commonwealth immigrants, and the fact that their children began to attend schools in significant numbers, forced national and local governments to act.[16] Education soon became the area to which local authorities across Britain arguably awarded the most attention, potentially because it fell firmly within their remit, it was deemed central to shaping an individual's future place and opportunities within society, and they received clear national-level directive, and Wiltshire was certainly no different. It is important to discuss Wiltshire's approaches to, and strategies and policies regarding, the education of immigrant children within the local migration context at the time. Whilst the number of immigrant schoolchildren in the county during this period is not known,[17] according to an Education Committee report from April 1970, Swindon had 533, 572, 650 and 603 immigrant pupils in 1967, 1968, 1969 and 1970 who constituted 2.65%, 2.84%, 3.17% and 2.89% of the total number of pupils, respectively, and who were predominantly of Indian, Italian, Pakistani, Polish and West Indian backgrounds.[18] Needless to say, the situation in Swindon was a far cry from Birmingham's primary and secondary schools that were 9.6% and 8% immigrant, respectively, in 1968, the Inner London boroughs of Islington and Hackney that had 24% and 26% immigrant children on roll in 1969, and the situation that developed in Bradford during the 1960s in which the overwhelming majority of Bangladeshi and Pakistani schoolchildren became concentrated in just six schools.[19]

Yet despite the low numbers of immigrant pupils and the lack of accompanying concerns and pressures in comparison to what was the case in cities across Britain, Swindon's local authority did not shy away from addressing the education of ethnic minority schoolchildren. To the contrary, already by 1962, special English-language classes for immigrant pupils had been set up. Initially established for ten children at one school and run by a part-time teacher, they soon began to attract children from other schools in the town. The overall aim was that these pupils would attend English-language classes, whilst simultaneously remaining in their mainstream classrooms as much as possible so as to become integrated into what was referred to as 'the normal life of the school'.[20] During the years that followed, Swindon witnessed an ever-increasing concentration of immigrant children in local schools. There were reports about secondary school immigrant pupils attending English-language classes that detailed the difficulties they experienced and the progress they made.[21] The Schools' Council launched an enquiry into the prevalence of, and the problems regarding, the teaching of English to immigrant children, with the hope it would result in recommendations regarding specific teaching materials, teacher training, and the necessary organisation involved both within and between schools.[22] Furthermore, there were efforts to ascertain the total number of both immigrant pupils in schools and those with little or no knowledge of the English language, and peripatetic teachers and part-time staff members were appointed especially to work with them.[23]

Towards the end of 1966, there were only six schools in the Borough of Swindon that had more than ten children of Commonwealth immigrants on roll. Largely infant and junior schools, the heads felt that assimilation would be achieved quicker if these immigrant children were placed in mainstream classrooms with their English counterparts. Only children who arrived at secondary school age were placed into a separate classroom until they were ready to join mainstream classes. Furthermore, schools with a 'substantial' number of immigrant pupils received extra members of staff, and attempts were made to ensure that teachers who had immigrant children in their classrooms attended relevant conferences and courses.[24] In 1968, two specialist teachers of immigrant pupils were appointed who were to each visit four schools per day in order to provide help to children who were struggling to keep up in mainstream classrooms due to their lack of proficiency in the English language. Some of the schools who were to receive this assistance were Clarence Junior School, Clarence Infants School, Queenstown Infants School and Gorse Hill Junior School, each of which had between four and twenty immigrant pupils who were in need of such additional help.[25]

Towards the end of 1968, the Assistant Education Officer offered a fairly positive account of developments regarding the schooling of immigrant pupils in Swindon. Firstly, it was argued that immigrant children were integrated in that they only left mainstream classes for short periods in order to receive additional language tuition, a practice that was no different from English children leaving when they needed additional help with reading from a remedial teacher. Secondly, it was reported that the town was not home to a 'colour problem' in that immigrant children were treated in the same way as their English counterparts, and that teachers had not reported any difficulties that implied that a 'colour problem' existed. Thirdly, there were steps being taken to teach English to the parents of immigrant children, which consisted of offering evening classes as well as classes at the local college.[26] By the spring of 1970, the Education Committee reported that the work of the two teachers of immigrant pupils that had started in September 1968 had been successful. Not only had immigrant children and their class teachers welcomed their visits and assistance, but it was found that infant children were settling in well to the mainstream classrooms and required very little assistance. As a result, these specialist teachers had stopped their work early at a number of schools because they were no longer needed. Overall, the number of immigrant children receiving special instruction had fallen, meaning that the teachers had been able to both visit a greater number of schools and limit the size of their classes, which had led to more positive results. In fact, the report went as far as to suggest that the work carried out by these teachers had been such a success that it was probable that the retention of both teachers would not be necessary for much longer.[27]

These positive accounts of the situation in local schools continued to be stressed in the years that followed. Firstly, in May 1971, the Borough Education Officer declared that 'there is no great immigrant problem in Swindon' and that immigrant pupils constituted only 2–3% of the town's total school population. Furthermore, it was emphasised that even in those three schools in which immigrants exceeded 20% of the total number of pupils, the majority required no additional support. Overall, it was judged that there was 'little need for special provision' and that 'the vast majority of the relatively small number of immigrants there are in the schools are well integrated'.[28] Secondly, in September 1974, prompted by the Burnham Committee,[29] Wiltshire County Council's Schools Sub-Committee prepared a list of its schools that were located in socially deprived areas. In order to measure social deprivation, it used a list of criteria, which included the schoolchildren's parents' economic and social status, the percentage of children receiving free school meals, and the proportion of children with severe language difficulties. It was established that, although the county did have schools that experienced some level of social deprivation, these tended to not be the schools that had the highest proportions of immigrant pupils. For example, whilst there were a number of primary schools especially that had a high proportion of immigrant children, including Holy Rood Infants School in Swindon and Trinity Infants School in Trowbridge, which were 39% and 14.3% immigrant, respectively, these were not amongst those schools the sub-committee chose to list, opting instead to prioritise schools in army garrison areas.[30]

However, local problems and setbacks did develop and, whilst they potentially called into question the positive and successful accounts that have been outlined, they were nevertheless clearly recognised and addressed. In March 1972, for example, it was acknowledged that an estimated sixty immigrant children had such difficulties with the English language that their ability to successfully pursue education was under threat.[31] A report from the following month pointed out that there had been cases in which immigrant secondary school pupils had spent two years in local schools before it had been realised that they were suffering from severe educational difficulties. The fact that they had what the report termed 'limited learning potential' had been concealed by what were referred to as 'cultural and linguistic handicaps'. It was stressed that such cases amongst immigrant children needed to be identified quickly after their arrival in local schools, and it was decided that they would undergo medical examinations as well as tests that would ascertain their abilities to learn. Any children who showed signs of having learning difficulties were to then undergo further examination with an educational psychologist. This exercise was to be applied to children arriving at a school in Swindon from abroad, to those being admitted to a local junior or secondary school who either did not arrive in the British Isles until after the age of five or who had spent time since the age of five in the 'homeland', and to children being admitted to junior and secondary schools who it was known were undergoing language difficulties and thus whose learning potential proved difficult to measure. The Principal Borough School Medical Officer was to be notified of any child who fell into one of these three categories, as well as of those who were already attending school in Swindon and had language difficulties or had spent time since the age of five abroad.[32] It was also recognised that more needed to be done to learn about the cultural and religious backgrounds of the different immigrant communities, as well as about the differences that existed between them, and that there were cases of children leaving school with a lack of proficiency in the English language.[33]

In Swindon, local political deliberations regarding the education of immigrant children did not focus solely on English-language proficiency and acquisition, but rather also stretched to religious considerations. In 1971, the Borough Education Officer reported that, despite the fact that Swindon experienced a higher level of immigrant concentration than other areas in Wiltshire, there did not appear to be any problems either in schools as a result of immigrants' different faiths or regarding the religious education of immigrant children. It was thought that the majority of the Asians were Muslim and, whilst some of the Muslim girls did not take part in physical education classes, most did so and wore modest clothing. Furthermore, there had been no reports of problems regarding the provision of school meals. The Education Officer put this absence of difficulties down to three factors. Firstly, the town was home to a small number of immigrants, and non-Christian immigrants in particular. Secondly, the *imam* of the local Muslim community was described as being tolerant, and as not opposing Muslim schoolchildren participating in religious activities within schools. It was believed that this resulted in Muslims not making the demands that other areas of the country had witnessed. Thirdly, the Swindon Committee for Community Relations took an accommodating approach, and both the local authority and individual schools made efforts to address any developing problems. Overall, it is clear that, in describing the situation in Swindon as 'one of peaceful co-existence', the town was seen as not experiencing the conflicts and tensions regarding the education of Muslim pupils that seemed to be developing elsewhere in Britain.[34]

West Wiltshire also featured in local political discussions about the education of immigrant schoolchildren during this period. During the mid-1970s, it was felt that due to the residential concentration of ethnic minority families in the west of the county, and in Trowbridge in particular, special educational provision needed to be put in place. In July 1974, the Wiltshire County Council Schools Sub-Committee estimated that there were 113 children who were in need of extra help, especially with English, and that even though they were spread across 21 schools, 36 of them were concentrated in an infant and junior school in Trowbridge. Furthermore, it was recognised that there existed many different levels of ability amongst the immigrant pupils, even amongst those who were not yet proficient in the English language. Whilst such cases had previously been addressed through additional part-time teachers, it was felt that more needed to be done to contend with what was a wider problem. Instead of setting up a language centre, it was deemed that these children would be best helped within mainstream schools where they would mix with, and learn from, other children. Thus, it was decided that schools would be given the necessary support by means of additional teaching staff, and particularly a specialist peripatetic teacher who would be shared amongst schools, teach individual or groups of children, and offer advice and guidance on how children's needs could be adequately met.[35]

These local discussions and approaches regarding the education of immigrant children during the 1960s and the early to mid-1970s did not emerge in isolation, but rather in accordance with, and in response to, Britain-wide developments. Not only did this period witness both a commitment in Wiltshire to cater for the educational needs of immigrant pupils and a lively dialogue on the topic, but also a regular inflow of information regarding policies and approaches that were being implemented in other areas, and especially in cities with substantial ethnic minority populations. In January 1967, for example, a report was received from the Inner London Education Authority, which outlined its need for a full-time centre to provide for immigrant children from a range of schools. It was decided that the situation in Swindon did not require a full-time centre, not least because immigrant families were residentially scattered throughout the town, which meant that there was 'no "ghetto" area to justify the housing of a Centre in any particular place'.[36]

In 1968, reference was again made to the correlation between discrimination in the housing sector and the difficulties encountered when educating immigrant children, and the dispersal policy that had been launched by the Borough of Ealing in London was mentioned specifically. It was felt that Ealing's policy of dispersing immigrant children from the older areas of Southall who were not proficient in the English language to reception classes in primary schools that were serving the newer, and predominantly white, areas of Ealing was a practice worth considering in Swindon. It was thought that such a policy might be particularly relevant for Queenstown Infants School, with the suggestion being that new immigrant children could be initially sent to a different school nearby that had fewer non-English-speaking pupils. The Borough Education Officer raised a number of potential options, including that the number of immigrant children in any given school class should not be allowed to exceed five.[37] Yet despite this discussion, there is no evidence to suggest that such a dispersal policy was ever deemed necessary and implemented. There was also a local interest in developments that were taking place in Birmingham. A late

1967 meeting of the Education Committee's Sub-Committee on Immigrants, for example, reported on the situation of non-English-speaking immigrant school pupils in this West Midlands city. It discussed its high numbers of specialist teachers and peripatetic schools, the fact that its Indian and Pakistani children especially required extra tuition, and how with more than 80% of some junior schools' pupils being 'coloured', there were some 'frightening aspects' to developments in the city.[38] Overall, the available archival material clearly shows that, in comparison to the situations that were unfolding elsewhere, local government officials perceived that in Wiltshire in a positive light.

As well as looking to other localities for policy developments and reference points, Wiltshire's initiatives and practices were simultaneously firmly rooted within the national-level mandate. On the whole, they reflected the assimilationist approach to the education of immigrant schoolchildren that was adopted by the British government during the 1960s and early 1970s. This approach was based on the belief that ethnic minorities should assimilate into a British majority culture, and education was seen as a crucial area in which to pursue this assimilation. This meant that the acquisition of the English language was prioritised over minority languages and cultures. Furthermore, in an attempt to preserve individual schools' British characters and principles and promote assimilation, the Department for Education and Science (DES) 1965 circular recommended that ethnic minority children should not constitute more than one-third of any school or class's total number of pupils, and that local authorities should introduce a dispersal policy through which surplus immigrant children were dispersed to schools in other neighbourhoods.[39] The emphasis placed on English-language classes in Wiltshire, as well as the consideration given to both the occasional concentration of immigrant pupils and the notion of dispersal, have already been discussed. A further aspect of this assimilationist agenda in Britain during the 1960s and early 1970s, and one for which it has long been criticised, is the manner in which it frequently portrayed immigrant children, rather than individual schools or the education system, as the problem. The historiography has repeatedly stressed how ethnic minority pupils were seen to disrupt, and lower the standards of, mainstream classrooms, and were often perceived to be 'backwards' and 'subnormal'.[40] Indeed, not only did Wiltshire local authority documentation employ the terms 'backward' and 'backwardness', but it also frequently discussed immigrant schoolchildren during this period in a tone that suggested they were a 'burden' and a 'problem' that needed to be 'dealt with' and 'solved'.[41]

It would, however, be unfair to render Wiltshire's policies regarding the education of ethnic minority children during the 1960s and early 1970s mere reflections of national-level directive. In fact, in some ways, local discussions and measures were quite forward thinking and progressive. For example, they recognised the correlation between residential segregation and the concentration of ethnic minority children in certain schools, as well as the educational demands and needs of Muslim pupils specifically, considerations that it has often been argued were largely absent from government focus in Britain until much later.[42] On the whole, it is clear that not only was education a key area of local authority concern in relation to Wiltshire's experience of immigration during this era, but also that the policy responses that were drawn up, considered and implemented, whilst shaped by a top-down assimilationist agenda, were simultaneously firmly rooted within the local migration context. Thus, they focused largely on Swindon and, to a lesser extent, on Trowbridge. Such a fusion of national mandate and local priorities and concerns informing migration policies was seen across a range of areas during this period, not least regarding the resettlement of Ugandan Asians to which this chapter now turns.

The resettlement of Ugandan Asians

When Idi Amin announced in August 1972 the expulsion of more than 50,000 Asians who had lived in Uganda for generations, Edward Heath's Conservative government, albeit somewhat reluctantly, decided that it had a moral and legal duty to offer residence to these British passport holders. As a result, the Uganda Resettlement Board was established and charged with resettling the Ugandan Asian refugees across Britain. Initially housed in transit camps, the idea was that the refugees would then be directed to areas that did not already have large ethnic minority populations. The county of Wiltshire was undoubtedly seen as a 'green area', an area suitable for resettlement, as it was not home to significant South Asian communities nor to strained local resources like the so-called 'red areas', which included Leicester and parts of London.[43] As such, Wiltshire's local authorities devoted a significant amount of attention to the arrival and settlement of Ugandan Asians during the early to mid-1970s.[44] The resettlement of Ugandan Asians is being included in this chapter for two key reasons. Firstly, it is widely recognised that, whilst many of the Ugandan Asians were Hindus, there were also Muslims amongst them, and thus these refugees have long been considered part of Britain's post-war history of Muslim immigration and settlement.[45] Secondly, this resettlement process was a significant part of Wiltshire's local authority's approach to immigrant communities during the early to mid-1970s, and offers an insight into the extent to which it implemented national directive at the local level.

In September 1972, Salisbury Housing Committee, for example, reported that the Uganda Resettlement Board was 'well aware of the apprehension felt in several parts of the country that any substantial influx of additional families from overseas might place severe strains on the housing, education and social services', and that thus the aim was 'to encourage the fresh arrivals to choose areas in which these problems were likely to be less severe'.[46] A Swindon Ugandan Bulletin from August 1973 went as far as to declare that 'in cities like London, Leicester, and Birmingham, evidence suggests that many evacuees are living under great stress' and that, in comparison, 'Swindon is in a favourable position.'[47] The Ugandan Asian refugees in question were primarily the 1,500 who were residing at a camp near Newbury in the neighbouring county of Berkshire. Consisting of Muslims, Hindus and Sikhs of all ages and from a range of employment backgrounds, it was hoped that suitable work and housing could be arranged for them in Wiltshire, and that local people would invite them both into their homes and to partake in social activities, including music and sports events.[48]

Yet despite there being pockets of a positive local reaction to the resettlement of Ugandan Asians, in Salisbury, numerous concerns were raised. It was pointed out that there were limited employment opportunities in the area, especially in no-skill or low-skill jobs, and that unless the Ugandan Asians had skills that were attractive to local employers, their success in the labour market would be limited. Concerning the local housing situation, it was stressed that there was a two-year wait for council housing and that no new homes were due to be ready until the spring of 1973.[49] Despite these local constraints, a number of initiatives were put in place to assist with the resettlement of Ugandan Asians. A series of almshouses were offered as accommodation on a temporary basis, and it was proposed that in order to overcome the council housing shortage, the council could purchase a small number of private houses and make them available to Ugandan Asians.[50] It was also suggested that the Finance Committee review applications from Ugandan Asians for either a council loan for a mortgage or a guarantee for a building society loan with 'special and sympathetic consideration'.[51] Local government documentation also discussed the formation of a Resettlement Co-ordination Committee that was set up in order to explore how support for the Ugandan Asians could be provided, and appeals for local people and organisations to offer assistance and hospitality were made.[52] The available archival material does not disclose the total number of Ugandan Asians who ended up settling in and around Salisbury, though a letter received from the Ugandan Asian Relief Trust in London confirms that it was at least twenty by early December 1972.[53]

Swindon's reaction to the Ugandan Asian refugees was more proactive, conscientious and considered than that of Salisbury. Writing in September 1972, the Swindon District Council for Community Relations argued that the taking of refugees was a 'moral obligation', and that offering 'something positive would be worth a great deal at a time when there is so much negative feeling'.[54] It felt that, because Swindon experienced less of a strain on housing than the cities as well as moderate employment opportunities, the town was a suitable place for resettlement. It was argued that, in contrast to cities, houses in Swindon were cheaper to purchase, the town experienced little multi-occupation, and that there was an availability of both council housing and properties in the private rental market. Regarding the labour market, it was stressed that, despite some unemployment and forthcoming redundancies, Swindon's unemployment rate was lower than the national average, and there was a growing number of commercial firms in the town and an ever-increasing amount of business opportunities.[55]

The arrival and settlement of Ugandan Asian refugees in Swindon and the surrounding area was overwhelmingly portrayed in a positive light. Regarding housing, for example, offers and possible solutions regarding temporary accommodation included an army camp, a hostel, a hotel and council housing. Furthermore, around 30 local English and Asian families offered to temporarily open their homes to some of the refugees.[56] By August 1973, an estimated 35 Ugandan Asian families, comprising 155 individuals, were living in and around Swindon, of which 20 families were in housing provided by Swindon Borough Council, four families were living in the area of Highworth Rural District Council, and the rest were largely residing either with family or friends or in rented accommodation. With regard to employment, local companies offered to employ a number of Ugandan Asians, whilst others found work as bus conductors, machine assistants and operators, and warehousemen, and were expected to quickly move onto more skilled work or establish businesses. By the summer of 1973, there were more than forty Ugandan Asians working either full- or part-time, ten of whom were women, and there was only one family without a wage earner.[57]

Like in Salisbury, Ugandan Asians arriving in Swindon also experienced a number of problems and obstacles, and there was some local concern expressed about their settlement. Due to a shortage of properties with two or three bedrooms, there were some Ugandan Asian men whose families were still living in the Resettlement Centre and who were thus separated from them for long periods of time. A lack of proficiency in the English language, amongst some of the Ugandan Asian women in particular, as well as an absence of paper qualifications, were highlighted as being significant barriers to securing employment. The collection and distribution of furniture and other household items for refugee families was considerably hindered by a shortage of funding and thus a lack of the necessary transport. Some families were separated and undergoing considerable distress as a result of official immigration and passport procedures, and there were some instances of local hostility towards them. Furthermore, the overall process of securing employment and accommodation for the Ugandan Asians had been incredibly slow-moving.[58]

Yet despite these difficulties, it is clear that Swindon's dedicated and proactive approach prevailed. A Ugandan Asian Welfare Committee was established in order to cater for the needs and interests of local Ugandan Asians, and meetings were arranged between the Ugandan Asians and local council staff and councillors. There was an awareness that the resettlement process stretched far beyond the initial securing of accommodation to a range of potential problems, including those regarding income tax forms and rent rebates, and it was suggested that Ugandan Asian families receive visits at home in order to try to handle any difficulties that arose more effectively. English classes were arranged for those who wanted language help, and it was thought that efforts should be made to spread children across local schools so that staff did not become overwhelmed.[59] There were opportunities for young adults to partake in a range of social activities alongside members of other ethnic minority communities, including film and bowling evenings.[60] Reflecting on what had been an overwhelmingly welcoming attitude, donations of clothing and furniture, and volunteers offering to teach English, the August 1973 Swindon Ugandan Bulletin reported that 'Swindon can be genuinely proud of the way in which local people have responded to the situation.'[61]

Whilst Salisbury and Swindon did indeed dominate Wiltshire's resettlement of Ugandan Asians, other towns also played a small part. There was discussion, for example, about making council houses in Chippenham, Devizes, Melksham, Pewsey, Trowbridge and Warminster available, even though they were overwhelmingly in poor condition, and there is some evidence that families did eventually settle in such towns.[62] On the whole, the county's, and especially Swindon's, response to the Ugandan Asians was arguably more positive than the opposition they encountered in Britain more widely that has been documented in the historiography. This hostile response was perhaps best captured by the infamous advert taken out by Leicester City Council, but there were numerous local authorities across Britain that were reluctant to accept Ugandan Asian evacuees, including those of Birmingham, Brent, Ealing and Southampton.[63] Furthermore, despite the fact that the dispersal policy ultimately failed and many Ugandan Asians settled in red areas, and particularly in Leicester and London,[64] it has been argued that some were forced into more remote, and often rural, parts of Britain where they experienced isolation and a lack of a cultural and religious support network.[65]

Yet in Wiltshire, the reaction to the Ugandan Asians was carefully considered, and occasionally proactive and conscientious. Although there is no record of the impact that initiatives and proposals had, many of which were recorded in correspondence, the local response is to be commended for having gone some way towards looking beyond the Ugandan Asians' immediate employment and housing needs, and for recognising the more social aspects of the resettlement process. Moreover, the refugees' long-term settlement was at times carefully thought through, and their particular assets and strengths, and thus their potential contribution to the county, were discussed.

In Swindon, it was pointed out that they were businessmen with entrepreneurial skills and experience, and that they overwhelmingly spoke English and were likely to want to purchase their own properties,[66] with the Executive Committee of the Swindon and District Council for Community Relations stressing that the town 'is a place with opportunities for people of enterprise and education'.[67] Thus, whilst the arrival and settlement of Ugandan Asians in Britain received a clear national-level response, both local conditions and clear pockets of commitment and determination nevertheless unquestionably shaped Wiltshire's reaction to the refugees.

Community relations

A final area that received a significant amount of attention during the 1960s and early 1970s in Wiltshire, and one that was again firmly rooted in national developments regarding immigration and race relations, was community relations. The second Race Relations Act, which came into force in November 1968, led to the establishment of both the Community Relations Commission and a series of local Community Relations Councils, which were charged with promoting harmonious race relations. Thus, the responsibility for community and race relations was decentralised and passed to local institutions, and the importance that the Community Relations Councils played in Britain's political approach to immigration at the local level has been widely recognised.[68] Yet whilst it has been acknowledged that local authorities did go some way towards supporting the work of these local councils, this support has often been described as having been limited, and the local councils themselves as having been underfunded, understaffed and lacking in any real political power.[69] Formed in 1968, the Swindon Council for Community Relations was, to some extent, no exception.[70] It repeatedly lamented that it lacked resources and manpower, and in May 1970, it maintained that the funding it received from the local authority was 'enough to tread water on', but 'not enough to advance our work'. The council regretted that it was 'only scratching at the surface' and 'treating symptoms rather than the complaint', and asked 'what price good race relations?'[71]

However, despite these constraints, as a result of both national and local funding, and the fact that it advised, and worked closely with, local government, the Swindon Council for Community Relations appears to have both been ambitious and to have made an impact in a number of areas beyond playing a role in the resettlement of Ugandan Asians. Its aim was to gain an insight into the situation of local migrant communities and it challenged the 'no problem here' mentality that it recognised was often prevalent in areas with small immigrant populations, and offered advice and training in a range of areas, from racial discrimination and the welfare of immigrant children to race relations in the education and employment sectors.[72] It is clear that the council saw its work as central to the development of community relations in the area. In a December 1969 letter written by its Community Relations Officer to the Borough of Swindon in which it requested additional funding, it was argued that the council's work was 'vital to Swindon' and 'able to… prevent the immigrant groups from becoming too isolated', and warned that 'if our office did have to close, Swindon could well suffer the terrible racial problems and tensions that the Midland industrial towns are facing now, in the future'.[73] It recognised the need to enable a 'two-way system of communications', and that community relations entailed working with both minority groups and the majority population in order to address misconceptions and encourage good relations.[74] Furthermore, despite being the consequence of national race relations legislation, the council clearly believed that it had a duty to compensate for restrictive national-level policy. As a reaction to the 1971 Immigration Act, for example, it reported that 'positive measures must be taken to reassure immigrant groups of their rightful place in our society'.[75]

Indeed, whilst recognising that the situation in Swindon was 'better than in many towns with higher numbers of newcomers',[76] the council nevertheless became engaged in a wide range of initiatives during the late 1960s and early 1970s. It investigated cases of alleged racial discrimination, emphasised the need to combat the isolation of ethnic minority communities, and devised a programme that aimed to bring together members of all local communities. Regarding the employment sector specifically, it educated employers on local ethnic minority communities in an attempt to help the younger generation secure work, offered advice on relationships and possible tensions between different ethnic groups in factories, and reviewed the progress of immigrant school leavers. It argued that immigrant workers' skills and abilities were not being fully utilised in the workplace, and brought representatives of management, unions and immigrant organisations together to discuss possible ways forward.[77]

With regard to housing, the council stressed that migrants faced a range of barriers, including the suspicion that some people had about 'the arrival of a coloured neighbour', and the lack of available flats and rooms to rent.[78] It highlighted the need to monitor the arrival of Commonwealth immigrants to Swindon and to ensure that the necessary housing stock was available, arguing that 'decent housing is a major factor in creating good community relations'.[79] It also considered, corresponded about and investigated individual cases of migrants being refused housing on the basis of their skin colour, and the fact that some landladies preferred 'professionals' and people who did not come from different cultural backgrounds and have special diets. It also offered advice on relationships and possible tensions in cases involving landlords and tenants, as well as on home improvement grants and mortgages.[80] In the area of education, it pledged to explore the progress of children who were recent arrivals in the UK, maintaining that they experienced a particular set of problems, as well as migrant parents' attitudes towards school. It organised school assemblies, which emphasised commonalities between world religions and aimed to teach children about the religious backgrounds of their peers, and spoke to school pupils about the importance of positive race relations. Despite fearing that drawing attention to race relations in schools could potentially create a problem where there was not one, the council continued to push ahead with such initiatives. Furthermore, for immigrant wives, and especially those of Asian origin, recognising that it could be difficult for them to spend time outside of the house due to either their husbands working long hours or cultural reasons, the council arranged for English-language classes to take place in their homes.[81]

Whilst the council's work in community relations was largely discussed and carried out with ethnicity and race in mind, there were numerous occasions on which it considered religious minorities and Muslims in particular. For example, it stressed the need for a council-run community centre, arguing that it would offer the local Muslim, as well as Sikh, community a space in which to pray. Pointing out that Muslims had to hire a number of different rooms for prayer, it maintained that not only could this accommodation prove difficult to secure, but also that the lack of one guaranteed place in which to pray led to an absence of a positive atmosphere and religious environment.[82] The council also worked with the Education Department and negotiated both the wearing of suitable clothing for girls in physical education classes and school canteen meals for Muslim children more widely.[83] Additionally, it recognised the local Muslim population's religious affiliation in other ways, such as by including information on Eid prayers and Ramadan in its newsletter.[84]

As previously mentioned, this devolution of the responsibility for community and race relations to local Community Relations Councils during the late 1960s in Britain was problematic for a number of reasons. There is no doubt that Swindon's lacked funding and the necessary staff, and the exact impact it had on local policymaking is unclear. Furthermore, it was most certainly at least partially composed of what Andrew Geddes has referred to as 'the local "great and good"', though there is evidence that representatives of immigrant communities were sought and secured.[85] On the whole, the council was a pivotal part of Wiltshire's local authority response to migration and ethnic diversity during this period, and an important local actor in addressing community relations. It demonstrated an understanding of local ethnic minority populations, a grasp of the key barriers to harmonious race relations, and a commitment to cater for immigrants' needs and well-being. Furthermore, once again, we can see that, despite the existence of a clear national political framework, local ambitions, concerns and initiatives shone through.

Conclusion

Local authorities across Britain have frequently been criticised for showing little interest in developing and implementing migration policies during this period.[86] Yet much like the aforementioned cities of Newcastle, Birmingham and Leicester, Wiltshire was, to a certain extent at least, also home to its own particular approach to migration during the 1960s and early 1970s. Although much of the work was done by and through the local Community Relations Council, whether with regard to the education of ethnic minority school-children, the resettlement of Ugandan Asians or community relations more broadly, the county's political dialogues and measures were both frequently positive and conscientious. Firmly framed within national-level concerns, developments and legislation, it did not lag behind the status quo, nor did it shun its responsibility for its migrant communities and adopt a 'no problem here' mentality as more rural and peripheral areas with small ethnic minority populations have so often been accused of. Furthermore, breaking away from the race relations model that dominated Britain at this time in which colour and ethnicity were central to how ethnic minority integration was framed and discussed,[87] Wiltshire's local authority also went some way towards considering the religious affiliations and needs of its Muslim communities specifically.

Yet Wiltshire's immigrant, integration and diversity policies and strategies of the 1960s and early 1970s were not without their constraints and limitations, and there are three in particular that are worth considering. Firstly, Wiltshire's political deliberations and measures were firmly framed within national-level developments and policies. As such, the county's local authorities were prac-tically forced into action by a mandate that trickled down from the national level within the unitary British state. In other words, whilst applying this mandate in a way that suited local aims, contexts and needs, Wiltshire's pol-itical approach towards its ethnic minority communities was nevertheless the result of national-level policy decisions. In fact, it is difficult to imagine that the county would have had a clear and proactive political agenda with regard to migrant communities were it not for the framework, and at times the funding, bestowed to it by the overarching assimilationist approach to the education of ethnic minority schoolchildren, and the establishment of the Uganda Resettlement Board and the local Community Relations Councils. Secondly, there is no doubt that Swindon dominated local authority initiatives in Wiltshire during this period. As has been discussed, whilst other towns like Devizes, Salisbury and Trowbridge, as well as Wiltshire County Council more widely, also played a role, Swindon and the town's surrounding district featured in all three of the policy areas discussed in this chapter. Not only does this highlight the diversity with regard to the political approach that existed within the county of Wiltshire, a theme that runs throughout subsequent chapters, but it also perhaps further exposes the extent to which certain towns and parts of the county, and by extension their immigrant populations, appear to have been largely absent from local authority focus at this time.

The third and final limitation, and one that is linked to the first two, is that there was arguably much missing from Wiltshire's local authority's approach to its migrant communities. There was no direct mention at all, for example, of the Moroccans who had begun to work and live in Trowbridge, and there were no more than a few brief references to the South Asian communities who were settling in towns across the county. It seems that being driven by a top-down agenda resulted in Wiltshire's political approach and focus lacking somewhat in local particularism. Yet despite these constraints, the county's local authority should be recognised for having gone some way towards responding to migrant communities' disadvantage and racial inequality, and for having promoted positive race relations. This meant that by the time of the passage of the Race Relations Act 1976, which placed a particular duty on local authorities to act in the areas of discrimination and equality of opportunity, Wiltshire had a good foundation on which to build. The impact of this third Race Relations Act will be assessed in the next chapter.

Notes

1 Hansen, *Citizenship and Immigration in Post-war Britain*, p. 16. For more details about Britain's post-war immigration and citizenship legislation, also see Kathleen Paul, *Whitewashing Britain: Race and Citizenship in the Postwar Era* (Ithaca, NY: Cornell University Press, 1997); Ian R.G. Spencer, *British Immigration Policy since 1939: The Making of Multi-Racial Britain* (London: Routledge, 1997); Joppke, *Immigration and the Nation-State*; Andrew Geddes, *The Politics of Migration and Immigration in Europe* (London: SAGE, 2003); and James Hampshire, *Citizenship and Belonging: Immigration and the Politics of Demographic Governance in Postwar Britain* (Basingstoke: Palgrave Macmillan, 2005).

2 For an insight into Britain's race relations framework, see Anthony M. Messina, *Race and Party Competition in Britain* (Oxford: Clarendon, 1989); Tessa Blackstone, Bhikhu Parekh and Peter Sanders (eds), *Race Relations in Britain: A Developing Agenda* (Abingdon: Routledge, 1998); Erik Bleich, *Race Politics in Britain and France: Ideas and Policymaking since the 1960s* (Cambridge: Cambridge University Press, 2003); and Solomos, *Race and Racism in Britain*.

3 For example, see Caponio and Borkert (eds), *The Local Dimension of Migration Policymaking*; Rianne Dekker, Henrik Emilsson, Bernhard Krieger and Peter Scholten, 'A local dimension of integration policies? A comparative study of Berlin, Malmö, and Rotterdam', *International Migration Review*, 49:3 (2015), 633–58; Maria Schiller, *European Cities, Municipal Organizations and Diversity: The New Politics of Difference* (Basingstoke: Palgrave Macmillan, 2016); and Ricard Zapata-Barrero, 'Intercultural policy and multi-level governance in Barcelona: mainstreaming comprehensive approach', *International Review of Administrative Sciences*, 83:2 (2017), 247–66.

4 See Hackett, *Foreigners, Minorities and Integration*; and Hackett, 'The "local turn" in historical perspective'.

5 See Seán McLoughlin, 'Discrepant representations of multi-Asian Leicester: institutional discourse and everyday life in the "model" multicultural city', in Seán McLoughlin, William Gould, Ananya Jahanara Kabir and Emma Tomalin (eds), *Writing the City in British Asian Diasporas* (Abingdon: Routledge, 2014), pp. 89–113.

6 Garbaye, *Getting into Local Power*, p. 103.

7 It has frequently been argued that it is federal countries like Belgium and Germany that are home to local-level variation in migration and integration policy. For example, see Christian Joppke and F. Leslie Seidle (eds), *Immigrant Integration in Federal Countries* (Montreal: McGill-Queen's University Press, 2012). However, some scholars have pointed out that, because Britain is a decentralised unitary state and migrant integration policies have traditionally developed at the local level, local authorities have in fact implemented a plethora of different policies since the early 1960s. For example, see Vertovec, 'Multiculturalism, culturalism and public incorporation'; and Peter Scholten, 'The multilevel dynamics of migrant integration policies in unitary states: the Netherlands and the United Kingdom', in Eve Hepburn and Ricard Zapata-Barrero (eds), *The Politics of Immigration in Multi-level States: Governance and Political Parties* (Basingstoke: Palgrave Macmillan, 2014), pp. 150–74.

8 For an insight into this literature, see Jay, '*Keep Them in Birmingham*'; Derbyshire, *Not in Norfolk*; Dhalech, *Challenging Racism in the Rural Idyll*; Henderson and Kaur (eds), *Rural Racism in the UK*; Neal, 'Rural landscapes, representations and racism'; de Lima, 'John O'Groats to Land's End'; and Neil Chakraborti, 'Beyond "passive apartheid"? Developing policy and research agendas on rural racism in Britain', *Journal of Ethnic and Migration Studies*, 36:3 (2010), 501–17.

9 See WSHC, 1802/115/2, Community Council for Wiltshire, Correspondence: Community Care and Social Services, Newcomers to Devizes Leaflet, 1968–1974; WSHC, F8/933/E.B.26, reports of Italian children learning English, 1963; and WSHC, F8/933/H.Y.88(a), Swindon Borough Education Committee, Correspondence Higher Education, Immigrants and Youth Service, 1967–1973, Swindon Youth Committee, minutes of meeting, 18 September 1967. For a brief insight into Swindon's Italian and Polish communities, see Hudson, *An Awkward Size for a Town*, pp. 166–71.

10   For example, see WSHC, F1/100/39, Wiltshire County Council Development Committee Minutes, 1963–1969, meeting of 17 May 1966; and WSHC, F1/100/39, Wiltshire County Council Development Committee Minutes, meeting of 8 November 1966.

11   Census 1961 England and Wales County Report Wiltshire, statistics provided by the Office for National Statistics (ONS). It must be recognised that, because these figures include only those people born in these countries, and not any descendants born in Britain, the real numbers of these ethnic minority populations are undoubtedly higher. Figures for residents in Swindon born in Kenya and Pakistan are not available because there are fewer than 50 persons in each category.

12   Census 1971 England and Wales County Report Wiltshire, statistics provided by the Office for National Statistics (ONS). As was the case for the 1961 Census, these figures include only those people born in these countries and not any descendants born in Britain.

13   Census 1971 England and Wales County Report Wiltshire for the Municipal Borough of Swindon, statistics provided by the Office for National Statistics (ONS). Again, the size of these Indian and Pakistani communities was undoubtedly higher as these figures do not include descendants born in Britain.

14   See Garbaye, *Getting into Local Power*, p. 98; and Tim Butler and Chris Hamnett, *Ethnicity, Class and Aspiration: Understanding London's New East End* (Bristol: The Policy Press, 2011), p. 60.

15   WSHC, F8/933/H.Y.88(b), Swindon Borough Education Committee, Correspondence Higher Education, Swindon Council for Community Relations, 1968–1976, 'Swindon and District Council for Community Relations Annual Report, 1972–1973'.

16   For an insight into policies regarding the education of immigrant children during this period, see Sally Tomlinson, *Ethnic Minorities in British Schools: A Review of the Literature, 1960–82* (London: Heinemann, 1983); and Tomlinson, *Race and Education*.

17   The Wiltshire County Council Education Committee Schools Sub-Committee argued in July 1974 that 'statistics on the number of immigrant families in an area can, for educational purposes, be misleading'. See WSHC, F1/201/10/3, Wiltshire County Council Schools Subcommittee, meeting of 15 July 1974.

18   WSHC, F8/933/E.B.26, Swindon Education Committee Report No. 70, 'Immigrant Pupils', 14 April 1970.

19   See Ian Grosvenor, *Assimilating Identities: Racism and Educational Policy in Post 1945 Britain* (London: Lawrence & Wishart, 1997), p. 97; Ansari, 'The Infidel Within', p. 299; and Tomlinson, *Race and Education*, p. 31. As Sally Tomlinson points out, the accuracy of these figures for London boroughs is disputed.

20   WSHC, F8/933/E.B.26, Governors of Secondary Schools, Secondary Education Sub-Committee, 'Special Class for Non-English-Speaking Pupils', 27 November 1962.

21   WSHC, F8/933/E.B.26, reports about immigrant children attending English classes at St. Joseph's School in Swindon from a range of different secondary schools (1963).

22   WSHC, F8/933/E.B.26, letter from Swindon Education Committee to a range of schools, 2 December 1965.

23   WSHC, F8/933/E.B.26, letter from Borough Education Officer, 11 November 1966.

24   WSHC, F8/933/E.B.26, note to the National Committee for Commonwealth Immigrants, 29 November 1966.

25   WSHC, F8/933/E.B.26, Swindon Education Committee circular to school members of staff, 19 June 1968.

26   WSHC, F8/933/E.B.26, letter from Assistant Education Officer, 4 November 1968.

27   WSHC, F8/933/E.B.26, Swindon Education Committee Report No. 70.

28   WSHC, F8/933/E.B.26, letter from Borough Education Officer, 13 May 1971.

29   Established in 1919, the Burnham Committee negotiated teachers' salaries at the national level until it was abolished in 1987.

30   WSHC, F1/201/10/3, Wiltshire County Council Schools Sub-Committee, 'Burnham Report 1974. Teachers in Schools in Socially Deprived Areas', 16 September 1974.

31   WSHC, F8/933/E.B.26, letter from Borough Education Officer, 10 March 1972.

32   WSHC, F8/933/E.B.26, Handbook, Education Department, Swindon, 10 April 1972.

33   WSHC, F8/933/H.Y.88(a), Swindon Youth Committee, minutes of meeting, 4 September 1967; and WSHC, F8/933/H.Y.88(a), Swindon Youth Committee, minutes of meeting, 25 September 1967.

34   WSHC, F8/933/E.B.26a, Swindon Borough Education Committee, Elementary Education Correspondence Files, Basic Subjects – General, 1965–1974, letter from Borough Education Officer to Headmaster of Moredon Secondary School in Swindon, 13 May 1971.

35   See WSHC, F1/101/10/1, Wiltshire County Council Education Committee Minutes, 1973–1981, meeting of 26 July 1974; and WSHC, F1/201/10/3, Wiltshire County Council Schools Sub-Committee, meeting of 15 July 1974.

36   WSHC, F8/933/E.B.26, Swindon Education Committee Report No. 70. As will be discussed in Chapter 5, this prevalence of residential dispersal amongst migrant communities in both Swindon and Wiltshire more widely was emphasised by a number of oral history interviewees.

37   WSHC, F8/933/E.B.26, note by Borough Education Officer, 31 May 1968.

38   WSHC, F8/933/H.Y.88(a), Swindon Education Committee, Sub-Committee on Immigrants, minutes of meeting, 11 December 1967. Discussions about developments in Birmingham also took place on other occasions. For example, see WSHC, F8/933/E.B.26, Swindon Education Committee Report No. 70. There was also an awareness of, and interest in, a range of other initiatives across Britain at this time, including a course in Liverpool that prepared teachers for education in a multiracial society and a conference on religious education in schools in Bristol. See WSHC, F8/933/H.Y.88(b), Swindon Education Committee, Swindon Council for Community Relations, various.

39 For an insight into this assimilationist approach, see Christopher Bagley, 'Immigrant children: a review of problems and policy in education', *Journal of Social Policy*, 2:4 (1973), 303–15; David L. Kirp, 'The vagaries of discrimination: busing, policy, and law in Britain', *The School Review*, 87:3 (1979), 269–94; and Tomlinson, *Race and Education*, pp. 19–41.

40 For example, see Bernard Coard, *How the West Indian Child is Made Educationally Subnormal in the British School System: The Scandal of the Black Child in Schools in Britain* (London: New Beacon for the Caribbean Education and Community Workers' Association, 1971); John Tierney (ed.), *Race, Migration and Schooling* (Eastbourne: Holt, Rinehart & Winston Ltd, 1982); Grosvenor, *Assimilating Identities*, pp. 116–29; and Richard Race, *Multiculturalism and Education* (London: Continuum, 2011), pp. 17–18.

41 See WSHC, F8/933/E.B.26, letter from Borough Education Officer, 11 November 1966; and WSHC, F8/933/H.Y.88(b), 'Swindon and District Council for Community Relations Annual Report, 1972–1973'.

42 For example, see Ansari, *'The Infidel Within'*, pp. 298–302; and Tomlinson, *Race and Education*, pp. 19–20, 24–5.

43 For an insight into the Ugandan Asian Crisis and the dispersal policy, see Tony Kushner and Katharine Knox, *Refugees in an Age of Genocide: Global, National and Local Perspectives during the Twentieth Century* (London: Frank Cass, 1999), pp. 265–81; Vaughan Robinson, 'Dispersal policies in the UK', in Vaughan Robinson, Roger Andersson and Sako Musterd (eds), *Spreading the 'Burden'? A Review of Policies to Disperse Asylum Seekers and Refugees* (Bristol: The Policy Press, 2003), p. 112; and Emma Robertson, '"Green for come": moving to York as a Ugandan Asian refugee', in Panikos Panayi and Pippa Virdee (eds), *Refugees and the End of Empire: Imperial Collapse and Forced Migration in the Twentieth Century* (Basingstoke: Palgrave Macmillan, 2011), pp. 245–67.

44 East African Asians from Kenya and Tanzania also settled in Wiltshire, but there are only a few sporadic references to these groups in the available archival material. For example, see WSHC, G6/132/105, Highworth Rural District Council, Clerk's Correspondence, Resettlement of Ugandan Asians, 1972–1973, letter from the Executive Committee of the Swindon and District Council for Community Relations to the Uganda Resettlement Board in London, 14 September 1972.

45 See Gilliat-Ray, *Muslims in Britain*, p. 51; and Tahir Abbas, *Islamic Radicalism and Multicultural Politics: the British Experience* (Abingdon: Routledge, 2011), p. 48.

46 WSHC, G23/132/89, Salisbury City Council, Clerk's Correspondence, Resettlement of Ugandan Asians, 1972, report by Salisbury Housing Committee, 14 September 1972.

47 WSHC, G6/132/105, Swindon Ugandan Bulletin No. 2, August 1973.

48 See WSHC, G23/132/89, letter from Swindon and District Council for Community Relations to Salisbury, 30 October 1972; and WSHC, G23/132/

89, minutes of Resettlement of Ugandan Asians Co-ordinating Committee, 29 December 1972.

49   See WSHC, G23/132/89, letter from Salisbury to Uganda Resettlement Board, 11 September 1972; and G23/132/89, report by Salisbury Housing Committee, 14 September 1972.

50   See WSHC, G23/132/89, letter from the Trustees of the Salisbury Municipal Charities to the Ugandan Resettlement Board in London, 28 September 1972; and WSHC, G23/132/89, letter from Salisbury Town Clerk to the Uganda Resettlement Board in London, 3 October 1972.

51   See WSHC, G23/132/89, minutes of Resettlement of Ugandan Asians Co-ordinating Committee, 11 December 1972.

52   See WSHC, G23/132/89, various.

53   WSHC, G23/132/89, letter from the Ugandan Asian Relief Trust in London to local authorities (received by Salisbury Town Clerk's Office), 4 December 1972. For a list of Ugandan Asians who had settled in Salisbury by November 1972, see WSHC, G23/132/89, lists of newcomers from Uganda who have settled in Salisbury, November 1972.

54   WSHC, G6/132/105, letter from the Swindon District Council for Community Relations to the Clerk of the Council, Highworth Rural District Council, Swindon, 11 September 1972.

55   See *Ibid.*; and WSHC, G6/132/105, letter from the Executive Committee of the Swindon and District Council for Community Relations to the Uganda Resettlement Board in London, 14 September 1972.

56   See WSHC, G6/132/105, letter from the Swindon District Council for Community Relations to the Clerk of the Council, Highworth Rural District Council, Swindon, 11 September 1972; WSHC, G6/132/105, letter from the Executive Committee of the Swindon and District Council for Community Relations to the Uganda Resettlement Board in London, 14 September 1972; WSHC, G6/132/105, letter from Clerk of the Swindon Council to the Uganda Resettlement Board in London, 22 September 1972; and WSHC, G6/132/105, Swindon Ugandan Committee Bulletin No. 1, Christmas 1972.

57   See WSHC, G6/132/105, letter from the Swindon District Council for Community Relations to the Clerk of the Council, Highworth Rural District Council, Swindon, 11 September 1972; WSHC, G6/132/105, Swindon Ugandan Committee Bulletin No. 1, Christmas 1972; and WSHC, G6/132/105, Swindon Ugandan Bulletin No. 2, August 1973.

58   See WSHC, G6/132/105, Swindon Ugandan Committee Bulletin No. 1, Christmas 1972; and WSHC, G6/132/105, Swindon Ugandan Bulletin No. 2, August 1973.

59   See WSHC, G6/132/105, letter from the Executive Committee of the Swindon and District Council for Community Relations to the Uganda Resettlement Board in London, 14 September 1972; WSHC, F8/933/E.B.26, Memo to the Housing Manager, 'Ugandan Asians', 9 October 1972; WSHC, G6/132/105, Swindon Ugandan Committee Bulletin No. 1, Christmas 1972; and WSHC, G6/132/105, Swindon Ugandan Bulletin No. 2, August 1973.

60 See WSHC, F8/933/H.Y.88(b), report by Swindon and District Council for Community Relations, 9 January 1974.

61 WSHC, G6/132/105, Swindon Ugandan Bulletin No. 2, August 1973. See also WSHC, F8/933/H.Y.88(b), Swindon and District Council for Community Relations Annual Report, 1972–1973.

62 For example, see WSHC, G23/132/89, letter from County Hall in Trowbridge, Wiltshire County Council to town clerks and offices across the region, 16 October 1972; and WSHC, G15/100/61, Trowbridge Urban District Council, Printed Council and Committee Minutes, 1972–1973, meeting of the Health and Housing Committee of 6 March 1973.

63 The 1972 advert was taken out in the *Ugandan Argus* and read as follows: 'The city council of Leicester, England, believes that many families in Uganda are considering moving to Leicester. If YOU are thinking of doing so it is very important that you should know that present conditions in the city are very different from those met by earlier settlers. They are: Housing: several thousands of families are already on the council's waiting list. Education: hundreds of children are awaiting places in schools. Social and health services: already stretched to the limits. In your own interests and those of your family you should accept the advice of the Uganda Resettlement Board and not come to Leicester'. For an insight into Leicester's and other local responses to the arrival of Ugandan Asians, see Knox and Kushner, *Refugees in an Age of Genocide*, pp. 276–81; and McLoughlin, 'Discrepant representations of multi-Asian Leicester', p. 96.

64 See Robinson, 'Dispersal policies in the UK', p. 112.

65 See Avtar Brah, *Cartographies of Diaspora: Contesting Identities* (London: Routledge, 1996), p. 34; and Anjoom Mukadam and Sharmina Mawani, 'Excess baggage or precious gems? The migration of cultural commodities', in Peter Hopkins and Richard Gale (eds), *Muslims in Britain: Race, Place and Identities* (Edinburgh: Edinburgh University Press, 2009), p. 161. By no means was Wiltshire the only county of a more remote and rural nature to adopt an accommodating and proactive approach to the settlement of Ugandan Asians, with Eastleigh Borough Council and Winchester Rural Council, for example, also putting local measures in place. See Knox and Kushner, *Refugees in an Age of Genocide*, pp. 276–7.

66 See WSHC, G6/132/105, letter from the Swindon District Council for Community Relations to the Clerk of the Council, Highworth Rural District Council, Swindon, 11 September 1972.

67 See WSHC, G6/132/105, letter from the Executive Committee of the Swindon and District Council for Community Relations to the Uganda Resettlement Board in London, 14 September 1972.

68 See Geddes, *The Politics of Migration and Immigration in Europe*, p. 45; Garbaye, *Getting into Local Power*, pp. 48–9; and Scholten, 'The multilevel dynamics of migrant integration policies in unitary states'.

69 See Jim Bulpitt, 'Continuity, autonomy and peripheralisation: the anatomy of the centre's race statecraft in England', in Zig Layton-Henry and Paul B.

Rich (eds), *Race, Government and Politics in Britain* (Basingstoke: Macmillan, 1986), pp. 33–4; and John Solomos, *Race and Racism in Contemporary Britain* (Basingstoke: Macmillan, 1989), pp. 91–2.

70 The committee's name changed various times in subsequent years. For example, in 1970, it became the Swindon and District Council for Community Relations.

71 WSHC, G24/132/1095, Swindon Borough Council, Finance and Law Committee Correspondence Files, Swindon Council for Community Relations, 1968–1972, newsletter, May 1970.

72 See WSHC, F8/933/H.Y.88(b), Swindon and District Council for Community Relations, Annual Report 1970–71; WSHC, F8/933/H.Y.88(b), Swindon Council for Community Relations, undated report; and WSHC, F8/933/ H.Y.88(b), Swindon and District Council for Community Relations Annual Report 1972–1973.

73 WSHC, F8/933/H.Y.88(b), letter from Community Relations Officer of the Swindon Council for Community Relations to the Borough of Swindon, 5 December 1969.

74 See WSHC, F8/933/H.Y.88(b), Swindon and District Council for Community Relations, Annual Report 1970–71.

75 WSHC, G24/132/1095, Swindon Council for Community Relations newsletter, July 1971. The Immigration Act 1971 attempted to put a stop to large-scale immigration from New Commonwealth countries. For an insight into the Act, see Spencer, *British Immigration Policy since 1939*, pp. 143–4.

76 See WSHC, F8/933/H.Y.88(b), Swindon Council for Community Relations newsletter, October 1969.

77 See WSHC, F8/933/H.Y.88(b), letter from Community Relations Officer of the Swindon Council for Community Relations to the Borough of Swindon, 5 December 1969; WSHC, F8/933/H.Y.88(b), Swindon and District Council for Community Relations, Summary of Annual Report 1971–1972; WSHC, F8/933/H.Y.88(b), Swindon and District Council for Community Relations Annual Report 1972–1973; and WSHC, F8/933/H.Y.88(b), Swindon Council for Community Relations, undated report.

78 WSHC, F8/933/HY88(b), Swindon and District Council for Community Relations, Community Relations Newsletter, January 1972.

79 WSHC, F8/933/H.Y.88(b), Swindon and District Council for Community Relations Annual Report 1972–1973.

80 See WSHC, G24/132/1095, Swindon Council for Community Relations newsletter, October 1971; WSHC, G24/132/1095, letter from Swindon Council for Community Relations, 24 November 1972; WSHC, G24/132/1095, reply from Chief Executive, 13 December 1972; and WSHC, F8/933/H.Y.88(b), Swindon Council for Community Relations, undated report.

81 See WSHC, F8/933/H.Y.88(b), letter from Community Relations Officer of the Swindon Council for Community Relations to the Borough of Swindon, 5 December 1969; WSHC, F8/933/H.Y.88(b), report of discussion on race and community relations in the syllabus at the Curriculum Development

Centre, 3 May 1971, meeting held under the auspices of the Education Panel of Swindon and District Council for Community Relations; WSHC, F8/933/H.Y.88(b), Education and Community Relations bulletin, September 1971; WSHC, F8/933/H.Y.88(b), Swindon and District Council for Community Relations, Community Relations newsletter, January 1972; WSHC, F8/933/H.Y.88(b), letter from Swindon and District Council for Community Relations to Swindon Education Office, 3 February 1972; WSHC, F8/933/H.Y.88(b), Swindon and District Council for Community Relations, summary of Annual Report 1971–1972; and WSHC, F8/933/H.Y.88(b), Swindon Council for Community Relations, undated report.

82 See WSHC, G24/132/1095, letter from Swindon and District Council for Community Relations to Swindon Civic Offices, 'Re Urban Aid Phase 3', 24 September 1970. In 1973, Muslims were granted the use of a room in a Methodist Church, which they used for at least 20 years. See WSHC, 3299/42, Swindon: Manchester Road, Correspondence about the use of rooms by the Moslem community, 1992–1996, letter issued by Manchester Road Methodist Church in Swindon detailing the history of Muslim use, 12 October 1995.

83 See WSHC, F8/933/H.Y.88(b), Swindon Council for Community Relations, undated report.

84 See WSHC, G24/132/1095, Swindon and District Council for Community Relations newsletter, November 1971.

85 Geddes, *The Politics of Migration and Immigration in Europe*, p. 45. See WSHC, G24/132/1095, Swindon and District Council for Community Relations Constitution; and WSHC, G6/132/105, letter from the Executive Committee of the Swindon and District Council for Community Relations to the Uganda Resettlement Board in London, 14 September 1972.

86 See Solomos, *Race and Racism in Contemporary Britain*, p. 91; and Rob Witte, *Racist Violence and the State: A Comparative Analysis of Britain, France, and the Netherlands* (Abingdon: Routledge, 2014), p. 40.

87 For example, see Rex and Moore, *Race, Community and Conflict*; and Tariq Modood, 'British Muslims and the politics of multiculturalism', in Tariq Modood, Anna Triandafyllidou and Ricard Zapata-Barrero (eds), *Multiculturalism, Muslims and Citizenship: A European Approach* (Abingdon: Routledge, 2006), p. 38.

3

Local government policy: race relations, multiculturalism and integration, 1976 to the late 1990s

The Race Relations Act 1976 can be seen to have been something of a turning point in the politics of migration and race in post-war Britain. Rooted in a perception that local authorities were not sufficiently active in this area, the act placed the responsibility of promoting positive race relations and tackling racial disadvantage firmly in their hands. Whilst the precise impact of the act is unclear and the notion that it yielded immediate results is disputed, with some arguing that action was also spurred on by the 1981 riots rather than by the act alone, local authorities began implementing a plethora of initiatives and responses.[1] The race relations legislation of the 1960s and 1970s paved the way for multiculturalist policies, which gradually began to emerge during the late 1970s and then in earnest during the 1980s, and lasted well into the 1990s. These multicultural policies sought to provide for minorities' cultural, ethnic and religious needs and demands, and took the form of programmes that showcased ethnic minority distinctiveness, pursued anti-racism and combatted ethnic disadvantage. Although the exact definition and manifestation of British multiculturalism, as well as its success and longevity, have long been the topics of academic debates and disagreements, this political response is nevertheless key to understanding the development of ideas surrounding the concept of integration.[2] Furthermore, it was often Labour-led local authorities across Britain that spearheaded these multicultural policies and initiatives, which it has frequently been argued flew in the face of some segments of Thatcher's government.[3] Throughout these decades, race relations legislation and multiculturalism developed against a backdrop of restrictive immigration policies, an ever-increasing diversification of migrant communities due to family reunification and the emergence of a British-born generation, and the persistent shift in the construction of difference from a focus on 'race' to 'ethnicity' to 'faith'.

This chapter focuses on local government policy in Wiltshire from the immediate aftermath of the passing of the Race Relations Act 1976 to the late 1990s. It charts an increase and diversification in the county's immigrant, integration and diversity policies within the national context of an ever-growing emphasis on multiculturalism, integration and positive race relations, and the local context of increasingly settled and visible migrant populations. As with the 1960s and early 1970s, the historiography has gone some way towards examining migration policies and measures devised and implemented at the local level in Britain during the late 1970s, the 1980s and the 1990s, albeit frequently in relation to urban, rather than more rural, case studies. Local authorities in Birmingham, Manchester and Wolverhampton, for example, put a range of measures into effect that attempted to promote multiculturalist agendas and equality of opportunity during the 1980s.[4] Newcastle upon Tyne's city council implemented equal opportunities policies, made attempts to improve its own recruitment of ethnic minorities, and both promoted positive race relations and combatted discrimination in the housing and education sectors.[5] In Leicester, in a departure from the status quo of the 1960s and 1970s, the city's local authority took a firm stand against racism, and strove to hire a greater number of ethnic minority employees and ensure that council services met the needs of local migrant communities.[6] On the whole, the post-1976 period witnessed an increase in local authority responses to migration and diversity across Britain, as well as a continuation of local particularism being reflected in policies and measures as had already started to be the case during the 1960s and early 1970s.

It was also during this period that local authorities started to recognise the religious affiliations of their migrant populations. In Hampshire, for example, a policy regarding the teaching of religious education in schools from a multi-faith perspective was introduced during the late 1970s, and in Birmingham, state schools did more to cater for the religious needs and identities of Muslim pupils and incorporated some aspects of Islamic studies into the curriculum during the 1980s.[7] In 1981, Bradford's local authority set up the Bradford Council for Mosques, which granted the city's Muslims greater recognition and representation, particularly in the areas of education and anti-racism.[8] By the late 1980s, numerous local authorities across Britain were offering *halal* meat in schools and most were allowing Muslim female pupils to wear modest clothing.[9] The 1989 Rushdie Affair, often seen as a pivotal and unprecedented turning point in the relationship between Britain and its Muslim communities, led to Muslims being perceived as having a collective identity and being set firmly apart from other ethnic and religious minority groups.[10] With regard to race politics at the local level specifically, it resulted in Muslim political activists gaining prominence in cities like Birmingham, Bradford and Leicester, and it had a clear impact on local authorities' debates on ethnicity and race, forcing them to consider religious identity in a way they had not done so previously.[11] Indeed, due to Britain's decentralised system of government, it was the decisions and policies of local authorities that often had the greatest impact on Muslim migrants' lives and integration.[12]

Yet despite these developments taking place largely amongst urban local authorities, it has long been argued that a very different story unfolded in rural areas. With regard to the Race Relations Act 1976, rural local authorities have been accused of either being slow, reluctant or entirely non-committal when it came to their race relations duties and responsibilities, with studies finding that some had still not taken any action by the 1990s.[13] Concerning religion specifically, there is an absence of research on rural local authorities' recognition of migrant communities' religious affiliations during this period. Yet as a successor to race and ethnicity as an acknowledged marker of identity, the underlying assumption seems to be that the religious identities and practices of their migrant communities were also not considered nor catered for. This chapter considers the extent to which these findings and assumptions hold true for Wiltshire. In doing so, it exposes a number of inter-county variations, both in terms of policy area and geographical region. On the whole, it shows that whilst continuing to be rooted in national-level mandate, and often directed at migrant populations as a whole rather than at Muslim minorities specifically, the late 1970s, 1980s and 1990s witnessed policies and measures that grew in both number and scope, and reflected an increased awareness of Muslim religious life and practices.

The local immigration context

Wiltshire's experience of immigration continued to develop differently and at a much slower pace than what was the case in many areas across Britain during this period. By the time of the 1981 Census, the county was home to 5,616 people who had been born in New Commonwealth countries, including in India (1,228), Pakistan (210), Bangladesh (55), and Caribbean (727) and East African (558) countries.[14] In Swindon District Unitary Authority there were 2,984 residents who had been born in New Commonwealth countries, with 1,416, 408, 341, 209 and 70 in India, the Caribbean, East Africa, Pakistan and Bangladesh, respectively.[15] At the time of the 1991 Census, the first to include a question on ethnic identity, Wiltshire had residents who described themselves as Black Caribbean (840), Indian (545), Black Other (484), Asian (434), Bangladeshi (183) and Pakistani (50), as well as 984 who identified their ethnic groups as 'Other'.[16] Swindon District Unitary Authority was also home to a range of ethnic groups, including Indian (1,668), Black Caribbean (758), Asian (439), Pakistani (394), Bangladeshi (204), and 869 people who identified as 'Other'.[17] Indeed, the 1% and 3% of Wiltshire and Swindon's populations, respectively, that were of ethnic minority origin at the time of the 1991 Census were a far cry from the figures for some of the London boroughs, including Brent (44.8%) and Tower Hamlets (35.6%), as well as of cities like Leicester

(28.5%) and Birmingham (21.5%), and they fell well below the figure of 5.5% for Britain as a whole.[18]

Yet behind these small figures and percentages, captured in what is a purely quantitative source,[19] lies a far more complex local history of immigration, as well as a series of vibrant political deliberations on how to respond to and manage migration, integration and diversity. During this period, Wiltshire's sense of duty to adhere to what was an increasingly top-down political agenda concerned with the promotion of race relations and multiculturalism and the combatting of racial discrimination intensified, despite its position as an English rural 'white' county with small migrant communities. It experienced the arrival and settlement of Vietnamese refugees and Bangladeshi immigrants, and its local authority both acknowledged and considered the responsibilities placed upon it by the Race Relations Act 1976, and fully committed itself to recognising cultural, ethnic and religious diversity within what it saw as a British multicultural society.[20] As was the case during the 1960s and early 1970s, local policies and practices in Wiltshire during this period continued to be a mixture of national mandate and local particularism. They predominantly addressed community relations and racial equality, Muslim communities' religious needs and demands, education, and equal opportunities and anti-discrimination, areas to which this chapter now turns.

Community relations and racial equality

The 1976 Race Relations Act made it unlawful to discriminate on the grounds of race, colour, nationality or ethnic or national origins, and established the Commission for Racial Equality (CRE). With a lack of a clear unitary policy structure for integration, the CRE worked through a network of local-level Racial Equality Councils (RECs) (formerly Community Relations Councils or CRCs). Whilst the RECs were technically voluntary organisations, they worked closely with local authorities to combat racial discrimination and ensure that migrant communities' needs and problems were addressed. Although they often suffered from a lack of funding and resources, RECs were an intrinsic part of Britain's local-level political approach to migration and race relations, and have been commended for the role some of them played. Not only did they offer an insight into local authority policies, but their own work was often integral to, and thus difficult to separate from, that of local government. Furthermore, in addition to RECs, some local authorities also set up their own committees and units in order to comply with their duty to promote equal opportunities and combat discrimination as outlined in Section 71 of the Race Relations Act 1976.[21]

The 1976 Act had an immediate impact on considerations and debates regarding the establishment and roles of committees, councils and working groups in Wiltshire, as well as on the working relationships between these groups and local government. Already in December 1976, a working group on community relations, comprised of representatives of Wiltshire County Council, the county's five district councils, the CRE and local RECs, was set up.[22] In July 1978, it issued a report, which stressed the duty that the 1976 Race Relations Act had placed on local authorities 'to eliminate unlawful discrimination and promote equality of opportunity and good relations between different racial groups', offered an overwhelmingly positive overview of the local situation, and made a number of suggestions.[23] It recorded people born in New Commonwealth countries in the county dispersed across the areas of Thamesdown (2,435), Salisbury (1,780), North Wiltshire (1,650), West Wiltshire (1,320) and Kennet (1,110). Despite the county's relatively small migrant population, it stressed that Wiltshire was 'part of a multi-racial society', and was home to three race relations organisations as well as to over a dozen religious and minority welfare associations located in Chippenham, Swindon and Trowbridge. Other initiatives included a full-time Community Relations Officer in Thamesdown and a part-time Community Liaison Officer in West Wiltshire.[24]

The report outlined the role that local authorities played in shaping the experiences of, and catering for, individual community groups, and emphasised the need for 'an agreed process whereby policy, practice and priorities may be considered to ensure that provision is made to meet the needs of ethnic minorities'.[25] The working group decided that a Wiltshire Committee for Racial Equality should be established, maintaining that such a county-wide committee would enable the necessary cooperation, whilst allowing the district organisations to focus on the more routine local issues. The suggested roles and responsibilities that the committee would assume included developing relationships with statutory, voluntary and ethnic minority organisations across Wiltshire; acting as an advisory service with regard to immigration, discrimination and language; enabling the discussion of policy issues with local government and private and public agencies; and supporting projects that addressed issues affecting migrant communities. The report also identified education and housing as being priority focus areas, and seemed to assume that this would become a Wiltshire-wide initiative despite Kennet and Salisbury not yet being home to Community Relations Councils.[26]

The reaction to the working group's report and suggestion to create a county-wide committee was met with elements of a 'no problem here' mentality. Kennet District Council, for example, saw 'no particular problem in their area' and, whilst the council approved the formation of a Wiltshire Committee for Racial Equality, it was not interested in establishing a local Kennet Council for

Racial Equality. Salisbury District Council did not want to have to financially support a county-wide committee, and pointed out that its district did not have a Community Relations Officer, maintaining that there was no need for one.[27] North Wiltshire District Council expressed concerns about the financial implications a county structure for community relations involved and decided not to make a financial contribution towards the North Wiltshire Council for Racial Equality's budget.[28] Wiltshire County Council's Local Government Joint Committee maintained that it wished to continue supporting community relations work in the county but, potentially as a result of the lack of available resources and the district councils' positions, felt that it was not the right time to establish another committee in this area. Instead, it hoped that the CRE's work in the county would continue and that local authority representatives would remain involved in the work carried out by district-level Community Relations Committees.[29]

Indeed, what might be perceived to be a lack of commitment to issues of migration and race was present in Wiltshire's local authority's interaction with local RECs in a number of ways. In January 1980, for example, a Thamesdown and District Council for Racial Equality Community Relations Officer wrote to Salisbury District Council on behalf of the Wiltshire Federation of Councils for Racial Equality confirming a request for a modest grant of £150 in order to carry out 'exploratory work' into the needs of Salisbury's ethnic minority communities. The officer explained that, as a result of a lack of funding and staff, little contact had previously been made with Salisbury's migrant populations, and that the aim of this proposed work was to establish contact with ethnic minority organisations, and representatives of schools, youth groups and social services, and consider whether a community relations organisation was needed in the area. After considering the request, Salisbury District Council's Finance Committee reaffirmed that 'it was not aware of any need for community relations work in the District and was satisfied that the interests of all its inhabitants were adequately safeguarded'.[30]

Similarly, throughout the 1980s, the North and West Wiltshire Council for Racial Equality struggled to secure financial support, especially from North Wiltshire District Council, despite the fact that it carried out work across North Wiltshire, including in Calne, Chippenham and Marlborough. Whilst North Wiltshire District Council put this down to financial constraints,[31] the Council for Racial Equality accused the district council of having 'no time for black and ethnic minority communities', of being 'under the misapprehension that there are no racial problems in their area', and of generally not fulfilling their obligations as outlined in Section 71 of the Race Relations Act 1976.[32] West Wiltshire Council for Racial Equality also conveyed a frustration with local government and, at its Annual General Meeting in July 1983, the Community Relations Officer stressed that 'we must encourage the councillors to realise that community relations is not just for black people, but the whole community'.[33] Wiltshire's RECs also frequently hinted that they were disappointed with what they perceived to be a range of local authority shortcomings throughout the 1990s, including the failure to secure an outreach worker to engage with ethnic minority youth, and a lack of commitment to dealing with cases of racial discrimination and harassment in schools and the housing sector, and implementing and updating equal opportunities policies.[34] Overall, it is clear that, regarding the district councils especially, they felt that they displayed what the Chair of Wiltshire Racial Equality Council referred to in 1994 as 'inertia and indifference to our policies and cause', and that there existed 'a great deal of inertia and resistance to change in rural areas' more broadly.[35]

However, whilst by no means suggesting that the RECs' frustrations and grievances lacked justification, it would be wrong to reduce Wiltshire's local government's engagement with them to one characterised by complete indifference. On the contrary, it is clear that there were a number of ways in which policies and the local authority's general approach towards the county's migrant communities were shaped either by REC advice, suggestions and pressure, or by working closely with them. In 1980, the Borough of Thamesdown Community Planning Committee set up a Working Party on Youth in Multi-Racial Society,[36] which comprised councillors and representatives of both the Thamesdown and District Council for Racial Equality and ethnic minority groups. Its 1982 report made a series of policy recommendations across a range of areas, including employment, housing, education, the youth service and the police. More specifically, it recommended that local government implement equal opportunities policies and encourage other employers to do the same; that staff be trained in the housing problems prevalent amongst ethnic minority communities; a programme in schools that reflected the local multicultural society with regard to staff training, school meals and the monitoring of ethnic minority pupils; additional support for ethnic minority youth organisations; and the recruitment of more ethnic minority police officers and improved relations between the police and migrant youth. Regarding Muslim communities in particular, it advocated a closer collaboration between the Social Services Department and Muslim organisations as a way of promoting an understanding of the issues and opportunities that result from the meeting of different cultures, and it supported the need for improved premises for both the Thamesdown Islamic Association and the Pakistan Muslim Association's mother-tongue language classes, religious ceremonies and social gatherings.[37] This report acted as the immediate foundation for political discussion and action by both Swindon Borough Council and Wiltshire County Council.[38]

The interaction between RECs and local government also led to a range of other policies and measures. For example, action was taken jointly to improve the situation of ethnic minority tenants in council housing who were waiting for repairs or transfers, a range of local authority equal opportunities and anti-discriminatory policies were drawn up and implemented, and plans were put in place to develop ethnic minority, and particularly Asian, businesses.[39] During the 1990s, with the assistance of the Wiltshire Racial Equality Council, West Wiltshire District Council implemented a new code of practice in an attempt to ensure racial equality in the distribution of council housing, a step that the Wiltshire Racial Equality Council Chair referred to as 'a major move forward for a local authority in the rural South-West'.[40] Furthermore, made possible by both CRE and local government funding, RECs constituted an integral part of the local equalities infrastructure and played a key role in helping Wiltshire's local authority fulfil its duties as outlined in Section 71 of the Race Relations Act 1976. Their work covered a range of areas and issues, including discrimination suffered by ethnic minority youth in Melksham, Arabic language classes for the Moroccan community in Trowbridge, individual cases of alleged racial discrimination and opportunities to raise racial awareness at schools in Chippenham and Corsham, equal opportunities policies in local schools and companies like Airsprung and Bowyers, and Islamic classes and mosque planning applications.[41]

Both the prevalence of Wiltshire's RECs and their working relationships with local government were characterised by a great deal of diversity. The RECs' work was often patchy in its geographical reach and was much slower to develop in some areas of the county than in others. Furthermore, whilst recognising the backing they received from Wiltshire County Council, the RECs were quick to criticise the district councils for their lack of support, something they often attributed to a 'rural attitude'. Nevertheless, it is evident that the responsibility placed on local authorities by the Race Relations Act 1976 had a clear impact on their presence and status, as well as on the role they played in combatting discrimination and promoting equality of opportunity along both racial and religious lines. Overall, there are two key ways in which Wiltshire's RECs stood apart from those in other more rural areas in Britain. Firstly, despite the aforementioned limitations, they enjoyed far greater support and resources than has been suggested was the case in counties like Cornwall, Devon and Dorset.[42] Secondly, far from having the local-level responsibility for migrant communities simply offloaded onto them by local government,[43] Wiltshire's local authority independently played an active and important role in addressing migration and integration during the post-1976 years. One way in which it did this was by accommodating Muslim communities' religious needs and demands.

Muslim communities' religious needs and demands

As a result of religious demands made by Muslim minorities, Wiltshire's local authority had to decide to what extent it wished to accommodate the religious needs of local Muslims already by the mid-1970s. In November 1976, a sub-committee of West Wiltshire District Council's Environmental Committee considered a request issued by the Trowbridge Moroccan Islamic Association for an area of Trowbridge cemetery to be reserved for Muslim graves. More specifically, the Association asked for a section in the cemetery that was separated by a divider in the form of a fence or a screening, that the deceased be buried facing Mecca, that it be permitted to dig the graves itself, and that graveside ceremonies include a reading from the Koran. In return, the Association pledged to adhere to council regulations regarding the depth of graves, and burials taking place on Sundays and Christian feast days, and to pay for both the divider and the graves' upkeep. Although approving the request in principle, the committee decided to inquire about the procedures for Muslim burials in Bristol, presumably as it was the closest urban centre with a significant Muslim population.[44]

The Environmental Committee continued this discussion in July 1978 following its receipt of information about Muslim burials in Bristol. Upon learning that Muslims in Bristol did not insist that all Islamic rules and customs be adhered to, but did request separate facilities, the committee felt that the Trowbridge Moroccan Islamic Association would accept similar conditions. Thus, it decided to offer the local Muslim community a separate burial section that would be divided from the rest of the cemetery by a hedge and to allow the deceased to be positioned facing Mecca. Yet it also set a number of conditions, which included the stipulations that graves be dug by a council employee, that a body could not be washed by the graveside, and that raised kerbs that protected a grave from people walking across it not be permitted.[45] Whilst not meeting all of the Muslim community's demands, the fact that these considerations and discussions regarding Muslim burials were taking place in mid- to late-1970s Wiltshire is notable. Not only have they traditionally been portrayed as a matter for cities like Birmingham, Bradford and London, but it has been argued that it was generally not until the 1980s that such cities' local authorities with sizeable Muslim populations began to recognise that special provisions for Muslim burials needed to be made.[46]

In January 1977, in the midst of local political discussions about Muslim burials, a sub-committee of West Wiltshire District Council's Environmental Committee also considered a request received from the Trowbridge Moroccan Islamic Association regarding the *halal* method of animal slaughter. The Association sought permission to use a licensed slaughterhouse in Steeple Ashton, a village around four miles east of Trowbridge, for occasional events, such as religious festivals, and wished to slaughter the animals, usually sheep, without pre-stunning. The committee recognised that 'by English standards no member of the Association has had slaughtering experience, other than the ritual performed by every Islamic family',[47] and that there existed some opposition to slaughter without prior stunning. Following some discussion between the committee and the Islamic Association over the following months, the committee agreed to accept applications for slaughterman licences from individuals only if they agreed to the pre-stunning of animals, to a trial period of three months, and to being supervised by an experienced licensed slaughterman and a meat inspector. The first two applications for slaughterman licences were approved subject to these conditions in March 1977.[48] Similar to discussions regarding Muslim burials, those on *halal* slaughter during this period have tended to be associated with urban centres, and perhaps especially with Bradford where during the early 1980s the local authority agreed to provide children with *halal* meat in schools, a decision that captured the attention of both right-wing political parties and animal welfare groups.[49]

A request received by West Wiltshire District Council from the Trowbridge Islamic Association to purchase a piece of land in the town for the construction of an Islamic meeting hall or mosque during the mid-1980s proved to be somewhat more contentious. Having had their request refused by the council's Environmental Committee in December 1985,[50] the Association tried again in 1986, this time having identified a different site that was co-controlled by the council's Environmental and Housing Committees. In a letter to the Environmental Committee written in June 1986, the Association's president pointed out that they had 'struggled to find suitable accommodation or land on which to build a meeting hall for several years' for the town's sixty Arabic families, something he put down to 'planning objections or plain religious prejudice'[51]. He emphasised that the meeting hall would be used to teach Muslim children about the Islamic religion and to speak, read and write Arabic, and to host religious gatherings and prayer meetings. He stressed that it would not have a minaret or a loudspeaker calling people to prayer, and that it would not be used for entertaining nor would it disrupt the surrounding neighbourhood.[52] Having considered the request, the Environmental Committee approved the sale of the land in their ownership to the Islamic Association and recommended that the Housing Committee do the same.[53]

West Wiltshire District Council's Housing Committee discussed and considered the request in September 1986. One of the items included in their agenda papers was a letter written by Trowbridge Islamic Association's president to the *Wiltshire Times*. In the letter, he stressed his concern about the 'totally unfair and unjustified' objections to the proposed Islamic meeting hall, emphasised that 'Muslim families have lived in Trowbridge for the past 20 years with no trouble whatsoever,' and asked why it was that the community was encountering 'such blind prejudice'.[54] He went on to explain that 'many people imagine that upon the building of such a hall, there will be nothing but smells of eastern cooking, noise, crowds, a minaret with someone calling people to prayer at dawn and even the slaughtering of animals on the doorstep', pledged that 'none of the aforementioned will take place', and pointed out that mosques in Bristol and Cardiff's residential areas did not pose any problems.[55] The proposed meeting hall was also clearly a source of contention between the local Muslim community and some councillors. A second letter, written by the Chairman of the Moroccan Islamic Association, accused one local councillor who had supposedly once supported the meeting hall of suddenly backing the objectors 'in exchange for their votes'.[56] Yet notwithstanding these tensions, and despite having received a petition from local residents who opposed the construction of a mosque in the area, the Housing Committee agreed to sell the land. Three councillors, including the one referred to in the letter above, requested that their opposition to the committee's decision be logged.[57] North and West Wiltshire Council for Racial Equality referred to the collaboration between the district council and the Islamic Association in the securing of a site for a mosque as 'inspiring'.[58]

Similar local government support for a mosque was seen during the 1990s. In 1996, Wiltshire County Council agreed to sell the former Queenstown Infants School site in Swindon to the town's Islamic Association at 50% of the open market value with the understanding that it would become a mosque. Furthermore, when the Association struggled to raise the necessary funds and had not obtained the required planning consent and approvals, the local authority granted it extensions.[59] It is well known that mosques have long sparked controversy in towns and cities across Britain and local authority reactions have varied. Some local authorities, like that of Birmingham, have been accused of adopting a hostile and restrictive stance towards mosque applications at times. Others have been commended for their more inclusive and liberal approach, an example of which is Leicester City Council which, during the early 1990s, like Wiltshire County Council, sold some of its land at a heavily reduced price in order to enable a new mosque to be built.[60] Yet regardless of how individual cities have been depicted, accounts of local-level discussions and negotiations regarding mosques have been firmly rooted in the city landscape, with it being stressed that mosques have gradually become symbols of British multicultural urban narratives.[61]

The 1980s are commonly seen as a turning point in local authorities meeting the particular religious demands of Muslim communities. Perhaps as a result of the wider political context of the time, which comprised the development of multiculturalism, the greater recognition of cultural and ethnic diversity, and the Rushdie Affair, British Muslims became more organised and local governments increasingly responded to Islamic needs.[62] Although taking place on a much smaller scale and not enjoying the same level of national, and even local, attention as Muslim institutionalisation and policymakers' decisions in cities with larger Muslim populations, it is clear that Wiltshire was no exception. Already during the mid-1970s, as a direct result of the Moroccan presence in and around Trowbridge, Wiltshire's local authority began to debate, and respond to, the religious needs and practices of local Muslims. Furthermore, whilst Muslim burials, *halal* slaughter and mosques were the three topics that received the most attention, the county's Muslim communities' religious needs and demands were also accommodated in other ways. Local authority grants, for example, supported a range of initiatives, including a cultural programme organised by Swindon's Pakistan Muslim Association, a celebration of the birthday of Prophet Muhammad hosted by the Jamia Mohammadia organisation, and an event to mark the end of Ramadan coordinated by Thamesdown Islamic Association.[63] There were also a number of other areas through which Wiltshire's local authority responded to the arrival and settlement of Muslim migrants, and ethnic minority communities in general, during the late 1970s, 1980s and 1990s, not least that of education.

Education

During the late 1970s, 1980s and 1990s, education was again the most complex and discussed topic regarding migrant communities in Wiltshire. In order to fully understand the county's local authority's policies and practices, it is necessary to recognise overarching national-level proposals and direction. As well as the Race Relations Act 1976, which outlawed racial discrimination in education specifically, there were a number of other developments that caused a shift in the political attitude to the education of ethnic minority schoolchildren in Britain during this period. The assimilationist approach, which it had initially been believed would result in the quick absorption of ethnic minority pupils into British society and which was discussed in the last chapter, was increasingly challenged and criticised. It was felt, for example, that it reinforced the notion that ethnic minority schoolchildren were the cause of educational problems, and that it did not adequately cater for the ethnic and cultural diversity present within the education system.[64] As the 1970s unfolded, it was gradually recognised that more needed to be done to prepare children for a multicultural British society. A 1977 Green Paper emphasised that Britain was home to ethnic minority communities and that schools had a duty to teach their pupils about this British multi-racial society.[65]

A few years later, the 1981 Rampton Report explored the causes of educational underachievement amongst West Indian schoolchildren, exposed the prevalence of racism in the education system, and made a series of recommendations pertaining to a range of areas, including the curriculum, teaching materials, and the relationship between schools and the wider community.[66] Yet it was with the publication of the Swann Report in 1985 that a multicultural approach to the education of ethnic minority schoolchildren really began to take hold.[67] The report addressed numerous areas, including achievement, language and teacher training, the needs of individual ethnic minority groups, and religion and religious education, and advocated a new 'education for all' approach. Whilst the report has been criticised, not least for failing to both recognise religion as a marker of identity and provide for the needs of Muslim communities, there is no doubt that it constituted a significant turning point in the political approach to the education of ethnic minority pupils in Britain.[68]

As a result of the decentralised nature of the British educational system, it largely fell to local education authorities to invoke change. Yet with regard to the Race Relations Act 1976, it has often been argued that immediate changes of direction in policies and practices regarding racial discrimination and equality of opportunity were seen in few local authorities.[69] Concerning education specifically, and with a few exceptions aside, it was generally not until the 1980s that local government began to act in earnest and local policy responses addressing education in a multicultural society really took off.[70] The policies and guidelines of a number of local education authorities in urban areas with substantial ethnic minority communities, such as Bradford, Inner London and Manchester, have been recognised.[71] Wiltshire also gets a fleeting mention, with Sally Tomlinson referring to the county as a 'pioneer' of multicultural education in a predominantly white area alongside Cumbria and Lincolnshire.[72] Although she does not go into any detail, an assessment of local policies and practices certainly goes some way towards explaining this commendation. That Wiltshire was a rural leader in catering for the education of ethnic minority schoolchildren during this period should perhaps not come as a surprise. As seen in the previous chapter, not only was education a key area of focus in relation to the county's local authority approach to ethnic minority communities during the 1960s and early 1970s, but it also had experience with the education of Cambodian and Vietnamese refugee families during the late 1970s to draw upon.[73]

Already in June 1978, in response to a Department for Education and Science (DES) circular, Wiltshire County Council's Education Committee's Schools Sub-Committee clarified its position on education and race. Despite not having an official policy on the promotion of racial understanding and the overall small number of ethnic minority pupils in the county's schools, it stressed that there was nevertheless a local commitment to ensuring that these schoolchildren were not subject to educational disadvantage. Conferences on the topic were organised and attended by local teachers, members of the local education authority and the race relations officer. The needs of non-English-speaking children in the county were surveyed annually, and help and advice were offered to individual teachers and schoolchildren within schools.[74] Whilst local political debates and measures regarding multicultural education overwhelmingly developed with all migrant schoolchildren in mind, there were some deliberations that addressed the local Muslim communities specifically. During the late 1970s, for example, the Chief Education Officer offered an insight into some aspects of education that touched upon Muslim pupils. He painted a fairly positive picture, stressing that parents had the right to withdraw their children from religious education instruction and collective worship, that revised school uniform rules allowed Muslim girls to wear trousers, and that a representative from Swindon's Muslim community had been invited to attend the teachers' panel on religious education.[75] Furthermore, it was emphasised that the religious education curriculum should reflect Britain's multi-faith society in order to prevent ignorance, intolerance and prejudice, and some schools soon began to hold assemblies that addressed other faiths and cultures.[76]

Wiltshire's local authority's commitment to multicultural education intensified during the 1980s despite acknowledging that the county was not home to large migrant communities. In December 1980, for example, the number of New Commonwealth immigrant pupils in the Thamesdown area stood at 800 (2.9%), whilst ethnic minority children were estimated to constitute between 2% and 3% of Wiltshire's school population during the mid-1980s.[77] Yet there was nevertheless a local commitment to do more to meet the needs of ethnic minority schoolchildren. The council's Finance and General Purposes Sub-Committee felt that the local education authority's work focused largely on pupils' basic language needs and that more support needed to be offered if these pupils were to fulfil their educational potential.[78] In November 1982, the council's Education Committee's Schools Sub-Committee acknowledged that multicultural education could no longer be perceived as being a concern only for those schools with significant numbers of ethnic minority pupils. Referring to the DES's January 1980 document entitled 'A Framework for the School Curriculum', it recognised that the curriculum should promote 'respect for the religious and moral values and a tolerance of other races, religions and ways of life, to help pupils understand the way in which they live, and the interdependence of individuals, groups and nations'.[79] It understood multicultural education as having two key aims. The first was to guarantee that schoolchildren of all ethnic backgrounds were able to fulfil their educational potential. The second consisted of ensuring that all children gained an understanding and appreciation of the various cultures and ways of life that comprised British society. The committee stressed that this constituted a shift from the assimilationist agenda that had shaped the education of ethnic minority pupils from the 1960s, and that this multicultural approach was central to children's education on both a social and personal level, and should thus be reflected throughout the entire curriculum.[80]

It was these ideals and values that shaped Wiltshire's local authority's approach to the education of migrant children throughout the 1980s. In January 1982, a Multicultural Education Team comprised of three teachers was formed as a result of funding secured through the Section 11 scheme.[81] Its aim was 'to meet the specific needs of children from ethnic minority groups and to make a positive response to the implications of a multicultural society for all pupils in the county', and it carried out its work in three key ways.[82] Firstly, a small unit was set up in Swindon for children who had recently arrived in the area and were in need of intensive English-language instruction. By November 1982, there were ten children making use of this facility on a part-time basis. Secondly, team members taught around thirty children, either individually or in groups, within their own schools. Their work with schools also consisted of offering advice to teachers on the teaching of English as a second language, and working to create positive relationships with the parents of ethnic minority schoolchildren. Thirdly, the team also carried out a number of functions beyond English-language teaching, including collecting learning materials that could be used by teachers across Wiltshire, helping with the translation of materials into a number of minority languages, and offering advice on the cultural backgrounds of the county's migrant populations.[83]

The early 1980s also saw Wiltshire County Council pursue two further initiatives on multicultural education. The first was the awarding of grants to groups in the Thamesdown area that organised and delivered the teaching of mother-tongue languages. One of these groups was the Pakistani Muslims Association, which offered Urdu classes to around thirty schoolchildren. The second was the drafting of a policy statement on multicultural education. Taking note of the fact that a number of neighbouring counties, including Avon and Berkshire, had already adopted such a policy, Wiltshire's local authority felt that it was necessary for its education sector to recognise both the multicultural nature of society and its educational needs. Its proposed policy consisted of four key objectives: 'to educate pupils and teachers towards an understanding of, and respect for, one another's cultural, ethnic and religious differences; within its many different educational activities, to draw upon, encourage and support the cultural heritage of the communities within our society; to take positive steps to promote equality of opportunity and harmony and to combat discriminatory practices; to endeavour to meet the particular needs of all children within its schools, having regard to their diverse cultural backgrounds.'[84] In the end, this policy was not adopted, yet the fact that such a policy was drawn up and considered in Wiltshire before the publication of the

Swann Report is an indication of how progressive its local political approach to the education of ethnic minorities was.[85]

During the early 1980s, Wiltshire County Council also solicited advice and guidance on race and immigration in schools from external experts. More specifically, it sought information with which to challenge misconceptions about the causes and levels of immigration to Britain, and on the media content through which pupils in areas with small migrant populations tended to learn about immigration, as well as on how race might be addressed in schools without the need for vast amounts of extra resources.[86] The Education Committee officially recognised the need for specialist workers to meet migrant pupils' educational needs, as well as a school curriculum that did more to educate white pupils about multi-racial Britain. Both racism and the celebration of cultural diversity became key issues in schools across Wiltshire. Chippenham's Sheldon School and Melksham's George Ward School, for example, discussed racism as part of social education courses. In Trowbridge, Paxcroft School introduced work on the West Indies and teachers from schools across the town met regularly to consider a number of issues regarding multicultural education, including racism. The county also witnessed increased support for mother-tongue teaching through grants, the provision of educational premises, and multi-racial primary schools making use of children's bilingualism in the classroom. Furthermore, Newton School in Trowbridge became the first school in Wiltshire to print its brochure in two languages, and did so both in English and Arabic, with the choice of Arabic undoubtedly being as a result of the local Moroccan community.[87]

Some of the local political discussions on multicultural education in Wiltshire during the early to mid-1980s were led by the Advisory Group for Multi-cultural Education. Comprised of representatives from primary and secondary schools, the local education authority, the Council for Racial Equality, and ethnic minority communities, the group was charged with creating a space for discussion between its various members, and with advising both the Chief Education Officer and schools across the county on matters relating to multicultural education.[88] The topics and issues the group addressed included mother-tongue teaching, the educational progress of ethnic minority pupils, teaching materials and resources, racism awareness sessions for teachers, and applications for, and the subsequent distribution of, Section 11 posts. More localised measures and initiatives were also considered and discussed, such as a sixth-form conference on race in Marlborough, difficulties meeting the needs of ethnic minority pupils at a secondary school in Swindon, and the allocation of additional teaching resources to a centre in Devizes.[89]

Although Wiltshire's local authority was already active in the area of multicultural education, the publication of the 1985 Swann Report nevertheless had an immediate impact in the county. For example, a report was produced that drew comparisons between the Swann Committee's findings and recommendations and the local situation. It recognised that, in accordance with the national picture, Bangladeshi and West Indian children in Wiltshire tended to educationally underachieve, and that this underachievement was partly caused by wider socio-economic disadvantage. Furthermore, it stressed that there was a tendency to perceive multicultural education 'in ethnic minority terms' rather than in relation to the education of all children, that racism caused by both the stereotyping of migrant communities and institutional practices was prevalent, and that aspects of multiculturalism were still often simply tagged on to the curriculum rather than constituting an inherent part of it.[90]

Regarding the Swann Report's recommended strategies for bringing about change, the report acknowledged that neither the local education authority nor any school in Wiltshire had an official policy pledging a commitment to 'Education for All', and that additional support, resources and awareness training were needed if schools were expected to review their curricula and implement anti-racism policies, especially as many denied that racism existed. It also recognised that secondary schools were not teaching community languages as part of their curricula, that schools and communities did not tend to work together on the provision of religious education, that Wiltshire's local education authority was not officially an equal opportunities employer, that there were difficulties recruiting ethnic minority teachers with overseas qualifications, and that statistics on migrant pupils were not up to date and widely kept. Yet the publication of the Swann Report also provided the opportunity to record the ways in which its recommendations were already being met in Wiltshire. For example, South Asian language classes were taking place and were being supported by the local education authority, and the county was home to what was referred to as 'a surprisingly high number of "black" teachers', some of which were at deputy head level. There was also some emphasis on Muslim pupils specifically, with the committee recognising that the lack of single-sex schools occasionally caused problems with Muslim families and pledging that plans were in place regarding the extent to which local schools catered for the pastoral needs of Muslim children.[91]

As a direct result of the 1985 Swann Report, the Working Party on Multicultural Education was set up by the council's Schools Sub-Committee the following year. At the very core of its rationale were the Swann Report's beliefs that all children needed to be prepared for life in a multicultural society, and that this society should be pluralist rather than be based on an expectation that ethnic minority communities would assimilate. The working party's central aim was to devise a policy statement on multicultural education for the county, which reflected the local education authority's commitment to combatting racial discrimination, and ethnic minority disadvantage and underachievement in schools, and supporting the preservation of minority languages and cultures. Its recommended policy consisted of four principles. The first was that the curriculum of all schools should reflect Britain's racially and culturally diverse society, and that schoolchildren should be taught to understand and respect this diversity. The second recognised that all children are equal and that schools had a duty to draw upon children's diverse ethnic and cultural backgrounds in a way that led to the appreciation of the inherent link between individuals, communities and nations. Making reference to the Race Relations Act 1976, the third stressed that the local education authority's services were to be delivered without racial discrimination, and with the aim of promoting positive community relations and equality of opportunity. In the fourth, the working party emphasised that members of ethnic minority groups had been consulted in the policy's development, and that it intended to consult these communities in the implementation and monitoring stages.[92] This statement was adopted by Wiltshire's local authority as the basis of its future official policy on multicultural education in April 1987.[93]

The working party outlined a number of ways in which these principles would translate into practice. It would, for example, continue to offer English-language tuition to ethnic minority pupils in primary and secondary schools. It felt that there were a significant number of children in Wiltshire who arrived at school with low levels of English-language proficiency. Furthermore, as was often the case in more rural areas, these children were increasingly found dispersed across the county and from a range of linguistic backgrounds. The party was also committed to supporting the teaching of mother-tongues, both in schools and across the wider community. It felt that fostering mother-tongue languages was a central part of valuing ethnic minority communities, and recognised that there were many spoken across the county, including Bengali, Punjabi and Urdu. It was suggested that some of Wiltshire's more prevalent minority languages could be offered in schools either through the curriculum or extra-curricular classes, and that some schools might even consider offering the option of learning a South Asian language to all pupils.[94]

The working party also highlighted the importance of providing training for teachers regarding the teaching of children from a range of ethnic and cultural backgrounds. It maintained that, whilst some progress had been made, in the Salisbury area in particular, further initiatives were needed in order to ensure that teachers were equipped with the necessary materials and methods. Furthermore, it felt that more needed to be done to both recognise and combat racial prejudice. Ethnic minority schoolchildren in Wiltshire were subjected to racist incidents carried out by their peers, but also to low educational expectations held by teaching staff. Whilst the working party recognised that changing such behaviour and perceptions was a long-term process, it stressed its commitment to doing so. Its proposed measures included the securing of a premise for ethnic minority communities to use for educational as well as cultural, religious and social purposes; the involving of members of ethnic minority communities in the development and monitoring of a multicultural education policy, believing that their advice would be invaluable and their participation would promote trust and positive relations; and the outlining of a rationale for additional English-language and mother-tongue teaching posts.[95]

This multicultural approach to education continued throughout the late 1980s and 1990s. Initiatives included a grant application for a pilot project to enhance multicultural awareness in an all-white area in Salisbury, and discussions about Section 11 provision in towns across Wiltshire, including Swindon and Trowbridge.[96] It was proposed that clear guidelines on how to address racial harassment in schools be drawn up once it was seen that other local authorities had done so, specialist teachers were hired through an expanded Multicultural Service to look after ethnic minority pupils' needs, and a Wiltshire–Kenya link was established through schools in Corsham and Melksham.[97] By 1996, the Multicultural Education Service offered support to 375 pupils across the county and was praised for encouraging students to be proud of their cultural backgrounds and its high-quality teaching, one school had introduced mother-tongue languages to its curriculum, and there was a continued commitment to the recommendations that had been outlined in the 1985 Swann Report.[98] Furthermore, individual schools liaised with the Wiltshire Racial Equality Council regarding the development of their equal opportunities policies, mother-tongue community language classes continued to receive funding, ways in which to address the bullying and expulsion of ethnic minority pupils were discussed, and local Muslim communities gained representation on the Standing Advisory Council on Religious Education (SACRE).[99]

As was the case during the 1960s and early 1970s, the late 1970s, 1980s and 1990s also saw Wiltshire's local authority look to other localities' developments and responses, and be influenced by national-level direction and mandate especially. The Race Relations Act 1976 and the 1985 Swann Report in particular guided the shift in Wiltshire from an assimilationist to a multicultural approach to the education of ethnic minority pupils, an approach that continued to develop throughout the late 1990s. Its policies and practices were rooted in the notions that even 'white' schools in 'white' areas had a duty to promote a pluralistic education, and that multiculturalism was to be advanced through providing an 'Education for All'. Indeed, as was the case for many local authorities, education became a, and perhaps *the*, key focus of Wiltshire's political approach to migrant communities, almost certainly as a result of a combination of factors, including clear national-level direction, Britain's decentralised education system, the availability of central government funding, and the fact that it was an area where a real difference could be made.[100] Moreover, whilst Wiltshire had addressed the education of ethnic minority schoolchildren already from the early 1960s, its policies and practices during the post-1976 period became greater in number, range of priorities and geographical scope. Whilst Muslim pupils were by no means the exclusive focus of these political discussions and measures, they were at the centre of some of them, and their educational needs were reflected in practically all of them, from those enabling an acquisition of English and mother-tongue languages to those supporting an appreciation of cultural, ethnic and religious differences. Despite its more rural setting and small migrant communities, and influenced by a top-down multiculturalist agenda, initiatives pursued in other areas and counties, and the local context, Wiltshire's local authority demonstrated a proactive and persistent commitment to migrant education during this period.

Equal opportunities and anti-discrimination

Wiltshire's local authority's response to the arrival and settlement of migrant communities extended to pursuing equal opportunities and anti-discrimination in a number of areas during the post-1976 period. In comparison to those regarding the education sector, these measures, policies and responses developed on a more ad hoc basis and, whilst firmly rooted in the Race Relations Act 1976, as has been argued was the case for local authorities in general, these changes in local policies and practices were by no means immediate.[101] Furthermore, they did not address Muslim migrant communities in particular, but rather were aimed at ethnic minorities in general. As has been established was the case in urban areas like Birmingham and Harrow, and arguably because this was an area in which local government felt it could make a real difference,[102] Wiltshire's local authority placed a large emphasis on developing and implementing its own equal opportunities policies, primarily with the view to hiring a greater number of ethnic minority employees.

Citing the Race Relations Act 1976 and the duty it placed upon local authorities, equal opportunities policies started to be drafted from the mid-1980s. Policy statements were drawn up, as were lists of specific aims and rationales. Thamesdown Borough Council stressed that such a policy would enable the eradication of direct and indirect discrimination and the identification of underrepresented groups in certain areas and types of work, and would allow staff to fulfil their potential.[103] West Wiltshire District Council's aims included reducing the effect of racial discrimination in employment, tackling the prevalence of high unemployment amongst ethnic minorities, and allowing individuals the opportunity to develop their abilities and the council to make full use of its staff.[104] Wiltshire County Council was driven by national-level directive, the benefits associated with attracting a wider proportion of the local labour force and, as the largest single employer in the county, by a perceived duty to adhere to high employment practice standards.[105] There were a number of ways in which equality of opportunity was to be promoted. These included offering training and guidance to all council employees involved with the recruitment and selection process; drawing up job advertisements that stressed that the council was an equal opportunity employer and were placed in publications available to ethnic minority communities; ensuring that all promotion decisions were rooted in fair and objective criteria; taking the cultural backgrounds of employees into account in discipline and dismissal matters; ensuring that policies of equality of opportunity and anti-discrimination were on display for all staff across all worksites; and implementing recruitment monitoring procedures through which to continuously assess the effect of policies and practices.[106]

These policy proposals do not appear to have been mere tokenistic attempts to comply with the equal opportunities and anti-discrimination agenda. Rather they were carefully considered, revised and updated, and there seems to have been a genuine commitment to being equal opportunities employers and to fulfilling the local duty placed upon local authorities more broadly. The Borough of Thamesdown's Race Relations Sub-Committee, for example, referred to the equal opportunities policy as 'an initial step towards the adoption of the spirit and intention of the Race Relations Act 1976'.[107] West Wiltshire District Council updated its policy in 1992, this time citing religion alongside race, colour and ethnic origins as a basis on which discrimination was opposed.[108] Wiltshire County Council recognised the need for further developments and procedures as ethnic minority applicants were less likely to be shortlisted and appointed for council jobs than their white counterparts.[109]

Furthermore, like many local authorities across Britain,[110] equal opportunities and anti-discrimination policies in Wiltshire also extended to service provision. Arguing that there were ethnic minorities in the county whose particular needs were not being met, Wiltshire's local authority pledged a commitment to developing a clear and comprehensive multicultural policy in the area of social services during the early 1990s and consideration was given to how individual services might be improved. It stressed that staff should be helped to acquire an understanding of service provision with regard to ethnic minority groups, and with reference to culture, religion and dietary requirements in particular, and it recognised the importance of involving ethnic minorities in the consultation and planning stages, as well as the need to secure carers and foster carers for ethnic minority communities. Proposed applications for central government funding included a mental health project for Asian women and young Asian and Afro-Caribbean men, and projects that supported elderly New Commonwealth (NCW) migrants and sought to break down cultural and linguistic barriers across a range of services, and addressed the recruitment of NCW child-minders and foster parents. Furthermore, a Social Services Anti-Discriminatory Steering Group was set up, which made a series of recommendations regarding the monitoring of ethnic data, the securing of funds to develop services to meet the needs of ethnic minorities, and promoting greater awareness amongst staff. These local developments were framed within national legislation, including the Race Relations Act 1976 and the Children Act 1989.[111]

Another area that received a significant amount of local authority attention with regard to ethnic minority communities securing equal opportunities was employment. During the early 1990s, Wiltshire County Council, Thamesdown Borough Council and Kennet District Council funded a labour market research project that explored those groups experiencing difficulties securing employment and ways in which employers could maximise recruitment potential.[112] People of ethnic minority origin were cited as being one of Wiltshire's 'disadvantaged employment groups', alongside people with disabilities, women returning to work and people over the age of fifty. The report estimated that there were around 1,000 people of ethnic minority origin in the county who were unemployed and seeking employment. It highlighted that there were a number of examples of good practice taking place in companies across the county, including anonymising applicants during the shortlisting process, ensuring that equal opportunities policies had the support of senior management and became part of the company culture, and recognising religious observance when planning holidays and shifts. Nevertheless, Wiltshire's local authority concluded that there existed barriers preventing people from ethnic minorities from securing employment, and that more needed to be done to make local employers aware of the benefits of both positive employment practices and of having a greater labour force to recruit from.[113] Furthermore, as part of its proposed economic development strategy for the county, the Joint Consultative Forum on Economic Development pledged to monitor the training and employment opportunities of minority groups, and to subsequently offer any necessary targeted support. How this was going to be implemented, however, was not specified.[114]

During the late 1980s and early 1990s especially, discussions also took place regarding the development of ethnic minority entrepreneurship. During the late 1980s, Thamesdown Borough Council financially supported a 'Black Business Conference', through which it wished to ascertain how it could help meet the needs of potential ethnic minority businessmen, and from which it aimed to draw up a series of recommendations for improving the prospects for developing 'Black businesses' and relevant services.[115] It also set up a working group, which surveyed local agencies in order to establish whether black people experienced particular problems and obstacles when setting up and running businesses, such as discrimination and racism, and thus required additional support.[116]

In 1993, Wiltshire County Council addressed the idea of developing ethnic minority, and particularly Asian, entrepreneurship. It recognised the extent to which Wiltshire was benefitting from ethnic minority businesses and investment, 'from the Japanese at Honda in Swindon, to an Afro-Caribbean cosmetics boutique in Trowbridge and an Asian corner shop in Salisbury'.[117] It argued that more needed to be done to help develop and support these business activities, and proposed holding a series of seminars aimed at ethnic minority businessmen specifically, in conjunction with a range of national and local bodies and organisations, including the Prince of Wales Trust, the Wiltshire Training and Enterprise Council, and the county's Racial Equality Councils and multicultural education advisors. Furthermore, it suggested inviting established ethnic minority businessmen to be speakers and considered targeting potential female entrepreneurs as well.[118] This local authority support for 'Black' or ethnic minority businesses reflected a wider political culture of promoting ethnic minority entrepreneurship in Britain during the late 1980s and early 1990s. Often perceived to be a way of combatting unemployment and economic difficulties and promoting urban regeneration and social cohesion in the shadow of the 1981 inner-city riots, such political backing and encouragement developed at both a national and local level.[119]

The 1981 urban riots, along with a number of other factors, including the Race Relations Act 1976 and reports and recommendations issued by the CRE, also played a role in prompting local authorities across Britain to consider equal opportunities in housing.[120] Wiltshire was no different in that housing became steadily more significant in its local authority's approach to ethnic minorities across the post-1976 period. Initially, this area does not seem to have been a pressing concern, with migrant communities' housing conditions and experiences only being addressed in a very impromptu and unplanned manner. In 1980, for example, an area in Trowbridge that was selected to undergo significant environmental improvements happened to be home to thirteen households 'of foreign origin'.[121] In 1981, West Wiltshire District Council stepped in to help secure housing for a Bangladeshi family, though stressed that it was unusual to encounter immigrant families faced with homelessness 'in this part of England', and feared that 'the question of creating precedents may loom in many people's minds'.[122] Indeed, it was not until the mid-1980s that policies and practices addressing ethnic minorities in the housing sector truly began to develop in earnest in the county. In 1982, for example, Thamesdown's Race Relations Sub-Committee argued the importance of council housing application forms being available in Urdu and Punjabi, of keeping and monitoring ethnic records, and of the particular needs of ethnic minorities being considered during a period of redevelopment.[123] A few years later, following a CRE report on the housing allocation policy in Hackney,[124] the Housing Management Sub-Committee was asked to carry out a full evaluation of the council's housing application policies and procedures despite there being no evidence of discrimination.[125]

The CRE again shaped local policy a few years later, this time in West Wiltshire as a result of its code of practice in rented housing.[126] Despite maintaining that ethnic minorities comprised less than 2% of the population and that therefore racial discrimination was 'not a major issue', West Wiltshire's District Council's Housing Committee was in favour of adopting the code.[127] It recognised that its aims were to offer guidance on how to implement the objectives and visions of the Race Relations Act 1976 and combat racial discrimination in the rented housing sector, whilst providing examples of good practice with regard to equal opportunities. It highlighted the ways in which the code outlined that direct and indirect racial discrimination might unfold, including with regard to housing access and quality, service delivery and harassment, as well as the examples of good practice it suggested, namely that all housing providers have equal opportunities policies, housing organisations review their policies and procedures, records of the ethnic origins of housing applicants and tenants be kept and monitored, and that staff be trained in equal opportunities. Furthermore, it was felt that adopting the code would reflect the local authority's commitment to equal opportunities more broadly.[128]

During the early 1990s, in the Borough of Thamesdown, the Ethnic Monitoring and Research Working Party of the Housing and Health Committee helped the Housing Department address the problems encountered by ethnic minorities with regard to housing services. Furthermore, a training programme on equality in housing was organised for staff, and a leaflet outlining the council's policy on racial harassment was created in an attempt to both discourage possible offenders and offer assurance to local ethnic minority communities.[129] During the mid-1990s, research into the housing needs of ethnic minorities in Thamesdown led to a local authority commitment to further address the housing of these communities in a range of ways, and considerations and recommendations included exploring the issue of overcrowding prevalent amongst Pakistani and especially Bangladeshi families, reviewing the ethnic records and monitoring system, undertaking future consultation with ethnic minority groups, and using renovation grants to improve the housing conditions of migrant groups.[130] Overall, these developments in Wiltshire during the 1980s and 1990s reflected what was a much wider trend of incorporating housing into the local government racial equality agenda, and the county's policies and practices mirrored those introduced by urban local authorities across Britain.[131]

Conclusion

There is no doubt that the Race Relations Act 1976 had a clear and wide-ranging impact on Wiltshire's local authority's political approach to its migrant communities. Despite the county's rural nature and small and dispersed ethnic minority populations, the local duty to promote positive race relations and address racial disadvantage prevailed and led to vibrant deliberations, policies and practices in a range of areas. Yet, as was seen to be the case during the 1960s and early 1970s, these were also not without their limitations and shortcomings. Firstly, there was clear inter-county variation, with Thamesdown and Trowbridge often being the frontrunners in addressing migration and integration, and more rural and 'white' areas like Kennet and Salisbury lagging behind and on occasion maintaining that there was no need for policy intervention. Secondly, the lack of commitment and support the RECs received from the district councils in comparison to Wiltshire County Council shows that there were also inconsistencies across different tiers of government. Both of these traits suggest that elements of a 'no problem here' mentality, or a 'rural attitude', were present in the county. Thirdly, whether a response to national-level directive or local Muslim communities' demands, or spurred on by other local authorities' actions and initiatives, Wiltshire's local authority's immigrant, integration and diversity policies and strategies were often active and conscientious. Yet they were simultaneously led and shaped by these numerous external influences without which it proves difficult to imagine what the county's political approach might have been or indeed whether it would have had one at all. Fourthly, although not easy to determine with the documentation available, it should nevertheless be recognised that the policies and practices discussed in this chapter were not necessarily always effective or successful. In fact, similar policies implemented by other local authorities, be it regarding equal opportunities, racial equality or multi-cultural education, have at times been deemed ineffective and weak, and have been heavily criticised.[132]

Nevertheless, Wiltshire's local authority did not display the apathy or ignorance during the late 1970s, 1980s and 1990s often associated with more rural areas. To the contrary, this period witnessed an intensification in the county's immigrant, integration and diversity policies, both in number and in scope. Firmly rooted within a national context marked by multiculturalism, equal opportunities and a growing appreciation of Muslim minority communities' religious identities and demands, Wiltshire's policies and practices were influenced by this national agenda, whilst simultaneously responding to local needs and issues. Furthermore, the county's local authority's political approach was concurrently embedded within a clear rural dimension. This was seen in the manner in which it looked to other rural areas as well as cities for precedence, in that its policies were often entrenched in the notion that Wiltshire was a 'white' county that was home to small ethnic minority populations, and in how there was at times a deliberate effort to not succumb to the 'no problem here' mentality frequently associated with rural Britain.

Overall, Wiltshire's RECs appear to have received more support than was the case in some rural counties, its Muslim communities' religious practices and traditions were recognised and accommodated from the late 1970s, and the county witnessed clear strategies regarding equal opportunities in a range of areas, including employment, housing and service provision. Furthermore, it is easy to see why Wiltshire has been referred to as a 'pioneer' of multicultural education in a predominantly white area.[133] Not only did Wiltshire's local authority devise and implement this political agenda despite its small ethnic minority communities and the frequently held belief that there were few problems or difficulties in the county as a result of migration, but it also often kept pace with its urban counterparts when doing so. The extent to which this commitment and dedication continued into the twenty-first century will be assessed in the next chapter.

Notes

1 The 1981 urban riots started in Brixton and spread throughout England, particularly to other inner-city areas in London, Liverpool and Manchester. The Scarman Report, the result of an investigation into the riots, found that they had been sparked by long-term issues such as a general mistrust in the police and racial disadvantage. For an insight into various arguments regarding the impact the Race Relations Act 1976 had on local authorities, see Ken Young and Naomi Connelly, 'After the Act: local authority policy reviews under the Race Relations Act 1976', *Local Government Studies*, 10:1 (1984), 13–25; Solomos, *Race and Racism in Contemporary Britain*, pp. 92–3; and Bleich, *Race Politics in Britain and France*, p. 108.

2 For some of the key works on British multiculturalism, see Yasmin Alibhai-Brown, *After Multiculturalism* (London: Foreign Policy Centre, 2000); Bhikhu Parekh, *Rethinking Multiculturalism: Cultural Diversity and Political Theory* (Basingstoke: Macmillan, 2000); Tariq Modood, *Multiculturalism: A Civic Idea* (Cambridge: Polity, 2007); and Nasar Meer, *Citizenship, Identity and the Politics of Multiculturalism: The Rise of Muslim Consciousness* (Basingstoke: Palgrave Macmillan, 2010).

3 See Roger Hewitt, *White Backlash and the Politics of Multiculturalism* (Cambridge: Cambridge University Press, 2005), pp. 30–2; and Amir Ali, *South Asian Islam and British Multiculturalism* (Abingdon: Routledge, 2016), pp. 44–6.

4 See Candappa and Joly, *Local Authorities, Ethnic Minorities and "Pluralist Integration"*.

5   See Hackett, *Foreigners, Minorities and Integration.*

6   See Paul Winstone, 'Managing a multi-ethnic and multicultural city in Europe: Leicester', *International Social Science Journal,* 48:147 (1996), 33–41.

7   See Ansari, *'The Infidel Within',* pp. 314, 325.

8   See Philip Lewis, 'The Bradford Council for Mosques and the search for Muslim unity', in Steven Vertovec and Ceri Peach (eds), *Islam in Europe: The Politics of Religion and Community* (Basingstoke: Macmillan, 1997), p. 110.

9   See Jørgen S. Nielsen and Jonas Otterbeck, *Muslims in Western Europe* (Edinburgh: Edinburgh University Press, 2016), p. 61.

10 See, for example, Tariq Modood, 'British Asian Muslims and the Rushdie Affair', *The Political Quarterly,* 61:2 (1990), pp. 143–60; and Nicole Falkenhayner, *Making the British Muslim: Representations of the Rushdie Affair and Figures of the War-on-Terror Decade* (Basingstoke: Palgrave Macmillan, 2014).

11 See Solomos, *Race and Racism in Britain,* p. 213.

12 It should be recognised, however, that despite this recognition of religious affiliation on behalf of many local authorities, there was often a perception amongst Muslim communities during this period that not enough was being done to meet Muslims' religious needs and demands, as well as a prevalence of local-level institutional discrimination. See Ansari, *Muslims in Britain,* pp. 8–9; Ansari, *'The Infidel Within',* pp. 325–7; and Eren Tatari, *Muslims in British Local Government: Representing Minority Interests in Hackney, Newham, and Tower Hamlets* (Leiden: Brill, 2014), p. 150.

13 For example, see Jay, *'Keep Them in Birmingham';* de Lima, 'John O'Groats to Land's End', p. 49; and Paul Connolly, ' "It goes without saying (well, sometimes)": racism, Whiteness and identity in Northern Ireland', in Sarah Neal and Julian Agyeman (eds), *The New Countryside?: Ethnicity, Nation and Exclusion in Contemporary Rural Britain* (Bristol: The Policy Press, 2006), pp. 21–2.

14 Census 1981 England and Wales, country of birth, statistics provided by the Office for National Statistics (ONS). As was the case for the 1961 and 1971 Censuses, these figures include only those people born in these countries and not any of their descendants born in Britain. As such, these communities were most certainly larger. Other residents in Wiltshire who had been born in New Commonwealth countries included those born in the Far East (1,419) and the Mediterranean (1,199).

15 Census 1981 England and Wales, country of birth, statistics provided by the Office for National Statistics (ONS). Again, the size of these communities was undoubtedly higher as these figures do not include descendants born in Britain. Both Wiltshire and Swindon were also home to significant numbers of people who had been born in Scotland, Wales and in other European countries.

16 Census 1991 England and Wales, ethnic group, statistics provided by the Office for National Statistics (ONS). Much has been written about the constraints and shortcomings of the ethnic group question in the 1991 Census. Not only has it been accused of conflating nationality, geographical origin and

skin colour, but also of failing to adequately capture smaller and less visible minorities, such as Moroccans. For example, see Roger Ballard, 'Negotiating race and ethnicity: exploring the implications of the 1991 Census', *Patterns of Prejudice*, 30:3 (1996), 3–33; and Cherti, *Paradoxes of Social Capital*, pp. 73–4.

17 Census 1991 England and Wales, ethnic group, statistics provided by the Office for National Statistics (ONS).

18 See David Owen, 'The demographic characteristics of people from minority ethnic groups in Britain', in David Mason (ed.), *Explaining Ethnic Differences: Changing Patterns of Disadvantage in Britain* (Bristol: The Policy Press, 2003), p. 40; Tahir Abbas, 'Sparkbrook, housing classes & the market situation: forty years on', in Tahir Abbas and Frank Reeves (eds), *Immigration and Race Relations: Sociological Theory and John Rex* (London: I.B. Tauris, 2007), p. 133; and Herbert, *Negotiating Boundaries in the City*, pp. 21–2.

19 For an insight into the advantages and limitations of using 1991 Census data to measure ethnicity, see Valerie Karn, Angela Dale and Peter Ratcliffe, 'Introduction: using the 1991 Census to study ethnicity', in Valerie Karn (ed.), *Ethnicity in the 1991 Census. Volume Four: Employment, Education and Housing among the Ethnic Minority Populations of Britain* (London: The Stationery Office, 1997), pp. xi–xiii.

20 For example, see WSHC, F1/201/10/3, Wiltshire County Council Schools Sub-Committee, meeting of 17 December 1979; WSHC, F1/101/5/1, Wiltshire County Council Policy, later Policy and Resources, Committee Minutes, 1973–1986, meeting of the Policy Committee of 10 November 1981; and WSHC, F1/201/10/3, Wiltshire County Council Schools Sub-Committee, meeting of 15 November 1982, 'Multi-cultural Education'.

21 For an insight into the RECs and the importance awarded to the local level, see Yasemin Nuhoğlu Soysal, *Limits of Citizenship: Migrants and Postnational Membership in Europe* (Chicago: University of Chicago Press, 1994), pp. 73–4; and Muhammad Anwar, Patrick Roach and Ranjit Sondhi, 'Introduction' in Muhammad Anwar, Patrick Roach and Ranjit Sondhi (eds), *From Legislation to Integration? Race Relations in Britain* (Basingstoke: Macmillan Press, 2000), p. 17.

22 The five district councils were North Wiltshire District Council, Kennet District Council, Salisbury District Council, Thamesdown Borough Council and West Wiltshire District Council. The County Local Government Joint Committee regretted that, beyond the establishment of the working group, there existed limited resources for community relations work. See WSHC, F1/102/1–4/7–8/11, Wiltshire County Council Miscellaneous Joint Committees, Minutes and Agenda Papers, 1977–1996, a meeting of the County Local Government Joint Committee, 9 December 1976, 'Community Relations in Wiltshire'.

23 See WSHC, G29/1/1/15/1, Salisbury District Council, Finance Committee Agendas, June 1975–September 1980, meeting of 6 November 1978, 'Community Relations in Wiltshire', Report of the Working Group for the County Local Government Joint Committee, July 1978, p. 1.

24   *Ibid.*, pp. 1–2. The three race relations organisations at the time were Thamesdown and District Community Relations Council, North Wiltshire Council for Racial Equality, and West Wiltshire Council for Racial Equality. However, it should be noted that the names of these councils often changed. For example, the North Wiltshire and West Wiltshire councils merged during the mid-1980s and became the North and West Wiltshire Racial Equality Council. From 1990, it was joined by Kennet and Salisbury, and became the Wiltshire Racial Equality Council in 1991.

25   *Ibid.*, pp. 2–3.

26   *Ibid.*, pp. 3–5.

27   See WSHC, F1/102/1–4/7–8/11, a meeting of the County Local Government Joint Committee, 7 March 1979, 'Community Relations in Wiltshire'.

28   See WSHC, G28/1/1/23/1, North Wiltshire District Council – Policy and Resources Committee Volume 1, Minutes and Agenda Papers, July 1974–April 1979, meeting of 31 October 1978.

29   See WSHC, F1/102/1–4/7–8/11, a meeting of the County Local Government Joint Committee, 11 July 1979, 'Community Relations in Wiltshire'.

30   WSHC, G29/1/1/15/1, Salisbury District Council, meeting of the Finance Committee, 3 March 1980.

31   See, for example, WSHC, G28/1/1/5/5, North Wiltshire District Council – Community Services Committee Volume 5, Minutes and Agenda Papers, May 1987–March 1988, meeting of 21 July 1987.

32   See WSHC, 3231/10, Wiltshire Racial Equality Council, Annual Reports with Annual General Meeting Minutes for the North and West Wiltshire Council for Racial Equality, 1983–1991, North and West Wiltshire Councils for Racial Equality, Annual Report 1983–1984, North Wiltshire Council for Racial Equality, minutes of the Annual General Meeting, 20 November 1983; WSHC, 3231/10, North and West Wiltshire Councils for Racial Equality, Annual Report 1983–1984, Community Relations Officer's Report; WSHC, 3231/7, Wiltshire Racial Equality Council, Council Agenda Papers, 1988–1997, North and West Wiltshire Council for Racial Equality, Monitoring and Evaluation of the Work Programme 1988/1989; and WSHC, G28/1/1/5/8, North Wiltshire District Council – Community Services Committee Volume 8, Minutes and Agenda Papers, May 1990–April 1991, meeting of 17 July 1990.

33   WSHC, 3231/10, North and West Wiltshire Councils for Racial Equality, Annual Report 1983–1984, West Wiltshire Council for Racial Equality, minutes of the Annual General Meeting, 20 July 1983.

34   See, for example, WSHC, 3231/11, Wiltshire Racial Equality Council, Annual Reports with Annual General Meeting Minutes, 1991–2000. North and West Wiltshire, Kennet, Salisbury Racial Equality Council, minutes of the Annual General Meeting, 25 June 1991; WSHC, 3231/3, Wiltshire Racial Equality Council, minutes of Executive Committee Meeting, 11 October 1993; WSHC, 3231/7, Wiltshire Racial Equality Council, Racial Equality Officer's Report, December 1995–March 1996; and WSHC, 3231/3, Wiltshire Racial Equality Council, minutes of Executive Committee Meeting, 17 March 1997.

35 WSHC, 3231/7, a letter from Richard Martin (Chair of the Wiltshire Racial Equality Council), 18 January 1994. See also WSHC, 3231/3, Wiltshire Racial Equality Council, minutes of Executive Committee Meeting, 14 July 1994.

36 This Working Party was inspired by the 1980 CRE report entitled *Youth in Multi-racial Society: The Urgent Need for New Policies; the Fire Next Time* (London: CRE, 1980).

37 WSHC, G30/Box811, Swindon Borough Council, Community Development: Race Relations, Agenda Papers, 1980–1996, 'Report of the Working Party on Youth in Multi-Racial Society', 22 February 1982.

38 See, for example, WSHC, G30/Box811, Race Relations Sub-Committee of the Community Planning Committee, 3 November 1982; and WSHC, F1/101/5/1, meeting of the Policy Committee, 9 November 1982.

39 See WSHC, 3231/10, North and West Wiltshire Council for Racial Equality, Annual Report 1985–1986, Community Relations Officer's Report; WSHC, 3231/7, Wiltshire Racial Equality Council, Racial Equality Officer's report, September–November 1992; WSHC, F1/201/5/1, Wiltshire County Council Policy and Resources Committee Agenda Papers, 1973–2002, meeting of 22 February 1994, 'Social Services Anti-Discriminatory Policy'; and WSHC, F1/102/1–4/7–8/11, Consultative Forum on Economic Development, 15 April 1993, 'Developing Ethnic Minority, Particularly Asian, Businesses'.

40 WSHC, 3231/7, a letter from Richard Martin (Chair of the Wiltshire Racial Equality Council), 18 January 1994.

41 See, for example, WSHC, 3231/2, Wiltshire Racial Equality Council, Council Minutes, 1988–1991, North and West Wiltshire Council for Racial Equality, minutes of Executive Meeting, 19 September 1988; WSHC, 3231/3, Wiltshire Racial Equality Council, Racial Equality Officer's report, February–May 1993; WSHC, 3231/7, Racial Equality Officer's Report, September–November 1994; WSHC, 3231/3, Wiltshire Racial Equality Council, minutes of Executive Commission Meeting, 27 November 1995; WSHC, 3231/3, Wiltshire Racial Equality Council, minutes of Executive Committee Meeting, 1 April 1996; and WSHC, 3231/3, Wiltshire Racial Equality Council, minutes of Executive Committee Meeting, 17 March 1997.

42 See Dhalech, *Challenging Racism in the Rural Idyll.*

43 See, for example, Dhillon, 'Rethinking rural race equality', p. 225.

44 WSHC, G31/1/2/7, West Wiltshire District Council Signed Minutes, January–December 1977, No. 2 Sub-Committee of the Environmental Committee, 'Trowbridge Cemetery – Muslim Burials', 25 November 1976.

45 WSHC, G31/1/2/9, West Wiltshire District Council Signed Minutes, November 1977–November 1978, Environmental Committee, 'Muslim Burials – Trowbridge Cemetery', 5 July 1978. There does not appear to be any further discussion in the council minutes on this topic.

46 See Danièle Joly, *Making a Place for Islam in British Society: Muslims in Birmingham*, Research Papers in Ethnic Relations No. 4 (University of Warwick: Centre for Research in Ethnic Relations, 1987), p. 13; and Nazneen Ahmed, 'Marking a good death: Muslim burial sites and practices in Britain

from 1800 to the present', in Jane Garnett and Alana Harris (eds), *Rescripting Religion in the City: Migration and Religious Identity in the Modern Metropolis* (Abingdon: Routledge, 2013), p. 111.

47　See WSHC, G31/1/1/9/4, West Wiltshire District Council, Environment Sub-Committees Agendas, January–November 1977, agenda item 6: 'Muslim Slaughter', report from West Wiltshire District Council Technical Services Department, meeting of 27 January 1977.

48　See WSHC, G31/1/2/7, West Wiltshire District Council, minutes of the No. 2 Sub-Committee of the Environmental Committee, 27 January 1977; and WSHC, G31/1/2/7, West Wiltshire District Council, minutes of the No. 2 Sub-Committee of the Environmental Committee, 3 March 1977.

49　See Ronald Kaye, 'The politics of religious slaughter of animals: strategies for ethno-religious political action', *New Community*, 19:2 (1993), 235–50; and Ansari, 'The Infidel Within', pp. 354–5.

50　See WSHC, G31/1/1/9/12, West Wiltshire District Council, Environment Sub-Committees Agendas, February–December 1985, Environmental Committee, 18 December 1985; and WSHC, G31/1/2/23, West Wiltshire District Council Signed Minutes, January–December 1985, Environmental Committee, meeting of 18 December 1985.

51　See WSHC, G31/1/1/9/13, West Wiltshire District Council, Environment Sub-Committees Agendas, February–December 1986, Environmental Committee, meeting of 25 June 1986.

52　*Ibid.*

53　See WSHC, G31/1/2/25, West Wiltshire District Council Signed Minutes October 1985–December 1986, Environmental Committee, meeting of 25 June 1986.

54　WSHC, G31/1/1/2/14, West Wiltshire District Council, Housing and Sub-Committee Agendas, February–December 1986, meeting of Housing Committee of 3 September 1986.

55　*Ibid.*

56　*Ibid.*

57　See *Ibid.*; and WSHC, G31/1/2/25, West Wiltshire District Council minutes, Housing Committee, meeting of 3 September 1986.

58　See WSHC, 3231/10, North and West Wiltshire Council for Racial Equality, Annual Report 1985–1986, Chairman's Report.

59　See WSHC, F1/101/7/5, Wiltshire County Council Economic Development and Environment Committee and Subcommittees Minutes 1996–1998, Economic Development and Environment Committee, meeting of 6 May 1998, 'Swindon: Former Queenstown Infants School Site, Fleming Way'; and WSHC, F1/201/7/4, Wiltshire County Council Economic Development and Environment Committee Agenda Papers, 1996–1998, meeting of 6 May 1998, 'Swindon: Former Queenstown Infants School Site, Fleming Way'.

60　See Gilliat-Ray, *Muslims in Britain*, pp. 199–200.

61　See, for example, Richard Gale and Simon Naylor, 'Religion, planning and the city: the spatial politics of ethnic minority expression in British cities and towns', *Ethnicities*, 2:3 (2002), 387–409; and Gale, 'The multicultural city and the politics of religious architecture'.

62 See Ansari, '*The Infidel Within*', pp. 353–4; and Timothy Peace, 'British Muslims and the anti-war movement', in Timothy Peace (ed.), *Muslims and Political Participation in Britain* (Abingdon: Routledge, 2015), pp. 125–6.

63 See WSHC, G30/Box811, Swindon Borough Council, Race Relations Sub-Committee of the Community Planning Committee, 21 August 1984; WSHC, G30/Box811, Swindon Borough Council, Race Relations Sub-Committee of the Community Planning Committee, 21 December 1988; and WSHC, G30/Box811, Swindon Borough Council, Race Relations Sub-Committee of the Community Planning Committee, 14 June 1989.

64 See Kevin Myers and Ian Grosvenor, 'Policy, equality and inequality: from the past to the future', in Dave Hill and Mike Cole (eds), *Schooling and Equality: Fact, Concept and Policy* (Abingdon: Routledge, 2004), p. 259; Race, *Multiculturalism and Education*, pp. 17–18; and Gajendra Verma, Paul Zec and George Skinner, *The Ethnic Crucible: Harmony and Hostility in Multi-Ethnic Schools* (Abingdon: Routledge, 2012), p. 13.

65 The Green Paper was entitled *Education in Schools: A Consultative Document*. See Gajendra Verma, 'Cultural diversity in primary schools: its nature, extent and cross-curricular implications', in Gajendra Verma and Peter Pumfrey (eds), *Cross Curricular Contexts, Themes and Dimensions in Primary Schools* (London: The Falmer Press, 1994), pp. 6–7.

66 See Department of Education and Science, *West Indian Children in Our Schools: A Report from the Committee of Enquiry into the Education of Children from Ethnic Minorities (The Rampton Report)* (London: HMSO, 1981). See also Janet McKenzie, *Changing Education: A Sociology of Education since 1944* (Abingdon: Routledge, 2014), p. 257.

67 Department of Education and Science, *Education for All: Report of the Committee of Enquiry into the Education of Children from Minority Groups (The Swann Report)* (London: HMSO, 1985).

68 For various insights into the Swann Report, see T.S. Chivers, *Race and Culture in Education: Issues Arising from the Swann Committee Report* (Windsor: NFER-Nelson, 1987); Gajendra Verma (ed.), *Education for All: A Landmark in Pluralism* (London: The Falmer Press, 1989); and Tomlinson, *Race and Education*, pp. 83–5, 93–4. For some criticisms of the Swann Report with regard to Muslim communities specifically, see Peucker and Akbarzadeh, *Muslim Active Citizenship in the West*, p. 126; and Choudhury, *Muslims in the UK*, pp. 162–4.

69 See Solomos, *Race and Racism in Britain*, p. 102.

70 Local education authorities were also encouraged to act as a result of other developments, including the 1981 urban riots and the subsequent Scarman Inquiry. See Tomlinson, *Race and Education*, pp. 86–7.

71 See Wendy Ball, William Gulam and Barry Troyna, 'Pragmatism or retreat? Funding policy, local government and the marginalisation of anti-racist education', in Wendy Ball and John Solomos (eds), *Race and Local Politics*

(Basingstoke: Macmillan, 1990), pp. 83–5; and Tomlinson, *Race and Education*, pp. 86–91.

72 Tomlinson, *Race and Education*, p. 87.

73 See WSHC, F1/201/10/3, Wiltshire County Council Schools Sub-Committee, meeting of 17 December 1979, 'Education of Vietnamese Refugees in Wiltshire'; and WSHC, F1/201/10/3, Wiltshire County Council Schools Sub-Committee, meeting of 15 November 1982, 'Multi-cultural Education'.

74 WSHC, F1/201/10/3, Wiltshire County Council Schools Sub-Committee, meeting of 12 June 1978.

75 See WSHC, F8/100/109, Wiltshire County Council Education Department, Schools Policy Correspondence, Curriculum Development – Religious Education, 1974–1979, Chief Education Officer to Chief Executive, 'Community Relations Commission "Between Two Cultures"', 26 January 1977.

76 See WSHC, F8/100/118, Wiltshire County Council Education Department, Schools Policy Correspondence, Religious Education Standing Advisory Council, 1978–1986, Wiltshire Agreed Syllabus of Religious Education, undated; and WSHC, F8/100/118, Wiltshire County Council Education Department, letter from Toothill School in Swindon to Mr. Slocombe, 17 July 1986.

77 See WSHC, F1/201/10/2 Wiltshire County Council Finance and General Purposes Subcommittee of Education Committee Agenda Papers, 1973–1990, meeting of 13 April 1981; and WSHC, F8/100/124, Wiltshire County Council Education Department, Schools Policy Correspondence, Multicultural Advisory Group, 1983–1992, 'Idiot's Guide to the Swann Report', undated report.

78 See WSHC, F1/201/10/2, Wiltshire County Council Finance and General Purposes Subcommittee of Education Committee, meeting of 13 April 1981.

79 WSHC, F1/201/10/3, Wiltshire County Council Schools Sub-Committee, meeting of 15 November 1982, 'Multi-cultural Education', p. 1.

80 *Ibid.*, p. 1.

81 Under Section 11 of the Local Government Act 1966, local authorities in areas of substantial ethnic minority concentration could apply for central government funding in order to employ extra staff on projects aimed at helping migrant schoolchildren overcome educational barriers and disadvantage. Whilst the scheme no doubt made many initiatives and projects possible, it has also been widely criticised for a number of reasons, including for being inconsistent, having limited benefits, and for perceiving ethnic minority children as being a 'burden' on local authorities. For example, see Gideon Ben-Tovim, John Gabriel, Ian Law and Kathleen Stredder, 'A political analysis of local struggles for racial equality', in John Rex and David Mason (eds), *Theories of Race and Ethnic Relations* (Cambridge: Cambridge University Press, 1986), p. 141; and Christina Julios, *Contemporary British Identity: English Language, Migrants and Public Discourse* (Aldershot: Ashgate, 2008), p. 102. Using the Section 11 scheme, Wiltshire's local authority applied for, and secured, funding for two peripatetic teachers and one advisory teacher. See WSHC,

F1/101/10/1, Wiltshire County Council Education Committee, meeting of 24 April 1981.

82 WSHC, F1/201/10/3, Wiltshire County Council Schools Sub-Committee, meeting of 15 November 1982, 'Multi-cultural Education', p. 2.

83 *Ibid.*, p. 2.

84 *Ibid.*, pp. 2–3.

85 See WSHC, F8/100/124, Wiltshire County Council Education Department, 'Idiot's Guide to the Swann Report', undated report. There were local authorities that implemented policies on multicultural education before the publication of the 1985 Swann Report. However, these were often in areas with sizeable migrant populations, such as Berkshire, Bradford and London. See Barry Troyna and Jenny Williams, *Racism, Education and the State* (Abingdon: Routledge, 1986); and Tomlinson, *Race and Education*, pp. 86–91.

86 See WSHC, F8/100/118, Wiltshire County Council Education Department, announcement of a conference, 'Education for a Multi-Racial Society' to be hosted by Wiltshire County Council Education Department, 9 July 1981.

87 See WSHC, 3231/10, North and West Wiltshire Councils for Racial Equality, Annual Report 1983–1984, Multicultural Education in Wiltshire – Report by John Fisher (Advisory Teacher for Multicultural Education).

88 See WSHC, F8/100/124, Advisory Group for Multi-cultural Education, meeting of 9 May 1984.

89 See WSHC, F8/100/124, Advisory Group for Multi-cultural Education, meeting of 16 June 1983; WSHC, F8/100/124, Advisory Group for Multi-Cultural Education, meeting of 18 January 1984; WSHC, F8/100/124, Advisory Group for Multi-cultural Education, meeting of 9 May 1984; WSHC, F8/100/124, Advisory Group for Multi-cultural Education, meeting of 24 September 1984; and WSHC, F8/100/124, Advisory Group for Multi-cultural Education, meeting of 21 January 1985.

90 WSHC, F8/100/124, 'Idiot's Guide to the Swann Report', undated report.

91 *Ibid.*

92 WSHC, F1/201/10/3, Wiltshire County Council Schools Sub-Committee, meeting of 13 April 1987.

93 See WSHC, F1/101/10/2, Wiltshire County Council Education Committee, meeting of 24 April 1987.

94 WSHC, F1/201/10/3, Wiltshire County Council Schools Sub-Committee, meeting of 13 April 1987.

95 *Ibid.*

96 See WSHC, F8/100/124, Advisory Group for Multicultural Education, meeting of 9 September 1985; WSHC, F8/100/124, Advisory Group for Multicultural Education, meeting of 13 January 1986; and WSHC, F8/100/124, Advisory Group for Multicultural Education, meeting of 21 April 1986.

97 See WSHC, F8/100/124, Multicultural Centre, Memo to County Advisory Group for Multicultural Education, 8 September 1988; and WSHC, F8/100/124, Multicultural Education in Wiltshire (by John Fisher, Advisory Teacher for Multicultural Education), undated.

 98 WSHC, F1/201/10/1, Wiltshire County Council Education Committee, 1973–2001, meeting of 19 January 1996.
 99 See WSHC, F1/201/10/1, Wiltshire County Council Education Committee, meeting of 23 April 1993; WSHC, F1/201/10/1, Wiltshire County Council Education Committee, meeting of 29 October 1993; WSHC, 3231/8, Wiltshire Racial Equality Council, Education Action Group Minutes and Correspondence, 1998–1999, correspondence between schools and Wiltshire Racial Equality Council; and WSHC, 3231/8, Wiltshire Racial Equality Council, notes on education meeting, 26 January 1998.
100 For an insight into the important role local government has long played in the education of ethnic minority schoolchildren in Britain, even when having its responsibilities diminished, see Tomlinson, *Ethnic Minorities in British Schools*; David Gillborn, 'Anti-racism: from policy to praxis', in Ben-Miriam Peretz, Sally Brown and Bob Moon (eds), *Routledge International Companion to Education* (London: Routledge, 2000), pp. 476–88; and Tomlinson, *Race and Education*.
101 See Solomos, *Race and Racism in Britain*, pp. 102–3.
102 See Iris Kalka, 'Striking a bargain: political radicalism in a middle-class London borough', in Pnina Werbner and Muhammad Anwar (eds), *Black and Ethnic Leaderships: The Cultural Dimensions of Political Action* (London: Routledge, 1991), p. 143; OECD Proceedings, *Immigrants, Integration and Cities: Exploring the Links* (Paris, OECD: 1998), p. 181; and Garbaye, *Getting into Local Power*, p. 58.
103 See WSHC, G30/Box807, Swindon Borough Council, Community Development Committee Agenda Papers, 1974–1984, Borough of Thamesdown, meeting of the Community Planning Committee, 28 July 1983, 'Equal Opportunities Policy'.
104 See WSHC, G31/1/2/27, West Wiltshire District Council Signed Minutes, January 1987–December 1987, Management Sub-Committee, 14 December 1987, Appendix 1, 'Equal Opportunity Policy'.
105 See WSHC, F1/201/5/1, Wiltshire County Council Policy and Resources Committee, 27 September 1994, 'Corporate Policy on Equal Opportunities and Anti Discrimination'.
106 See *Ibid.*; WSHC, G30/Box807, Swindon Borough Council, 'Equal Opportunities Policy', 28 July 1983; WSHC, G31/1/2/27, West Wiltshire District Council Signed Minutes, Management Sub-Committee, 'Equal Opportunity Policy', 14 December 1987; and WSHC, F1/101/5/3, Wiltshire County Council Policy, later Policy and Resources, Committee Minutes, 1993–1995, meeting of 27 September 1994, 'Corporate Policy on Equal Opportunities and Anti-Discrimination. Statement of Policy Objectives'.
107 See WSHC, G30/Box807, Borough of Thamesdown, meeting of the Community Planning Committee, 24 November 1983, Race Relations Sub-Committee, 'Equal Opportunities Policy and Employment Code of Practice', 8 November 1983. It is worth noting that there was some disagreement within the local authority regarding the need for an equal opportunities policy, with the Management Services Sub-Committee not supporting it.

108 See WSHC, G31/1/1/53/20, West Wiltshire District Council, Local Joint Consultative Committee and Sub-Committees, Minutes and Agenda Papers, February–September 1992, Local Joint Consultative Committee, meeting of 6 July 1992, 'Equal Opportunities Policy'.

109 Statistics for 1993/1994 showed that, out of the 16,679 applicants who had applied for employment at the Council, 175 (1%) were from an ethnic minority background, a figure slightly lower than the 1.7% of Wiltshire's population recorded in the 1991 Census. Of the 175 applicants, 45 (26%) were shortlisted, compared to 29% of the white applicants, and 10 (6%) were appointed, compared to 9.5% of the white applicants. See WSHC, F1/201/5/ 1, Wiltshire County Council Policy and Resources Committee, 27 September 1994, 'Corporate Policy on Equal Opportunities and Anti Discrimination'.

110 See Ken Young, 'The space between words: local authorities and the concept of equal opportunities', in Richard Jenkins and John Solomos (eds), *Racism and Equal Opportunity Policies in the 1980s* (Cambridge: Cambridge University Press, 1989), p. 93; and Kalka, 'Striking a bargain', p. 143.

111 See WSHC, F1/201/14/1, Wiltshire County Council Social Services Committee Agenda Papers, 1973–2001, meeting of 14 February 1991, 'Proposed Applications for Section 11 Funding'; WSHC, G31/1/1/2/19, West Wiltshire District Council, Housing and Sub-committee Agendas, January–November 1991, West Wiltshire District Council Housing Performance Review Sub-Committee, meeting of 14 March 1991, 'Wiltshire Social Services Department Community Care Plan 1991'; WSHC, F1/201/14/1, Wiltshire County Council Social Services Committee, meeting of 7 November 1991, 'Developing a Multi-cultural Policy for Wiltshire Social Services'; WSHC, F1/201/14/1, Wiltshire County Council Social Services Committee, meeting of 13 February 1992, 'Section 11 Homefinding Project (Child Care)'; and WSHC, F1/201/14/1, Wiltshire County Council Social Services Committee, meeting of 2 February 1994, 'Social Services Anti-Discriminatory Policy'.

112 This research project was also funded by the Allied Dunbar Charitable Trust, a charitable arm of a UK-based life assurance company.

113 WSHC, F1/202/8, Wiltshire County Council Joint Consultative Forum on Economic Development Agenda Papers, 1987–1995, meeting of 22 February 1991, 'Wiltshire Employment Update Report'.

114 See WSHC, F1/202/8, Wiltshire County Council Joint Consultative Forum on Economic Development, 'Economic Development Strategy for the County', draft report, undated, p. 12.

115 See WSHC, F8/194/33, Wiltshire County Council Education Department, Youth Employment Correspondence, Equal Opportunities – Racial Equality – Gender Disability, 1986–1992, 'Black White: An Anti-Racist Newsletter', August 1988; and WSHC, G30/Box811, Swindon Borough Council, Race Relations Sub-Committee of the Community Planning Committee, 21 December 1988, 'Black Business Conference'.

116 See, for example, WSHC, G30/Box811, Swindon Borough Council, Race Relations Sub-Committee of the Community Planning Committee, 21

December 1988, 'Some Questions Asked, Some Questions Answered: A Survey of Service Providers to Small or Start Up Businesses within the Wiltshire Area'.

117 WSHC, F1/202/8, Wiltshire County Council Joint Consultative Forum on Economic Development, 'Developing Ethnic Minority, Particularly Asian, Businesses', 15 April 1993.

118 *Ibid.*

119 See Giles A. Barrett, Trevor P. Jones and David McEvoy, 'Socio-economic and policy dimensions of the mixed embeddedness of ethnic minority business in Britain', *Journal of Ethnic and Migration Studies*, 27:2 (2001), 249; Monder Ram and David Smallbone, *Ethnic Minority Enterprise: Policy in Practice* (Small Business Service Report, 2001); and Hackett, *Foreigners, Minorities and Integration*, pp. 44–57.

120 Examples include the local authorities of Hackney, Haringey and Newcastle upon Tyne. See Solomos, *Race and Racism in Contemporary Britain*, pp. 93–4; and Hackett, *Foreigners, Minorities and Integration*.

121 See WSHC, G31/1/1/2/8, West Wiltshire District Council, Housing and Sub-Committee Agendas, January–December 1980, meeting of 7 March 1980, 'Proposed General Improvement Area No. 4 Ashton Street, Trowbridge'.

122 See WSHC, G31/1/1/2/9, West Wiltshire District Council, Housing and Sub-Committee Agendas, January–December 1981, meeting of 1 May 1981, 'Homelessness Report – Immigrant Families'.

123 See WSHC, G30/Box811, Swindon Borough Council, Race Relations Sub-Committee of the Community Planning Committee, 3 November 1982.

124 See Commission for Racial Equality, *Race and Council Housing in Hackney: Report of a Formal Investigation* (London, 1984).

125 See WSHC, G30/Box811, Swindon Borough Council, Race Relations Sub-Committee of the Community Planning Committee, 17 January 1984.

126 See Commission for Racial Equality, *Code of Practice in Rented Housing: For the Elimination of Racial Discrimination and the Promotion of Equal Opportunities* (London, 1991).

127 See WSHC, G31/1/1/2/21, West Wiltshire District Council, Housing and Sub-Committee Agenda Papers, 1993, minutes of the Housing Committee, 10 March 1993, 'Commission for Racial Equality – Code of Practice in Rented Housing'.

128 See *Ibid.*; and WSHC, G31/1/1/2/19, West Wiltshire District Council, Housing Committee, 12 June 1991, 'Commission for Racial Equality – Statutory Code for Rented Housing'.

129 See WSHC, Box G30/922, Swindon Borough Council, Annual Reports, Standing Orders and Bye-Laws, Race Relations Advisory Sub-Committee, Annual Report 1990–1991, Community Development Borough of Thamesdown.

130 See WSHC, G30/Box811, Swindon Borough Council, Race Relations Advisory Panel of the Community Development Committee, 26 June 1996, 'Housing Needs of Ethnic Minorities in Thamesdown'. See also WSHC,

G30/Box811, Swindon Borough Council, Race Relations Advisory Panel of the Community Development Committee, 29 June 1994, 'Homelessness Survey 1993'.

131 See John Solomos and Gurharpal Singh, 'Racial equality, housing and the local state', in Wendy Ball and John Solomos (eds), *Race and Local Politics* (Basingstoke: Macmillan, 1990), pp. 99, 108–10; and Richard Skellington, *'Race' in Britain Today* (London: SAGE, 1996), p. 139.

132 See Troyna and Williams, *Racism, Education and the State*; Solomos, *Race and Racism in Britain*, pp. 104–5; and Romain Garbaye, 'British cities and ethnic minorities in the post-war era: from xenophobic agitation to multi-ethnic government', in Ahmed Al-Shahi and Richard Lawless (eds), *Middle East and North African Immigrants in Europe* (Abingdon: Routledge, 2005), p. 210–11.

133 Tomlinson, *Race and Education*, p. 87.

4

Local government policy: anti-racism, equal opportunities, community cohesion and religious identity in a rural space, 1999 onwards

Whilst multiculturalism remained the backbone of official policy regarding the settlement and integration of migrant communities in Britain throughout the 1980s and 1990s, the 2000s have seen it gradually fall out of favour. Indeed, the rather optimistic take on the prevalence and future of multiculturalism in Britain promoted by the Commission on the Future of Multi-Ethnic Britain during the late 1990s soon made way for what has often been referred to as a 'multiculturalism backlash', which was spurred on by a number of events and developments.[1] The institutional racism exposed by the 1999 Macpherson Inquiry into the murder of Stephen Lawrence, for example, was at odds with the aims, ideals and promises of 'multicultural Britain'.[2] The government-commissioned Cantle Report following the 2001 riots in northern cities maintained that Britain was divided, allowing migrants to lead 'parallel lives'.[3] In September 2005, in the aftermath of 7/7, Trevor Phillips, Chair of the then Commission for Racial Equality (CRE), famously professed that multicultural politics had impeded integration and warned that Britain was 'sleepwalking to segregation'.[4] In a February 2011 speech on Islamic extremism, then Prime Minister David Cameron spoke of the failure of the 'doctrine of state multicul-turalism', which had 'encouraged different cultures to live separate lives' and led to the toleration of 'these segregated communities behaving in ways that run completely counter to our values'.[5]

Since the early 2000s, Britain has gradually adopted a policy framework based on the importance of common British values and identities and com-munity cohesion,[6] a political approach that has received significant academic criticism.[7] In a Britain that, as Steven Vertovec argues, could be seen to be both 'post-multicultural' and 'super-diverse', there has been a focus on for-ging a stronger national identity and securing increased integration, and specific measures have included citizenship and English-language tests for new citizens, the inclusion of citizenship education in school curricula, and classes for immigrants on British customs and history.[8] Often blamed for the failure of multiculturalism as a result of cases of radicalisation and so-called 'homegrown terrorism', and a perceived lack of integration more generally, Britain's Muslim communities have found themselves at the centre of this policy drive for commonality.[9] The widely criticised Prevent strategy, the 2016 government-commissioned Casey Review, and frequent allegations of social and economic isolation, low levels of English-language proficiency, and regressive religious and cultural practices ensured that Muslims continued to be the main focus of the community cohesion agenda.[10] There was also a simultaneous number of changes with regard to Britain's anti-discrimination legislation. As a direct result of the Macpherson Report's recommendations, the Race Relations (Amendment) Act 2000 extended the 1976 Act in relation to public authorities, placing a duty upon them to promote equal opportunities and positive relations between ethnic groups. Furthermore, partly as a result of European Union policy directives, anti-discrimination also extended to religion as seen with the Employment Equality (Religion or Belief) Regulations 2003, the Racial and Religious Hatred Act 2006, and the Equality Act 2010.[11]

This is the final chapter to examine local government policies and measures in Wiltshire and it focuses on the county's local political approach to immigration, integration and diversity since the turn of the twenty-first century. It traces changes and continuities as Wiltshire's local administration once again balanced national-level directive and mandate with local circumstances and particularism. As was the case during previous decades, local authorities were once again counted on to play an important role in delivering national-level policy. The 2001 Cantle Report requested that they 'prepare a local community cohesion plan', which was to 'include the promotion of cross cultural contact between different communities at all levels, foster understanding and respect, and break down barriers'.[12] Similarly, the Local Government Association's 2002 *Guidance on Community Cohesion* stressed that 'local authorities have a key role to play in driving this agenda forward',[13] and the government's 2012 approach to integration maintained that 'integration is a local issue' that 'requires a local response'.[14]

Local authority measures have been both plentiful and varied. Through the Pathfinder Programme, for example, which focused on increasing cross-cultural interaction, some local authorities received government funding in order to implement policies and practices that promoted cohesion, whilst others put similar initiatives into practice despite not receiving external financial support.[15] Oldham and Rochdale pledged to promote community cohesion by enabling greater chances of residential mobility and building more sustainable multi-ethnic neighbourhoods.[16] The London borough of Tower Hamlets has been recognised for mainstreaming its community cohesion measures into its broader policies and services, including those addressing education, housing and community grants.[17] Leicester's initiatives have involved engaging with local Muslim communities, including young people and women, and challenging violent extremist ideologies.[18] Bristol's local authority has recognised diversity as being one of the city's key strengths, and has pledged to create an inclusive city where everyone has a sense of belonging, a voice and equal opportunity.[19] Regarding local-level anti-discrimination measures during the 2000s, measures implemented by local authorities included race awareness training programmes, efforts to foster engagement with ethnic minority communities, and the recognition of religious celebration and Muslim and Sikh pupils' religious and cultural needs.[20]

In some ways, the gap between local authority action and policy in urban and rural Britain has not been as pronounced since the turn of the twenty-first century. Ted Cantle argued that the community cohesion agenda could be applied to more rural areas with small ethnic minority and faith communities and, rather than continue to predominantly focus on centres of diversity, the Race Relations (Amendment) Act 2000 placed a duty on all public authorities in the UK.[21] Indeed, some local authorities that cover rural areas, such as those of Lancashire and Peterborough, have demonstrated a commitment to community cohesion.[22] Yet some scholars have pointed out that, despite the opportunities presented by the community cohesion agenda, policy responses in rural areas have continued to be inadequate, with Philomena de Lima going as far as to argue that 'the presence and contribution of rural minority ethnic dwellers has largely been ignored'.[23] Others have maintained that the post-Macpherson rural context continues to be plagued by poor responses to rural racism.[24] Some of the reasons given for these shortcomings include neglect, lack of political commitment or resources, and incompetence.[25] This chapter considers the extent to which these arguments on rural Britain can be applied to Wiltshire by assessing how the county's local authority responded to both national influences and top-down policy, and local Muslim communities' efforts with regard to their recognition, integration and religious needs.

The local immigration context

Wiltshire's experience of migration during the 2000s has been one of increased diversity. Whilst at the time of the 2001 Census, the UK White population constituted 96.2% of the county's population, by the 2011 Census this figure had fallen to 93.4%. The number of people belonging to certain ethnic groups in Wiltshire increased during this ten-year period, including Other Asian (2,611; +874%), African (1,418; +389%), Bangladeshi (595; +145%), Indian

(1,547; +112%) and Pakistani (215; +68%). The 2011 Census also recorded 288 people who identified their ethnic group as Arab, which was an option for the first time, as well as a significant increase in the number of people born in Poland as a result of Poland joining the European Union in 2004 (from 328 in 2001 to 3,546 in 2011). The most diverse settlements were the military areas of Amesbury and Tidworth, as well as Chippenham, Salisbury and Trowbridge.[26] Regarding the county's Muslims specifically, according to the 2001 Census, the first to include a question on religious affiliation, there were 1,177 Muslims in Wiltshire who constituted 0.3% of the population.[27] By the time of the 2011 Census, these figures had risen to 2,074 and 0.4%, respectively.[28]

Regarding Swindon's unitary authority, the 2001 Census recorded 91.5% of people who described themselves as White British, a figure that had fallen to 84.6% by 2011. In 2011, 5.9%, 5.2% and 1.4% described themselves as Asian or Asian British, White (non-British) and Black or Black British, respectively.[29] More specifically, the figures for the Indian, Pakistani and Bangladeshi communities at the time of the 2011 Census stood at 6,901, 1,292 and 936, respectively, and smaller ethnic groups identified by respondents included Turkish (308), Arab (200) and Iranian (125).[30] With regard to Muslims specifically, the 2001 Census recorded 1,850 Muslims who comprised 1.03% of the total population, figures that had risen to 3,538 and 1.7%, respectively, by the time of the 2011 Census.[31] Whilst in both Swindon and Wiltshire Muslims made up the largest religious group after Christians, they nevertheless constituted far smaller percentages of their local surroundings than the national average (4.8%).[32]

As in earlier years, despite Wiltshire's relatively small ethnic minority communities, the post-1999 period was also marked by a series of political debates, measures and responses regarding migration in the county. As well as increasingly settled, diverse and growing Muslim communities, for example, the county's local authority also catered for the arrival of Eastern European, and especially Polish, migrant workers from the mid-2000s and, subsequently, the settlement of Syrian refugees.[33] It considered and acted upon both the Macpherson Report and the Race Relations (Amendment) Act 2000 with great commitment, as was witnessed through the devising and implementation of its first Race Equality Scheme, and it supported the partnership agreement between Trowbridge and Oujda, thus resulting in Wiltshire's county town becoming the first in Britain to be twinned with a Muslim Arab city.[34] Overall, Wiltshire's local government's political approach during the post-1999 era both recognised the county's position as a place where migrant communities had settled, and indeed continued to do so, and bestowed a greater emphasis on the more rural context in which their lives unfolded.

National influences and top-down policy

As was the case in earlier decades, Wiltshire's local political approach to its migrant communities during the post-1999 period was also heavily shaped by national influences and top-down policy. The county's policies and measures have reflected the national level in three key ways: first and foremost, by implementing the Macpherson Report and subsequent Race Relations (Amendment) Act 2000, but also through its gradual shift to both promoting community cohesion and extending anti-discrimination policy to include religion. The 1999 Macpherson Report made seventy recommendations on how to address institutional racism, some of which referred to the vital role local government and the local level more widely were expected to play in this process.[35] It also led to the New Labour government passing the Race Relations (Amendment) Act 2000, which required all public authorities 'to eliminate unlawful racial discrimination; and to promote equality of opportunity and good relations between persons of different racial groups'.[36] These top-down duties and recommendations soon captured the attention of local authorities across Britain, and Wiltshire was no exception, with the Wiltshire Racial Equality Council, for example, professing in its 2000 annual report that the Macpherson Report provided 'a unique opportunity to make a difference within a rural area like Wiltshire'.[37]

Wiltshire's local authority did not hesitate in responding. As was already the case from the 1960s, education once again became central to the political approach to migration and race in 'post-multicultural Britain'. Stressing that the effort to combat racism needed to stretch beyond the police services, the Macpherson Report argued that 'our education system must face up to the problems, real and potential, which exist', and included four recommendations in the area of education that centred around 'valuing cultural diversity and preventing racism'.[38] The 2000 Act placed a duty on local authorities to draw up race equality schemes, which addressed education as well as a number of other areas, and schools were asked to prepare race equality policies.[39] Wiltshire County Council's Education Committee commissioned research into ethnic minority pupils in the county's schools in July 1999. Amongst a range of findings, this research concluded that ethnic minority pupils underachieved in a number of subjects, but especially in English;[40] that little was being done to analyse examination and test results according to ethnicity; that parents felt that schools did not fully grasp their children's needs with regard to culture, religion and language; and that there was a need to have ethnic minority role models in schools, to keep statistics on ethnic minority pupils in order to measure their attainment and progress, and to improve contacts between schools and the homes of ethnic minority schoolchildren. There were also two ways in which ethnic minority educational achievement in Wiltshire was found to be lacking. Firstly, the average level of attainment for ethnic minority pupils securing five or more GCSE grades A* to C was below both the national and county-level average. Secondly, the targets set for ethnic minority pupils completing statutory education fell below those for other pupils.[41]

Alongside these findings there was a sense that Wiltshire's schools were not sufficiently committed to meeting the needs of ethnic minority pupils. Only 54% of them had responded to the Education Committee's research brief, which it assumed was the result of 'a lack of interest' or 'an assumption that these issues relate only to schools with a comparatively large number of ethnic minority pupils'.[42] Furthermore, despite most schools reporting that their ethnic minority children experienced underachievement, the majority were unable to provide accurate figures. Moreover, the Education Committee maintained that some of the county's schools demonstrated what it termed 'a considerable misunderstanding' regarding religious affiliation, cultural diversity and language acquisition, did not understand the need to monitor and analyse educational achievement along ethnic lines, and that some schools' small numbers of ethnic minority pupils had led them to adopt a 'no problem here' mentality.[43]

Yet despite almost half of Wiltshire's schools not responding to the research brief and the fact that the county was home to only a small number of ethnic minority pupils (1,089 in 1998),[44] the Education Committee persevered and findings were considered and acted upon. It made a series of recommendations, including asking schools to analyse examination entries and results according to ethnicity, to keep a logbook of racist incidents, and to ensure that the celebration of cultural diversity was embedded throughout the school curriculum. It also pledged to monitor ethnic minority underachievement, to develop curriculum materials that promoted ethnic minority engagement, and to assess how local schools were applying the Macpherson Report's recommendations.[45] The committee also recognised a number of measures that the schools that took part in the research outlined as having the potential to improve ethnic minority educational achievement, as well as combat exclusion and truancy. These included offering more support for English as a second language, making staff aware of ethnic minority needs, employing ethnic minority adults as role models, celebrating cultural and religious diversity, and developing a flexible and inclusive curriculum.[46] Similarly, as a direct consequence of the Stephen Lawrence Inquiry, the Swindon and Wiltshire Multicultural Education Service decided to appoint an advisory teacher who was to be responsible for 'raising achievement of ethnic minority pupils'.[47] Furthermore, citing the Race Relations (Amendment) Act 2000, Wiltshire County Council's first Race Equality Scheme extended to the area of education, amongst others, and pledged a commitment to monitoring and improving access to services, implementing Ofsted's specific recommendations on race equality and, through the Wiltshire Racial Equality Council, working with schools.[48] Overall, these measures and recommendations were in line with the Macpherson Report and the Race Relations (Amendment) Act 2000, as well as with those adopted by other local authorities across Britain, both in urban centres like Birmingham and the London borough of Merton and in more rural areas like Devon and North Lincolnshire.[49]

The Macpherson Report and Race Relations (Amendment) Act 2000 had an impact on policy in Wiltshire beyond the area of education. As a direct result of both, and also influenced by the Human Rights Act 1998, the Parekh Report, and pressure from central government on public authorities to implement anti-discriminatory measures, a working group was established in the county in December 1999.[50] Comprised of representatives from the county council, the Wiltshire Racial Equality Council, the Black Police Association, the Wiltshire Black Workers' Group and the Diversity Coordinator of the Wiltshire Constabulary, the group was responsible for assessing the implications of the Macpherson Report for the county council, and for preparing the corresponding action plans addressing both council services and its position as an employer.[51] It drew up a statement outlining the county council's commitment to anti-racist practices that was approved by the Policy and Resources Committee in December 2000.[52] The statement asserted that 'all persons have the inalienable right to be treated with equal dignity, respect, consideration and without prejudice and to be given equal access to all our services without regard to race, colour, nationality, culture, languages spoken, religious beliefs, creed, ethnicity'.[53]

Furthermore, it pledged that 'we in Wiltshire County Council will not tolerate any form of discriminatory behaviour by our employees or by those using our services', and that 'we in Wiltshire celebrate, encourage and enjoy the benefits that come from our people's ethnic, cultural, language, religious and other diversities'.[54] In order to achieve this, the statement vowed that the council would implement a series of anti-discriminatory measures, devise a long-term action plan that would ensure its services and employment practices were anti-discriminatory, and adopt the Macpherson Report's definitions of both 'racist incident' and 'institutional racism'.[55] Finally, the statement also demonstrated a commitment to establishing a 'human rights culture' across the county,[56] an initiative that undoubtedly reflected the increasing recognition that human rights legislation could play a role in achieving race equality as outlined by the Parekh Report and the Equalities Review Panel, and as witnessed in the establishment of the Commission for Equality and Human Rights (CEHR) in 2007.[57]

This commitment to, and subsequent statement on, anti-racism and equal opportunities led to the drawing up of Wiltshire County Council's first Race Equality Scheme in 2002.[58] Pointing out that 'Wiltshire is a diverse, significantly rural County, with half of the population living in villages and small towns', it argued that 'this diversity is a strength, but we also need to ensure that there is access to the Council's services for the whole population, including those groups such as minority ethnic people who may experience greater isolation'. It went on to stress that 'there is a need for a rural focus and action at strategic level and also at the level of local community planning. Minority ethnic people may experience isolation in smaller communities'.[59] Citing both the Macpherson Report's recommendations and the duty placed upon all public authorities by the Race Relations (Amendment) Act 2000, the scheme outlined a number of priorities and measures. These included increasing the number of ethnic minority council employees, making an effort to integrate race equality objectives into wider council plans and targets, the continuous monitoring of its operations, services and culture, making access to information and services available to all local communities, and ensuring that staff are adequately trained in the areas of equality and diversity.[60] A central aspect to the scheme was the council's commitment to consult local ethnic minority communities in order to be able to better cater for their aspirations and needs. This was seen especially through a research report it published entitled *Hidden Voices*, which offered an insight into the experiences and needs of ethnic minority communities in the county, the results of which were to inform the Race Equality Scheme's implementation. This research stemmed from the belief that there was a need to shed light on 'hidden' ethnic minorities' needs and views, and that these should be reflected in the council's initiatives and strategies. It also exposed incidents of discrimination and racism, and thus combatted the 'no problem here' mentality it recognised was often held by authority figures in more rural areas.[61]

There are a number of ways in which, spurred on by both the Macpherson Report and the Race Relations (Amendment) Act 2000, Wiltshire's local authority has gradually framed its dedication to meeting the needs of what it has feared are potentially isolated and vulnerable ethnic minorities within the context of the county's rural nature. Set up in 2000, for example, the Children and Families Divisional Working Group was tasked with both assessing the services provided by the council's Children and Families Division to children from ethnic minority communities, and considering the implications of the Macpherson Report and preparing an action plan. The working group drew up a policy statement, which recognised the duty placed on the division by the 2000 Act, and pledged a commitment to anti-racism and equal opportunities.[62] It stressed that it was necessary to 'recognise the needs of people from black and ethnic minority communities living in a rural context', and pointed out that 'Wiltshire's small numbers of looked after children from black and other minority ethnic groups can be particularly isolated and vulnerable'.[63] It outlined a range of initiatives, including consulting ethnic minority communities and community organisations, securing and retaining ethnic minority staff members, and providing placements that helped ethnic minority children maintain contact with their families and communities and reach their full educational potential.[64]

Wiltshire County Council's June 1999 update of the 'Wiltshire Community Care Plan, 1997–2000' stressed the importance of ensuring that community care services, such as social and health services, reached ethnic minority communities in especially rural locations. For example, it proposed an ethnic record-keeping and monitoring system, which assessed the correlation between quality of service and the rurality of a user's home, and a continued commitment to promoting awareness regarding the impact of the racism, isolation and exclusion suffered by ethnic minority communities in rural areas.[65] Similarly, a 2013 report on the extent to which health, public and social care services were meeting the cultural, ethnic and religious needs of migrant communities that was commissioned and funded by Wiltshire Council exposed the rural dimension of their experiences. With regard to the county's Muslim communities specifically, it showed that there existed a lack of awareness concerning religious rules and practices, including in relation to prayer rituals, burials and *halal* meat despite local-level discussions having been held previously.[66] Likewise, a Swindon Borough Council report on its achievements and objectives in the area of equality, including in relation to children and health services, recognised that around 75% of the borough was rural, including the market town of Highworth and the villages of Blunsdon and Wroughton.[67]

Whilst by no means to the same extent, the Macpherson Report and the Race Relations (Amendment) Act 2000 also triggered policies and measures at the district council level. Salisbury District Council introduced a race equality policy for housing, which aimed to promote equality of opportunity and combat discrimination with regard to accessing housing, quality of housing and service delivery. Specific actions and measures included the keeping of ethnic records, considering the particular needs of ethnic minority communities when devising plans and policies, removing racist graffiti, including an anti-racist clause in tenancy agreements, and translating leaflets into minority languages and using trained interpreters.[68] North Wiltshire District Council argued that, due to the area's small ethnic minority population, it made more sense 'to see the Lawrence Inquiry report as an investigation into white racism rather than black disadvantage', and it stressed the need to resist both the fact that ethnic minorities often constituted 'invisible' communities and the notion that there was scarce anti-racism work to be carried out.[69] It drew up a race equality policy that aimed 'to create a culture of change' through which it could combat institutional racism and promote equal opportunities.[70] Furthermore, it actively sought, and financed, the assistance of the Wiltshire Racial Equality Council in order to be able to fulfil the duties and obligations expected of local authorities.[71] Similarly, West Wiltshire District Council adopted a Corporate Equalities Strategy and Race Equality Scheme, drew up a form for reporting racist incidents in consultation with Wiltshire Racial Equality Council, and discussed both devising an ethnic minority housing strategy and offering guidance on equality issues to staff.[72]

Whilst not to the same extent, as well as the Macpherson Report and the Race Relations (Amendment) Act 2000, Wiltshire's local authority also responded to national-level mandate through both its promotion of community cohesion and its gradual inclusion of religion in anti-discrimination policy. Indeed, as was the case for local governments across Britain, 'cohesion' is a term that increasingly featured in its documentation throughout the 2000s, and integration has come to be measured against the cohesiveness of a given neighbourhood or society.[73] On the whole, local authorities have attempted to deliver the community cohesion agenda by trying to bring different communities together, concentrating on equalities, promoting community engagement, and constructing what has been referred to as 'a positive narrative to change attitudes'.[74] Furthermore, it is widely acknowledged that these local measures and strategies stretched to areas with small ethnic and religious minority communities and that, despite the fact that local authorities in rural areas had less experience addressing migration and diversity than those in urban ones, they nevertheless awarded significant efforts and resources to fostering integration and community cohesion.[75] As will be seen in the next chapter, community cohesion was not just endorsed and pursued by local government in Wiltshire, but also by the county's Muslim communities themselves.

Wiltshire's authority fully adhered to the wider local government approach. The *Wiltshire Compact*, a set of principles that sought to acknowledge and value diversity in the county, stressed the correlation between recognising the importance of equality and diversity and securing a cohesive society, and identified both ethnic minority needs and rural isolation as key issues to address.[76] Similarly, an overview of the progress made in the county regarding equality and diversity emphasised that cohesion was being encouraged by working with BME communities in order to identify areas for improvement in relation to health and social services, and through activities that sought to raise awareness regarding the issues they faced and remove barriers that discouraged cohesion.[77] Wiltshire Council's 2010 report on inclusive communities recognised the emphasis the national government had placed on the local level, driving cohesion and integration through initiatives such as the local government White Paper entitled *Strong and Prosperous Communities* (2006) and the *Our Shared Future* report (2007).[78] As a result, it suggested that its development plans aim to create socially inclusive societies and equal opportunities for everyone, and stressed that all of Wiltshire's communities must have the opportunity to play a role in the county's future development.[79] Similarly,

Swindon Borough Council's 2010 Equality Policy placed the promotion of social cohesion within its broader anti-discrimination and equality aims.[80]

Measures promoting community cohesion were also carried out at the sub-county level. Regarding North Wiltshire District Council, for example, it was stressed that, albeit in small numbers, all of its wards were home to ethnic minority communities, yet its population's diversity 'lacked acknowledgement and visibility'.[81] A local cultural strategy was proposed in an attempt 'to integrate communities and encourage community cohesion by recognising the increasing multicultural nature of North Wiltshire and the immense diversity of people residing within the District'.[82] It hoped to do this through various measures, which included doing more to inform the local population about the district's diversity and promoting the reporting of hate crimes.[83] The boosting of community cohesion was seen to be beneficial to a multi-racial ward in Melksham that suffered socio-economic deprivation, something it was hoped could be achieved through a proposed community centre that was to offer a variety of education, health and sport and leisure services.[84] A series of 2011 reports on different community areas, including Malmesbury and Westbury, stressed that community cohesion was essential to a community's success, whilst simultaneously acknowledging that recognising cultural and religious diversity and ethnic minority needs in a rural county like Wiltshire in which migrant communities were often isolated and did not constitute organised groups proved difficult.[85] The Ethnic Minority Achievement Service (EMAS) also played an important role and, amongst other things, ran training days and events on community cohesion, citizenship and the Prevent strategy for pupils and school staff members across Wiltshire, including in Calne and Trowbridge.[86]

The way in which Wiltshire's local authority's political approach to its diverse communities during the post-1999 period was shaped by the national level, through the extension of anti-discrimination policy to cover religion, has already briefly been touched upon. Yet this went beyond the council's aforementioned 2000 anti-racist statement that covered religious beliefs. Indeed, the 2002 Race Equality Scheme that did so much to frame anti-racism and equal opportunities within Wiltshire's rural context also included religion.[87] Making reference to both the Equality Act 2010 and the Equality and Human Rights Commission, and the fact that the county's rurality meant that engaging with community groups was often more challenging, Wiltshire Council expressed a commitment to recognising, and catering for, its staff's religious beliefs and practices. Individual considerations addressed workforce monitoring, the provision of a prayer room for staff, and fasting and religious dress in the workplace.[88] Furthermore, the Wiltshire Community Plan made reference to the Moroccan community specifically and stressed that there was a need for greater awareness regarding the county's cultural and religious diversity and minority groups' needs, especially as they can be subject to isolation and a lack of community organisation in their rural surroundings.[89]

Similarly, citing the Equality Act 2010 and recognising the rural nature of much of the borough, Swindon Borough Council cited religion and belief as key characteristics inherent in its equality objectives, which included community engagement, and staff training and monitoring.[90] The council also considered religious identity and rurality with regard to public transport needs, acknowledging that a Department for Transport paper had shown that ethnic minority groups were often dependent on public transport, yet were disadvantaged by religious harassment, timetables that revolved around Christian holidays and a lack of understanding regarding the transport needs of minority faith communities. It pledged to address the issues of communication and the safety and security concerns regarding transport services and ethnic and religious minorities in the local transport plan.[91] Wiltshire's local authorities at the sub-county level also gradually recognised religion. Those in the districts of Salisbury and North Wiltshire and the town of Devizes, for example, incorporated religious belief into their housing, recruitment and wider equal opportunities policies, respectively.[92] Overall, the measures and policies implemented by Wiltshire's local government addressing anti-discrimination, equal opportunities and community cohesion conformed to what was expected of, and indeed prepared by, local authorities at the turn of the twenty-first century. The key difference is that they frequently considered and made attempts to cater for what were small, and potentially isolated and vulnerable, ethnic minority communities on the county's rural landscape.

The response to local Muslim communities: recognition, integration and religious needs

As well as reacting to policy and guidance that trickled down from the national level, Wiltshire's local authority also continued to respond to its Muslim communities' cultural, religious and social needs and demands. These responses addressed a range of areas and initiatives, stemmed from various levels of local government, and went some way towards officially acknowledging and honouring the Muslim presence in the county. For example, during the early to mid-2000s, Wiltshire County Council considered a request submitted by the Trowbridge-based Moroccan Community Association of Southern England and Wales (MCA) to lease council-owned land to them for a nominal price on which they wished to build a Moroccan community centre. It was intended that the centre cater for both British Moroccans and other residents of Trowbridge and the surrounding area, and that, amongst other initiatives, it offer sports facilities, a space for social functions, including weddings and women's groups, and classes on ethnic minorities' languages, histories and cultures.[93] The MCA's business plan stressed that the centre was 'for the use of all residents of the area, irrespective of race or religion', that it 'would demonstrate the gratitude the British Moroccans of the district feel for their kindly reception by the host community over the past four decades', and that it 'would be a bridge to improve relations between the Islamic world and the West at a time of great tension'.[94] For example, it planned to use the centre as an educational resource for those interested in learning about both Moroccan and Arabic culture more widely.

Wiltshire County Council responded favourably to the MCA's request. Whilst, from a financial perspective, it made sense to sell the site on the open market, the council agreed to lease it to the MCA at a peppercorn rent providing that it catered for all segments of the local community. On the whole, the council was committed to helping the MCA offer community provision to the Moroccan and other ethnic minority populations in the area. Furthermore, it felt that the centre would contribute to Trowbridge and the wider district's multicultural community as well as fit in with its broader community policies.[95] Similarly, Trowbridge Town Council also appeared to back the centre, stressing both the importance of integration and that Trowbridge had the second-largest Moroccan community in the country after London.[96] Finally, the centre also had the strong support of Wiltshire MP Andrew Murrison who not only petitioned that Wiltshire County Council allow the centre to go ahead, but also hoped that it would 'act as a beacon for other communities' and argued that 'the Moroccan community in Trowbridge is a valued and well-respected part of the community and other areas can learn from that'.[97]

Trowbridge Town Council also responded positively to a request it received from the MCA regarding the twinning of Trowbridge with Oujda, the city in which the majority of Wiltshire's Moroccan community had its roots.[98] Signed in 2009, the partnership aimed to develop positive collaboration and relationships between the two councils and the towns' communities more widely in the areas of culture, education, hospitality, sport and tourism.[99] There were reciprocal visits of local government delegations between the two towns, and Trowbridge Town Council spoke about continuing to improve links with this north-eastern Moroccan city. This partnership agreement, the first ever between a British town and one in a Muslim Arab country, captured the attention of both the local and national press. It was about looking back at, and indeed recognising, the area's migration history, and it paid tribute to the local Moroccan community that began settling during the 1960s. Yet it was also about showcasing how well integrated the community was and about looking to the future. One local councillor who was involved in the twinning arrangements hoped to 'show the rest of the country how Muslim and Christian communities can get on together' and how communities in Trowbridge have 'lived side-by-side for many years without any problems',[100] whilst another argued that it would help 'dispel prejudice and misconceptions'.[101]

Wiltshire's local authority's recognition of local Muslim populations, and its response to their needs and demands, stretched beyond the Moroccan community in and around Trowbridge. Muslim burials, for example, continued to be an area of discussion and provision in a number of towns. In 2017, Melksham Town Council received a request regarding the possibility of providing an area for Muslim burials in the town. Whilst citing that this fell under the jurisdiction of Wiltshire Council, the town's Policy and Resources Committee stressed 'that persons of the Muslim faith are very much an established, growing and welcome part of Melksham's community', and thus decided to liaise with the council to see if an appropriate piece of land could be identified.[102] Despite recognising that, according to the 2011 Census, only 105 Muslims lived in the Melksham Community Area, thus comprising less than 0.5% of the population, the Melksham Area Board's response was positive.[103] It decided to grant a separate space in the town's cemetery for Muslim burials in which the graves would be orientated to face Mecca. A number of other towns had already allocated Muslim areas in their cemeteries, including Trowbridge and Warminster.[104] Furthermore, a planning application for a new cemetery in Salisbury that was drawn up by Salisbury City Council and approved by Wiltshire Council in 2018 had an allocated Muslim burial area. The cemetery was located on what was once farmland, and was to serve Salisbury, Wilton and the surrounding area.[105]

There are also a number of other ways in which Wiltshire's local authority recognised, catered for and supported the county's Muslim communities. Trowbridge Area Board, for example, awarded funding to the Wiltshire Islamic Cultural Centre in order to enable it to run a BME youth project that was partly a response to 'parents who are worried about their children not being able to socialise in a setting that conforms with their religious and cultural needs'.[106] It also granted funding to the Trowbridge Islamic Trust in order to support the Trowbridge Cultural Food Festival, maintaining that it fully supported 'the work of the mosque to aid integration of different cultures in the town'.[107] Roundway Parish Council approved an application made by local Muslims to use two portable buildings in a garden on the outskirts of Devizes as a prayer centre,[108] and a cultural strategy for Salisbury and South Wiltshire made reference to the area's Muslim population specifically.[109] Other considerations and initiatives included the tackling of Islamophobic crime in the county and ensuring Muslim communities were aware that they had the support of the police; the Wiltshire Standing Advisory Council on Religious Education (SACRE) recruiting a Muslim representative, and thus supporting the teaching and learning of Islam in the county's schools; and mayors of rural

Wiltshire market towns attending Ramadan celebrations.[110] The next chapter will offer an insight into many of these local Muslims' needs and demands, and the local recognition of Islam, including with regard to community and cultural centres, burial rituals and religious education, from the perspective of the Muslim communities themselves, as well as capture their views on, and commitment to, integration and community cohesion.

Conclusion

An assessment of Wiltshire's local authority's political approach towards its ethnic minority communities across the post-1999 period shows the extent to which it was influenced and shaped by national-level policy. The Macpherson Report and subsequent Race Relations (Amendment) Act 2000 and, to a lesser extent, the community cohesion agenda and the extension of anti-discrimination policy to include religion were all reflected in county-level actions, measures and schemes. Furthermore, as was the case during previous decades, whilst the county's Muslim communities were at the receiving end of these policies and practices together with other ethnic and religious minorities, they also received tailored attention and acknowledgement. During the post-1999 period, this consisted of responding to their cultural, religious and social needs, as well as an increased official recognition of their long-term presence, acceptance and integration in the county.

Once again, the local authority's political approach was not without its shortcomings. Whilst certainly being active and catering for its Muslim communities and ethnic minority populations more widely, it nevertheless continued to largely respond to a range of both national and local factors. Furthermore, it is difficult to ascertain the extent to which its policies and practices were the consequence of political will and dedication, or rather were merely symbolic efforts to comply with the duties placed upon public authorities. Wiltshire Racial Equality Council hints that it suspected that this might have been the case and when, for example, recognising the implications of the Macpherson Report 'in a rural district like Salisbury', it referred to the need for the entire county 'to embrace race and diversity issues fully and keep them high on the agenda, and not as a token'.[111] Nevertheless, despite these misgivings, it is clear that Wiltshire's local government continued to offer an active, considered and continuous approach to its ethnic minority communities in a range of areas during the post-1999 years. Moreover, local authority responses to Muslim communities, as well as ethnic minorities more generally, became much more of a county-wide endeavour, with district councils such as those of North Wiltshire and Salisbury, and town councils like those of Devizes and Melksham, playing an active part.

Yet it is perhaps the rural dimension of Wiltshire's local government's political approach that is most noteworthy. Not only did it continue to demonstrate a commitment to its ethnic and Muslim minority communities, but the post-1999 era increasingly saw policies and measures being implemented, not despite the county's rurality, but rather being embedded within it and, at times, emerging because of it. In other words, there was a gradual recognition amongst the local authority that small and scattered ethnic minorities within Wiltshire's otherwise white rural landscape might be susceptible to isolation, racism and vulnerability. Furthermore, in doing so, it pushed through pockets of a clear 'no problem here' mentality in the county, such as that adopted by a number of local schools, and it made a conscious effort to not fall into the trap of dismissing issues of race, equality and diversity that it was aware plagued so many rural areas across Britain.[112] Even its response to local Muslim communities, and their religious needs and practices, was often framed within a sense of inherent rurality, be it through its approval of makeshift cultural, social and prayer spaces,[113] or of Muslim burials in a rural market town with a small Muslim population. It would be unfair to conclude, as has often been argued was the case in rural Britain more generally, that ethnic minorities in Wiltshire lacked service provision or were invisible from a policy perspective.[114] Moreover, Rhys Dafydd Jones' observation that 'Muslims in rural areas encounter not only a visible absence, but also a discursive absence in which they are written out of rural space' does not appear to have held true for the county.[115] One of the reasons for this might have been the vibrant and proactive nature of the Muslim communities themselves, one of the many themes that will be explored in the next chapter.

Notes

1   See Commission on the Future of Multi-Ethnic Britain, *The Future of Multi-Ethnic Britain (The Parekh Report)* (London: Profile Books, 2000). For an insight into, and debates on, the multiculturalism backlash in Britain and further afield, see Steven Vertovec and Susanne Wessendorf (eds), *The Multiculturalism Backlash: European Discourses, Policies and Practices* (London: Routledge, 2010); Varun Uberoi and Tariq Modood, 'Has multiculturalism in Britain retreated?', *Soundings*, 53 (2013), 129–42; and Christian Joppke, *Is Multiculturalism Dead? Crisis and Persistence in the Constitutional State* (Cambridge: Polity Press, 2017).

2   William Macpherson, *The Stephen Lawrence Inquiry: Report of an Inquiry by Sir William Macpherson of Cluny* (London: Home Office, 1999).

3   Community Cohesion Independent Review Team, *Community Cohesion: A Report of the Independent Review Team, Chaired by Ted Cantle (Cantle Report)* (London: Home Office, 2001), p. 9.

4   Trevor Phillips, 'After 7/7: Sleepwalking to Segregation', Speech to the Manchester Council for Community Relations, 22 September 2005.

5   PM David Cameron's Speech at Munich Security Conference (5 February 2011).

6   See Home Office, *Improving Opportunity, Strengthening Society. The Government's Strategy to Increase Race Equality and Community Cohesion* (London, 2005); and Ted Cantle, *Community Cohesion: A New Framework for Race and Diversity* (Basingstoke: Palgrave Macmillan, 2005).

7   For example, see Derek McGhee, 'Moving to "our" common ground – a critical examination of community cohesion discourse in twenty-first century Britain', *The Sociological Review*, 51:3 (2003), 376–404; and Margaret Wetherell, Michelynn Laflèche and Robert Berkeley (eds), *Identity, Ethnic Diversity and Community Cohesion* (London: SAGE, 2007).

8   Steven Vertovec, 'Towards post-multiculturalism? Changing communities, conditions and contexts of diversity', *International Social Science Journal* 61:199 (2010), 83–95.

9   See, for example, Derek McGhee, *The End of Multiculturalism? Terrorism, Integration and Human Rights* (Maidenhead: Open University Press, 2008); and Paul Thomas, *Youth, Multiculturalism and Community Cohesion* (Basingstoke: Palgrave Macmillan, 2011), pp. 1–2.

10 For critiques of the Prevent strategy, see Charles Husband and Yunis Alam, *Social Cohesion and Counter-terrorism: A Policy Contradiction?* (Bristol: The Policy Press, 2011); and Paul Thomas, *Responding to the Threat of Violent Extremism: Failing to Prevent* (London: Bloomsbury, 2012). For the Casey Review, see Louise Casey, *The Casey Review: A Review into Opportunity and Integration* (London: Department for Communities and Local Government, 2016).

11 For an insight into this political landscape, see Chris Allen, 'Still a challenge for us all? The Runnymede Trust, Islamophobia and policy', in Dawn Llewellyn and Sonya Sharma (eds), *Religion, Equalities, and Inequalities* (Abingdon: Routledge, 2016), pp. 113–24.

12 Community Cohesion Independent Review Team, *Community Cohesion*, p. 11.

13 Local Government Association, *Guidance on Community Cohesion* (London, 2002), p. 5.

14 Communities and Local Government, *Creating the Conditions for Integration* (London, 2012), p. 7.

15 See Home Office and Vantagepoint, *Community Cohesion Pathfinder Programme: The First Six Months* (London: Vantagepoint/Home Office, 2003); Claire Worley, ' "It's not about race. It's about the community": New Labour and "community cohesion" ', *Critical Social Policy*, 25:4 (2005), 493; and Peter Ratcliffe, 'From community to social cohesion: interrogating a policy paradigm', in Peter Ratcliffe and Ines Newman (eds), *Promoting Social Cohesion: Implications for Policy and Evaluation* (Bristol: The Policy Press, 2011), p. 25.

16 See Deborah Phillips, Ludi Simpson and Sameera Ahmed, 'Shifting geographies of minority ethnic settlement: remaking communities in Oldham and

Rochdale', in John Flint and David Robinson (eds), *Community Cohesion in Crisis? New Dimensions of Diversity and Difference* (Bristol: The Policy Press, 2008), p. 83.

17 See Scholten, 'The multilevel dynamics of migrant integration policies in unitary states', 155; and Tower Hamlets Overview and Scrutiny Committee, *A More Cohesive Borough: A Scrutiny Challenge Report* (June 2017).

18 See Communities and Local Government Committee, *Preventing Violent Extremism: Sixth Report of Session 2009–10* (London: House of Commons, 2010), p. 145.

19 See Bristol City Council, *Equality and Inclusion Policy and Strategy 2018–2023* (2018), p. 4.

20 See Asifa Hussain and Mohammed Ishaq, 'Managing race equality in Scottish local councils in the aftermath of the Race Relations (Amendment) Act 2000', *International Journal of Public Sector Management*, 21:6 (2008), 586–610; Asif Afridi, *From Benign Neglect to Citizen Khan: 30 Years of Equalities Practice in Birmingham* (Birmingham: BRAP, 2015), pp. 18–9; and North East Derbyshire District Council Single Equality Scheme (2016–2019).

21 See Cantle, *Community Cohesion*, p. 159; and Charlotte Williams and Mark R. D. Johnson, *Race and Ethnicity in a Welfare Society* (Maidenhead: Open University Press, 2010), pp. 128–9.

22 See Hannah Jones, '"The best borough in the country for cohesion!": managing place and multiculture in local government', *Ethnic and Racial Studies*, 37:4 (2014), 605–20; and Lancashire County Council, *Equality, Cohesion and Integration Strategy 2014–2017* (Preston, 2014).

23 de Lima, 'John O'Groats to Land's End', p. 42.

24 See Garland and Chakraborti, 'Racist victimisation, community safety and the rural'.

25 See Williams and Johnson, *Race and Ethnicity in a Welfare Society*, p. 137.

26 See Wiltshire Council, *Wiltshire's Diverse Communities*.

27 See Wiltshire County Council, *A Summary of the 2001 Census for the County of Wiltshire* (Economic Research and Intelligence Unit, 2006), p. 12.

28 These figures were obtained from the 2011 Census for England and Wales.

29 See Swindon Joint Strategic Needs Assessment, *Census 2011 Profile Number One*.

30 These figures were obtained from the 2011 Census for England and Wales.

31 See Swindon Borough Council, *Swindon Population by Equality Groups* (undated); and 2011 Census for England and Wales.

32 See Office for National Statistics, *Religion in England and Wales* (11 December 2012).

33 For example, see WSHC, G31/1/1/8/8, West Wiltshire District Council, Cabinet Agendas, January–November 2008, meeting of 5 November 2008, 'Migrant Workers and Houses in Multiple Occupation in West Wiltshire 2008'; Wiltshire Council, 'Wiltshire Part of Pilot Scheme to Help Support Refugees' (22 July 2016); and Wiltshire Council, *The Corporate Equality Plan*, January 2017. Furthermore, Swindon Borough Council helps fund *The*

Harbour Project, an organisation that offers support to asylum seekers and refugees.

34 See WSHC, F1/201/20, Wiltshire County Council Cabinet Agenda Papers, 2001–date, meeting of 23 May 2002, 'Wiltshire County Council Draft Race Equality Scheme May 2002–5'; Trowbridge Town Council, meeting of 15 November 2005; and *BBC News,* 'Market Town Twins with Arab City'.

35 Macpherson, *The Stephen Lawrence Inquiry.*

36 Race Relations (Amendment) Act 2000.

37 WSHC, 3231/11, Wiltshire Racial Equality Council, Annual Report 2000.

38 Macpherson, *The Stephen Lawrence Inquiry.*

39 For an insight into the influence the Macpherson Report and the Race Relations (Amendment) Act 2000 had on the education sector, see Sally Tomlinson, 'Race, ethnicity and education under New Labour', *Oxford Review of Education,* 31:1 (2005), 153–71; Tomlinson, *Race and Education,* pp. 129–30, 132; and Race, *Multiculturalism and Education,* pp. 30–2. However, it should be noted that the actual impact the 1999 Report and the 2000 Act had on policymakers has at times been questioned. For example, see Tomlinson, *Race and Education,* p. 146; and David Gillborn, *Racism and Education: Coincidence or Conspiracy?* (Abingdon: Routledge, 2008).

40 The results also found that the type of underachievement differed according to ethnicity and gender. For example, Bangladeshi boys underachieved in general, whilst Asian girls suffered from low self-esteem, and Asian and Turkish pupils underachieved in English.

41 See WSHC, F1/201/10/1, Wiltshire County Council Education Committee, meeting of 17 December 1999, 'Implications of the Macpherson Report'.

42 *Ibid.,* Appendix A, 'The Macpherson Report Research Findings'. As the report recognised, the figures and insights attained were not representative of all schools in the county.

43 *Ibid.*

44 *Ibid.*

45 See WSHC, F1/201/10/1, Wiltshire County Council Education Committee, meeting of 2 July 1999, 'Implications of the Macpherson Report'; WSHC, F1/201/10/1, Wiltshire County Council Education Committee, meeting of 17 December 1999, 'Implications of the Macpherson Report'; and WSHC, F1/201/5/1, Wiltshire County Council Policy and Resources Committee, meeting of 19 December 2000, 'The County Council's Response to the Macpherson Report'.

46 See WSHC, F1/201/10/1, Wiltshire County Council Education Committee, 'Implications of the Macpherson Report', 17 December 1999, Appendix A, 'The Macpherson Report Research Findings'.

47 See Swindon Borough Council Unsigned Minutes, 1999–2000, Education Committee, 9 June 1999, 'Swindon and Wiltshire Multicultural Education Service: Implications of Stephen Lawrence Inquiry'.

48 WSHC, F1/201/20, Wiltshire County Council Cabinet, meeting of 23 May 2002, 'Wiltshire County Council Draft Race Equality Scheme May 2002–5', pp. 4, 14, 21.

49 See Merton Council, *The Stephen Lawrence Inquiry – Merton Council's Response to the Macpherson Report* (October 2000); Devon County Council, *Devon County Council Race Equality Scheme, May 2002–5*; North Lincolnshire Council, *The Promotion of Race Equality Guidance for Schools* (2004); and Tahir Abbas and Muhammad Anwar, 'An analysis of race equality policy and practice in the city of Birmingham, UK', *Local Government Studies*, 31:1 (2005), 53–68.

50 Published in 2000 and the product of two years of deliberation carried out by the Commission on the Future of Multi-Ethnic Britain, *The Parekh Report* offered an insight into multi-ethnic Britain and made a series of policy recommendations across a range of societal areas. See Commission on the Future of Multi-Ethnic Britain, *The Future of Multi-Ethnic Britain*.

51 See WSHC, F1/201/5/1, Wiltshire County Council Policy and Resources Committee, meeting of 19 December 2000, 'The County Council's Response to the Macpherson Report'.

52 See WSHC, F1/101/5/5, Wiltshire County Council Policy, later Policy and Resources, Committee Minutes, 1998–2001, meeting of 19 December 2000.

53 WSHC, F1/201/5/1, Wiltshire County Council Policy and Resources Committee, meeting of 19 December 2000, 'Appendix A: Statement of County Council's Commitment to Anti-Racist Practices'.

54 *Ibid.*

55 The adopted definition of a 'racist incident' was 'any incident which is perceived to be racist by the victim or any other person'. The adopted definition of 'institutional racism' was 'the collective failure of an organisation to provide an appropriate and professional service to people because of their colour, culture or ethnic origin. It can be seen or detected in processes, attitudes and behaviour which amount to discrimination through unwitting prejudice, ignorance, thoughtlessness and racist stereotyping which disadvantages minority ethnic people'. See *Ibid.*

56 *Ibid.*

57 See Commission on the Future of Multi-Ethnic Britain, *The Future of Multi-Ethnic Britain*, pp. 90–102; Department of Trade and Industry, *Fairness for All: A New Commission for Equality and Human Rights* (London, 2004); and The Equalities Review, *Fairness and Freedom: The Final Report of the Equalities Review* (2007).

58 The Scheme was approved by Cabinet and published in May 2002. The progress of the Scheme's implementation was tracked across the following years. For example, see WSHC, F1/201/20, Wiltshire County Council Cabinet, 'Race Equality Scheme 2003–04', meeting of 6 September 2004.

59 WSHC, F1/201/20, Wiltshire County Council Cabinet, meeting of 23 May 2002, 'Wiltshire County Council Draft Race Equality Scheme May 2002–5', pp. 3, 6.

60 *Ibid.*, pp. 4, 11, 14, 16, 18, 24.

61 *Ibid.*, pp. 3, 12, 16; and Wiltshire County Council and Wiltshire Racial Equality Council, *Hidden Voices: A Study of Wiltshire's Minority Ethnic Residents* (April 2002). The results of this research report will be further discussed in the

following chapter. Whilst the report addresses the experiences and views of Wiltshire's ethnic minority residents as a whole, some of the respondents were Muslim.

62   WSHC, F1/201/20, Wiltshire County Council Cabinet, meeting of 1 February 2002, 'Services to Children and Families from Black and Other Minority Ethnic Communities', pp. 1–3.

63   *Ibid.*, pp. 3–4.

64   *Ibid.*, p. 4.

65   WSHC, F1/201/14/1, Wiltshire County Council Social Services Committee, meeting of 17 June 1999, 'Wiltshire Community Care Plan, 1997–2000' (Final Draft, 3 June 1999).

66   Wiltshire and Swindon Users' Network, *Diverse Communities*. As with the *Hidden Voices* report, the results of this research report will be further discussed in the following chapter.

67   See Swindon Borough Council, *Equality Duty Publication Report* (January 2015).

68   See WSHC, G29/1/1/1/4, Salisbury District Council, Cabinet Minutes and Agenda Papers, September 2002–November 2002, meeting of 25 September 2002, 'Race Equality Policy for Housing', September 2002. See also WSHC, G29/1/1/8/4, Salisbury District Council, Housing Committee Minutes and Agenda Papers, May 2000–September 2001, meeting of 30 January 2001, Report of Head of Housing Strategy, 'CRE Code of Practice in Rented Housing'.

69   See WSHC, G28/1/1/3/2, North Wiltshire District Council – Cabinet Committee Volume 2, Minutes and Agenda Papers, September 1999–January 2000, meeting of 5 January 2000, Report from Head of Environmental Health to Cabinet, 'Institutional Racism and Racist Incidents – The Stephen Lawrence Inquiry'.

70   See WSHC, G28/1/1/2/8, North Wiltshire District Council – Executive Committee Volume 8, Minutes and Agenda Papers, September–December 2001, meeting of 20 December 2001, 'Policy Statement: Race Equality'.

71   See WSHC, G28/1/1/2/5, North Wiltshire District Council – Executive Committee Volume 5, Minutes and Agenda Papers, February–March 2001, meeting of 8 March 2001, 'Wiltshire Racial Equality Council – Service Level Agreement'.

72   See WSHC, G31/1/1/8/2, West Wiltshire District Council, Cabinet Agendas, January–December 2002, meeting of 25 September 2002; WSHC, G31/1/1/8/2, meeting of 25 September 2002, 'West Wiltshire District Council, Foundations for the Future Housing Strategy 2003–2008'; WSHC, G31/1/1/8/3, West Wiltshire District Council, Cabinet Agendas, January–December 2003, meeting of 12 March 2003; and WSHC, G31/1/100/132, West Wiltshire District Council, Local Joint Consultative Committee and Subcommittees, Signed Minutes, February–November 2000, Local Joint Consultative Committee, meeting of 15 May 2000.

73   See Nissa Finney and Ludi Simpson, *'Sleepwalking to Segregation'? Challenging Myths about Race and Migration* (Bristol: The Policy Press, 2009), p. 9.

74   Rose Doran and Michael Keating, 'Social cohesion in the local delivery context: understanding equality and the importance of local knowledge', in Peter Ratcliffe and Ines Newman (eds), *Promoting Social Cohesion: Implications for Policy and Evaluation* (Bristol: The Policy Press, 2011), p. 144.

75   See *Ibid.*, pp. 144–5; and Jill Rutter, *Moving Up and Getting On: Migration, Integration and Social Cohesion in the UK* (Bristol: The Policy Press, 2015), pp. 29–30.

76   WSHC, F1/360/9, Wiltshire County Council, The Wiltshire Compact – a strategy to improve working arrangements between Wiltshire County Council and the voluntary and community sector, 2005, Wiltshire Compact, Code of Practice on Equality and Diversity, September 2005.

77   See WSHC, F1/360/12, Wiltshire County Council, 'No Barriers Week' (1–5 December): Disability Equality Wiltshire, brochure, 2008–2011, 'Key Equality and Diversity Achievements, April 2008–March 2009' (Wiltshire Council).

78   Department for Communities and Local Government, *Strong and Prosperous Communities: The Local Government White Paper* (2006); and Commission on Integration and Cohesion, *Our Shared Future* (2007).

79   Wiltshire Council, *Wiltshire Sustainability Appraisal Scoping Report. Topic Paper Ten: Inclusive Communities* (April 2010), pp. 5, 9.

80   Swindon Borough Council, *Equality Policy* (Cabinet, 14 April 2010).

81   WSHC, G28/1/1/2/15, North Wiltshire District Council – Executive Committee Volume 15, Minutes and Agenda Papers, September–November 2003, meeting of 4 September 2003, 'Suggested Changes to the Local Cultural Strategy for North Wiltshire', p. 1. The diversity referred to was in reference to both 'ethnic minorities and gay communities'.

82   *Ibid.*, p. 1.

83   *Ibid.*, p. 2.

84   See WSHC, G31/1/1/8/4, West Wiltshire District Council, Cabinet Agendas, January–December 2004, meeting of 7 April 2004, 'Proposed Community Centre at Awdry Avenue, Melksham'.

85   Wiltshire Public Services Board, *Joint Strategic Assessment for Malmesbury Community Area* (2011); and Wiltshire Public Services Board, *Joint Strategic Assessment for Westbury Community Area* (2011).

86   For example, see Wiltshire Council, *Equality Matters (for Schools)* (June 2010: No. 3).

87   WSHC, F1/201/20, Wiltshire County Council Cabinet, 'Wiltshire County Council Draft Race Equality Scheme May 2002–5', p. 9.

88   For example, see Wiltshire Council, *Religion and Belief in the Workplace Policy and Procedure* (2011); and Wiltshire Council, *Equalities Information and Objectives* (2015).

89   Wiltshire Assembly, *People, Places and Promises*, p. 6.

90   See Swindon Borough Council, *Equality Duty Publication Report* (January 2015).

91 See Swindon Borough Council, *Swindon Local Transport Plan 3: 2011–2026* (April 2011).
92 See WSHC, G29/1/1/8/4, Salisbury District Council, minutes of the Housing Committee, meeting of 5 September 2001, 'Review of Tenancy Conditions'; WSHC, G28/1/1/69/2, North Wiltshire District Council – Local Joint Consultative Committee Volume 2, Minutes and Agenda Papers, October 2004–December 2005, meeting of 14 December 2005, 'Recruitment and Selection Guidelines'; and WSHC, 3332/29, Devizes Town Council, Council Minutes with Agenda Papers, 2007–2008, meeting of 18 December 2007, 'Devizes Town Council Equal Opportunities Policy'.
93 See WSHC, F1/201/20 (box 3637), Wiltshire County Council Cabinet, meeting of 12 July 2002, 'Request for the Use of Land in Innox Road Trowbridge for a Moroccan Community Centre'.
94 WSHC, F1/201/20 (box 3639), Wiltshire County Council Cabinet, meeting of 19 December 2006, 'Trowbridge: Land at Innox Road', Appendix A: 'The MCA Community Centre Business Plan', p. 2.
95 See WSHC, F1/101/20, Wiltshire County Council Cabinet Minutes, meeting of 12 July 2002, 'Request for the Use of Land in Innox Road Trowbridge for a Moroccan Community Centre'; WSHC, F1/201/20, 'Request for the Use of Land in Innox Road Trowbridge for a Moroccan Community Centre'; and WSHC, F1/201/20, 'Trowbridge: Land at Innox Road', Appendix A: 'The MCA Community Centre Business Plan'.
96 See Trowbridge Town Council, Community Development Committee, meeting of 11 December 2001, 'Proposed Moroccan Community Centre'.
97 See 'VIP in Visit to Mosque', *Gazette & Herald* (28 January 2005); and WSHC, F1/201/20, 'Trowbridge: Land at Innox Road', Appendix B: Letter from Dr Andrew Murrison MP to the Chief Executive of Wiltshire County Council, 18 October 2006. Andrew Murrison MP visited the site with the MP for the Greater London constituency of Old Bexley and Sidcup who wished to learn more about the area's flourishing Moroccan community.
98 For Trowbridge Town Council's response to the request and discussion about the partnership, see Town Council meeting, 20 September 2005, 'Twinning'; Town Council meeting, 15 November 2005, 'Twinning with Oujda, Morocco'; Trowbridge Town Council, Town Clerk's Report to Policy and Resources Committee, 9 January 2007; Trowbridge Town Council meeting, 17 March 2009, 'Visit of Delegation from Morocco'; and Trowbridge Town Council, Town Clerk's Report to Policy and Resources Committee meeting, 1 March 2011.
99 The Partnership Agreement is on display at Trowbridge Town Council.
100 'Trowbridge in Wiltshire First in Britain to be Twinned with Muslim Arab Town', *Telegraph* (27 March 2009); and 'Pork Pies Help Build Civic Links with Muslim Town', *Independent* (28 March 2009).
101 'Market Town Twins with Arab City', *BBC News* (3 October 2006). For a write-up of some of the partnership's activities and ambitions in the local press, see 'Moroccan Town Link Bid Takes Big Step Forward', *Wiltshire Times* (22 March 2006).

102 Melksham Town Council, Policy and Resources Committee, meeting of 16 January 2017, 'Email from Mr C Pickett Concerning Burial Arrangements within the Town'.

103 Area Boards consist of Wiltshire Council staff and councillors, and local organisations and residents. Their aim is to enable closer collaboration and working between the local authority and local communities.

104 See Wiltshire Council, Melksham Area Board, meeting of 6 September 2017, minutes, 'Melksham Burial Space'; and Wiltshire Council, Melksham Area Board, meeting of 6 September 2017, report entitled 'Melksham Cemetery – Grave Space Allocation'. A spokesman for the town's Muslim community gratefully welcomed the decision, stating that 'we see this as the fullest of integration as it will now be both in this life and the next'. See 'Muslim Community Welcomes Cemetery Decision', *Wiltshire Times* (14 September 2017).

105 The planning application and supporting documents, including site plans and drawings, can be accessed via Wiltshire Council, planning number 18/00239/FUL. See also Rebecca Hudson, 'New Cemetery Planned for City as Existing Graveyards Reach Capacity', *Salisbury Journal* (5 February 2018).

106 See Wiltshire Council, Trowbridge Area Board, 15 March 2012, 'Community Area Grants Scheme 2011/12', minutes and grant application.

107 See Wiltshire Council, Trowbridge Area Board, 16 July 2015, 'Community Area Grants', minutes.

108 See Roundway Parish Council minutes, meeting of 20 October 2014, 'Report for Information and Decision Regarding Planning Matters: Bedborough Farm, London Road'. The plan was withdrawn due to objections made by neighbours and the fact that the Highways Department opposed the proposal on traffic grounds. See 'Mosque Bid Withdrawn After Devizes Residents Object to London Road Location', *Gazette & Herald* (18 December 2014). This use of portable buildings is mentioned by an interviewee in the following chapter.

109 See WSHC, G29/1/1/1/4, Salisbury District Council Cabinet, meeting of 27 November 2002, ' "Ways of Life": Cultural Strategy for Salisbury and South Wiltshire'.

110 See Wiltshire Council, Wiltshire Police and Crime Panel, 4 February 2016, 'Hate Crime'; Wiltshire Council, Wiltshire Standing Advisory Council on Religious Education (SACRE) Annual Report, September 2016–August 2017; and Highworth Town Council minutes, meeting of 19 June 2018, 'Mayor of Highworth Attended Functions'. Highworth's mayor's visit to a mosque in Swindon also received some attention in the local press. See 'Mayors Celebrate Ramadan at Swindon Mosque', *Swindon Advertiser* (7 June 2018).

111 WSHC, 3231/11, 'Wiltshire Racial Equality Council Annual Report 2000', Development Worker (Community Care)/Social Policy Development Officer's Report.

112 The Wiltshire County Council and Wiltshire Racial Equality Council *Hidden Voices* report, for example, made reference to the findings of a number of

key works on ethnic minorities in rural counties, including Eric Jay's '*Keep Them in Birmingham*' and Mohammed Dhalech's *Challenging Racism in the Rural Idyll.*

113 For an insight into the presence of makeshift sacred spaces amongst Muslims in and around market towns in West Wales, see Jones, 'Negotiating absence and presence'. Notions and images of rurality have also been employed in local governments' responses to religious minorities further afield. For examples of exclusionary responses, see Laura Bugg, 'Religion on the fringe: the representation of space and minority religious facilities in the rural–urban fringe of metropolitan Sydney, Australia', *Australian Geographer*, 43:3 (2012), 273–89.

114 For an insight into these arguments, see Neal, 'Rural landscapes, representations and racism'; and Neil Chakraborti and Jon Garland (eds), *Rural Racism* (Cullompton: Willan Publishing, 2004).

115 Jones, 'Negotiating absence and presence', p. 336.

5

Muslim migrant histories, personal narratives and experiences of integration

Writing in 1999, Alistair Thomson maintained that 'migration emerges as one of the most important themes of oral history research.'[1] From the 1990s, oral history has increasingly been recognised as an invaluable resource for uncovering the experiences and lives of migrants in Britain, which are often not documented in more conventional sources, and thus as having the potential to reveal what are otherwise 'hidden' histories.[2] Overall, the historiography has stressed the extent to which oral history offers a more in-depth historical understanding of migration, and has shown its capacity for exposing the role that age, immigrant generation, culture, ethnicity, gender, religion and location of settlement, amongst other factors, play in the migrant experience.[3] Furthermore, existing research has argued that oral history often leads to a sense of advocacy, empowerment, recognition and self-worth amongst ethnic minority populations, enables the challenging of the more traditional top-down approach to the study of migrant communities and, perhaps most importantly, allows the capturing of histories that would otherwise be disregarded or lost to history as they do not feature in written sources.[4] Indeed, Paul Thompson's argument that oral history's ability to focus on 'the under-classes, the underprivileged, and the defeated' leads to both 'a much fairer trial' and 'a more realistic and fair reconstruction of the past' has most certainly struck a chord with migration historians.[5]

This chapter draws upon oral history interviews conducted with members of Wiltshire's Muslim migrant communities. Through the interviews, migrants' narratives and histories, and thus the 'human' side of the migration process, are detailed, and subjective perceptions and important events and themes in the interviewees' migratory experiences emerge. A number of insights into Muslim migrant integration in rural Britain are offered, as are interviewees' experiences, views and observations across a range of areas. The material presented in this chapter is not intended to challenge that addressing Wiltshire's local authority's political approach to migration, integration and diversity outlined in the previous three chapters. Instead, the oral history interviews complement the archival material, reconstructing parts of the county's post-war history of Muslim minorities' settlement, experiences and integration that are simply not captured in written sources.[6] Alongside the interviews, three existing research reports, which offer an insight into the experiences and views of Wiltshire's ethnic minority communities, are also drawn upon in later sections.[7] The chapter will discuss the benefits, potential shortcomings and prevalence of using oral history within migration studies before going on to introduce the oral history research carried out in Wiltshire.

Oral history and beyond: lived experiences and the study of migration

Oral history has potentially been critiqued more than any other methodo-logical approach within the discipline of history. Indeed, oral historians working in the field of migration have themselves acknowledged some of the criticisms and challenges they face. These include the issues of potential bias, interpretation, reliability, subjectivity and fading memories, the way in which an individual's recollections and perceptions can be shaped according to class, ethnicity and gender, and the need to have an understanding of the cultural dynamics and the migration and settlement contexts of the community or communities in question. Yet others consist of cultural and language barriers, the difficulties involved in trying to access what are often perceived to be 'hard to reach' communities, and the fact that the experiences and stories disclosed can be sensitive, and even traumatic, in nature. Some of these factors have the potential to cause anxiety, suspicion and issues of trust amongst respondents, whilst all have a direct impact on the material they are willing to share in their oral testimonies.[8]

Yet despite these limitations, migration historians have successfully championed the important role oral history can and does play. They have argued that the benefits stretch beyond recording what is the migrant's other-wise untold story, offering a more balanced insight into the process of migra-tion, and granting recognition to members of what can sometimes constitute marginalised communities. Oral history also allows, for example, the cap-turing of the inherent complexity and diversity of the migration process, and the uncovering of experiences and stories at the individual, rather than just the community, level. It permits the study of migration through a cultural, gender and social lens as well as through the more traditional economic one.[9] Amongst other things, it explores individual reasons for migration, migrant journeys, experiences of settlement, the prevalence of transnational family connections, and how migrants' behaviour and identities are shaped by age, gender and religious affiliation, and it goes beyond facts to offer an unpre-cedented insight into what can be very personal, unique and powerful testi-monies of migration.[10] Furthermore, in some cases, oral history has enabled the collection and preservation of the memories and stories of increasingly elderly first-generation migrant settlers, thus preventing them from potentially becoming lost forever.[11] The contribution that oral history has made to British migration studies since the turn of the twenty-first century is irrefutable. Notable works include that of Myriam Cherti on Moroccan immigrants in London, which sheds light on a migrant community that is too often overlooked in written sources; that of Joanna Herbert on the city of Leicester, which examines how both migrants and their white British-born counterparts negotiate boundaries and the everyday human experiences of migration; and that of Linda McDowell, which captures the voices of migrant women in the UK since the Second World War, and documents their diverse lives and work experiences.[12]

Yet the collection and preservation of migrants' experiences and stories is not confined to history nor to the practice of oral history, but rather stretches to other disciplines and methodologies. In fact, with regard to race, ethnic minorities and Muslim communities in the rural context, it has often been scholars in a range of other disciplines, including criminology, geography and sociology, who have captured the migrant perspective through a variety of methodological approaches, such as focus groups, interviews, life stories and postal questionnaire surveys. Existing research has uncovered the diverse experiences of migrant communities and the importance of locality in shaping the rural racism encountered in Mid Wales; assessed racial harassment and racist victimisation amongst ethnic minorities in Northamptonshire, Suffolk and Warwickshire; and investigated experiences of community, racism and mobility amongst both asylum seekers and migrant groups in East Kent.[13] The few existing studies that draw upon rural Muslims' experiences and perspectives have addressed how they constitute both visibly absent and physically present communities, the strategies they use to cater for their religious needs and practices, and the difficulties they encounter in attempting to develop a local sense of community.[14] It has largely been such works that have paved the way in both calling for a greater policy response to racist prejudice, and giving a voice to Muslim communities, in rural Britain.

The research

This chapter draws upon thirty-eight interviews with members of Wiltshire's Muslim migrant communities that were conducted during 2016 and 2017.[15] The interviewees were first-generation, 1.5-generation and second-generation migrants who overwhelmingly had long-term experience of living in the county and had witnessed their communities develop over time. Therefore, they were able to offer first-hand insights into the migration and settlement process on an individual basis, but also often in relation to their families and the Muslim population more widely. Some, such as the Bangladeshis, Moroccans and Pakistanis, belonged to Wiltshire's more well-established and visible ethnic minority populations. Others, including Saudi Arabians, Tunisians and Turks, belonged to smaller, and often more invisible, Muslim minority communities. They migrated to and were born, lived, worked, socialised and attended a mosque or prayer room in and around towns across the county, including Amesbury, Bradford-on-Avon, Calne, Chippenham, Devizes, Melksham, Royal Wootton Bassett, Salisbury, Swindon, Trowbridge and Warminster.

They were a diverse group, not just according to ethnicity and area of settlement, but also age, gender, migration history, educational attainment, socioeconomic status and class. They also displayed different levels of religiosity and religious practice. Most were religiously active Muslims, with some placing a stricter adherence to religious activity than others, whilst a few had inherited their religion and did not always follow Islamic practices, yet being Muslim nevertheless constituted an important part of their identities. Rather than impose any kind of strict definition of 'Muslim', this research draws upon the oral history testimonies of those migrants who labelled themselves as such. Furthermore, some interviewees, acting as politicians, community leaders and prominent businessmen and women, were highly visible and well known within both their immediate and wider communities. They included a Salisbury City Council and Wiltshire Council councillor and a politician who has since become Swindon's first Muslim mayor, active members of the Wiltshire Islamic Cultural Centre and mosques, and the owners of locally celebrated and valued businesses. Yet on the other hand, some of the respondents chose to live their lives in a more private, and even anonymous, manner.

The participants were overwhelmingly contacted through various leading and trusted members of the communities. Whilst it must be acknowledged that the use of such so-called gatekeepers can potentially influence the representativeness of the communities interviewed, it is widely recognised that they reduce mistrust and suspicion amongst potential respondents, and can help build a rapport between interviewer and interviewee. After the initial interviews, the so-called snowball sampling technique was used to recruit additional participants.[16] The interviews revolved around open-ended questions that invited interviewees to speak on a range of topics, from their migration histories and senses of identity and integration, to their experiences of practising Islam, and working and living in the county. The questions allowed for a range of possible responses, and enabled the respondents to expand on themes and subjects they deemed important, and thus reveal their personal migratory experiences. The aim was not to establish patterns or generalisations, although some did emerge, but rather to allow for the participants' inherent diversity, and for individual and unique histories and voices regarding their past and ongoing experiences as Muslims in Wiltshire. All of the interviews were conducted in English, and were recorded and transcribed. They varied in length and largely took place in the respondents' homes, but also at other locations, including places of work and worship.[17]

The interviews were unquestionably shaped by my own behaviour, identity and status in a number of different ways.[18] In general, my position as an academic researcher appeared to gain me a certain amount of prestige and respect, especially amongst the first-generation male participants. As an outsider in both ethnic and religious terms, some of the female interviewees, and some of the younger ones in particular, seemed to feel as though they could confide in me, with some sharing personal stories as well as criticisms of their communities. My feeling was that being a relatively young female helped me appear less intimidating and threatening, and not being from Wiltshire, or even originally British, helped me build a rapport with the participants. Furthermore, my participation in community activities, including mosque open days, Eid celebrations, food festivals, and events on hate crime, integration and race relations, sometimes as an invited participant or speaker, allowed me to become familiar to some of the local Muslim communities' members.

Yet the interviews were also undoubtedly hindered in some ways. Familiarity and rapport, for example, did not necessarily always equate to complete disclosure and trust. It was clear that several of the respondents were not willing to be completely open with an 'outsider', with some being more guarded than others. A few of the participants seemed reluctant to offer too many details about their lives and personal experiences in general, especially as they were being recorded.[19] A more common trait was an unwillingness to admit vulnerability by being ambiguous and vague about some of the more negative aspects of their migratory experiences, such as incidents of Islamophobia and hardship, preferring instead to focus on what they perceived to be the more positive features and their successes. Furthermore, the fact that Islam and the presence and integration of Muslim minority communities are topics of much contention, debate, and even anxiety, in early twenty-first-century Britain most certainly played a role in shaping some of the interviews, and some of the interviewees made direct reference to these wider political and popular deliberations.

Overall, these were some of the factors that influenced how the participants constructed their own narratives, causing them to focus overwhelmingly on the past or the present, on their own experiences or those of their parents and families, or on the positives or the negatives, and prompting some to be overwhelmingly cautious and others extremely open with the information they were willing to divulge. Yet regardless of each respondent's approach or the direction an interview took, the experiences and stories that emerged were, for the most part, being shared for the first time. Moreover, amongst the interviewees there was often a sense of pride, delight, and sometimes intrigue, that there existed an interest in capturing the voices of such small rural Muslim communities. The material from the interviews has been organised around key areas and themes that came across throughout them. This chapter will now offer an insight into the interviewees' migration histories and stories of settlement in Wiltshire before addressing their post-settlement experiences in relation to a range of topics, including identity, employment, housing, education, racism and discrimination, cross-community relations, and religious practices and recognition.

Migration histories and settlement

South Asian communities

The migration histories and settlement patterns of South Asian communities in post-war Britain have been widely documented. Largely for socio-economic reasons, but also a range of other push and pull factors, Indians, Pakistanis and Bangladeshis began arriving during the 1950s and 1960s, often as single men who had left their wives and children back in the 'homeland'.[20] Many Indians and Pakistanis originated from Gujarat State, the Mirpur District and the Punjab, whilst the majority of Bangladeshis came from the rural district of Sylhet. Indians and Pakistanis frequently started out working in the West Midlands' metal-bashing industries and the north's woollen textile mills, whilst the Bangladeshis were often employed in heavy industry before moving to London during the 1970s and 1980s to work in the capital's garment and restaurant industries. Few initially intended to settle in Britain permanently, though many eventually called for their families to join them. The subsequent communities that have formed have been strongly shaped by the process of chain migration and their geographical distribution across Britain has been uneven. Significant Indian communities are located in London, Birmingham, Leicester and Wolverhampton, and sizeable Pakistani communities in London, Birmingham, Bradford and Manchester. Significant Bangladeshi communities are found in London, with a large concentration in the borough of Tower Hamlets, but also in Birmingham and Oldham.[21]

On the whole, Britain's South Asians have largely been seen as urban communities. Indeed, many of my interviewees had either themselves lived in London or in the industrial cities of the Midlands and the north, and thus amongst more established and sizeable Muslim communities, before moving to Wiltshire or had parents who had done so. Furthermore, for many, Wiltshire had not been a chosen or preferred place of settlement, but rather was one that had often come about as a result of work, marriage, and unforeseen and unplanned circumstances. The county had frequently been a random, and even accidental, destination about which they had little, if any, previous knowledge. Mahmood, for example, who migrated to Britain from Pakistan in 1962 with the intention of studying at the Northampton Light Manufacturing Institute, described how having boarded a train in London for Wales, he spontaneously decided to get off at Swindon. He took a taxi to Gorse Hill police station where he asked if there were any Asians living in the town and, having been given directions, he knocked on the door of an Indian man who helped him find work as a bus conductor.[22] Atiff, a second-generation Pakistani, was born and raised in Wiltshire because his father, having grown up in Birmingham, found work as an engineer in Swindon during the late 1970s.[23] Similarly, Farzana's family migrated to London from Pakistan when she was a teenager, yet she has lived in Bradford-on-Avon since 1990 when the bank she worked for decided to relocate some of its business to Wiltshire.[24] After getting married around ten years ago, one Birmingham-born second-generation British Bangladeshi moved to Melksham to be close to her husband's family.[25]

Yet most decisions to migrate to Wiltshire were linked to self-employment and business formation,[26] and often the 'Indian' restaurant trade in particular,[27] some of which were more spontaneous and unplanned than others. One Bangladeshi female who grew up in Wiltshire, for example, explained how her father was driving through Salisbury with friends during the late 1960s when they noticed that the area's ruralness reminded them of Bangladesh.[28] They subsequently decided to open a restaurant collectively in the city. In her words:

> [S]o they were driving through the countryside and Wiltshire reminded them of back home, the countryside and all the rolling hills and all the fields... so they stopped in Salisbury, the rivers and the water and every-thing else, they liked it. And then I think the idea came from there that they banded together, collected all their money together, I think four or five of them started a restaurant.[29]

Similarly, Junab, a British Bangladeshi who also grew up in Wiltshire, described how he believed his father initially worked in a textile mill somewhere in the north before moving to Royal Wootton Bassett during the late 1970s. His uncle began working in restaurants across a number of counties and, needing help managing and running them, Junab's family was allocated the restaurant in this North Wiltshire market town. As he explained:

> He needed people to manage and look after it so each family, extended family, whoever, 'Could you go there? Could you go there?' It's through that organic... Initially when my uncles or my grandfathers came before, they came straight to the factories, or some being bus drivers or cleaners,

whatever, but us moving into Wootton Bassett or other areas is because the next phase after the factories was restaurants. That's why we are in Wootton Bassett.[30]

Likewise, Atiqul, who was born in the Sylhet region of Bangladesh and migrated to London during the mid-1980s, had planned to move to Birmingham, but was invited to Salisbury by his brother-in-law to gain work experience in a local restaurant.[31] Wali explained how he was born in India and his family migrated to the UK when he was two years old, initially settling in Taunton. His father had worked in the Merchant Navy, and saved up enough money to go into business and buy a number of restaurants in partnership in Somerset. In 1984, Wali's family moved to Warminster in western Wiltshire because his father, keen to branch out on his own, happened to find a restaurant in the town he wanted to purchase.[32]

For others, the decision to move to Wiltshire to run a business was more planned and strategic, and was made based on the entrepreneurial opportunities they felt the county could provide them with. One British Bangladeshi whose father migrated to London during the post-war years and worked as a tailor, explained how his family gradually got involved in the restaurant trade. Having gained experience, as a chef and a waiter, through his uncle who owned an East London restaurant, his older brother, together with a friend, made a conscious decision to leave the capital and relocate somewhere they could afford to open their own restaurant. Initially settling in Cheltenham for a number of years, they decided upon Melksham during the early 1980s. With regard to his brother, he explained:

[H]e was working with a friend of his and they decided that they wanted to open their own restaurant and they didn't have a lot of money so London has always been expensive because it's the capital and anywhere else like Bath and Bristol is also expensive. So, whilst they were doing their search and driving round and sort of thing, they came across Wiltshire and Wiltshire didn't have any restaurant whatsoever, nothing. This is countryside, people didn't even know anything about Indian food.[33]

Likewise, although his family initially settled in Luton when they arrived from Bangladesh in 1980, Ala moved to Wiltshire during the 1990s to pursue a business opportunity, and initially purchased an Indian restaurant in Westbury before opening two in Calne. Describing the county as 'a good place for a business', he explained how there were not many Indian restaurants and thus not much competition initially.[34] Shahid, who is of a Pakistani background and who moved to the UK during the late 1990s and spent some time in Manchester, also explained how his family's move to Wiltshire was the result of a good business opportunity through which he bought a textile recycling business in Devizes.[35] Overall, perhaps unsurprisingly, Wiltshire was not the initial destination for its South Asian Muslim communities. Instead, they overwhelmingly migrated to the county having first lived in, and experienced, key urban areas of settlement, often London and Birmingham. Furthermore, their choices of residential settlement have not been shaped by the factors it has long been argued play a role in the city context, such as the prevalence of affordable housing and racial discrimination, and a desire to live amongst established and visible ethnic minority populations that offer support mechanisms and shared cultural, linguistic and religious practices.[36] In Wiltshire, the arrival and settlement of South Asian Muslims has largely been the result of work, and predominantly entrepreneurial, opportunities.

The Moroccan community

Compared to the Indians, Pakistanis and Bangladeshis, the remainder of the interviewees belong to what have been referred to as Britain's 'hidden' or 'invisible' Muslim communities, and primarily include Moroccans and Turks, but also individuals from Saudi Arabia, Sri Lanka and Tunisia.[37] With regard to the Moroccan community, many arrived in Britain as unskilled workers during the 1960s and often worked in the hotel and catering industries, with family reunification starting to take place from the 1970s. Chain migration has had a clear impact on their residential patterns, with those from the Larache region, Meknes and Oujda predominantly settling in West London, Crawley and Trowbridge, respectively. What began as temporary economic migration gradually developed into long-term settlement and, for many, the initial 'myth of return' slowly faded away. Yet unlike the South Asians who migrated from former colonies, Britain's Moroccan communities found themselves trying to integrate into a society and way of life with which they had no substantial prior connection. Often referring to first-generation migrants especially and overwhelmingly to the community in London, the small existing body of scholarship has emphasised the prevalence of a language barrier and low education levels, but also the gradual emergence of community associations and informal networks that promote community cohesion.[38]

With regard to Trowbridge, it was not the hotel and catering industries, but rather initially the available factory work and subsequently the increasingly settled Moroccan community that attracted Moroccans to this Wiltshire town. Furthermore, whilst the South Asians' entrepreneurial activity was organised and led by men, Moroccan men and women appear to have carried out factory work equally. Some migrated directly to Trowbridge, whilst others had initially lived elsewhere in the UK. Jilali, for example, migrated to the UK in 1969 and lived in various places, including Southend-on-Sea and

Southampton, where he worked a number of jobs, including as a handyman in schools and colleges and in a railway yard, before moving to Trowbridge in 1974. He decided to settle in Trowbridge after having visited the town and seeing that it had both work available and a Moroccan community, some of whom he knew from back home in Oujda. He worked at the Bowyers meat factory for about a year, first in the pie room and then as a chopper man, before moving to the Airsprung mattress factory.[39] Abdel, who is of a Moroccan background and who arrived in Trowbridge at a young age, explained how his father initially migrated to Wiveliscombe near Taunton in Somerset during the late 1960s where he worked in a chicken factory for around four years.[40] He explained that the factory issued quite a few contracts for labour migrants. In his words:

> There was a chicken factory and there were contracts, there was a company called Ross Chickens, and Ross Chickens wanted to employ only Spaniards, Italians and Moroccans for some reason and the contracts were sent to those three countries and everyone who worked there was either English, Spanish, Moroccan or Italian.[41]

His family then moved to Trowbridge where his father worked in the Bowyers slaughterhouse for around seven years, before finding a job at the Avon Rubber plant. Abdel's mother, Zoubida, explained how she had only stayed in Taunton for three months when she arrived in 1970 before returning to Morocco to give birth to her daughter. When she returned to the UK, she described how, compared to how difficult she had found it in Taunton because of the language barrier and there being 'no Moroccans', Trowbridge was home to a number of Moroccans who also came from Oujda. She began working in sausage production at Bowyers where she remained for 25 years before taking up a cleaning job in a college.[42]

Like Zoubida, many of the other Moroccan women also followed their husbands who had made the journey to Trowbridge first.[43] One migrated to Trowbridge from Morocco in 1969 to join her husband who had arrived six months earlier. She explained how they both began working at the Ross chicken factory, her husband loading lorries whilst she packaged chickens. She went on to work at the Bowyers meat factory where she wrapped sausages and operated machinery, as well as at a beauty product factory in the town, whilst her husband worked as a forklift and lorry driver at Ushers Brewery and then spent a few years at Bowyers.[44] Similarly, another Moroccan female had followed her husband from Oujda to Trowbridge during the late 1960s, and they both initially worked in the Ross chicken factory. Her husband then worked at the Airsprung mattress factory, whilst she worked a number of cleaning jobs as well as in a school cafeteria.[45] This pattern of female migration and factory work was not confined to the late 1960s. Touria, for example, migrated to Wiltshire in 2000 soon after getting married to join her husband who had lived in the town for decades, having been attracted to Trowbridge due to the availability of factory work and the opportunity to live amongst a Muslim community. When she first arrived, she worked rolling sausages at Bowyers and as a supermarket cleaner before moving on to a job packaging at a beauty product factory.[46] Overall, the first generation of Moroccans largely came from a farming background in rural Oujda, and arrived in the county with low education levels and a poor command of the English language, as well as what was most certainly a lack of confidence and firm professional aspirations.[47] As such, their settlement was dominated by both an initial and long-term concentration in unskilled, and largely factory, work.

Turkish and other 'hidden' communities

As with Moroccans, the academic literature on Turkish and Turkish-speaking migrants in Britain has also overwhelmingly focused on London. Often originating from rural areas, many began to arrive during the 1970s and worked in the capital's textile and food industries, with migration continuing into the 2000s.[48] In Wiltshire, much of the Turkish community appears to have begun to settle much later but, as elsewhere, it has overwhelmingly been shaped by both chain migration and business formation, especially in the area of Turkish food.[49] Mehmet, for example, migrated to the UK from Aksaray in the Central Anatolia region of Turkey in 1991 when he was still a teenager and was drawn to Wiltshire because he had family living in Salisbury. He began working in Chippenham where he found a job washing up in an Italian restaurant, before moving to Trowbridge and then Salisbury to work in kebab shops. With business ownership being his long-term ambition, he opened his first business in 2001 and has since owned a number of takeaways in both Melksham and Corsham. Much like the South Asians who arrived during the 1960s, 1970s and 1980s plugged a gap in Wiltshire's rural market with curry restaurants, Mehmet did the same with kebab shops and takeaways in a couple of the county's small market towns during the 2000s.[50]

Having been born in what she described as a fairly rural area of Turkey, Selvi's family migrated to the UK in 2000 in search of socio-economic security when she was almost eight years old. They initially settled in Bristol where they remained only a few weeks before moving to Swindon. Selvi explained that they were attracted to this Wiltshire town both because it was small and thus reminded them of where they were from in Turkey and because it had a Turkish community, which included her uncle who had arrived a few years earlier. As she summarised, 'It's like a small town and where we're from originally back in Turkey, it's exactly the same. It's a small place, everyone's friendly, everything's quite local...'[51] Also reflecting upon his family's decision to move to Swindon, Selvi's brother, Ozay, explained the role that social networks had played in the Turkish community's initial settlement patterns more broadly. In his words: 'So, when you first move to England, if you don't know anybody, when there's someone you know, then you go and you stay with them. You won't leave them.'[52] Their family had long been involved in the Turkish food business, with Swindon acting as a base for their entrepreneurial activities that were often family and community ventures that stretched across the wider South West.[53]

Onder was born in Ankara and migrated to Bristol in 2007 where he worked as a project manager for a charity, which sent him to Swindon after seven or eight months. He has since also been involved in the Turkish kebab business, both as a business owner and as a part-time worker in a friend's takeaway. However, a key reason that Onder's family was drawn to Swindon was because they were invited by the town's Turkish community to teach their children Turkish language and Islamic religious education classes. Unlike in London where there have been Turkish mosques for decades, which have long acted as important community institutions where religious and social activities are carried out and children can access language and religious classes,[54] Swindon did not have such provision. As Onder explained:

> [W]hen we were in Bristol we were coming to Swindon to meet some Turkish people who work in kebab business, and they invited us here to help their children, because they weren't able to teach their children, to teach Turkish language or religious studies and they were worried about this issue, 'cause lots of them have children here... their children was growing up and they didn't speak Turkish properly when we came here and they would like us firstly to teach Turkish language and teach Qur'an 'cause they are religious people.[55]

With regard to Muslims from other ethnic backgrounds, it has largely been education and employment opportunities that have shaped their settlement in Wiltshire. Omar, for example, migrated from Saudi Arabia to the UK in 1976 and studied engineering in both Poole and Bath, and has lived between Saudi Arabia and Wiltshire since the late 1970s, first in Corsham and then in Melksham.[56] Kamel grew up in Tunisia and moved to Trowbridge from London in 1991 because of his wife's work. Despite being a qualified accountant, he went on to study business at a local college, before working in IT both in Melksham and then for the Ministry of Defence.[57] Shazuli, a first-generation Sri Lankan, moved to Wiltshire from Kingston-upon-Thames in 2005 as Head of Finance in a charity and has since set up his own accounting business in Trowbridge.[58]

Overall, the migration histories and initial settlement patterns of Muslim ethnic minority communities in post-war Wiltshire have been diverse. Many were drawn to the county as a result of businesses opportunities and chain migration. The Moroccans valued the available factory work and the increasingly settled Moroccan community in the Trowbridge area. For some Muslim migrants, their arrival and settlement were the result of spontaneous or unplanned circumstances rather than decisions rooted in Wiltshire's characteristics and attributes. Yet for others, it was the county's ruralness, and the prevalence of small towns rather than larger urban areas, that appealed and influenced both decisions to migrate and initial experiences of settlement: the county was reminiscent of 'back home', and was perceived to provide opportunities in a way cities could not. The chapter will now turn to examining Wiltshire's Muslim communities' experiences post-settlement, and the impact living in a rural county amongst small Muslim minority populations has had on their lives in a variety of ways. It will first introduce how it has shaped how they identify and perceive themselves before offering an insight into how it has influenced their attitudes, perceptions and behaviour with regard to a range of areas, including employment and entrepreneurship, housing and the neighbourhood, and the formation of multi-ethnic Muslim communities that seek to promote community cohesion and integration. It will then turn to exposing how living in smaller and more rural Muslim communities has had an effect on their experiences of racism, discrimination and prejudice, and the extent to which there exists a local understanding of Islam, and a provision for religious education and practice in Wiltshire.

Small Muslim communities, self-perceptions and identities

Being part of small rural Muslim and ethnic minority communities clearly shaped the interviewees' identities and how they perceived themselves. Many were keen to emphasise just how small Wiltshire's migrant populations were, often pointing out that they and their families did in fact frequently comprise their respective towns' ethnic and Muslim communities. This assertion was often made with reference to their initial settlement, or to their experiences growing up, in the county, and with regard to the 1960s and 1970s, although some interviewees also discussed it in relation to more recent, and even contemporary, experiences, with many describing themselves as the 'first' or 'only' Muslims or migrants in their neighbourhoods and towns. Mahmood, for example, referred to himself as having been 'the first Muslim immigrant in Swindon' in 1962, whilst Omar described himself as being 'the only Arab in Melksham', and Ala stressed that he was not aware of there being other Muslims in Calne.[59] On growing up in Warminster, Wali recalled how: 'I think for many years, we were the only Asian family, not even Asian, but non-white!'[60] Reflecting upon her childhood in Salisbury during the 1970s, Kantha confirmed that there was a time when, including her own, there were only two or three Bengali families locally.[61] Similarly, Junab maintained that his was the only Muslim family when growing up in Royal Wootton Bassett,[62] and Mehmet stressed that, when he arrived in Chippenham during the 1990s, it was 'very, very rare' to see other Turks in the area.[63] Atiqul described his family as the being the only Asians in his otherwise 'white' neighbourhood in Salisbury, Touria explained that hers was the only Muslim family on her estate in Trowbridge and, in Melksham, one interviewee described his neighbours as 'all English'.[64]

Some of the respondents also stressed the small size of their ethnic and Muslim communities by sharing their experiences in Wiltshire's schools. A British Pakistani who was born and brought up in Swindon, for example, emphasised how small the town's Muslim community was when she attended school. As she explained:

> In fact it was me and two other Asians in the school I went to. I think one was a Muslim. The other one wasn't a Muslim, she was a Sikh. It was a very small community.[65]

Similarly, thinking back to her childhood in Chippenham, Radia, whose family settled in the town during the 1980s, maintained that, alongside her sister, she had been 'the first Asian person, first black person, first coloured person' at school.[66] Also reflecting upon his school years, Abdel remarked upon the small number of other Moroccan children who had attended his school in Trowbridge. He recalled:

> Yeah, there was a couple or one in every year group, not many. So, in 100 there was one or two and generally you weren't in the same class.[67]

Likewise, one second-generation Bangladeshi female described how she was one of the only Bengalis at her school in Melksham. As she explained:

> [I] was the only Bengali girl in my year… the only other Bengalis there – in that school, at the time – were two of my older sisters and this other Bengali girl that lives local.[68]

The manner in which the interviewees' identities and self-perceptions were shaped by being part of small rural Muslim and ethnic minority communities was perhaps best seen through their employment experiences and careers, which were at times pioneering and groundbreaking. Indeed, the manner in which they brought South Asian and Turkish food to rural Wiltshire through their restaurants and takeaways, for example, has already been touched upon. When discussing the Indian restaurant that her father had opened with friends, for example, one female interviewee claimed that it had potentially been the first one, not just in Salisbury, but also in the entire county. As she explained:

> [T]hey were one of the first, back in the sixties there weren't any Indian restaurants like there are now, now there's millions of them but they were the only ones in Salisbury to start with and I think they were the only ones in the whole of Wiltshire for a long time.[69]

Mehmet stressed that people in Melksham did not even know what kebabs tasted like before his takeaways opened, and Radia, who had owned and run an Indian restaurant in Chippenham alongside her husband for around eleven years at the time of her interview, described herself as 'the first woman in [the] Indian restaurant business' in the town.[70] This sense of accomplishment and pride in breaking new ground also stretched to politics. Atiqul, for example, acting as both a city and a county councillor, referred to himself as 'the very first Muslim in the history of Wiltshire Council'.[71] Similarly, Junab, who has since become Swindon's first Muslim mayor, described himself as having been 'the first British Muslim Asian councillor in Swindon', and subsequently 'the first British Bangladeshi candidate for the Labour party in the European election in the south-west of England'.[72]

The fact that being part of small rural Muslim communities was discussed by many of the interviewees is not surprising. Yet what is perhaps more noteworthy is the extent to which this was often at the centre of their identities and achievements, and how they spoke about themselves and their families. Whilst some of their claims that they were the 'first' or 'only' Muslims in their respective towns might be questionable, and perhaps even statistically refutable, they were nevertheless often central to their relationships with, and experiences within, their rural Wiltshire localities. Furthermore, not only was belonging to small rural Muslim communities at times tied up in their achievements and accompanying pride, be it with regard to entrepreneurialism or politics but, as will be discussed in the following sections, it also led to both cross-community engagement and integration, and a sense amongst the interviewees that their experiences had frequently differed from those of Britain's urban Muslim populations.

Employment and entrepreneurship

The manner in which their employment and entrepreneurship activities and experiences resulted in, and often depended on, cross-community engagement and integration within Wiltshire's wider society was stressed by a number of interviewees. Both the Moroccans who arrived in Trowbridge during the late 1960s and early 1970s, as well as those who arrived in later decades, and were employed in the town's factories described how they worked alongside some fellow Moroccans, but also English people and migrants from India, Italy, Jamaica, Poland, Spain and Yugoslavia.[73] Jilali recalled how he had worked with English colleagues at Bowyers before moving to the Airsprung mattress factory where he helped train a few of the English employees on the job.[74] Zoubida described her colleagues at Bowyers, who were English, Indian, Jamaican, Moroccan and Spanish, as 'nice people' and she expressed her regret that the factory had closed.[75] It was not just the Moroccan respondents who stressed the extent to which their employment experiences in Wiltshire had allowed them to engage with people outside their own ethnic and religious groups. Farzana explained how she was one of only two Asian women who had moved to Wiltshire when the bank she worked for relocated some of its business to the county.[76] Atiff, who was employed as a market analyst at a technology company in Swindon, described his colleagues as being largely British, but also from Russia, South Asia and across Europe.[77] When sharing her experiences as a teacher in a North Wiltshire town, one interviewee explained that practically all of her colleagues and pupils were white and that, despite being the school's only Muslim teacher, she felt integrated. In her words:

> I'm the only Muslim, yeah. I might be the only Muslim in the school. I don't know if there's any Muslim children either. There's Indians but don't know any… yeah, I don't think there is any Muslims… Muslim children. So I'm the only Muslim teacher in school, yep… I love it <laughs>. I love it because everyone gives me so much attention… I do feel really integrated. I know quite a lot of teachers and I get along with everybody and I get along with all the kids.[78]

Those interviewees who owned businesses were also eager to stress the extent to which their entrepreneurialism enabled, and relied on, engagement beyond their immediate communities. As has long been recognised to be the case regarding South Asian curry houses across Britain, for example, those in Wiltshire have largely served a white British clientele.[79] Azad and Ala pointed out that the majority of the customers at their curry houses in Salisbury and Calne, respectively, were white British.[80] One interviewee explained that, not only were his customers at his restaurant in Devizes largely white locals, but that when he moved to the market town in 2000, through his business was one way he socialised and got to know people in the area.[81] Radia went as far as to stress that she has gradually come to consider her white English customers in Chippenham as friends and family. She also proudly shared how the town's MP had visited her restaurant and given a speech.[82] Describing what were the restaurant's tenth anniversary celebrations, a local newspaper article reported how the speech proclaimed that the restaurant had 'become part of the community' and that Radia was 'a stalwart in our community'.[83] Whilst the academic literature on Turkish takeaways in Britain is less sizeable, the extent to which they cater for white British customers has gradually been documented, as has the way in which many have diversified into other food products in an attempt to attract a wider clientele.[84] Mehmet's customers in Melksham, for example, were predominantly English, though they also consisted of people of Bangladeshi, Pakistani and Jamaican backgrounds, and a number of the Turkish interviewees involved in the kebab business also served pizza and chicken.[85]

Wiltshire's Muslim migrants' businesses also acted as conduits of cross-community engagement through their recruitment of employees. Whilst many of Wiltshire's Muslim migrant entrepreneurs had initially depended on work in other restaurants and takeaways until they had saved up the necessary capital to purchase their own businesses or the right opportunity presented itself in the county, and many of their businesses began as community ventures and were co-owned and co-run amongst partners comprised of family and friends,[86] they did not merely hire co-ethnic employees and depend on family members. Indeed, many stressed that their employees were from a range of ethnic backgrounds. Radia, for example, explained that she had employed English and European workers, one first-generation Bangladeshi businessman had hired 'local people' from time to time, and Sohidul had taken on English, Indian and Romanian employees at his restaurant in Devizes.[87] Similarly, as well as Turks, Mehmet hired Bulgarians, and Shahid's textile business was made up of what he referred to as English, Indian, Arabic and African employees.[88]

Overall, there is no doubt that this practice of business owners hiring staff from beyond their immediate ethnic groups was necessary due to the county's small migrant populations. A few of the interviewees made this point, with Azad describing a shortage of staff in the county, and Sohidul explaining that the situation was getting 'tougher and tougher' and stressing the difficulty of attracting suitable restaurant staff from cities like London or Birmingham to Wiltshire.[89] It has long been pointed out that many ethnic minority businesses in Britain, and arguably in the restaurant sector in particular, have traditionally often relied on family members and co-ethnic employees.[90] Whilst it has at times proved difficult for migrant entrepreneurs in Britain generally to secure ethnic staff,[91] this has been even more of a challenge in Wiltshire where the business owners and their families have often constituted the majority of their respective towns' ethnic minority populations. As such, they have been compelled to recruit workers from other ethnic and religious backgrounds, thus making their businesses centres of workforce diversity.

Housing and the neighbourhood

Housing and neighbourhood experiences were also central to the interviewees' narratives about their lives and integration in Wiltshire. During the 1960s and 1970s, they often began with renting single rooms and living in cramped conditions above restaurants. Khan and Mahmood, for example, initially rented rooms from Indian families in Swindon, and a first-generation Moroccan female and Jilali from fellow Moroccans and a Jamaican landlady, respectively, in Trowbridge, whilst Kantha and another second-generation Bengali female respondent both spent some time during their childhoods living above their fathers' restaurants in Salisbury.[92] For many, home ownership was a clear ambition from the outset, and an important step in the settlement and integration process. One female interviewee in Salisbury explained how, for her parents, purchasing property was a status symbol and that, in her words, it was about 'what people think if you rent… you're higher up the status if you own your own house rather than renting'.[93] Muhammad stressed that, for the community in Swindon, purchasing property had made financial sense and had brought a feeling of security in that it meant not being at the mercy of landlords.[94] One Moroccan female interviewee explained that she had worked hard to be able to buy a house, and that owning property had been part of feeling comfortable and at home in Wiltshire.[95] Ala emphasised the importance of home ownership for him, and how he owned a second house that he rented out, a practice that he perceived to be part of his entrepreneurial portfolio alongside his businesses.[96] This prevalence of multi-occupation and a community-based housing support system, and increasingly widespread pursuit of owner-occupation, have long been recognised in the academic literature, with regard to South Asian communities in particular.[97]

Yet there were a number of ways in which the interviewees' housing and neighbourhood experiences were shaped by living in a rural county with small Muslim minority communities. Unlike has often been argued regarding Muslim migrant populations in Britain more widely, they did not become residentially concentrated in certain areas or districts, either as a result of low socio-economic status, a lack of housing opportunities or the draw of cultural and religious facilities, nor did they pursue or endure segregation and residential isolationism and thus live what have been termed 'parallel lives'.[98] It appears as though, compared to their urban counterparts, their housing and neighbourhood experiences have been marked by greater levels of residential dispersal, mixing and integration. Be it in Bradford-on-Avon, Devizes, Melksham, Salisbury, Swindon or Trowbridge, the interviewees discussed their neighbours and neighbourhoods across Wiltshire as having long been predominantly 'white' and 'English'.[99] Looking back to his initial years in Swindon, for example, Mahmood stressed how it was 'a small town' with few immigrants where securing housing was not often a problem. Talking about the first property he bought in Swindon, he emphasised the good rapport he had with people in what he referred to as his 'English white neighbourhood'. In his words:

> Neighbourhood was English families both sides, they were very good, they were very helpful, very helpful. This old couple was always helped me, if I'm away they were looking after my children, taking sometimes to school, was telling my wife where to buy things, how the shops are like. They were very good families.[100]

Similarly, one second-generation female respondent used her experiences at the neighbourhood level in Swindon and her relationship with her non-Muslim neighbours as one example through which to explain why she felt that she and her family were integrated in the town. As she described:

> I do feel we are integrated and I think, touch wood, we are quite lucky… Both my neighbours, one goes to Church of England, an elderly couple, but we'll stand there in the garden talking, trying to put the world right at times… we both respect each other's faiths. He respects what I believe in, I respect what he believes in. The other couple, they're a fairly young couple with a son and they're equally nice. We like to… for example Christmas we'll give each other Christmas cards and Christmas presents because we know that's what they're celebrating.[101]

Likewise, expanding on hers being the only Muslim family on her estate in Trowbridge, Touria also emphasised the good rapport she had with her English neighbours. She shared how she was very close to, and fond of, one set of neighbours in particular, explaining how the older son was like a third son to her and he saw her as a second mother.[102] For a few of the interviewees, living amongst the local English community made sense because it was in these areas that their businesses were located. Mehmet explained that, as his customers in Melksham were English, it made sense to live amongst English neighbours.[103] For Ala, it was important to live in close proximity to his businesses in Calne and thus be able to easily visit them when necessary.[104] Both clearly saw themselves as integrated within their neighbourhoods, with Mehmet discussing the ways in which he and his neighbours helped and looked out for each other, and Ala proudly pointing out that 'probably most of the people in Calne know me and my name, it's like they treat me as a friend, businessman'.[105]

For some of the interviewees, an important aspect of Wiltshire's Muslim communities' housing patterns was that they had always been residentially dispersed. Referring to the Moroccan community in Trowbridge, for example, Abdel pointed out how unlike in other places, and London in particular, it had never been residentially concentrated in certain districts. Reflecting on the Moroccan families' residential distribution when growing up in the town, he explained:

> They were scattered. In Trowbridge it's quite... they were all scattered across the town. They were not in any particular area. It's quite strange actually. If you go to places like London or somewhere the communities are all in certain areas. But in Trowbridge they're all over the place. It's a few houses on this estate, a few houses on that estate, and it's all over and that's how it's been.[106]

Similarly, with regard to Melksham's Bengali families, one female interviewee explained how they are 'spread out across town'.[107] In fact, quite a few of the interviewees dismissed the notion of residential clustering in Wiltshire more broadly, pointing out either that its Muslim communities were small and dispersed throughout the county, or that its towns were not large and thus everyone lived in close proximity to each other regardless. Furthermore, some spoke out against ethnic minority and Muslim residential concentration, a practice that they associated with urban areas, and Birmingham and London in particular, and they argued that, in comparison, their residential dispersal and patterns had led to greater levels of integration. Contrasting the situation in Wiltshire with that in Birmingham, Wali explained:

> [I]f you go to somewhere like Birmingham where there's lots of Muslim communities and it's kind of... I think there's more of a separation, so I'm more comfortable living within a wider community, integrated. So from that point of view I think it's good to be in Wiltshire.[108]

At a later stage in the interview, when asked about whether he perceived Muslims in Wiltshire as having had different experiences to larger communities in cities, he again emphasised residential dispersal, arguing that 'because there's not much of a chance to be ghettoised so I think they're more integrated'.[109] Kamel also drew comparisons with Birmingham and with the area of Small Heath in particular. In his words:

> [T]here is an area there called Small Heath, I call it Small Karachi, because you go there it is Karachi. And hence the kids there, they've got a mixed

identity, do they call themselves Pakistanis or British?... We don't have it here.[110]

Likewise, Junab also explained how he felt uncomfortable with ethnic residential segregation, a feeling that he put down to having grown up in rural Wiltshire, and one which clearly shaped his choice of neighbourhood in Swindon. As he explained:

> I wanted to be in west Swindon because I dunno, growing up and having families, extended families in the urban areas I didn't like staying with the Asian community in one ghettoised area. I used to go to East London, whatever, it's like the whole block was all Bangladeshis, whole blocks was Pakistanis or Africans. For me, it's very uncomfortable... I think by growing up in a rural area I wasn't used to it and I felt uncomfortable... That's why I chose... In west Swindon then there was just my family and another family.[111]

For some interviewees, Wiltshire's ruralness offered a sense of safety and security compared to urban centres. Some ethnic minority respondents of Wiltshire Council's 2008 *Qualitative Consultation* report, for example, maintained that they did not suffer as much racism because of their communities' rural dispersed nature.[112] One female interviewee's family had lived in Bradford-on-Avon before moving to Birmingham where they settled in what she termed an 'English area' of the city.[113] Having suffered racial harassment, they returned to Wiltshire after only a few months, this time to Trowbridge, which she described as a 'small town' where she could be 'close with people'.[114] As she saw it, the difference between Birmingham and Wiltshire was that, in Birmingham, white residents wanted to live in white neighbourhoods apart from ethnic and religious minority communities.[115] Even within Wiltshire, there existed what were perceived to be varying levels of protection from racial harassment depending on the ruralness of the surrounding area. For one male interviewee, the way in which to escape incidents of racial harassment that he and his family had occasionally suffered on the outskirts of Melksham was to move to a more rural part of the county. As he summarised:

> We've had both of our cars egged and so on... I was going to treat myself to... a substantial car, electric car, and I haven't bought it because I don't want my vehicle to be damaged. And now we're putting that money towards it and we're going even more rural. We're just in the process of purchasing something. There will be no neighbours, nothing there.[116]

Overall, it is clear that Wiltshire's Muslim communities long perceive there to have been a rural dimension to their housing and neighbourhood experiences.

They emphasised how they formed part of otherwise white neighbourhoods, were residentially scattered across various areas and districts, and how the county's rurality, and small towns and Muslim populations, shaped their housing choices. Furthermore, not only did they believe that these traits and characteristics set them apart from what they perceived to be the norm in urban areas, but they also often felt that they enjoyed comparatively higher levels of integration.

Multi-ethnic Muslim communities and integration

British Muslims are correctly portrayed as inherently diverse, with their attitudes and behaviour with regard to community formation, socialising and worship often being divided along cultural, ethnic, linguistic and religious lines. It has long been argued that religious proliferation amongst Britain's Muslim communities reflects both ethnic groups and religious tendencies. Mosques, for example, which often act as centres of community identity, have continued to drive both ethnic and sectarian divisions by establishing links with the countries of origin, acting as community centres, and offering educational and mother-tongue language provision.[117] As Humayun Ansari argued with regard to Britain's industrial towns and cities, what had emerged by the late 1970s was 'a patchwork of communities', each with 'its particular national, ethnic, linguistic and doctrinal character'.[118] Indeed, overwhelmingly referring to urban areas with sizeable Muslim populations, a number of studies have emphasised the importance and prevalence of clear-cut identities, places and spaces for individual Muslim communities.[119]

Yet in Wiltshire, the existence of these separate and disparate Muslim communities does not appear to be as certain or straightforward. In fact, many of the male interviewees especially emphasised that cross-community engagement and integration beyond their immediate co-ethnics were the norm, something they often attributed to their communities' small rural characters. A few, for example, used the mosque and their prayer spaces to describe how the county's Muslim communities came together regardless of ethnicity. Junab recognised that the situation in Swindon had since changed as more mosques had been established, but he fondly reflected on how all Muslims used to converge to pray in the town's only mosque. As he explained:

Used to be only one mosque. For me that was really great. You had Muslims from all over the world praying at the same mosque. It's the first time I saw an Indonesian. You see Indonesian, you see Nigerian, you see Somalis, Arabs... This is the Muslim people. Doesn't matter. Irrespective of where you're from you're all in the Muslim world, Muslim and other Muslim is like brother and sisters.[120]

Whilst Swindon's mosques have grown in number and thus gradually become more fragmented along ethnic lines, those in the rest of Wiltshire have largely continued to be home to more diverse and inclusive congregations. Discussing the mosque in Trowbridge, for example, Jilali explained how Muslims of various ethnic backgrounds came together 'all in one mosque… The head of the mosque now is… from Tunisia. And we got Bangladeshis, we got Iranians… We still pray the same. That's why I keep telling people… we all praying to one God.'[121] Kamel, who had been heavily involved in the Trowbridge mosque since it had been built in 1997, including as a trustee and as the secretary, was also eager to make this point, and was proud to convey that the mosque acted as a space that brought worshippers from a diverse range of ethnic backgrounds together. In his words:

> We have got at our mosque about twenty-two different nationalities. When they get together you can see it's the friendship, it's… we chat, we laugh, we eat together especially during the month of Ramadan, that's beautiful.[122]

Similarly, Anser pointed out that Devizes' Muslim congregation of around 25 to 30 people, which came together at the town's Quaker Meeting House for Friday prayer, consisted of Bangladeshis, Indians and Pakistanis.[123] Ala explained that Chippenham's mosque was used by a range of different communities, including Bengalis and Moroccans. Atiqul described Salisbury as catering largely for Bengalis, but also Indians, Pakistanis and Turks, and in Melksham, Turkish-born Mehmet attended the Bangladeshi community centre for prayers.[124] Indeed, beyond at a handful of central mosques located in British cities, such multi-ethnic, inclusive and integrated congregations are the product of small Muslim communities located in towns and rural areas. Whilst due to an absence of mosques and prayer rooms this convergence has often been through necessity rather than choice for these small, and often dispersed, Muslim populations, these spaces have nevertheless acted as sites of social bridging between local Muslims, fostering a sense of community and integration, and helping with feelings of isolation.[125] Furthermore, the importance of these types of social bonds and relationships for the wider integration process has been recognised.[126]

The female interviewees, however, often held a different view. Perhaps because they did not attend the mosque on a weekly basis, and certainly not as often as many of their male counterparts, many felt that more needed to be done to foster one single inclusive and integrated Muslim community in

Wiltshire. Farzana, for example, was of the opinion that Wiltshire's Muslims were 'behind' those of cities in this way and that, because the county's Muslim communities were small, this type of community work was more challenging and time-consuming. As she summarised:

> So I think the Wiltshire community is behind, for example, a bigger city, even if you take the nearest one, Bristol... In Bristol, there are lots of mosques because the community is large, and they have a council of Bristol mosques, so they tend to come together, so there is that unity. I just think there is not much sense of volunteering in our community... But that might be because they are so busy developing and working within the community. It's a small community, so you don't have much time to do anything else.[127]

Similarly, one interviewee who had grown up in Birmingham and often drew comparisons between Wiltshire's Muslim communities and those of the West Midlands city, maintained that Muslims in Wiltshire often tended to organise along ethnic lines. Discussing the Bangladeshi Community Centre in Melksham, for example, she recalled how when she first moved to the town, she had felt that the centre's name encouraged barriers and division. As she explained:

> ['C]ause they named the community centre The Bangladeshi Community Centre and I was like, 'Why would you name it...?' ... You do realise there's Turkish here, there's Moroccans here, you know, that other people will migrate and they will move here. You've labelled it Bangladeshi Community Centre. Somebody else will have to open another one because they won't feel welcome.[128]

Although there were diverging views on the extent to which Wiltshire was home to engagement and integration across ethnic lines within the county's Muslim communities, there was a clear sense that there was a strong commitment to community, integration and community cohesion work with the county's population more broadly. It has been argued that Muslims across Britain have attempted to challenge negative portrayals of their communities through community and public engagement activities, and those in Wiltshire were certainly no different.[129] Yet much of the interviewees' work to promote integration and social cohesion, which included organising community engagement activities and teaching the public about Islam, was nevertheless frequently rooted in their being part of small rural communities. Furthermore, they often drew upon and made use of their multi-ethnic bonds and organisations in order to promote community cohesion and integration with the wider local white population. Talking about the mosque community in Trowbridge and drawing comparisons with what he felt was the case in Birmingham, for example, Kamel explained that it was a small multi-ethnic community, that there was 'no cultural control by means of the elders', and that the mosque was able to teach and promote the importance of integration. In his words:

> [W]e are very much in control of what is being expressed… When people come and sit down and chat in a… We're not… we shouldn't be controlling what they say, no, we tell them in terms of sermons, in terms of lessons, that we need to integrate, it's important. Integration, I see it as key for the Muslim success.[130]

This commitment to integration has been seen, for example, through a series of open days, which aimed to invite non-Muslims from the local community into the mosque in order to promote both cross-community engagement and an understanding of Islam.[131] Yet it has not only been the mosque in Trowbridge that has devised activities aimed at fostering integration and community cohesion. Shazuli recalled how, encountering what he referred to as 'a gap' between communities when he first arrived to Wiltshire, he helped establish the Wiltshire Islamic Cultural Centre (WICC). The centre was set up and run by Muslims of different ethnic backgrounds in an attempt to offer religious education to local Muslim children, but also 'build a bridge' between Wiltshire's Muslim and non-Muslim communities.[132] Wali, who was also involved in the establishment of the WICC, explained that the organisation aimed 'to help with community cohesion' and promote an understanding of Islam amongst 'the wider public'.[133] The centre carried out a range of activities, including school visits and the delivery of diversity and cultural awareness training for the police and other statutory organisations. In 2010, the centre worked with the local council and police, and spoke out against plans for an extremist Islamic group to march through Royal Wootton Bassett with empty coffins in what the group claimed was an attempt to draw attention to Muslim deaths in Afghanistan and Iraq.[134] When asked why this work was so important, Wali stressed that there was a need for Wiltshire's dispersed rural Muslims to have a voice and to be able to promote community cohesion. In his words:

> [B]ecause we're in a unique situation being a minority community and even if you look in Wiltshire because it's so rural you've got people spread out all over the place and I thought it was important to have that voice, especially with regards to the school visits because we get so many requests and if we weren't providing that service, there could be others that are doing it, but we feel like we're doing it in a professional way and providing that information to break down those misconceptions and cultural barriers which can lead to hate crime, it can lead to Islamophobia, misunderstanding and so on. So

I just feel it's important from a community cohesion point of view and also it's allowed us to have a say.[135]

One Bengali female interviewee also talked about the importance for Wiltshire's small Muslim communities to play a role in promoting integration and offering an alternative to what she felt were often negative portrayals of Islam and Muslims in the media. She mentioned that one of the ways they did this was by organising community events to which all local communities were invited. As she explained:

We do all these different events and... multicultural... – we like to get everyone involved, even though the group's a Wiltshire Muslim one, but we like to plan these events, get posters out and then just have everyone come, regardless of what faith they are, what religion they are. It's just lovely meeting so many different people from different cultures. We don't see anyone differently; everyone's the same to us.[136]

For many, taking part in outward-facing activities that were organised and run by their local multi-ethnic Muslim communities, and aimed to engage with Wiltshire's population more broadly, constituted a key part of their integration in the county. When asked why he felt integrated, for example, Sohidul discussed an Eid celebration he had helped organise as part of the small Muslim community in Devizes to which people from a number of different communities and backgrounds, including the local MP, had been invited. As he summarised:

[W]e organised an event which was Eid for Muslims... the Devizes Muslim, like I say, six or seven of us only, so it was held in the leisure centre in Devizes, so we had a chance to invite people from say local Christian churches, local mayors, people from all backgrounds really, but mainly we invited the locals, regardless of the religion, regardless of the races. There were people from Caribbean, all races, Pakistani... most of them were English. The local MP came and the local police... They were all very happy.[137]

Whilst not all interviewees felt that Wiltshire was home to fully integrated and inclusive Muslim communities that crossed ethnic lines, it is evident that, when multi-ethnic Muslim communities, mosque congregations and organisations did come together, they gave a voice to what might otherwise have been dispersed, isolated and 'hidden' individuals. Not only was their community cohesion and integration work possible because of this cross-ethnic cooperation, but it was also often firmly rooted within, and shaped by, the Muslim communities' small rural nature. For many, this resulted in a clear commitment to building social bridges between communities, whilst others believed they had a responsibility to teach the county's wider population about Islam. On the whole, this community and civic engagement work was seen as being integral to the wider integration process.

Racism, discrimination, prejudice and the local understanding of Islam

That racism and discrimination are prevalent, and that local responses are needed, are perhaps the two most prevailing arguments in the academic literature on ethnic minority communities in rural Britain. On the whole, it has been contended that rural migrant communities are often more vulnerable and isolated and suffer greater levels of racist prejudice and racial exclusion than those in cities, lack local community support networks, and stand out in what are perceived to be 'white areas'.[138] Whilst research on the discrimination and intolerance encountered by Muslim minority communities specifically in rural Britain is practically non-existent, the extent to which Muslims have suffered rural racism and vulnerability has received a few sporadic mentions. Examples cited have included cases of racial harassment in rural Suffolk, a feeling of cultural and social isolation in rural Scotland, and a deterioration in how Muslims felt they were treated post-9/11 in semi-rural East Kent.[139] Regarding rural West Wales, Jones has argued that there was a lack of understanding of Islam due to a number of factors, including the area's small number of Muslims and an absence of visible traces of Islam.[140]

With regard to Wiltshire, the interviewees offered a range of insights into how the county's 'white' society has reacted to and treated them, both as ethnic and Muslim minorities. Whilst few maintained that they had suffered high levels of racism and discrimination, those who did discuss experiences of racist prejudice often framed them within the context of being part of small ethnic and Muslim communities in a rural area. Junab, for example, explained the difficulties he had encountered during his childhood as the only ethnic minority pupil at his school in Royal Wootton Bassett, and clarified that these had been down to his ethnicity, not his religion. As he summarised:

> Growing up, when I went to school in Wootton Bassett I was the only non-white in there so it was quite hard. Religion didn't play a part. As I say it was prejudice and racism, it was. I had to break barriers. I had to be twice as good as the white child to be involved in anything. I was left aside. Even the teachers… They just like, 'Oh, he's got a little problem with English. Put him in the bottom set, let him continue by himself, struggle himself.'[141]

One interviewee talked about having been the only Bengali girl in her year at school in Melksham and having her headscarf pulled off her head by a fellow pupil.[142] Touria explained that her son had suffered racist abuse at the hands of a neighbour in Trowbridge.[143] Wali described the multiple challenges and barriers he faced in employment and career progression in Wiltshire, which he put down to unconscious bias and racial and religious discrimination.[144] Abdel explained that some members of Trowbridge's Moroccan community had felt prejudiced against when the council did not erect a sign to officially recognise the town's twinning with Oujda like there were for some of its European partnerships.[145] A number of the ethnic minority respondents who took part in Wiltshire Council's *Qualitative Consultation* felt that it was a local 'small town mentality' that often led to incidents of prejudice and negative stereotyping in the county.[146] Yet despite these cases, many of the interviewees felt that they endured less racist prejudice and discrimination than their urban counterparts. Mahmood, for example, believed that Muslims in Wiltshire had always encountered fewer problems that those living in larger communities in cities like Birmingham and Leicester, and Onder maintained that he endured less racism in Swindon than he had done in Bristol.[147]

In fact, a large proportion of the interviewees were eager to stress that they had rarely suffered incidents of racism or Islamophobia in Wiltshire.[148] This chapter has already touched upon the occasional incidents of racial harassment one male interviewee suffered in Melksham. Yet despite these, reflecting on being part of what he called the town's 'only Asian family' when he first arrived during the early 1990s, he was of the opinion that standing out had actually benefitted him. He remembered how, at school, people were 'excited to see someone different' and that, in Melksham more generally, people saw him to be 'something exotic', and were 'intrigued to talk to me. They wanted me to say something in my own language'.[149] A second-generation Bengali female who grew up in Salisbury explained how people living in cities would often assume that she might have 'trouble living here because you're a small minority against all these English people', to which her response would be: 'No, we don't actually. Because... we were born and brought up here... we're still kind of doing the same things, learning the same things at school, and working together.'[150] Atiff emphasised that he had never experienced any problems in Swindon and, making reference to the aftermath of the EU referendum, he maintained that the racist and religious attacks and harassment that he was aware had manifested elsewhere had not done so in the town or in the county more broadly. As he explained:

> [I] mean this county's been very welcoming, I've never, ever experienced any sort of racial hatred or religious hatred within this town. I know last year, I think around this time, there has been an increase of attacks after Brexit...

I think a lot more Muslims live in fear because they feel that there may be some sort of animosity against them, but… living in Wiltshire, living in this town… it's been nice, it's always been nice living in Wiltshire.[151]

A number of the female interviewees discussed their perceptions regarding racism, prejudice and a local understanding and tolerance of Islam in Wiltshire through their experiences wearing the headscarf. Looking back, one Moroccan female talked about the comfort with which she had covered her head when working as a cleaner in a local factory.[152] Similarly, Zoubida stressed that she had never been victimised when wearing a headscarf because Trowbridge is home to 'really good people'.[153] Reflecting upon her childhood in Chippenham, Radia explained that despite having been, alongside her sister, the 'first coloured person' in her school during the late 1980s, she had never experienced any problems as a result of wearing a headscarf.[154] Yet wearing a headscarf was discussed by a number of women as a practice that they felt made them stand out in Wiltshire. The *Hidden Voices* report, for example, captured the voice of a South Asian female who remembered how she felt uncomfortable wearing a headscarf when she first moved to the county because people would stare at her, and one respondent of the *Qualitative Consultation* study shared how wearing a headscarf attracted attention in the county.[155] Similarly, as someone who chose to cover her head whenever leaving her house, a number of the personal experiences one interviewee shared were about wearing a headscarf. She recalled, for example, how when she first moved to Wiltshire, her in-laws warned her: 'Oh, you're not gonna get a job in Wiltshire,' 'cause of my headscarf'. Yet, refusing to give in, she explained: 'I wanna kind of prove that actually, you can be Muslim, you can wear a headscarf, you can follow your religion and live in Wiltshire.'[156] Despite her commitment, she acknowledged that wearing a headscarf in Wiltshire had not always been easy. For example, she discussed how wearing a headscarf had led to assumptions that she could not speak English and, in relation to a time she had attended a parents' meeting at a school in Melksham, she recalled:

The Head of Year said to me, 'Do you speak English?', even before I opened my mouth. And I was taken aback. I was like, 'Quite fluently, thank you very much'. So I carried on but he just assumed because I was brown and I was wearing a headscarf that I didn't speak English.[157]

This prejudicial assumption that the combination of their ethnicity and wearing of a headscarf meant that they would not understand English was also described by a number of female Muslim respondents in the *Diverse Communities* report in relation to their experiences using health, public and social care services in Wiltshire.[158] One interviewee also compared her experiences wearing a headscarf, and as a Muslim female more generally, in the county with those growing up in Birmingham. As she explained:

> And because I've been brought up in Birmingham and I don't really notice that I'm wearing a headscarf or that I'm brown and as the years have gone on, I've noticed actually I am like a sore thumb. And I stick out and I don't realise it until I walk past a mirror or… 'cause no one treats me any different but there are people in the streets that treat me different. And I don't realise that I'm different unless someone's looking at me funny or someone's said something. And it's a bit odd. Whereas in Birmingham, you wouldn't think twice how you're dressing, you just walk out.[159]

This feeling of standing out from the norm also came across in the uncertainty she felt about asking whether she could pray during her teacher training placement. Again, drawing comparisons with Birmingham, she described her hesitation:

> But I remember the first time I had to ask someone if I could pray in one of my PGCE placements. I was like, 'When do I do it? How do I do it?' And it was weeks of preparation to actually ask… To just get up the courage and say, 'You know what, I'm gonna need a room at this time'. And I always make sure that work doesn't come… I'm balancing so it'll be after I finished work or when I have a free period… I'm struggling a little bit. I think it's because I don't have that circle of friends and I think I'm not as good of a… I would define myself as not as good of a Muslim as I used to be when I lived in Birmingham. Like praying was just second nature, whereas now I'm sat here thinking, 'I've got a meeting now. I could technically go and pray but I'll just have a cup of tea instead'.[160]

Being the only Muslim and feeling like she lacked a support network, she tried to avoid having to ask for a space to pray, which led to her praying less and thus had an impact on how good of a Muslim she felt she was. This lack of prayer facilities was also highlighted in the *Diverse Communities* report in which respondents stressed that their use of Wiltshire's health, public and social care services was frequently made difficult by an absence of prayer rooms and spaces for pre-prayer wash, as well as a general lack of awareness regarding Friday prayers.[161] Wali gave an insight into how he felt wanting to perform Muslim prayers impacted where he could work. As he explained:

> [I] feel as a practising Muslim in somewhere like rural Wiltshire, I think the only place that someone like me unfortunately can be comfortable working is somewhere like big organisations, like the council or a university… if

you're in a private business, for example, you'd find it very difficult to be able to go for Friday prayers or have somewhere to pray your five daily prayers, things like that.[162]

Overall, when discussing religious practice, including attending the mosque and celebrating Ramadan, he referred to Wiltshire as a place that can be home to 'less tolerance… and also maybe less cultural awareness', arguing that 'if people are surrounded by more diverse people then they might have a better understanding'.[163] Others also recalled the general lack of awareness that existed regarding fasting during Ramadan and the feelings of 'otherness' that could cause. Ozay, for example, remembered how when fasting at school and college 'all my friends used to say, "What are you doing?"'[164] Similarly, Atiff had 'a tough time' fasting in school 'because people wouldn't understand why you're starving yourself'.[165] The *Hidden Voices* report also described a case of a secondary school pupil who, largely when younger, had been bullied and stereotyped because of a general lack of awareness and knowledge about Islam in the county.[166] Furthermore, Muslim participants in the *Diverse Communities* study reported that a lack of understanding of religious and cultural needs and practices in Wiltshire led to a range of service deficits, which included an absence of prayer rooms in public services, female-only leisure activities and social activities for Muslim teenagers, and adequate circumcision services in hospitals.[167]

Yet a few of the respondents discussed how their local surroundings accepted and respected their religious practices. Jilali and Azad, for example, both mentioned the provision of designated areas for Muslim burials in Trowbridge and Salisbury's cemeteries, respectively.[168] Others went as far as to stress that their religious practices were actively encouraged and endorsed in Wiltshire. Kantha described how, in Salisbury, one of her daughter's teachers enquired if she was going to take a day off school for Eid, thus almost surpassing her own expectations and sense of religious obligation. In her words:

[A]t my daughter's school, she wasn't gonna take Eid off, 'cause at her school it's quite pressurised and she'd have to make up the day off… But her RE teacher's like, 'Aren't you going to take Eid off?' and so I was like, 'I have to take Eid off 'cause Miss So-and-so knows that I'm Muslim and I'm not taking Eid off and she'll think it's really weird.' <Laughs> 'OK. You wanna take the day off, you can stay at home with me.' <Laughs>[169]

This notion that people in Salisbury tolerated and welcomed Islam and Islamic practice was strongly emphasised by Atiqul. Discussing his experiences attending functions in his role as a councillor, he described how efforts were made to ensure that he was given fish or vegetarian meals and was not placed in the proximity of alcoholic beverages. He put what he saw as a general acceptance of Islam down to the local history of Christianity. As he explained:

> I think Salisbury is a perfect place for any Muslim. I think the way the people has welcomed us and made us feel has been really superb. Wiltshire, I think, is a prime example of accepting Muslim people in the best form. End of the day they're looked at as they are people, and I think Salisbury has demonstrated that very well because the Cathedral city, you've got a background of history and all the love and the religion is there, and that's why I think that's how the people looked at it, is anybody can come in, they are very welcome.[170]

On the whole, the interviewees offered mixed views regarding how living in a more rural area amongst small Muslim communities had impacted their chances and experiences of suffering racism, discrimination and prejudice. Whilst the majority agreed that their rural surroundings played a part, there was a clear divergence regarding the type of impact they thought they had. Some felt they suffered the consequences of not having a community support network and a general local lack of understanding regarding Islam and Islamic practices, which in turn influenced where they could work, and the ease with which they could wear a headscarf, pray and fast. Others believed that living in Wiltshire had meant they endured less racism and discrimination than members of larger urban Muslim communities, and they maintained that they in fact benefitted from standing out in the rural county, and were surrounded by a welcoming white population and a sense of religious tolerance. Thus, the correlation between racism and prejudice and rural Britain, at least with regard to Wiltshire, has been somewhat more complex and multifaceted than the historiography has often asserted. Yet the ease or difficulty with which the interviewees felt they could practise Islam and 'be Muslim' in Wiltshire was not just influenced by the local presence, or absence, of racism, discrimination and a sense of understanding. To the contrary, it was also shaped by the extent to which their religious identities and practices were catered for in the county more widely, an area to which this chapter now turns.

Religious practice and 'being Muslim' in the rural landscape

The historiography has long reminded us that the Islamic presence in Britain has predominantly been an urban phenomenon, with cultural, religious and social amenities and facilities including mosques, community centres, Islamic and supplementary schools, *halal* butchers, and provisions for Muslim death and burial traditionally being associated with the city landscape.[171] To the contrary, as has been previously discussed, whilst there has been an impetus to contest the notion that the English countryside is white, and thus recognise both the presence and needs of ethnic minorities,[172] this has rarely extended to religion. Thus, the religious practice and identity of Muslim communities in rural Britain has received scarce academic attention. One notable exception is Jones' research, which found that Muslims often encountered difficulties practising Islam in rural West Wales, especially with regard to securing adequate spaces for prayer and religious rituals.[173]

Islam is frequently publicly perceived to be a barrier to integration, with mosques and visible religious identities often causing anxiety and concern.[174] Yet, as has been increasingly argued in relation to a range of geographical contexts, the important role that religion can play in the lives of Muslim migrants should be taken into account and considered as part of the wider integration process.[175] Furthermore, Islam and religious practice can help Muslim migrants adapt to their surroundings and, across both the first and younger generations, they offer social support, and a sense of self-esteem and cultural continuity.[176] Additionally, as has long been maintained to be the case regarding the United States, but also increasingly Britain, religious membership promotes a sense of belonging and civic integration and offers leadership prospects, and religious groups are often active in community and volunteer work and thus enable integration opportunities.[177] Indeed, the manner in which Wiltshire's Muslims have made use of their multi-ethnic collaboration and organisations in order to pursue community cohesion and integration more widely has already been discussed in this chapter.

Alongside race and ethnicity, religion played a central role in shaping the lived experiences of those interviewed in Wiltshire. For all, being Muslim constituted an important part of their identities, and frequently superseded ethnic and linguistic backgrounds.[178] Being a topic that first-generation, 1.5-generation and second-generation interviewees discussed in considerable detail,[179] it is clear that the extent to which they felt their religious identities were catered for in the county was often a crucial aspect of their migratory experiences and thus influenced their sense of belonging and integration. They spoke about the ease or difficulty with which they could practise Islam and 'be Muslim', and many explained how they felt living in a more rural setting with small Muslim communities had impacted their religious practices and identities. When doing so, as has already been discussed, they at times made reference to the views and attitudes of the local white society but, more often than not, they referred to Wiltshire more broadly and the opportunities and constraints they felt the county provided them with. At the centre of their lived experiences of migration was a constant process of negotiation with regard to the extent to which they could access the necessary amenities and facilities, and follow religious rules and teachings, in their rural surroundings.

The fact that factory work played a role both in drawing Moroccans to Wiltshire and in their post-settlement employment has already been explored. Yet what merits further attention is the fact that, because many worked at Bowyers and thus handled pork, their work experiences often come into direct conflict with their religious identities and practices. Some of the interviewees had sought permission to carry out this work and, although many had left Bowyers as soon as they had been able to find work in a different factory, they clearly felt they had to explain why they had taken on work at Bowyers in the first place. Jilali, who worked both in the pie room and as a chopper man, described how he wanted to work, but was unable to initially find a job elsewhere. In his words:

> [I]f you can't find any job, other jobs, you are allowed to do a job like that because you're not allowed to stay without, not by religion but I don't like stay without a job. But if there was another job going for me in that time, I wouldn't do it.[180]

Abdel, whose father had worked in Bowyers slaughterhouse for around seven years, explained that, because the Moroccans were economic migrants who had come to Wiltshire to work and in search of a better life, working with pork was accepted.[181] One Moroccan female sought the approval of her *imam* who, as she recalled, assured her: 'If you don't find no job anywhere else, you can work there.'[182] Similarly, Touria had sought the endorsement of her mother. Referring to working with pork, she explained how she told her mother that she needed the money to take care of her son. Once her mother confirmed that she would not be eating it, and that she would be touching pork on a temporary basis and out of necessity only, she told her to go ahead and do it.[183] Whilst working with pork was an experience that was particular to the Moroccans, it nevertheless highlights the extent to which, faced with limited employment opportunities on Wiltshire's labour market, the need to secure work and have an income at times superseded religious teachings and identities. There were also a number of other ways in which the interviewees more broadly had to negotiate their interests and needs as Muslims, as well as cope with the absence of Islamic features from the landscape, in rural Wiltshire. The specific areas that came to light in the interviews were the local access to mosques, opportunities for religious education, provisions for Muslim burials, and the availability of *halal* food.

Mosques

Mosques are naturally key to the development of Muslim communities in Britain, and they have long been centres of prayer, education, and Muslim identity and practice. It has been pointed out how their establishment has both reflected Muslim migrant communities' long-term commitment to Britain and awarded them a sense of belonging to, and a space within, their respective localities. Indeed, as Pnina Werbner has argued:

> [T]he conquest of space, its inscription with a new moral and cultural surface… is an act of human empowerment… in sacralising spaces, Muslims also root their identities qua Muslims in a new locality and embody the moral right of their communities to be "in" this new environment.[184]

Much has been written about the progress in mosque construction that has been made throughout the post-Second World War years; from 'house' or 'makeshift' prayer rooms and mosques during the 1950s and 1960s that were largely established by South Asian Muslim communities to the gradual emergence of purpose-built mosques and Islamic centres from the 1970s onwards that was undoubtedly linked to the process of family reunification and Muslim migrants' increasingly certain future in Britain. Mosques have been transformed from informal spaces where overwhelmingly male migrant workers could pray to highly organised centres that offer collective prayer led by *imams* as well as a range of amenities, including Islamic education for children, marriage and funeral services, and leisure and social activities for entire communities. Mosques have become community hubs that are often organised along ethnic, linguistic and political lines, and some have attracted foreign funding and sponsorship.[185]

Yet this narrative is one that is very much rooted within the city context and what John Eade termed 'the Islamization of local urban space'.[186] In contrast, studies on the establishment, development and characteristics of mosques in Britain's more rural areas are rare, and it would be a mistake to assume that they simply mirror their urban counterparts. In his research in rural West Wales, for example, Jones referred to 'storefront mosques' that 'occupy mundane buildings' and were thus 'visually absent' and 'subterranean sacred spaces', such as a gymnasium and a church hall, which were few and far between.[187] Whilst acknowledging that Muslims in British cities have also used such spaces, he argued that, in rural areas, they tend not to be owned or controlled by local Muslim communities, but rather are simply borrowed for the use of prayer. He pointed out that the Muslims who used these mosques often encountered difficulties and impracticalities, which included newcomers struggling to find them and long journey times. His respondents also felt that, due to their small numbers and dispersed nature, it proved difficult to make the case for establishing a designated mosque, and that the lack of a discernable Islamic presence in the surrounding landscape hindered a local understanding of Islam.[188] For Muslims in a semi-rural area in East Kent,

Larry Ray and Kate Reed found that the lack of an official mosque and community centre prevented a sense of belonging to a local Muslim community from developing.[189]

Muslims in rural Wiltshire often encountered similar, and even parallel, experiences. Some of the respondents discussed the lack of mosques upon arrival in Wiltshire or when growing up in the county. It was quite common amongst those respondents who had settled in the county during the 1960s and 1970s especially to emphasise that, although it had initially proved difficult to practise Islam, it had gradually become easier. Mahmood explained how, having arrived in Swindon during the early 1960s, it was not until the early 1980s that the town's small Muslim community bought a house to use as a mosque, and he gradually went from praying alongside only a handful of people to eventually being a member of an established religious congregation of a few hundred people.[190] Before there was a mosque in Trowbridge, Jilali recalled how he would either pray at home or travel to Bristol, and that eventually the local Muslim community began renting a room from a local community organisation for Friday prayers and Eid celebrations.[191] Zoubida and another Moroccan female interviewee remembered how Muslims from Trowbridge would travel to Bath for Ramadan and sometimes for Friday prayer.[192] One second-generation Bengali female recalled how the community in Salisbury used a space above an Indian restaurant as a mosque when she was growing up.[193]

This lack of local mosque provision was not just confined to the 1960s and 1970s, but rather extended into later decades. Junab, for example, explained how, growing up in Royal Wootton Basset during the 1980s and early 1990s and not having a mosque nearby meant having to pray largely at home. On special occasions, he attended prayers at 'a house' in Swindon. In his words:

> It's like in a house. Only time was Eid, end of Ramadan, and Eid-ul-Adha. That's the only two times growing up. I didn't really have that cultural upbringing of a Muslim where you'd attend the mosque say a few times a week for an hour and go to Friday ceremony... In that respect we didn't have a Muslim upbringing.[194]

Similarly, Wali shared his experiences growing up in Warminster during the 1980s and 1990s, which involved travelling to either Bath or Bristol, and sometimes Salisbury, for Eid and Ramadan prayers. As he explained:

> So when I was growing up, obviously being in Warminster there's no mosque there, the nearest mosque to us was Bath. I think initially... Bath and Bristol, so for special occasions like Eid we'd go to either Bath or Bristol to our prayers and during Ramadan; sometimes I recall going to Salisbury

where the Asian community would rent the town hall to hold the prayers…
so growing up it wasn't… the mosque really didn't play a part in my life.[195]

Likewise, Ala also described having to initially travel to either Bath or Bristol
when he first settled in Wiltshire during the 1990s, before beginning to
attend the mosque in Trowbridge, and eventually a repurposed building that
opened in Chippenham that he referred to as a mosque and was much closer
to his home in Calne.[196] Based in Devizes, one first-generation Bangladeshi
male discussed the inconvenience of travelling to the mosque in Trowbridge
before options for communal prayer became available closer to home, first in
Melksham, and then in Devizes itself.[197] As Shahid explained, Devizes' small
Muslim community had for some time used what he called a 'container', and
a local newspaper article referred to as 'two portable buildings in the garden
of a house he owns', for Friday prayers.[198] However, due to complaints from
neighbours and problems regarding planning permission, they stopped using
them and began hiring the town's Quaker Meeting House on Fridays instead.[199]
Some of the county's Muslims travelled even further in order to celebrate religious holidays at the mosque. Mehmet, for example, explained that there had
been a time when he had travelled to London for religious festivals due to the
lack of mosques in Wiltshire.[200] Thus, for many of Wiltshire's Muslims, the
initial lack of local provision meant undertaking long journeys to the nearest
mosque, often beyond county lines at first. This led to them attending less
frequently than they might have liked to, with some having prayed largely at
home and attending the mosque only on religious holidays.

As mosques and prayer spaces have gradually been established in Wiltshire,
they have largely taken the form of makeshift prayer rooms and converted
and rented buildings: one of Swindon's mosques is in a former working men's
club and Salisbury's is in a building that used to be a furniture store, whilst
Melksham's Bangladeshi Community Centre is located in what was once a
hair salon.[201] Furthermore, the interviewees often employed the term 'mosque'
loosely, with it often being used to describe a community centre or makeshift and contingent spaces that held Friday prayers. One exception was the
mosque in Trowbridge, which was purpose-built using funds raised by the
local Muslim communities and had a designated area for women.[202] It was,
nevertheless, fairly architecturally inconspicuous in that it was located in a
residential area and would not immediately be recognised as a mosque to
anyone from outside the local Muslim communities. Not only have these types
of mosques meant that there has long been a lack of visible markers reflecting
the presence of Muslims in Wiltshire, but their rural and multi-ethnic nature
has also led to other barriers and struggles with regard to the practice of Islam.
Referring to the situation in Salisbury, Kantha felt that some parts of the local
Muslim community struggled, and potentially even felt excluded, because

prayers were carried out in Bengali, meaning that not everyone could understand and follow. In her words:

> Well, because the mosque only does Bengali... There are other Muslims
> here – there are Turkish people, I know someone who's Kurdish, there are
> Indian Muslims as well – so there is no one Muslim... They go to Jummah
> prayer and they're like, 'Why are they speaking in Bangla? We don't know
> what they're talking about.' So the mosque is run by the Sylheti Bengalis, but
> there are other people who... The Turkish community contributes to the
> mosque, but I think some of them have stopped sending their kids, thinking,
> 'Well, they're not gonna understand what's happening.'[203]

Kamel, for example, spoke of the difficulty in securing an *imam* that spoke
both Arabic and English at the mosque in Trowbridge, and in even being able
to attract an *imam* to the area altogether. As he explained:

> Sometimes you find them, they speak fluent Arabic, their English is poor or
> vice versa, which is a pain, especially in our community, it's split into two.
> We've got a huge Moroccan community here and also we've got Bengalis and
> Pakistanis, so you need to be able to pass on the message in both languages
> unless one of... part of the community they're not going to understand,
> they're not going to engage... And we've got another issue which is the
> package we're offering, it's not competitive, we can't afford it. The only... the
> main income for us is our Friday box... we don't have people from overseas
> supporting us, no central organisation like in London they've got.[204]

In fact, at the time of the interview, Kamel was temporarily adopting the role
of the *imam* during Friday prayers at the mosque himself. The Muslim community in Devizes brought in an *imam* from Bristol for Friday prayers and,
in Melksham, Friday prayers were being led by someone who the interviewee
referred to as 'just another local person' because the former *imam*, who was
from Bangladesh, could not lead the prayers in English and thus cater for the
town's multi-ethnic community.[205]

Religious education

A common theme amongst many of the younger respondents, and one that
was often linked to mosque provision, was the frustration they expressed at
the lack of opportunities available to them in Wiltshire to acquire a greater
understanding of their religion. Furthermore, they frequently contrasted their
experiences with what they perceived to be very different circumstances in

British cities with larger Muslim communities. When invited to discuss her experiences of practising Islam when growing up in Salisbury, for example, one second-generation Bengali female admitted:

> It's quite difficult, I would say, because... because we haven't got the education here, there's some things that I don't know fully about our religion that I would have liked to... So we have a lot of cousins that live in London or Birmingham, and you learn a lot from just speaking to them, because they've got the incentive of having the education over there. But we don't have it here. We're sort of having to teach ourselves most of the time. We're still even learning new things every day.[206]

At a later stage in the interview, when asked whether there was anything else she wanted to add about her experiences growing up in Wiltshire, she again emphasised this point, maintaining:

> I think it's been quite challenging. You want to learn more about your religion, but you haven't got the facilities here to learn about it. It's more self-taught, sort of thing. What you're being taught at school is just basics about our religion, like the five pillars of Islam. But more insight into our religion probably would have been more beneficial, I think. I do really want to become a better Muslim.[207]

Similarly, another second-generation female interviewee in Swindon admitted that she sometimes lamented not living in Birmingham as she felt the West Midlands city was home to 'a lot more talks and Islamic stuff'.[208] Also discussing Swindon, Atiff outlined what he perceived to be the limitations to the depth to which he would be able to learn about Islam in the town. He explained:

> [I]f I wanted to study my religion more, study in greater detail and do like a course in some of the Islamic Sciences, I think Swindon doesn't have that opportunity or offer that kind of education, you'd have to travel out to Birmingham or to Coventry where there's a lot more established, Madrassas... I mean all the mosques locally offer you the basic teachings, so every mosque will have its class where they'll teach you how to read the Quran properly, the Arabic language, teach you how to pray, but if you wanted to learn in detail some of the finer aspects of the religion and actually get qualified, say like become a qualified *imam*, you'd have to go out of town to learn that, Swindon doesn't offer that, whereas if you go to Birmingham there's many places or many people you could study and learn from in that area.[209]

Likewise, whilst recognising that Muslims in any non-Muslim country were likely to encounter difficulties when it came to freely practising their religion, Abdel nevertheless felt that the opportunities to learn about Islam in Wiltshire were hampered by the county's small Muslim communities. He elaborated:

> [I] think it's got to be harder to practise maybe, harder to learn about your faith, maybe. Opportunities for learning and educational are going to be less. So, obviously, that's going to be the hindrance, if you like, whereas with a larger community there's more of you, there's more willingness to learn and probably local authorities are more willing to engage. With smaller communities, it's a bit in the background.[210]

One second-generation Bengali respondent reflected upon her experiences compared to those of Muslims living in Birmingham and London. She summarised:

> ['C]ause obviously with such a small community of Asians and… You go somewhere else – say, Birmingham, London – they're everywhere. There's such a wider community up there. And I think if I was… Like I was saying about reading the Quran and stuff, a lot of my cousins have memorised it because they've got mosques up there – girls-only mosques and whatnot – but we don't have that here. And we'd have to travel quite far just to get to one of them. In that sense, religious sense, I think we were deprived of a lot of things here.[211]

On the whole, the interviewees conveyed a belief that growing up in a more rural area with relatively small Muslim communities had directly limited their chances of learning about, and understanding, Islam. Unlike first-generation migrants who were often more concerned with the practical aspects of migration and settlement in Britain, and who brought their religion with them from their countries of origin, for those growing up in Wiltshire, religious education depended on immediate surroundings. Due to the fact that mainstream British schools did not provide this in-depth religious education, it was, and indeed still is, predominantly up to the Muslim populations themselves to plug this gap through what are largely independently organised and community-based initiatives.[212] As a result, many lamented the lack of religious opportunities Wiltshire had provided them with, believing that living amongst small Muslim communities had led to an overall absence of facilities, only a basic teaching of Islam, a limited motivation to learn and less interest from the local council, and that more extensive religious education was available in cities, the distance to which meant that regular travel was impractical. These feelings were perhaps accentuated by the fact that they were aware of the amenities available to their urban counterparts. One of the female respondents, for example, explained that she had family in Birmingham and described it as her 'second home',[213] whilst Atiff's father had grown up in the West Midlands city before relocating to Wiltshire, and thus he had visited regularly due to family affiliations and commitments. There was also a clear sense that growing up in Wiltshire had led to possessing a more basic understanding of Islam, which in turn impacted the type of Muslim one was.

The availability of halal *food, Muslim burial rituals and the importance of locality*

Whilst accessing mosques and opportunities for religious education were the two main areas of concern with regard to how their religious identities and practices were provided for in Wiltshire, the availability of *halal* food and Muslim burial rituals were also emphasised by a number of interviewees. Many of those who had grown up in Wiltshire recalled that their school canteens had not served *halal* food. One female interviewee remembered being given 'plates of cheese' to eat for lunch at her school in Salisbury and, in Trowbridge, Abdel reflected on how the lack of *halal* food had meant either eating the vegetarian school meals or taking sandwiches from home.[214] When discussing growing up in Royal Wootton Bassett, Junab emphasised how not being able to acquire *halal* food was a source of even more anxiety than not having access to a mosque for some of his family members. In his words:

> [T]hey were more worried with the food they were having because it wasn't *halal*. With praying at least they can do it at home. You don't need a mosque… You can pray anywhere… The mosque as a building or something, that wasn't the most important. For me growing up and listening to my family, mainly it was the food. Didn't want to eat non-*halal* food.[215]

When asked how his family handled this issue, Junab explained that they had travelled to London or Gloucester every couple of months, which he described as 'a long run before the dual carriageway was built'.[216] A few of the interviewees mentioned that it was possible to get *halal* meat from a number of slaughterhouses, and particularly one near Melksham and one in Frome in Somerset.[217] Yet many had long travelled outside of Wiltshire for this purpose, and continued to do so, and not only to London and Gloucester, but also to Bristol, Birmingham and Southampton.[218] For the first four or five years after he settled in Swindon, Onder went as far as to purchase *halal* meat from Belgium where he had family members living because of what he felt was a lack of available and trustworthy produce in the area.[219] This practice of travelling long distances to purchase *halal* meat was also found to be the case for Muslims in rural West Wales who journeyed to Birmingham and Swansea for this purpose.[220] The Muslim respondents who took part in the *Diverse Communities* study pointed out that local services that offered food across Wiltshire were not always aware of Muslim dietary requirements and thus did not provide *halal* meat.[221]

For some of the interviewees, it was the county's lack of provision for Muslim burial rituals that caused real concern and worry. Once again, Atiff contrasted the situation in Wiltshire with what he felt was available elsewhere. In his words:

> The idea is someone's passed away, you need to bury them as soon as possible, you need to start the funeral proceedings as soon as possible. And in places like Birmingham and Derby they are able to bury people on the weekend, if someone passes away on the weekend, they could be buried on the weekend, it's not so difficult. Where here if someone, say, passes away on the weekend or on a Friday or whatever, you have to wait 'til Monday, if it's a Bank Holiday, then Monday you can't do anything on a Monday, so it has to be done on a Tuesday.[222]

One Moroccan female, who had lived in Trowbridge since 1969, shared some anxiety about dying in Wiltshire. Despite describing her experiences in the county as 'happy' and explaining that, when moving back to Morocco in 1979, she and her family had lasted no more than six or seven weeks there because they soon realised that they felt more comfortable in Trowbridge, she was nevertheless clearly apprehensive about the lack of local provision for Muslim burial rituals. As she clarified:

> Because, to be honest with you, I no want die here. I no want... I want die today and buried that day. I no want doctor see me, I no want anybody, you know, that's the reason.[223]

As appeared to be the case amongst many of the respondents, the extent to which Wiltshire was able to cater for her religious practices, and the importance she awarded to them, formed part of a constant process of negotiation within the migratory experience. In other words, interviewees were at times willing to forego religious practices and weighed them up against other aspects of their lives in the county. Despite her apparent uneasiness with the burial practices available to her in Wiltshire, she admitted that returning to Morocco was 'wishful thinking', explaining that she had told her children: 'If I die here, I bury here. If I die in Morocco, I bury in Morocco. Whatever God decide to do for me, I'm happy with it.'[224] Similarly, the reason her family had contemplated moving back to Morocco in 1979 was because she wanted her children to study and learn Arabic and Islam yet, preferring life in Trowbridge, they returned despite such provisions clearly not being available in Wiltshire. She was also often eager to portray her experiences in a more positive light. Despite recalling, for example, that they initially went 'through hell' without a mosque, she was keen to stress that it was generally easy to practise Islam in the town, and talked about attending Friday prayers and celebrating Ramadan with the Muslim community. In fact, she expressed nostalgia for her early years in the county when, despite there being scant provision for religious practice, she felt there had existed a greater sense of community amongst local Muslims.[225] A few of the interviewees who had grown up in Wiltshire actually appreciated the lack of a formal Islamic provision and structure their small rural communities had provided them with. One female participant felt that it had enabled her to see a different way of thinking and living beyond that of her immediate community, whilst another had fond memories of learning about the Quran in a close-knit and informal setting.[226]

Yet others downplayed the importance of religious affiliation and identity, arguing that their religious practices had played little role in shaping their overall experiences and integration in Wiltshire. For some, locality appeared almost irrelevant and, discussing carrying out daily prayers specifically, they maintained that this was a private practice that could be done anywhere. This was evident in Kamel's interview who, when reflecting upon his life as a Muslim in Wiltshire, claimed: 'I'm happy, I'm… I'm easy, it doesn't make no difference for me whether I am a Muslim or not…'[227] He stressed the importance of prayer and the ease with which he could pray five times a day: 'of course, dawn, you know, pray, go back to sleep, get up to work, do a little prayer, an afternoon prayer. For me that aspect, prayer, is the most important things in my life.'[228] Likewise, when asked whether she had experienced any difficulties practising Islam and being Muslim in Salisbury, Kantha stressed that 'the Islam that I practise – the praying and that sort of stuff – is very private.'[229] In fact, instead of discussing religious practices, she added: 'The only thing I can think of is maybe it did hinder my social life, 'cause I couldn't say to friends, "Oh, I can't go to pubs", and so on.'[230] Shahid also focused on the ease and flexibility with which one could pray. Reflecting upon his experience in Devizes, he explained:

> To be a Muslim is not difficult anywhere… as a Muslim you can live anywhere… it's not necessary to have a mosque to practise it because Islam give us the freedoms, if we have mosque we can go to mosque, if we don't have mosque we can do prayer at home.[231]

A number of the interviewees were reluctant to admit vulnerability, and instead emphasised that their rural locality was not a hindrance and that they had long succeeded in practising Islam in Wiltshire. Nevertheless, the prevalence of inconspicuous and storefront mosques and prayer rooms, the general lack of provision regarding religious education, Muslim burial practices and *halal* products, and the necessity or willingness to relinquish aspects of their religious identities and practices by working with pork or not benefitting from the leadership and knowledge of an *imam* has meant that Wiltshire's Muslims have at times not been able to fully practise their faith nor completely enact their religious identities in the county's rural landscape. As a result, compared to their urban counterparts, these small and disparate Muslim communities have often practised a more private Islam and have thus remained less visible. In fact, the county's Muslim communities at times remained so 'hidden' that new arrivals were not aware that there even was a local Muslim community. Farzana, for example, explained how after moving to Bradford-on-Avon, 'it took about a year, I think, to discover there was a community in Trowbridge'.[232]

Conclusion

The oral history interviews have humanised the official archival narrative, and revealed the inherent and numerous complexities of Muslim migrant settlement, experiences and integration in post-1960s Wiltshire. Some interviewees' migration to the county was shaped by available entrepreneurial and employment opportunities whilst, for others, Wiltshire was more of an unexpected and unplanned destination. They were, on the whole, committed to being part of the wider local community, yet practising Islam and fully performing and enacting their religious identities in the county frequently proved inconvenient, and sometimes, impossible. There was a clear dedication to integration and community cohesion, both within the Muslim communities and beyond, yet there were simultaneously instances of divergence and division as a result of ethnic-specific community hubs and cases of discrimination and prejudice. There was often a pride in being the 'first' or 'only' Arab, Asian or Muslim in their classrooms, neighbourhoods and towns on an individual basis, yet a clear desire to gain further recognition and visibility at a community level. There were examples of standing out and attracting attention in rural Wiltshire, yet at the same time there was frequently an absence of a real tangible Islamic presence as seen through the prevalence of inconspicuous and storefront mosques and prayer rooms, and a local lack of provision for, and understanding of, Islam.

The complexities intrinsic to the settlement, experiences and integration of Muslim migrant communities in Wiltshire are also seen in the differences and variations that emerged between the interviewees, often according to ethnic background, gender, immigrant generation and location of settlement. The Moroccans' employment in the county, for example, was dominated by factory work, whilst that of the South Asian and Turkish populations was frequently steered by entrepreneurialism and business activity. Perhaps unsurprisingly, male interviewees tended to measure their experiences and communities' success in relation to the establishment of mosques, prayer rooms and community organisations, whereas female respondents focused on the ease with which they had worn headscarves and at times felt that more needed to be done to promote inclusivity across ethnic groups. First-generation migrants often conveyed a 'pioneer pride' in having settled in Wiltshire, whilst participants who had grown up in the county expressed concern about the lack of religious education available to them, often drawing comparisons with provision in cities. Salisbury was frequently portrayed as actively welcoming the practice of Islam, whereas in towns like Devizes and Melksham, Muslim communities were still working hard for recognition and acceptance. Furthermore, the oral history interviews also uncovered the complexities and diversity of the migration process at the individual level, with interviewees choosing to construct their narratives around a range of different personal experiences, feelings and stories. These included those in relation to the prevalence of institutional racism, anxiety about dying in Wiltshire due to the lack of local provision for Muslim burial rituals, and a feeling of delight in being the only Muslim in the workplace.

At the core of these varied and multifaceted individual- and community-level narratives often lay a strong sense of agency that can be traced from the interviewees' initial settlement in Wiltshire to all aspects and stages of their lived migratory experiences. Perhaps more than in cities with ready-made Muslim communities, Wiltshire's Muslims have portrayed clear self-determination when seeking, and securing, available factory work; taking advantage of, and filling, gaps in the market with curry restaurants and kebab shops and takeaways; succeeding in purchasing properties in the 'white' towns and neighbourhoods of their choice; and managing to establish multi-ethnic mosques, and community centres and organisations that offer a space and a platform for, and give a voice to, the county's small and dispersed Muslim populations. This agency and self-determination have also long been reflected in the constant process of negotiation that living as a Muslim in Wiltshire has entailed. In other words, Muslim migrants have frequently worked with pork, and foregone readily available access to mosques and prayer spaces, *halal* meat and religious education. Yet their sacrifices have often been soothed by employment opportunities, the prevalence of multi-ethnic and close-knit Muslim communities that work to promote community cohesion, and an affiliation with the rural landscape. Indeed, what is particularly of note are the ways in which the interviewees demonstrated a positive attachment to Wiltshire's rurality. Some had an emotional connection with the rural landscape, a landscape that, on the one hand, like much of rural Britain, has often been identified as 'white', pure, stable, unchanging and 'quintessentially English' yet, on the other, could conjure up memories of rural Bangladesh or Turkey. For others, the county's rurality was perceived to bring with it a sense of safety and security, and many felt that living in a more rural area with smaller Muslim communities meant not being susceptible to the problems they associated with cities, including ghettoisation, market saturation and fewer opportunities for integration.

The oral history narratives have also revealed a correlation between the small and rural nature of Wiltshire's Muslim communities and integration. Whether through necessity or choice, the interviewees' employment histories in the county have been embedded in cross-community contact with colleagues, employees and customers, and their education and housing experiences have been shaped by dispersal, contacts and friendships in 'white' schools and neighbourhoods. Furthermore, despite the difficulties encountered when trying to practise their religion, they have used Islam as a conduit of integration, with cross-community engagement and community cohesion activities often being central to the work carried out by mosques and community organisations. Thus, although they may be small in number and dispersed across the county, Wiltshire's Muslims have become increasingly vocal and visible communities whose lives are often firmly rooted in, and committed to, their rural surroundings.

Having spent time in London, for example, Wali claimed the countryside was 'calling me back' and thus returned to Wiltshire, whilst Ozay revealed how he felt like he arrived back in his 'hometown' whenever he returned to Swindon having been away.[233] Radia was adamant that her future was in Chippenham, maintaining that 'Wiltshire is my county', whilst Atiqul emphasised that he wanted to give something back to Salisbury as it had given him so much.[234] Looking to the future, one interviewee explained that she was committed to staying in Wiltshire, maintaining that it was important that local people, and the schoolchildren she taught in North Wiltshire in particular, had the opportunity to come into contact with a Muslim.[235] In Devizes, Anser believed that progress was still being made with regard to the recognition and acceptance of Islamic practices as people in this 'old English town… are coming to know Muslims'.[236] Overall, whilst acknowledging that being Muslim and practising Islam in Wiltshire had by no means always been straightforward, and that they have often had to work hard at it, they have risen to the challenge and have pursued, embraced and achieved integration in a variety of ways across their migration experiences in the county.

Notes

1 Thomson, 'Moving stories', 24.

2 See Rina Benmayor and Andor Skotnes (eds), *Migration & Identity* (Oxford: Oxford University Press, 1994); Brown, 'Moving on'; and Kathy Burrell and Panikos Panayi (eds), *Histories and Memories: Migrants and Their History in Britain* (London: I.B. Tauris, 2006).

3 For example, see Katy Gardner, 'Narrating location: space, age and gender among Bengali elders in East London', *Oral History*, 27:1 (1999), 65–74; Burrell, *Moving Lives*; Herbert, *Negotiating Boundaries in the City*; Joanna Herbert, 'Oral histories of Ugandan Asians in Britain: gendered identities in the diaspora', *Contemporary South Asia*, 17:1 (2009), 21–32; Alistair Thomson, 'Moving stories, women's lives: sharing authority in oral history', *Oral History*, 39:2 (2011), 73–82; and Jody Mellor and Sophie Gilliat-Ray, 'The early history of migration and settlement of Yemenis in Cardiff, 1939–1970: religion and ethnicity as social capital', *Ethnic and Racial Studies*, 38:1 (2015), 176–91.

4 See Thomson, 'Moving stories'; Myriam Cherti, 'Reconstructing the history of Moroccan migration to the UK: an oral history approach', *Beihefte der Francia*, 62 (2006), 169–78; and Paul Thompson with Joanna Bornat, *The Voice of the Past: Oral History* (Oxford: Oxford University Press, 2017).

5 Thompson with Bornat, *The Voice of the Past*, p. 6.

6 Alessandro Portelli, for example, argued that 'written and oral sources are not mutually exclusive', whilst Myriam Cherti's research on London's Moroccan community used oral history 'to reconstruct part of this recent history that remains to this day unavailable in written sources'. See Alessandro Portelli, 'What makes oral history different', in Robert Perks and Alistair Thomson (eds), *The Oral History Reader* (Abingdon: Routledge, 2016), p. 49; and Cherti, 'Reconstructing the history of Moroccan migration to the UK', 170.

7 See Wiltshire County Council and Wiltshire Racial Equality Council, *Hidden Voices*; Wiltshire Council, *Qualitative Consultation with Wiltshire's Minority Ethnic Residents*; and Wiltshire and Swindon Users' Network, *Diverse Communities*.

8 For example, see Herbert, *Negotiating Boundaries in the City*; David Palmer, '"Every morning before you open the door you have to watch for that brown envelope": complexities and challenges of undertaking oral history with Ethiopian forced migrants in London, U.K.', *The Oral History Review*, 37:1 (2010), 35–53; Joanna Herbert, 'Negotiating boundaries and the cross-cultural oral history interview', in Richard Rodger and Joanna Herbert (eds), *Testimonies of the City: Identity, Community and Change in a Contemporary Urban World* (Abingdon: Routledge, 2016), pp. 251–67; and Carol McKirdy, *Practicing Oral History with Immigrant Narrators* (Abingdon: Routledge, 2016).

9 See Thomson, 'Moving stories'; and Joanna Herbert, 'Migration, memory and metaphor: life stories of South Asians in Leicester', in Kathy Burrell and Panikos Panayi (eds), *Histories and Memories: Migrants and Their History in Britain* (London: I.B. Tauris, 2006), pp. 133–48.

10   For example, see Benmayor and Skotnes (eds), *Migration & Identity*; Katy Gardner, *Age, Narrative and Migration: The Life Course and Life Histories of Bengali Elders in London* (Oxford: Berg, 2002); A. James Hammerton and Alistair Thomson, *'Ten Pound Poms': Australia's Invisible Migrants* (Manchester: Manchester University Press, 2005); Mary Chamberlain, *Family Love in the Diaspora: Migration and the Anglo-Caribbean Experience* (New Brunswick, NJ: Transaction Publishers, 2006); Catherine Delcroix, 'Two generations of Muslim women in France: creative parenting, identity and recognition', *Oral History*, 37:2 (2009), 87–94; and Sarah Hackett, 'Turkish Muslims in a German city: entrepreneurial and residential self-determination', *Migration Letters*, 12:1 (2015), 1–12.

11   For example, see Gardner, 'Narrating location'; and Cherti, 'Reconstructing the history of Moroccan migration to the UK'.

12   Cherti, *Paradoxes of Social Capital*; Herbert, *Negotiating Boundaries in the City*; and Linda McDowell, *Migrant Women's Voices: Talking About Life and Work in the UK since 1945* (London: Bloomsbury, 2016).

13   See Chakraborti and Garland, 'England's green and pleasant land?'; Vaughan Robinson and Hannah Gardner, 'Unravelling a stereotype: the lived experience of black and minority ethnic people in rural Wales', in Neil Chakraborti and Jon Garland (eds), *Rural Racism* (Cullompton: Willan Publishing, 2004), pp. 85–107; Ray and Reed, 'Community, mobility and racism in a semi-rural area'; and Chakraborti, 'Beyond "passive apartheid"?'.

14   See Ray and Reed, 'Community, mobility and racism in a semi-rural area'; Jones, 'Islam and the rural landscape'; and Jones, 'Negotiating absence and presence'.

15   I met with one interviewee twice because, after the first interview, he contacted me to ask if we could meet again due to the fact that he had thought of further experiences he wanted to share. Two of the interviews were carried out with married couples. This was not planned, but rather just transpired. In one, the wife was the main interviewee and the husband contributed some of his experiences and impressions. In the other, I had initially made contact with the husband, but both the husband and wife were keen to participate.

16   These procedures for seeking and securing oral history respondents are both widely accepted and implemented in the migration studies literature, and I have used them in my own research previously. See Carol Lynn McKibben, *Beyond Cannery Row: Sicilian Women, Immigration, and Community in Monterey, California, 1915–99* (Urbana, IL: University of Illinois Press, 2006); Vilna Francine Bashi, *Survival of the Knitted: Immigrant Social Networks in a Stratified World* (Stanford, CA: Stanford University Press, 2007); Herbert, *Negotiating Boundaries in the City*; and Hackett, 'Turkish Muslims in a German city'.

17   The participants had varying levels of English-language proficiency. Whilst conducting the interviews in what, for some of the respondents, was not their mother-tongue language might potentially have impacted the extent to which they were able to freely express themselves, this did not appear to

be the case. Even those respondents who were comparatively less proficient in English were able to share their stories and make themselves understood. All interviewees were given a project information sheet, which outlined the purpose of the project, how and why the interviews were being carried out, the potential benefits and risks of taking part, and an explanation of how the interviews would be stored and used. They were also asked to sign a consent form, and they could choose to remain anonymous, to not be directly quoted, and to not answer certain questions or discuss particular topics. They were able to choose the locations of the interviews and review their transcripts. They also had the right to withdraw from the project at any point, though no one did. All interviews were transcribed using intelligent verbatim. Regarding those interviewees who consented to the use of their names, I use their first names only.

18   Joanna Herbert encountered some of these same factors and issues when interviewing members of Leicester's South Asian communities. See Herbert, *Negotiating Boundaries in the City*, pp. 9–10; and Herbert, 'Negotiating boundaries and the cross-cultural oral history interview'.

19   In fact, a few of the interviewees offered additional details about their personal lives, experiences and perceptions once the interviews were finished and the recorder had been turned off.

20   By no means am I suggesting that all South Asian migrants are Muslim. To the contrary, whilst the vast majority of Pakistani and Bangladeshi populations are Muslim, the same cannot be said for the Indian community. See Peach, 'South Asian migration and settlement in Great Britain, 1951–2001', 140.

21   For an insight into the arrival, settlement and development of South Asian communities in post-war Britain, see Vaughan Robinson, *Transients, Settlers, and Refugees: Asians in Britain* (Oxford: Clarendon, 1986); Roger Ballard (ed.), *Desh Pardesh: The South Asian Presence in Britain* (London: Hurst, 1994); Shaw, *Kinship and Continuity*; Gardner, *Age, Narrative and Migration*; John Eade and David Garbin, 'Competing visions of identity and space: Bangladeshi Muslims in Britain', *Contemporary South Asia*, 15:2 (2006), 181–93; Peach, 'South Asian migration and settlement in Great Britain, 1951–2001'; and Katy Gardner, 'Keeping connected: security, place, and social capital in a "Londoni" village in Sylhet', *The Journal of the Royal Anthropological Institute*, 14:3 (2008), 477–95.

22   Mahmood, 28 May 2016.

23   Atiff, 5 December 2016.

24   Farzana, 13 June 2016.

25   Anonymous interviewee, 18 November 2016.

26   Britain's South Asian communities have long been recognised for their involvement in business formation and entrepreneurial activity, and there exists a vast literature on the topic. See Pnina Werbner, 'Renewing an industrial past: British Pakistani entrepreneurship in Manchester', in Judith M. Brown and Rosemary Foot (eds), *Migration: The Asian Experience* (Basingstoke: Palgrave Macmillan, 1994), pp. 104–30; Anuradha Basu, 'An

exploration of entrepreneurial activity among Asian small businesses in Britain', *Small Business Economics*, 10:4 (1998), 313–26; Barrett, Jones and McEvoy, 'Socio-economic and policy dimensions of the mixed embeddedness of ethnic minority business in Britain'; Muhibul Haq, 'South Asian ethnic minority small and medium enterprises in the UK: a review and research agenda', *International Journal of Entrepreneurship and Small Business*, 25:4 (2015), 494–516; and Ken Clark, Stephen Drinkwater and Catherine Robinson, 'Self-employment amongst migrant groups: new evidence from England and Wales', *Small Business Economics*, 48:4 (2017), 1047–69.

27 Like elsewhere in the UK, 'Indian' restaurants in Wiltshire have also long often been owned and staffed by Bangladeshis. See Elizabeth Buettner, ' "Going for an Indian": South Asian restaurants and the limits of multiculturalism in Britain', *The Journal of Modern History*, 80:4 (2008), 865–901; and Panikos Panayi, *Spicing Up Britain: The Multicultural History of British Food* (London: Reaktion Books, 2008), pp. 172–3.

28 She was not sure whether her father was based in Halifax or Oldham at the time.

29 Anonymous interviewee, 28 November 2016.

30 Junab, 27 May 2016.

31 Atiqul, 9 December 2016.

32 Wali, 28 April 2016.

33 Anonymous interviewee, 28 June 2017.

34 Ala, 26 March 2017.

35 Shahid, 15 September 2016.

36 For an insight into Muslim geographical and residential distribution, see Ansari, *'The Infidel Within'*, pp. 172–9; Deborah Phillips, 'Parallel lives? Challenging discourses of British Muslim self-segregation', *Environment and Planning D: Society and Space*, 24:1 (2006), 25–40; and Peter Hopkins, 'Muslims in the West: deconstructing geographical binaries', in Richard Phillips (ed.), *Muslim Spaces of Hope: Geographies of Possibility in Britain and the West* (London: Zed, 2009), pp. 31–4.

37 See Madawi Al-Rasheed, 'The other-others: hidden Arabs?', in Ceri Peach (ed.), *Ethnicity in the 1991 Census, Volume 2: The Ethnic Minority Populations of Great Britain* (London: HMSO, 1996), pp. 206–20; Hussain, *Muslims on the Map*, pp. 28–37; Cherti, *Paradoxes of Social Capital*, p. 73; and Russell King, Mark Thomson, Nicola Mai and Yilmaz Keles, ' "Turks" in London: shades of invisibility and the shifting relevance of policy in the migration process', Sussex Centre for Migration Research, Working Paper No. 51 (September 2008).

38 See Cherti, *Paradoxes of Social Capital*; and Cherti, *British Moroccans – Citizenship in Action*. Moroccans in post-war Britain have also been discussed within the context of Arab communities more broadly. See Camillia Fawzi El-Solh, 'Arab communities in Britain: cleavages and commonalities', *Islam and Christian-Muslim Relations*, 3:2 (1992), 236–58; Caroline Nagel, 'Constructing difference and sameness: the politics of assimilation in London's Arab

communities', *Ethnic and Racial Studies*, 25:2 (2002), 258–87; and Hussain, *Muslims on the Map*.

39 Jilali, 30 January 2017.

40 Abdel explained that his understanding was that quite a few Moroccans migrated to Wiveliscombe. Ross Poultry appears to have had a number of factories in England, two of which were in Wiveliscombe and Trowbridge. This link may have encouraged some Moroccan migration from Wiveliscombe to Trowbridge, although none of the interviewees mentioned this. See also 'Market Town Twins with Arab City', *BBC News* (3 October 2006).

41 Abdel, 17 November 2016. This pattern of Moroccans working with Southern European migrants was also common in London's hotel and catering industries. See Cherti, *Paradoxes of Social Capital*.

42 Zoubida, 8 December 2016.

43 This finding deviates from Myriam Cherti's claim that many Moroccan women came to Britain as independent migrants. See Cherti, *Paradoxes of Social Capital*, p. 79.

44 Anonymous interviewee, 8 December 2016.

45 Anonymous interviewee, 1 December 2016.

46 Touria, 3 June 2016.

47 Low educational attainment and a poor command of the English language were traits that were stressed by the respondents. One Moroccan female interviewee, for example, never went to school, whilst Jilali and another Moroccan female did, but left at the ages of fourteen and fifteen, respectively. Before migrating to the UK, they spoke little, if any, English. The lack of confidence and initial low employment aspirations are traits that have been stressed with regard to Moroccan communities in England more broadly. See Communities and Local Government, *The Moroccan Muslim Community in England: Understanding Muslim Ethnic Communities* (London, 2009), pp. 31–2.

48 See Ansari, 'The Infidel Within', pp. 169–70; Asu Aksoy, 'Transnational virtues and cool loyalties: responses of Turkish-speaking migrants in London to September 11', *Journal of Ethnic and Migration Studies*, 32:6 (2006), 923–46; King, Thomson, Mai and Keles, '"Turks" in London'; and Tayfun Atay, '"Ethnicity within ethnicity" among the Turkish-speaking immigrants in London', *Insight Turkey*, 12:1 (2010), 123–38. It is important to note that Turkish-speaking communities in Britain tend to be divided into three main groups: mainland Turks, Turkish Cypriots and Kurds from Turkey.

49 For an insight into the prevalence of Turkish entrepreneurship in Britain, see Inge Strüder, 'Self-employed Turkish-speaking women in London: opportunities and constraints within and beyond the ethnic economy', *The International Journal of Entrepreneurship and Innovation*, 4:3 (2003), 185–95; Levent Altinay and Eser Altinay, 'Factors influencing business growth: the rise of Turkish entrepreneurship in the UK', *International Journal of Entrepreneurial Behavior & Research*, 14:1 (2008), 24–46; and Panayi, *Spicing Up Britain*, p. 168.

50   Mehmet, 16 June 2016.
51   Selvi, 29 January 2017.
52   Ozay, 29 January 2017.
53   *Ibid.*; Selvi, 29 January 2017.
54   See Communities and Local Government, *The Turkish and Turkish Cypriot Muslim Community in England: Understanding Muslim Ethnic Communities* (London, 2009).
55   Onder, 7 November 2016.
56   Omar, 28 September 2016.
57   Kamel, 6 May 2016.
58   Shazuli, 1 December 2016.
59   Mahmood, 28 May 2016; Omar, 28 September 2016; Ala, 26 March 2017.
60   Wali, 28 April 2016.
61   Kantha, 9 December 2016.
62   Junab, 27 May 2016.
63   Mehmet, 16 June 2016.
64   Atiqul, 9 December 2016; Touria, 3 June 2016; anonymous interviewee, 28 June 2017.
65   Anonymous interviewee, 28 May 2016.
66   Radia, 30 March 2017. Her father had been in Britain since the 1960s.
67   Abdel, 17 November 2016.
68   Anonymous interviewee, 26 September 2016.
69   Anonymous interviewee, 28 November 2016.
70   Mehmet, 16 June 2016; Radia, 30 March 2017.
71   Atiqul, 9 December 2016.
72   Junab, 27 May 2016.
73   Touria, 3 June 2016; anonymous interviewees (couple), 1 December 2016; anonymous interviewee, 8 December 2016; Zoubida, 8 December 2016; Jilali, 30 January 2017.
74   Jilali, 30 January 2017.
75   Zoubida, 8 December 2016.
76   Farzana, 13 June 2016.
77   Atiff, 5 December 2016.
78   Anonymous interviewee, 18 November 2016.
79   See Monder Ram, Trevor Jones, Tahir Abbas and Balihar Sanghera, 'Ethnic minority enterprise in its urban context: South Asian restaurants in Birmingham', *International Journal of Urban and Regional Research*, 26:1 (2002), 24–40; and Buettner, ' "Going for an Indian".
80   Azad, 28 November 2016; Ala, 26 March 2017.
81   Anonymous interviewee, 28 September 2016.
82   Radia, 30 March 2017.
83   Andrew Lawton, 'Cafe India Celebrates Decade of Business in Chippenham', *Gazette & Herald* (19 January 2016).
84   See Altinay and Altinay, 'Factors influencing business growth'; Panayi, *Spicing Up Britain*, p. 168; and Ibrahim Sirkeci, 'Transnational döner kebab taking over the UK', *Transnational Marketing Journal*, 4:2 (2016), 143–58.

85   Mehmet, 16 June 2016; Onder, 7 November 2016; Ozay, 29 January 2017.

86   For example, having previously lived elsewhere in Britain, including in Croydon and Luton, Azad moved to Wiltshire in 1989 in search of business opportunities with a group of partners, and went on to open a number of restaurants, including in Amesbury and Salisbury. Similarly, Sohidul opened his restaurant in Devizes with a partner, and Mehmet worked closely with his brother when buying and selling a number of takeaways. Azad, 28 November 2016; Sohidul, 30 October 2017; Mehmet, 16 June 2016.

87   Radia, 30 March 2017; anonymous interviewee, 28 September 2016; Sohidul, 30 October 2017.

88   Mehmet, 16 June 2016; Shahid, 15 September 2016.

89   Azad, 28 November 2016; Sohidul, 30 October 2017.

90   For example, see Monder Ram, Balihar Sanghera, Tahir Abbas, Gerald Barlow and Trevor Jones, 'Ethnic minority business in comparative perspective: the case of the independent restaurant sector', *Journal of Ethnic and Migration Studies*, 26:3 (2000), 495–510; Anuradha Basu and Eser Altinay, 'The interaction between culture and entrepreneurship in London's immigrant businesses', *International Small Business Journal*, 20:4 (2002), 371–93; and Anuradha Basu and Eser Altinay, *Family and Work in Minority Ethnic Businesses* (Bristol: The Policy Press, 2003).

91   See Trevor Jones, Monder Ram and Paul Edwards, 'Ethnic minority business and the employment of illegal immigrants', *Entrepreneurship & Regional Development*, 18:2 (2006), 133–50; and John Kitching, David Smallbone and Rosemary Athayde, 'Ethnic diasporas and business competitiveness: minority-owned enterprises in London', *Journal of Ethnic and Migration Studies*, 35:4 (2009), 689–705. Rahman, Ullah and Thompson argued that ethnic minority businesses in Aberdeen struggled to secure co-ethnic staff due to the city's small migrant communities. See Md Zillur Rahman, Farid Ullah and Piers Thompson, 'Challenges and issues facing ethnic minority small business owners: the Scottish experience', *The International Journal of Entrepreneurship and Innovation*, 19:3 (2018), 177–93.

92   Khan, 28 May 2016; Mahmood, 28 May 2016; anonymous interviewee, 8 December 2016; Jilali, 30 January 2017; Kantha, 9 December 2016; anonymous interviewee, 26 June 2016.

93   Anonymous interviewee, 28 November 2016.

94   Muhammad, 16 May 2016.

95   Anonymous interviewee, 1 December 2016.

96   Ala, 26 March 2017.

97   It must be recognised, however, that by no means have South Asian communities' housing tenure preferences and characteristics been homogenous. For example, see Alison Shaw, 'The Pakistani community in Oxford', in Roger Ballard (ed.), *Desh Pardesh: The South Asian Presence in Britain* (London: Hurst, 1994), pp. 35–57; Valerie Karn and Deborah Phillips, 'Race and ethnicity in housing: a diversity of experience', in Tessa Blackstone, Bhikhu Parekh and Peter Sanders (eds), *Race Relations in Britain: A Developing*

Agenda (London: Routledge, 1998), pp. 128–57; Ceri Peach, 'South Asian and Caribbean ethnic minority housing choice in Britain', *Urban Studies*, 35:10 (1998), 1657–80; and Hackett, *Foreigners, Minorities and Integration*.

98   For an insight into some of these debates, see Deborah Phillips, 'Black minority ethnic concentration, segregation and dispersal in Britain', *Urban Studies*, 35:10 (1998), 1681–702; Phillips, 'Parallel Lives?'; Deborah Phillips, Cathy Davis and Peter Ratcliffe, 'British Asian narratives of urban space', *Transactions of the Institute of British Geographers*, 32:2 (2007), 217–34; and Anthony Heath and Neli Demireva, 'Has multiculturalism failed in Britain?', *Ethnic and Racial Studies*, 37:1 (2014), 161–80.

99   Farzana, 13 June 2016; anonymous interviewee, 18 November 2016; anonymous interviewee, 1 December 2016; Hajra and Awais, 4 December 2016; Atiff, 5 December 2016; Atiqul, 9 December 2016.

100   Mahmood, 28 May 2016.

101   Anonymous interviewee, 28 May 2016.

102   Touria, 3 June 2016.

103   Mehmet, 16 June 2016.

104   Ala, 26 March 2017.

105   Mehmet, 16 June 2016; Ala, 26 March 2017.

106   Abdel, 17 November 2016.

107   Anonymous interviewee, 26 September 2016.

108   Wali, 28 April 2016.

109   *Ibid.*

110   Kamel, 6 May 2016.

111   Junab, 27 May 2016.

112   Wiltshire Council, *Qualitative Consultation with Wiltshire's Minority Ethnic Residents*, p. 11.

113   Anonymous interviewee, 18 May 2016.

114   *Ibid.*

115   *Ibid.*

116   Anonymous interviewee, 28 June 2017.

117   See Lewis, 'The Bradford Council for Mosques and the search for Muslim unity'; Ansari, '*The Infidel Within*', pp. 343–56; Samia Bano, *Muslim Women and Shari'ah Councils: Transcending the Boundaries of Community and Law* (Basingstoke: Palgrave Macmillan, 2012), pp. 31–3; and Innes Bowen, *Medina in Birmingham, Najaf in Brent: Inside British Islam* (London: Hurst & Co, 2014).

118   Ansari, '*The Infidel Within*', p. 343.

119   For example, see John Eade, 'Nationalism, community, and the Islamization of space in London', in Barbara Daly Metcalf (ed.), *Making Muslim Space in North America and Europe* (London: University of California Press, 1996), pp. 217–33; Pnina Werbner, 'Fun spaces: on identity and social empowerment among British Pakistanis', *Theory, Culture & Society*, 13:4 (1996), 53–79; and Hopkins and Gale (eds), *Muslims in Britain*.

120 Junab, 27 May 2016.
121 Jilali, 30 January 2017.
122 Kamel, 6 May 2016.
123 Anser, 15 September 2016.
124 Ala, 26 March 2017; Atiqul, 9 December 2016; Mehmet, 16 June 2016.
125 Such inclusive congregations have survived in some places more than in others. See Waqar Ahmad, '"Creating a society of sheep"? British Muslim elite on mosques and imams', in Waqar Ahmad and Ziauddin Sardar (eds), *Muslims in Britain: Making Social and Political Space* (Abingdon: Routledge, 2012), p. 175; and Jones, 'Negotiating absence and presence'.
126 See Alastair Ager and Alison Strang, 'Understanding integration: a conceptual framework', *Journal of Refugee Studies*, 21:2 (2008), 166–91.
127 Farzana, 13 June 2016.
128 Anonymous interviewee, 18 November 2016.
129 For example, see Hopkins and Gale (eds), *Muslims in Britain*; and Rahielah Ali and Peter Hopkins, 'Everyday making and civic engagement among Muslim women in Scotland', in Waqar Ahmad and Ziauddin Sardar (eds), *Muslims in Britain: Making Social and Political Space* (Abingdon: Routledge, 2012), pp. 141–55.
130 Kamel, 6 May 2016.
131 These open days were mentioned by Kamel. They have also received positive attention in the local press, and have been commended for attempting to break down community barriers and promote an understanding of Islam. See, for example, Tanya Yilmaz, 'Trowbridge Mosque Opens its Doors to Address Misconceptions of Religion', *Wiltshire Times* (3 August 2016).
132 Shazuli, 1 December 2016.
133 Wali, 28 April 2016.
134 The extremist group chose Royal Wootton Bassett as this Wiltshire town had become known for the manner in which it honoured fallen British soldiers. The way in which Wiltshire's Muslims, and the Wiltshire Islamic Cultural Centre in particular, spoke out against this planned march received both local and national media attention. For example, see Christopher Hope, 'Islamic March through Wootton Bassett Should not be Banned, Says Sir Hugh Orde', *Telegraph* (5 January 2010); and Nicola Curtis, 'Anger in Trowbridge at Islamic March', Wiltshire Times (8 January 2010).
135 Wali, 28 April 2016.
136 Anonymous interviewee, 26 September 2016.
137 Sohidul, 30 October 2017.
138 See Neal, 'Rural landscapes, representations and racism'; Chakraborti and Garland, 'An "invisible" problem?'; Chakraborti and Garland, 'England's green and pleasant land?'; Neal and Agyeman (eds), *The New Countryside?*; and Chakraborti and Garland (eds), *Rural Racism*.
139 See Ray and Reed, 'Community, mobility and racism in a semi-rural area', 228; de Lima, '"Let's keep our heads down and maybe the problem will go

away"', p. 87; and Neil Chakraborti and Jon Garland, 'Introduction: justi-fying the study of racism in the rural', in Neil Chakraborti and Jon Garland (eds), *Rural Racism* (Cullompton: Willan Publishing, 2004), p. 1.

140 Jones, 'Islam and the rural landscape', 759–60.
141 Junab, 27 May 2016.
142 Anonymous interviewee, 26 September 2016.
143 Touria, 3 June 2016.
144 Wali, 18 May 2016.
145 Abdel, 17 November 2016.
146 Wiltshire Council, *Qualitative Consultation with Wiltshire's Minority Ethnic Residents*, p. 17.
147 Mahmood, 28 May 2016; Onder, 7 November 2016.
148 Anser, 15 September 2016; anonymous interviewee, 8 December 2016; Ala, 26 March 2017.
149 Anonymous interviewee, 28 June 2017.
150 Anonymous interviewee, 26 June 2016.
151 Atiff, 5 December 2016.
152 Anonymous interviewee, 1 December 2016.
153 Zoubida, 8 December 2016.
154 Radia, 30 March 2017.
155 Wiltshire County Council and Wiltshire Racial Equality Council, *Hidden Voices*, p. 17; and Wiltshire Council, *Qualitative Consultation with Wiltshire's Minority Ethnic Residents*, p. 17.
156 Anonymous interviewee, 18 November 2016.
157 *Ibid.*
158 Wiltshire and Swindon Users' Network, *Diverse Communities*, pp. 29–30.
159 Anonymous interviewee, 18 November 2016.
160 *Ibid.* This placement was at a school in in a city outside Wiltshire. However, the interviewee's hesitation to ask for a space in which to pray was most likely at least partially shaped by the fact that she lived in Wiltshire at the time and thus did not have the support network she had done in Birmingham. Overall, many of the experiences she shared discussed the difficulties and unease that she felt being a Muslim in Wiltshire at times entailed, at least initially and when compared to Birmingham. When I sought clarification about this, she explained that her initial assumption had been that this city was like Wiltshire.
161 Wiltshire and Swindon Users' Network, *Diverse Communities*.
162 Wali, 18 May 2016.
163 Wali, 28 April 2016.
164 Ozay, 29 January 2017.
165 Atiff, 5 December 2016.
166 See Wiltshire County Council and Wiltshire Racial Equality Council, *Hidden Voices*, p. 52.
167 See Wiltshire and Swindon Users' Network, *Diverse Communities*.

168   Azad, 28 November 2016; Jilali, 30 January 2017. The request in Trowbridge and subsequent approval was discussed in Chapter 3 from the local authority's perspective.
169   Kantha, 9 December 2016.
170   Atiqul, 9 December 2016.
171   For example, see Stephen Barton, *The Bengali Muslims of Bradford: A Study of Their Observance of Islam with Special Reference to the Function of the Mosque and the Work of the Imam* (Leeds: University of Leeds, 1986); Lewis, *Islamic Britain*; Danièle Joly, *Britannia's Crescent: Making a Place for Muslims in British Society* (Aldershot: Avebury, 1995); Noha Nasser, 'Expressions of Muslim identity in architecture and urbanism in Birmingham, UK', *Islam and Christian-Muslim Relations*, 16:1 (2005), 61–78; and Humayun Ansari (ed.), *The Making of the East London Mosque, 1910–1951: Minutes of the London Mosque Fund and East London Mosque Trust Ltd* (Cambridge: Cambridge University Press, 2011).
172   For a few key works, see Agyeman and Spooner, 'Ethnicity and the rural environment'; Neal, 'Rural landscapes, representations and racism'; Chakraborti and Garland, 'An "invisible" problem?'; and Chakraborti and Garland (eds), *Rural Racism*.
173   Jones, 'Islam and the rural landscape'.
174   See, for example, Nasar Meer and Tariq Modood, 'Refutations of racism in the "Muslim question"', *Patterns of Prejudice*, 43:3–4 (2009), 335–54; and Alba and Foner, *Strangers No More*, pp. 118–25.
175   See Fetzer and Soper, *Muslims and the State*; and Jonathan Laurence and Justin Vaisse, *Integrating Islam: Political and Religious Challenges in Contemporary France* (Washington, D.C.: Brookings Institution Press, 2006).
176   See Karen Phalet, Mieke Maliepaard, Fenella Fleischmann and Derya Güngör, 'The making and unmaking of religious boundaries: comparing Turkish and Moroccan Muslim minorities in European cities', *Comparative Migration Studies*, 1:1 (2013), 123–45; and Alba and Foner, *Strangers No More*, p. 123.
177   See Siobhan McAndrew and David Voas, 'Immigrant generation, religiosity and civic engagement in Britain', *Ethnic and Racial Studies*, 37:1 (2014), 99–119; and Alba and Foner, *Strangers No More*, pp. 129–30.
178   The *Hidden Voices* report also found that 'religious affiliation was generally very strong' amongst the Muslim respondents. See Wiltshire County Council and Wiltshire Racial Equality Council, *Hidden Voices*, p. 15.
179   Whilst one might expect 1.5- and second-generation Muslim migrants in Britain to be less religious than their parents, regarding South Asians especially, a number of studies have argued that the younger generations are just as, or even more, religious than the first. Albeit with a few exceptions, this was certainly the case amongst my respondents. See Jessica Jacobson, *Islam in Transition: Religion and Identity among British Pakistani Youth* (London: Routledge, 1998); and Michela Franceschelli, *Identity and Upbringing in South Asian Muslim Families: Insights from Young People and their Parents in Britain* (London: Palgrave Macmillan, 2016).

180 Jilali, 30 January 2017.

181 Abdel, 17 November 2016.

182 Anonymous interviewee, 8 December 2016.

183 Touria, 3 June 2016.

184 Pnina Werbner, quoted in Gilliat-Ray, *Muslims in Britain*, p. 197. See also Gilliat-Ray, *Muslims in Britain*, p. 187; and Villis and Hebing, 'Islam and Englishness'.

185 For an insight into the development of mosque construction in Britain, see Gale, 'The multicultural city and the politics of religious architecture'; Gilliat-Ray, *Muslims in Britain*, pp. 181–205; and Shahed Saleem, *The British Mosque: An Architectural and Social History* (Swindon: Historic England, 2018).

186 Eade, 'Nationalism, community, and the Islamization of space in London', p. 231. For an insight into the development of mosques in British cities, see also Seán McLoughlin, 'Mosques and the public space: conflict and cooperation in Bradford', *Journal of Ethnic and Migration Studies*, 31:6 (2005), 1045–66; Gale, 'The multicultural city and the politics of religious architecture'; Gilliat-Ray, *Muslims in Britain*, pp. 187–94; and Mellor and Gilliat-Ray, 'The early history of migration and settlement of Yemenis in Cardiff'.

187 Jones, 'Islam and the rural landscape', 758; and Jones, 'Negotiating absence and presence'. The term 'storefront mosque' is taken from Susan Slyomovics, 'The Muslim World Day parade and "storefront" mosques of New York City', in Barbara Daly Metcalf (ed.), *Making Muslim Space in North America and Europe* (Berkeley, CA: University of California Press, 1996), pp. 204–16.

188 Jones, 'Islam and the rural landscape'; and Jones, 'Negotiating absence and presence'.

189 Ray and Reed, 'Community, mobility and racism in a semi-rural area'. There has also been a more popular interest recently in the provision of mosques for small rural Muslim communities. See, for example, Harriet Sherwood, 'First Mosque Opens on Outer Hebrides in Time for Ramadan', *Guardian* (11 May 2018); and Tom Rowley, 'The B-Road to Mecca: Britain's Rural Muslims are a Minority within a Minority', *The Economist* (17 May 2018).

190 Mahmood, 28 May 2016.

191 Jilali, 30 January 2017.

192 Anonymous interviewee, 8 December 2016; Zoubida, 8 December 2016.

193 Anonymous interviewee, 26 June 2016.

194 Junab, 27 May 2016.

195 Wali, 28 April 2016.

196 Ala, 26 March 2017.

197 Anonymous interviewee, 28 September 2016.

198 'Mosque Bid Withdrawn after Devizes Residents Object to London Road Location', *Gazette & Herald* (18 December 2014); Shahid, 15 September 2016.

199 Shahid, 15 September 2016; Anser, 15 September 2016.

200 Mehmet, 16 June 2016.

201 This information was attained from members of Wiltshire's Muslim communities and Wiltshire Council planning applications.

202 A few of the female interviewees really valued that women had access to the mosque; anonymous interviewee, 18 May 2016; and Farzana, 13 June 2016.

203 Kantha, 9 December 2016.

204 Kamel, 6 May 2016.

205 Shahid, 15 September 2016; anonymous interviewee, 28 June 2017.

206 Anonymous interviewee, 26 June 2016.

207 *Ibid.*

208 Anonymous interviewee, 28 May 2016.

209 Atiff, 5 December 2016.

210 Abdel, 17 November 2016.

211 Anonymous interviewee, 26 September 2016.

212 For example, see Ansari, 'The Infidel Within', pp. 344–5; Gilliat-Ray, *Muslims in Britain*, pp. 146–56; and Jonathan Scourfield, Sophie Gilliat-Ray, Asma Khan and Sameh Otri, *Muslim Childhood: Religious Nurture in a European Context* (Oxford: Oxford University Press, 2013), Chapter 5: 'Children in formal religious education'.

213 Anonymous interviewee, 26 September 2016.

214 Anonymous interviewee, 28 November 2016; Abdel, 17 November 2016.

215 Junab, 27 May 2016.

216 *Ibid.*

217 Anonymous interviewee, 1 December 2016; Jilali, 30 January 2017.

218 Anonymous interviewee, 18 May 2016; Atiqul, 9 December 2016. Respondents of Wiltshire Council's *Qualitative Consultation* report also explained how they travelled significant distances to purchase *halal* food. See Wiltshire Council, *Qualitative Consultation with Wiltshire's Minority Ethnic Residents*, p. 11.

219 Onder, 7 November 2016.

220 See Jones, 'Islam and the rural landscape', 760.

221 See Wiltshire and Swindon Users' Network, *Diverse Communities*, p. 31.

222 Atiff, 5 December 2016. The lack of local provision for the Islamic practice of burial was also raised in the Wiltshire and Swindon Users' Network *Diverse Communities* report. See Wiltshire and Swindon Users' Network, *Diverse Communities*, p. 28.

223 Anonymous interviewee, 8 December 2016.

224 *Ibid.*

225 *Ibid.*

226 Anonymous interviewee, 26 September 2016; anonymous interviewee, 28 November 2016.

227 Kamel, 6 May 2016.

228 *Ibid.*

229 Kantha, 9 December 2016.

230 *Ibid.*

231   Shahid, 15 September 2016.
232   Farzana, 13 June 2016.
233   Wali, 28 April 2016; Ozay, 29 January 2017.
234   Atiqul, 9 December 2016; Radia, 30 March 2017.
235   Anonymous interviewee, 18 November 2016.
236   Anser, 15 September 2016.

6

Migration, integration and Muslims
in rural Britain

Rural Britain, and England in particular, have long been perceived and portrayed as peaceful, picturesque, pure, romantic, safe and unchanging, as embodying national values and identity and a strong sense of community spirit, as a beacon of social cohesion and harmony, and as not being troubled by 'urban problems'.[1] Indeed, often conjuring up, and being associated with, terms and phrases such as 'an icon of Englishness',[2] 'the rural idyll',[3] and 'Green and Pleasant Land',[4] the English rural landscape has frequently been imagined as needing to be cherished, defended and protected. Scholars have argued that this romanticised, and even mythical, representation of the English country-side, used in clear opposition to that of the city or urban setting, has its roots in both historical and contemporary contexts. Raymond Williams, for example, argued that 'a contrast between country and city, as fundamental ways of life, reaches back into classical times',[5] a contrast that was most certainly reinforced by the period of urbanisation that took place from the sixteenth century, the changes brought about by the Industrial Revolution, and the urban expansion of both the inter-war years and the early twenty-first century.[6] Thus, for many, rural Britain represents a clear favourable contrast to its urban counterpart, which is often associated with crime, deprivation, disorder, isolation, loneliness, pollution and social exclusion.[7]

Whilst the rural idyll may well be a social construct rooted in nostalgia and idealism, it would be wrong to dismiss it as a mere illusion. To the contrary, it has had clear influence and consequences. For example, the image of the rural idyll has shaped identity formation and notions of belonging, has been recognised by parents as the ideal place to raise children, and has been used to defend the right to hunt and oppose the development of asylum centres and urban expansion.[8] It has also been argued that the concept of the rural idyll has at times led to the glossing over of problems that have at times developed in more rural areas, including crime, disadvantage, drug addiction, homelessness and poverty.[9] Furthermore, it has long been recognised that it has at times caused policymakers to neglect the issues facing, and the experiences of, certain segments of Britain's rural populations, for example women, youth and the homeless.[10] Regarding the academic sphere, whilst much work has been done since Chris Philo's 1992 claim that Britain was characterised by what he coined 'neglected rural geographies',[11] rural space nevertheless remains overlooked in comparison to urban settings across a range of disciplines and areas of research.

This chapter places the integration of Muslim migrant communities in post-1960s Wiltshire within this context of rural Britain. It builds upon previous chapters and offers an in-depth overview and assessment of the existing historiography, and addresses the extent to which there has existed a rural dimension to the integration process. An insight into the academic literature on migration, race and Muslim communities in rural Britain was offered in this book's introduction, and there are clear overlaps with that on rural Britain more broadly. The concept of the rural idyll has meant that rural settings have overwhelmingly been perceived as being untouched by immigration and ethnic minority communities, and thus as being white, with immigration being deemed an urban phenomenon and concern. As a result, the historiography's focus has largely remained on urban Britain and comparatively little work has been done on rural areas, especially with regard to Islam and Muslim minority communities specifically. The academic research that does exist on rural Britain has often argued that members of ethnic minority communities are, on the one hand, highly visible in the rural landscape and thus more likely to encounter prejudice and racism than their urban counterparts yet, on the other hand, are simultaneously invisible in terms of local policy and service provision. It is also argued that Muslim populations frequently encounter difficulties when trying to practise their religion, and suffer local opposition to mosques, fragmented communities and racial abuse.[12] This chapter now turns to assessing the extent to which this rural dimension has existed in Wiltshire, firstly from the perspective of the county's local authority and, secondly, from that of the Muslim migrant communities themselves.

The local authority perspective

That ethnic minority communities have remained largely invisible is certainly the most common argument amongst scholars investigating the rural policy context. Largely referring to rural racism specifically, they have asserted that efforts to address it are hindered by the small ethnic minority populations in question and the resulting unwillingness to act, the difficulties encountered when trying to gather statistics on migrant communities in rural areas, and the fact that racist incidents in rural settings are under-reported and thus under-recorded.[13] Furthermore, this notion of policy neglect has flown in the face of ever-increasing evidence of a widespread prevalence of discrimination and racism in rural areas, be it in Cornwall, Devon, Dorset, Kent, Northumbria, Somerset or rural Scotland.[14] Indeed, the dominant consensus is that this gradual recognition that it is ethnic minorities not in the inner cities, but rather in the more rural and low-density ethnic minority areas, that are often at greatest risk of experiencing racial attacks and abuse has done little to over-turn local authority complacency in rural Britain.

This complacency was perhaps best initially captured in Eric Jay's ground-breaking report, which recorded responses to requests for information from a range of organisations, including local and health authorities and voluntary sector organisations, in Cornwall, Devon, Dorset and Somerset during the early 1990s about the counties' ethnic minority communities and corresponding needs, problems, organisations, policies and services. Many of these responses reflected a lack of awareness of, and commitment to, ethnic minority com-munities and racial equality. The exact phrases used included 'the subject of racial equality does not play a significant role because of the paucity of ethnic groups', 'the ethnic dimension is not a significant element... due to the lack of sizeable ethnic communities', and one district council officer claimed that their area 'does not have a high ethnic minority population, so to a certain extent race relations problems are not so prevalent here'.[15] Furthermore, whilst the academic literature has acknowledged that, on the whole, more rural areas have increasingly begun to recognise the need for policy intervention that addresses racism and provides tailored support for their ethnic minority com-munities, this has largely been portrayed as a more recent development that did not begin to emerge in earnest until the 1990s.[16]

It would be unfair to render Wiltshire part of this wider rural paradigm.[17] To the contrary, Wiltshire's local authority has considered, responded to, and provided for, the arrival and long-term settlement of its ethnic minority, and Muslim, communities across the post-1960s period. Furthermore, it has often framed its political deliberations, measures and policies within both its rural nature and the fact that it is home to small migrant populations, and many examples have been addressed throughout this study. These include Swindon Borough's Education Officer concluding that one of the reasons there were not any problems as a result of immigrants' different faiths or regarding the religious education of immigrant children during the early 1970s was because the town was home to such small immigrant communities; West Wiltshire District Council's code of practice aimed at promoting racial equality in the distribution of council housing of the 1990s being referred to as 'a major move forward for a local authority in the rural South-West'; and Wiltshire County Council's Race Equality Scheme, and social, health and housing services, of the 2000s recognising that the county's rurality meant that its small and dispersed ethnic minorities were potentially susceptible to exclusion, isolation and vulnerability.[18]

Furthermore, Wiltshire's local authority frequently drew upon its surrounding rural context in order to conscientiously and forcefully devise its migration, integration and diversity policies, and thus resist falling into the 'no problem here' mentality that it was aware was prevalent in so many other British rural areas with small ethnic minority populations. Already during the early 1970s, for example, the desire of Swindon's Council for Community Relations to capture the situation and experiences of local migrant communities was at least partially based on this ambition.[19] During the 1980s and 1990s, Wiltshire County Council's Education Committee's policies and practices were rooted in the belief that 'white' schools in 'white' areas were not exempt from a responsibility to deliver a multicultural education.[20] Similarly, as reflected in its name, the 2002 *Hidden Voices* report emerged from a commitment to shedding light on the county's ethnic minority communities and thus avoiding the neglect their counterparts often experienced in other rural settings.[21] Regarding Muslim populations specifically, Wiltshire's local authority responded to local Muslim communities' needs and demands, with its political concerns, deliberations and provisions, from those regarding makeshift prayer spaces to Muslim burials, often being shaped by the county's more rural make-up.

Yet Wiltshire's local authority's approach to its Muslim migrant communities across the post-1960s period has by no means entirely escaped the allegations of complacency and neglect that have been so forcefully made regarding rural Britain more widely. There are five key ways in which there existed a rural dimension to the devising and implementing of the county's policies. Firstly, they have at times arguably been lacking in quantity, commitment and substance. Neither a political discussion of, nor direct response to, the Moroccan or South Asian communities that began to arrive and settle across the county in sizeable numbers during the 1960s and 1970s, for example, seems to have ever been initiated by Wiltshire County Council or any of the district councils, and explorations and analyses of individual migrant communities' experiences and needs never took place. On the whole, and as is to be expected, Wiltshire's local authority's initiatives did not match those of its urban counterparts across Britain, whether Brent's Community Relations Council during the 1960s or Lambeth's Race Unit of the late 1970s, the specialised units that were set up in cities like Birmingham, Bradford and Manchester during the mid-1980s to address local migration and race matters, or Newcastle upon Tyne's local council's considerations of the city's South Asians' self-employment and housing patterns during the 1980s and 1990s.[22] Moreover, the late 1970s and early 1980s witnessed a number of Wiltshire's district councils, including those of Kennet and Salisbury, reveal what appeared to be a clear disinterest in issues of racial equality.[23] Indeed, Wiltshire Racial Equality Council frequently became frustrated with what it perceived to be a lack of action displayed by Wiltshire's local authorities on a number of occasions, arguing during the

1990s that the district councils exhibited what it referred to as 'inertia and indifference to our policies and cause', and hinting during the 2000s that some local government efforts to address ethnic minority communities in the county appeared to be merely tokenistic.[24]

Secondly, the fact that the arrival and settlement of migrant populations to rural Wiltshire took place in small numbers, and that they have often constituted dispersed, 'hidden' and 'invisible' communities, meant that the local authority's response developed on a more uncoordinated and ad hoc basis compared to what was often the case in cities. There was, for example, no single unit or local government committee in the county that led on migration, integration and race issues to the extent that was the case regarding race units in urban areas like Brent, Ealing and Manchester.[25] Whilst bodies like the Swindon and District Council for Community Relations and the Wiltshire Racial Equality Council did play a role in many of the political discussions and initiatives regarding the settlement and experiences of ethnic minority communities in the county, and Swindon was home to a Race Relations Sub-Committee, issues of migration, integration and local Muslim populations' needs and demands permeated numerous levels and aspects of local government. These included county, district and town councils, and a wide range of committees and sub-committees, including those relating to community development, education, environment, finance, health, housing, policy and resources, social services, and youth.

Whilst this could be perceived to have been a benefit in that ethnic minority and race matters were not sidelined into one specific unit or committee, this was potentially at least partially the result of the fact that, unlike was the case in many British cities across the post-war decades, Wiltshire did not experience major local turning points or landmark developments that focused the minds of policymakers and thus played a part in coordinating and shaping subsequent migration and integration debates, policies and measures. Urban examples include the discussions and disputes that took place regarding the wearing of turbans and beards by busmen in Wolverhampton during the 1960s, the 1981 and 1985 race riots in Birmingham, the 1986 racist murder of a school pupil in Manchester, waves of racial harassment on council estates in Ealing and Newcastle, and the general settlement in significant numbers, and at times residential concentration, of ethnic minority communities in inner-city areas, all of which influenced local council policy and direction.[26]

Thirdly, and perhaps partially as a consequence of this somewhat unco-ordinated development of policy, there were variations in policy responses across both districts and towns and tiers of government within the county. Whilst Swindon's local government's committees and officers regularly made reference to the town's relatively small ethnic minority populations and its rural surroundings, this north-east Wiltshire town is that with the least rural profile. Potentially as a result, it was Swindon's local authority's measures and responses that were without a doubt the most numerous and persistent across the post-1960s period as a whole, ranging from those addressing the education of immigrant children and the resettlement of Ugandan Asians during the 1960s and early 1970s, respectively, to those focusing on ethnic minority businessmen during the 1980s, and on social cohesion and the inclusion of religion and belief in its equality policies of the 2000s.[27] Similarly, largely as a result of the settlement of the Moroccan community in Trowbridge, West Wiltshire District Council was also fairly active, and it responded to local Muslims' religious needs and demands, including regarding Muslim burials and *halal* slaughter, and it also devised and implemented racial equality policies and schemes.[28] To the contrary, with regard to the other district councils, the 'rural mentality' often prevailed, with those of Kennet and North Wiltshire occasionally displaying a lack of interest in, and thus commitment to, their small, rural and dispersed ethnic minority populations.[29]

At the county level, Wiltshire County Council's dedication to its ethnic minority communities progressively increased throughout the post-1960s period and seemed to respond to a growing awareness of the alleged neglect of migrant groups across the wider British rural policy context. In an attempt to not succumb to this 'rural norm', it pushed ahead with a range of initiatives and strategies, which were rooted in the notion that the rural nature of the county, and thus of the ethnic minorities themselves, needed to be acknowledged, considered and incorporated into its policy measures.[30] Furthermore, as decades passed, Wiltshire's political approach to the settlement, experiences and integration of its Muslim migrant communities gradually extended both down to its parish and town councils, including those of Melksham and Trowbridge, and to its more rural authorities, such as Roundway Parish Council and Highworth Town Council. Overall, Wiltshire's rurality acted as both a catalyst and inhibitor of policy and practical action, and went some way towards shaping policy discourses and chronologies across different localities and levels of government within the county.

Fourthly, arguably as a result of the fact that Wiltshire's local government was not the most experienced in the areas of migration, integration and diversity, it often looked to other local authorities, both urban and more rural, as a kind of policy marker or gauge. During the late 1960s, for example, Swindon's Education Committee considered the Inner London Education Authority's need for a full-time centre for immigrant children and the high concentration of non-speaking English-language immigrant school pupils in Birmingham, and clearly pitted both the situation in the town and the political action required against these city case studies.[31] During the mid-1970s, upon receiving a request for an area of Trowbridge cemetery to be reserved for Muslim graves, a sub-committee of West Wiltshire District Council's Environmental Committee looked to Bristol for direction.[32] Wiltshire County Council's Schools Sub-Committee felt compelled to draw up a policy statement on multicultural education during the early 1980s because neighbouring counties like Avon and Berkshire had done so.[33] The 2002 *Hidden Voices* report that was jointly produced by Wiltshire County Council and the Wiltshire Racial Equality Council, and the results of which were to inform the local authority's strategies moving forward, used the allegation that ethnic minority communities had remained invisible in other rural counties, including Cornwall, Devon, Dorset and Somerset, as a starting point and motivation to act.[34]

Fifthly, Wiltshire's local government's migration, integration and diversity policies across the post-1960s period were overwhelmingly reactive in that they largely conformed to top-down national mandate across a range of different policy areas, from education and housing to community and race relations. Progressively throughout the decades, Wiltshire's local authority tailored national-level mandate and legislation, whether the Race Relations Act 1976, the 1985 Swann Report, or the 1999 Macpherson Report and subsequent Race Relations (Amendment) Act 2000, to its local rural and low-density ethnic minority context. This stands in contrast to the proactiveness it has been argued emerged in some of Britain's more diverse cities that are renowned for their well-established and sizeable ethnic minority populations, and some of which have perceived their diversity as being an intrinsic part of their urban identities. In Birmingham, Bradford and London, for example, local integration policies and strategies were at times implemented before a clear national-level policy framework existed and some even deviated from the national model, thus resulting in what Maren Borkert and Tiziana Caponio have referred to as a distinct 'local dimension of migration policy and policy-making'.[35] In Wiltshire, whilst the local authority did at times respond to local factors and developments, largely in the form of Muslim communities' religious needs, a proactive local political approach to migration and integration did not emerge in this more rural county.

In his work highlighting the inadequacy of policy responses to racism in rural Britain, Neil Chakraborti argued that there is a need to recognise both 'the problem of rural racism' and 'the fallacy of the rural idyll', and that 'policymakers… remain largely unfamiliar with the dimensions of the first issue and transfixed by the appeal of the second'.[36] Yet despite the five ways outlined above in which there existed a rural dimension to the devising and implementing of Wiltshire's migration, integration and diversity policies, the county's policymakers do not appear to have been either 'unfamiliar' or 'transfixed'. Unlike some of their counterparts in other rural areas, they acted upon the Race Relations Act 1976, and implemented a series of policies and strategies long before the 1999 Macpherson Report and the Race Relations (Amendment) Act 2000.[37] Furthermore, they both recognised and drew upon the county's rurality when doing so, and progressively sought to counter the notion of the 'rural idyll'. Additionally, Wiltshire's local authority responded to the county's Muslim communities' needs and requests favourably and with a sense of commitment, and often kept up with initiatives and developments taking place in cities, be it when providing a separate cemetery section for Muslim burials or selling land at a heavily reduced price in order to enable the construction of a mosque.[38] Indeed, to focus solely on rural racism is to neglect many other aspects of local authority migration and integration policy.[39] In Wiltshire, a more comprehensive and historical assessment of the county's policies across the post-1960s period reveals a local authority that, despite pockets of indifference, has long pursued the integration, recognition and well-being of its small, rural and dispersed Muslim migrant communities.

The Muslim communities' perspective

The academic literature exploring the experiences of ethnic minority communities residing in rural Britain has been almost as unanimous as that investigating the rural policy context. Since the 1990s especially, there have been a number of localised studies that have gone some ways towards exposing the prevalence of racism, intolerance and prejudice in the 'rural idyll'. Helen Derbyshire offered an insight into racism and discrimination in Norfolk, Philomena de Lima uncovered racial discrimination and the lack of community networks amongst ethnic minorities in rural Scotland, and Helen Moore disclosed the 'othering' of Eastern European migrants in rural Worcestershire as a result of the fact that they were perceived as being 'not quite white enough' to integrate into their local surroundings.[40] In their research on Northamptonshire, Warwickshire and Suffolk, Neil Chakraborti and Jon Garland revealed how ethnic minorities felt unwelcome and not part of their local settings, were victims of racist discrimination and isolation at the hands of rural communities who were unwilling to accept 'the other', and generally struggled to achieve integration.[41] On the whole, existing studies have shown there exists a clear and distinct rural dimension to ethnic minorities' experiences and levels of integration in rural Britain and that, amongst other factors, this is shaped by the prejudice and racism they endure, the sense of anxiety and misgiving their encounters with rural areas stir up, and the fact that the rural landscape often continues to be perceived as a symbol of 'white' national identity.[42] Speaking in 2004, Trevor Phillips, former Chair of the Commission for Racial Equality (CRE), went as far as to claim that rural Britain was home to a 'passive apartheid', which resulted in members of ethnic minorities not feeling welcome.[43]

Compared to ethnicity and race, religion in Britain's rural landscape has received comparably less academic attention, and thus there is scant research on Islam and Muslims' experiences and integration in more rural areas. Indeed, Britain's Muslim communities continue to overwhelmingly be perceived solely as rural–urban migrants who uprooted from rural Mirpur or Sylhet and settled in Birmingham, Bradford or London.[44] Nevertheless, there does exist a small body of literature that has gone some way towards offering an insight into Muslim migrants' settlement and subsequent lives in rural Britain, much of which has been cited throughout this study. It has been argued, for example, that those Ugandan Asian refugees of the early 1970s who found themselves in rural areas suffered from isolation and an absence of a cultural and religious support system.[45] Larry Ray and Kate Reed's research on low-density ethnic minority communities in a semi-rural area in East Kent revealed a fragmented Muslim community that lacked mosques and community centres, and thus clear community markers.[46] Rhys Dafydd Jones' work found that there existed a clear rural dimension to rural Muslims' lives and experiences in West Wales. For example, they encountered a range of challenges and difficulties when trying to perform religious rituals and community-based activities, they had to make do with makeshift and contingent sacred spaces, they endured isolation and the absence of a local understanding of Islam, and they were 'physically present' in their rural surroundings despite Islam being largely 'visibly absent'.[47] Furthermore, unlike their urban counterparts who were often able to simply make use of existing religious services, they were compelled to arrange and establish their own, often having to prioritise and compromise due to available capacity and resources.[48]

With regard to Wiltshire's Muslim communities, the first and chief observation that can be made about their lived migratory experiences is that, whilst they have certainly been marked and shaped by the county's rurality, this correlation is by no means as straightforward as existing academic research suggests.[49] Nevertheless, many of the aforementioned arguments and findings do hold true for the experiences of Muslim ethnic minority communities in Wiltshire across the post-1960s period. Indeed, the oral history testimonies reveal how some of the interviewees felt that the small and rural nature of their communities had in fact led to instances of racism, intolerance and prejudice, and how it was not uncommon to experience difficulties accessing mosques and *halal* food, as well as a sense of uneasiness when attempting to pray at work, fast during Ramadan or wear a headscarf. Others discussed the consequences of not having a community support network, and the general lack of understanding regarding Islam and Islamic practices in their more rural surroundings. Furthermore, the prevalence of inconspicuous and storefront mosques and prayer rooms meant that there was often a clear absence of visible markers reflecting the presence of Muslims in Wiltshire, yet there were also a number of 'active citizens' who established community organisations, facilitated Friday prayers, and provided the county's small and dispersed Muslims with a voice.

However, the interviewees' oral testimonies also revealed that rurality has shaped Wiltshire's Muslims' migration and integration experiences in a number of different, multifaceted, and even contradictory, ways. Some sensed that their rural surroundings actually shielded them from what they perceived was discrimination, Islamophobia and victimisation endured by Muslims across urban Britain. Others stressed how rural Wiltshire had accepted, respected, and even welcomed, Islam and their religious practices. For a number of the interviewees and their families, it had been Wiltshire's rurality that had drawn them away from cities with larger Muslim populations to the county in the first place, and many emphasised how forming part of small rural Muslim and ethnic minority populations shaped their identities, and resulted in their employment, entrepreneurial, housing and neighbourhood experiences being comprised of what they felt were greater levels of diversity, community mixing and integration. For some, rural Wiltshire invoked notions of safety and security and memories of a foreign landscape left behind, whilst others felt uneasy about standing out in a rural environment. Some maintained that their rural surroundings had not hindered their religious identities and argued that Islam could be practised anywhere, whilst others lamented the lack of religious education opportunities available. Many stressed the prevalence of multi-ethnic Muslim communities and collaboration in the county, yet others felt that more needed to be done to enable engagement and cooperation across ethnic lines. Overall, whether because they formed part of small and dispersed Muslim communities, lived in 'white' neighbourhoods and attended 'white' schools, introduced South Asian and Turkish food to the county through their restaurants and takeaways, found themselves negotiating the absence and shortage of mosques, *halal* food and provisions for Muslim burials, or felt that they suffered comparably more or less racism and Islamophobia, the interviewees had a clear sense that their everyday experiences had frequently been different from those of their city equivalents. Furthermore, a common theme that materialised from the testimonies was an intrinsic commitment to community cohesion and integration that developed from the Muslim communities' small rural nature.

Additionally, differences between urban and rural experiences also emerged according to ethnic group. The South Asian groups, for example, were largely drawn to Wiltshire as a result of entrepreneurial opportunities, rather than chain migration, affordable inner-city terraced houses, and the appeal of community support networks as was often the case with regard to urban settings.[50] Furthermore, instead of comprising a visibly 'dominant' British Muslim minority, which resulted in them leading the way across the postwar period in the construction of mosques, Muslim supplementary schools and Islamic organisations, and the transformation of certain city districts and neighbourhoods, their cultural, ethnic and religious identities have remained far more hidden and private.[51] This rural case study has also shed light on what have often been referred to as Britain's 'hidden' Muslims or minorities, about which the existing historiography has often granted no more than a fleeting reference and has focused almost exclusively on those in London, thus rendering these more rural communities 'doubly hidden'.[52] The Moroccans who began to settle in Trowbridge during the 1960s, for example, have received scant academic attention despite being the largest Moroccan community in Britain outside of London, yet their migratory experiences have clearly set them apart from their counterparts in the capital.[53] They were employed in factories, not the hotel and catering industries, they have not become residentially concentrated in one particular area or neighbourhood and, despite being the area's 'dominant' minority, they lived without a purpose-built mosque and a developed religious infrastructure of any kind for years. Similarly, whilst London's Turkish community has long benefitted from an established visible presence and religious infrastructure, and their business ventures from the advice, support and networks of an ethnic economy,[54] Turks in Wiltshire have at times found themselves scattered around towns such as Melksham and Swindon, depending on staff from beyond their immediate ethnic group to run their businesses, and attending 'non-Turkish', and often Bangladeshi-run, Friday prayers where they encounter linguistic barriers. Furthermore, the individual voices of Saudi, Sri Lankan and Tunisian Muslims revealed how being part of small rural Muslim communities has shaped their identities and self-perceptions, led to an active commitment to community cohesion, and created difficulties in securing a suitable *imam* for the local mosque, respectively.

As well as these complex and varied manifestations of the rural dimension that have developed at the level of the individual and group, ethnic or otherwise, there are three broader observations that can be made about this study's rural Muslims' experiences on the whole that can go some way towards furthering our understanding of Islam and Muslim communities in Britain. Firstly, they showcase the extent to which the religious experiences and practices of British Muslims are by no means homogenous. Indeed, there exists a vast literature acknowledging their diversity with regard to denominational, doctrinal and sectarian differences, religious interpretations and traditions, and levels of religiosity in urban areas. For example, we have a solid grasp of the diverse day-to-day workings of *sharīa* councils in London and Birmingham, of the principles, priorities and teachings of the various Islamic institutions in Bradford, and of the diverse experiences and views of young British Muslims in cities like Cardiff, Leeds and Leicester with regard to a range of topics, from restrictions on women entering mosques to arranged marriage and Islamic dress.[55] Yet with regard to Wiltshire, the Muslims' testimonies revealed that there has also long been a clear rural sphere to Muslim heterogeneity and practising Islam in Britain consisting of a series of compromises, challenges, inconveniences, sacrifices and anxieties, but also multi-ethnic collaboration and cohesion, that has largely gone undocumented. This has included Moroccans working with pork; a sense of there being a lack of adequate religious education opportunities available for the younger generations; women feeling uncomfortable wearing a headscarf; not having access to, having to travel long distances for, and not understanding Friday prayer; anxieties about not being able to access *halal* food, secure a suitable *imam* and about dying in Wiltshire due to the absence of Muslim burial rituals; a shortage of prayer rooms and spaces for pre-prayer wash; apprehension about not being able to 'be Muslim' to the same extent as their urban counterparts; and the prevalence of multi-ethnic mosque congregations and Islamic organisations that pursue integration and community cohesion.

Secondly, Muslim communities and Islam in Wiltshire across the post-1960s period have been characterised by a deep-rooted tension between absence and presence. On the one hand, Muslims have been highly visible and noticeable on the county's 'white' rural landscape yet, on the other, as Jones argued was the case in West Wales, Islam has often not been 'present in a symbolic sense'.[56] Rather than being able to truly 'Islamisize' local space through a series of clearly visible indicators, including purpose-built mosques with domes and minarets, and more broadly by enacting their religious identities in certain neighbourhoods which it has been argued is crucial in the process of achieving a local urban sense of belonging, Wiltshire's small and dispersed Muslim communities have largely prayed in storefront and unspectacular mosques and prayer rooms, and used contingent spaces for Friday prayer.[57] Over the years, these have comprised mosques and community centres located in a former working men's club, hair salon and furniture store, and Friday prayers being held in a Quaker Meeting House and even in portable buildings placed in a garden.

This has meant that, whilst Wiltshire's Muslims have gradually been able to organise themselves as a collection of small religious communities and thus Islam has been present in what Jones called 'a lived, everyday sense', like his Muslim respondents in West Wales, they have nevertheless often suffered from a lack of 'an explicit presence of Islam' in the county's rural landscape.[58] This lack of visibility and religious markers has also created challenges and difficulties with regard to how Islam is practised and perceived. For example, as a result of constituting small communities that have not been able to mobilise, or secure resources, to the same extent as their urban counterparts, Wiltshire's Muslims have frequently depended on others in order to be able to practise their religion, whether on the local council to sell them land at a heavily reduced price on which to build a mosque or community centre, or on local community and religious organisations to provide them with the necessary space for Friday prayers. Furthermore, compared to the urban status quo, the absence of a visible Islamic presence in Wiltshire has meant that Muslims have often experienced a shortage of religious and social activities, Muslim newcomers have not immediately realised that an established local Muslim community existed, and there has often been a general local lack of understanding regarding Islam and Islamic practices.[59]

Thirdly, largely as a result of their small, dispersed and rural nature, Wiltshire's Muslims have long demonstrated a strong sense of agency, self-determination and active citizenship, both as ethnic and religious minorities. Their agency and self-determination was seen in that many migrated to Wiltshire with little to no prior knowledge of the county, and despite the absence of an ethnic or religious community support structure. They seized business opportunities and filled gaps in the restaurant and takeaway markets, settled and purchased properties in 'white' neighbourhoods, and developed a range of services through multi-ethnic mosques, and Islamic community centres and organisations that catered for their small and dispersed communities' needs. Furthermore, they have long been active citizens in the county and pursued positive engagement with wider society, expressed their ethnic and religious identities, a sense of belonging, and a long-term commitment to their local surroundings, and they have been proactive in developing services that meet their needs.[60]

In doing so, they have engaged with, and demonstrated an understanding of, local society in the form of institutions and non-Muslim stakeholders, in order to enable the gradual practice and recognition of Islam. This is seen in the way they have successfully negotiated the purchase, hiring and use of land, buildings and rooms for community centres, Friday prayers and Eid celebrations, the allocation of designated areas for Muslim burials in the county's cemeteries, and the successful application for slaughter licences. At the centre of this active citizenship was often a commitment to enacting their ethnic and religious identities in the county's rural landscape in a way that promoted integration and community cohesion, whether through community work and participation or their roles as business owners, politicians and British Muslims outside the major conurbations of Muslim settlement.

Islam might not always be immediately visible in Wiltshire, yet the county has long been home to settled Muslim communities whose rural surroundings have been reflected in every stage and aspect of their personal migratory experiences, from initial settlement and identity formation to encounters with discrimination and prejudice, religious practice and the development of Islam. Yet by no means has there existed one single homogenous 'rural experience' across the county,[61] with Muslims in towns like Calne, Devizes and Melksham undoubtedly living in more rural settings amongst smaller communities than those in Swindon or Trowbridge. Some of the interviewees themselves recognised the role that location and place had played in shaping their integration, with Salisbury's history of Christianity being employed to explain the manner in which one interviewee believed it has accepted Islam, for example, and Devizes' position as an 'old English town' with a small Muslim community being drawn upon to rationalise the delay in it accepting a more established place for Islamic worship.[62] Nevertheless, on the whole, the interviewees were resolute that their experiences as members of both ethnic and religious minorities had frequently differed from those of their urban counterparts, and from those in Birmingham and London in particular. Their voices and experiences join those of Muslims in Cambridge, East Kent and market towns in West Wales in teasing out the distinct nature of Muslims' lives and integration in rural and semi-rural areas with small migrant populations.[63]

Conclusion

It has long been the city, both in Britain and beyond, that has dominated academic and non-academic debates on ethnic and Muslim minority communities, and been perceived as a beacon of diversity, multiculturalism and social cohesion.[64] To the contrary, the constant neglect of rural Britain has only served to reinforce the notion of a pre-multicultural landscape that is devoid of Islam and has no place in these broader deliberations. Writing during the early 1990s, Chris Philo argued that scholarship had long been at risk of portraying rural Britons as what he referred to as 'Mr Averages... as white and probably English, straight and somehow without sexuality, able in body and sound in mind, and devoid of any other quirks of (say) religious belief or political affiliation'.[65] Whilst there has been a recognition that geography and locality play a role in the everyday lives of British Muslims, as well as a call to shift the focus away from the major conurbations of Muslim settlement, it remains the case that these academic debates and developments have rarely extended to more rural settings.[66]

Yet it is evident that rurality matters and that, with regard to Wiltshire, there is a story that deserves to be told. Not only is the county home to well-established, diverse and active Muslim communities that are largely absent from its dominant rural imaginary, but both its local authority's political approach and Muslims' experiences across the post-1960s period have frequently set it apart from the prevalent urban narrative and shown that rural developments have often been far more complex than has been recognised. Whilst rural areas may well be home to much smaller Muslim populations than urban settings, the experiences of, and local political responses to, rural Muslims across Britain as both ethnic and religious minorities are undoubtedly collectively significant. Indeed, the rural dimension has been neglected for too long. Not only does it offer an additional branch to the existing academic literature, but it is crucial if we are to reach a thorough and multidimensional understanding of the Muslim integration process.

Notes

1 For an insight into some of these perceptions and portrayals, see Raymond Williams, *The Country and the City* (Oxford: Oxford University Press, 1975); Stephen Daniels, *Fields of Vision: Landscape Imagery and National Identity in England and the United States* (Cambridge: Polity Press, 1993); Agyeman and Spooner, 'Ethnicity and the rural environment'; Hugh Matthews, Mark Taylor, Kenneth Sherwood, Faith Tucker and Melanie Limb, 'Growing-up in the countryside: children and the rural idyll', *Journal of Rural Studies*, 16:2 (2000), 141–53; and Brian Short, 'Idyllic ruralities', in Paul Cloke, Terry Marsden and Patrick Mooney (eds), *The Handbook of Rural Studies* (London: SAGE, 2006), pp. 133–48.

2 See Phil Hubbard, '"Inappropriate and incongruous": opposition to asylum centres in the English countryside', *Journal of Rural Studies*, 21:1 (2005), 12.

3 See Mark Shucksmith, 'Re-imagining the rural: from rural idyll to Good Countryside', *Journal of Rural Studies*, 59 (2018), 163.

4 See Grace Harrison and Ben Clifford, '"The field of grain is gone; it's now a Tesco superstore": representations of "urban" and "rural" within historical and contemporary discourses opposing urban expansion in England', *Planning Perspectives*, 31:4 (2016), 588.

5 Williams, *The Country and the City*, p. 1.

6 See Jeremy Burchardt, *Paradise Lost: Rural Idyll and Social Change since 1800* (London: I.B. Tauris, 2002); Harrison and Clifford, '"The field of grain is gone; it's now a Tesco superstore"'; and Nick Gallent, Iqbal Hamiduddin, Meri Juntti, Sue Kidd and Dave Shaw, *Introduction to Rural Planning: Economies, Communities and Landscapes* (Abingdon: Routledge, 2015).

7 See Neal and Agyeman (eds), *The New Countryside?*; John Horton, 'Producing Postman Pat: the popular cultural construction of idyllic rurality', *Journal of Rural Studies*, 24:4 (2008), 390; and Harrison and Clifford, '"The field of grain is gone; it's now a Tesco superstore"', 601.

8 See Gill Valentine, 'A safe place to grow up? Parenting, perceptions of children's safety and the rural idyll', *Journal of Rural Studies*, 13:2 (1997), 137–48; Jodi Wallwork and John A. Dixon, 'Foxes, green fields and Britishness: on the rhetorical construction of place and national identity', *British Journal of Social Psychology*, 43:1 (2004), 21–39; Hubbard, '"Inappropriate and incongruous"'; Sarah Neal and Sue Walters, 'Strangers asking strange questions? A methodological narrative of researching belonging and identity in English rural communities', *Journal of Rural Studies*, 22:2 (2006), 177–89; and Harrison and Clifford, '"The field of grain is gone; it's now a Tesco superstore"'.

9   See Paul Cloke, 'Knowing ruralities?', in Paul Cloke (ed.), *Country Visions* (Harlow: Pearson Education Limited, 2003), p. 3.

10 See Jo Little, 'Gender relations in rural areas: the importance of women's domestic role', *Journal of Rural Studies*, 3:4 (1987), 335–42; Paul Cloke, Paul Milbourne and Rebekah Widdowfield, *Rural Homelessness: Issues, Experiences and Policy Responses* (Bristol: The Policy Press, 2002); and Rosie Meek, 'Young people, social exclusion and inter-generational tension in a rural Somerset town', *Children & Society*, 22:2 (2008), 124–35.

11 Chris Philo, 'Neglected rural geographies: a review', *Journal of Rural Studies*, 8:2 (1992), 193–207.

12 See Jay, *'Keep Them in Birmingham'*; Neal, 'Rural landscapes, representations and racism'; Chakraborti and Garland, 'An "invisible" problem?'; Chakraborti and Garland, 'England's green and pleasant land?'; and Williams, 'Revisiting the rural/race debates'. With regard to Muslims specifically, see Ray and Reed, 'Community, mobility and racism in a semi-rural area'; Jones, 'Islam and the rural landscape'; Jones, 'Negotiating absence and presence'; and Villis and Hebing, 'Islam and Englishness'.

13 An overview of these arguments can be found in de Lima, 'John O'Groats to Land's End', pp. 42–6.

14 See Jay, *'Keep Them in Birmingham'*; Jay Rayner, 'The Hidden Truths Behind Race Crimes in Britain', *Observer* (18 February 2001); and de Lima, ' "Let's keep our heads down and maybe the problem will go away" '.

15 Jay, *'Keep Them in Birmingham'*, pp. 18–9.

16 For example, see Neal, 'Rural landscapes, representations and racism'; and de Lima, 'John O'Groats to Land's End'.

17 This section draws on the local authority policies, practices and strategies covered in Chapters 2–4.

18 See WSHC, F8/933/E.B.26a, letter from Borough Education Officer to Headmaster of Moredon Secondary School in Swindon, 13 May 1971; WSHC, 3231/7, a letter from Richard Martin (Chair of the Wiltshire Racial Equality Council), 18 January 1994; WSHC, F1/201/14/1, 'Wiltshire Community Care Plan, 1997–2000' (Final Draft, 3 June 1999); WSHC, F1/201/20, 'Services to Children and Families from Black and Other Minority Ethnic Communities'; and WSHC, F1/201/20, 'Wiltshire County Council Draft Race Equality Scheme May 2002–5'.

19 See, for example, WSHC, F8/933/H.Y.88(b), Swindon and District Council for Community Relations, Annual Report 1970–71.

20 For a discussion of these policies and practices, see the section on education in Chapter 3.

21 Wiltshire County Council and Wiltshire Racial Equality Council, *Hidden Voices*.

22 See Candappa and Joly, *Local Authorities, Ethnic Minorities and 'Pluralist Integration'*; Rahsaan Maxwell, *Ethnic Minority Migrants in Britain and France: Integration Trade-Offs* (Cambridge: Cambridge University Press,

2012), pp. 143, 146–7; Hackett, *Foreigners, Minorities and Integration*; and Fazakarley, *Muslim Communities in England 1962–90*, pp. 220–1.

23 For example, see WSHC, F1/102/1–4/7–8/11, 'Community Relations in Wiltshire', 7 March 1979; and WSHC, G29/1/1/15/1, Salisbury District Council, meeting of the Finance Committee, 3 March 1980.

24 For example, see WSHC, 3231/7, a letter from Richard Martin (Chair of the Wiltshire Racial Equality Council), 18 January 1994; and WSHC, 3231/11, 'Wiltshire Racial Equality Council Annual Report 2000'.

25 See Candappa Joly, *Local Authorities, Ethnic Minorities and 'Pluralist Integration'*; Garbaye, *Getting into Local Power*, pp. 57–8; and Maxwell, *Ethnic Minority Migrants in Britain and France*, pp. 143–4. Although the influence these units had on positively shaping policy and practice has been questioned, they have frequently been portrayed as an inherent part of urban Britain's local response to migration, integration and diversity.

26 See Candappa and Joly, *Local Authorities, Ethnic Minorities and 'Pluralist Integration'*; Deborah Phillips and Rachael Unsworth, 'Widening locational choices for minority ethnic groups in the social rented sector', in Peter Somerville and Andy Steele (eds), *'Race', Housing & Social Exclusion* (London: Jessica Kingsley Publishers, 2002), pp. 87–8; Hackett, *Foreigners, Minorities and Integration*, pp. 108–12; Camilla Schofield, *Enoch Powell and the Making of Postcolonial Britain* (Cambridge: Cambridge University Press, 2013), p. 216; and Kieran Connell, *Black Handsworth: Race in 1980s Britain* (Oakland, CA: University of California Press, 2019), pp. 24–6.

27 For example, see WSHC, F8/933/E.B.26, 'Special Class for Non-English-Speaking Pupils', 27 November 1962; WSHC, G6/132/105, letter from the Swindon District Council for Community Relations to the Clerk of the Council, Highworth Rural District Council, Swindon, 11 September 1972; WSHC, G30/Box811, 'Black Business Conference', 21 December 1988; Swindon Borough Council, *Equality Policy* (Cabinet, 14 April 2010); and Swindon Borough Council, *Equality Duty Publication Report* (January 2015).

28 See, for example, WSHC, G31/1/2/7, minutes of the No. 2 Sub-Committee of the Environmental Committee, 3 March 1977; WSHC, G31/1/2/9, minutes of the Environmental Committee, 'Muslim Burials – Trowbridge Cemetery', 5 July 1978; and WSHC, G31/1/1/8/2, West Wiltshire District Council Cabinet, meeting of 25 September 2002.

29 See the section on community relations and racial equality in Chapter 3.

30 This was arguably best seen in the 2002 Race Equality Scheme. See WSHC, F1/201/20, Wiltshire County Council Cabinet, 'Wiltshire County Council Draft Race Equality Scheme May 2002–5'.

31 See, for example, WSHC, F8/933/E.B.26, Swindon Education Committee Report No. 70; and WSHC, F8/933/H.Y.88(a), Swindon Education Committee, Sub-Committee on Immigrants, minutes of meeting, 11 December 1967.

32 See WSHC, G31/1/2/7, West Wiltshire District Council, 'Trowbridge Cemetery – Muslim Burials', 25 November 1976.

33 See WSHC, F1/201/10/3, Wiltshire County Council Schools Subcommittee, 'Multi-cultural Education'.

34 Wiltshire County Council and Wiltshire Racial Equality Council, *Hidden Voices*, pp. 4–5.

35 Maren Borkert and Tiziana Caponio, 'Introduction: the local dimension of migration policymaking', in Tiziana Caponio and Maren Borkert (eds), *The Local Dimension of Migration Policymaking* (Amsterdam: Amsterdam University Press, 2010), p. 24. See also Peter Scholten and Rinus Penninx, 'The multilevel governance of migration and integration', in Blanca Garcés-Mascareñas and Rinus Penninx (eds), *Integration Processes and Policies in Europe: Contexts, Levels and Actors* (Dordrecht: Springer, 2016), p. 99.

36 Chakraborti, 'Beyond "passive apartheid"?', 514. As well as policymakers, he also levelled this accusation against both rural agencies and academia.

37 See de Lima, 'John O'Groats to Land's End', pp. 42–3; and Connolly, ' "It goes without saying (well, sometimes)" ', pp. 21–2.

38 For city-level examples, see Joly, *Making a Place for Islam in British Society*, p. 13; Gilliat-Ray, *Muslims in Britain*, p. 199; and Ahmed, 'Marking a good death', p. 111.

39 As previously mentioned, many studies that have investigated the rural policy context have largely done so through the lens of rural racism. See Dhalech, *Challenging Racism in the Rural Idyll*; Henderson and Kaur (eds), *Rural Racism in the UK*; Neal, 'Rural landscapes, representations and racism'; Chakraborti and Garland (eds), *Rural Racism*; and Chakraborti, 'Beyond "passive apartheid"?'.

40 Derbyshire, *Not in Norfolk*; de Lima, *Needs Not Numbers*; and Moore, 'Shades of whiteness?', 15.

41 See Chakraborti and Garland, 'An "invisible" problem?'; Garland and Chakraborti, 'Racist victimisation, community safety and the rural'; Chakraborti and Garland, 'England's green and pleasant land?'; and Jon Garland and Neil Chakraborti, ' "Race", space and place: examining identity and cultures of exclusion in rural England', *Ethnicities*, 6:2 (2006), 159–77.

42 See Agyeman and Spooner, 'Ethnicity and the rural environment'; Neal, 'Rural landscapes, representations and racism'; and Chakraborti and Garland (eds), *Rural Racism*.

43 See Williams, 'Revisiting the rural/race debates', 741.

44 See Ballard (ed.), *Desh Pardesh*; Peach, 'South Asian migration and settlement in Great Britain, 1951–2001'; Gilliat-Ray, *Muslims in Britain*, p. 210; and William Gould, 'Diasporic cities in Britain: Bradford, Manchester, Leicester, London', in Joya Chatterji and David Washbrook (eds), *Routledge Handbook of the South Asian Diaspora* (Abingdon: Routledge, 2013), pp. 339–49.

45 See Mukadam and Mawani, 'Excess baggage or precious gems?', p. 161.

46 Ray and Reed, 'Community, mobility and racism in a semi-rural area'.

47 See Jones, 'Negotiating absence and presence', 340.

48 See *Ibid.*; and Jones, 'Islam and the rural landscape'.

49 The experiences discussed in this section draw on the oral history testimonies provided in Chapter 5.

50 See Badr Dahya, 'The nature of Pakistani ethnicity in industrial cities in Britain', in Abner Cohen (ed.), *Urban Ethnicity* (London: Tavistock, 1974), pp. 77–118; Peach, 'South Asian migration and settlement in Great Britain, 1951–2001'; and Gilliat-Ray, *Muslims in Britain*, pp. 46–8.

51 See Werbner, *Imagined Diasporas Among Manchester Muslims*; Eade and Garbin, 'Competing visions of identity and space'; and Gilliat-Ray, *Muslims in Britain*.

52 See Nagel, 'Constructing difference and sameness'; Ansari, '*The Infidel Within*', pp. 341–2, 351–3; Cherti, *Paradoxes of Social Capital*; King, Thomson, Mai and Keles, ' "Turks" in London'; and Gilliat-Ray, *Muslims in Britain*, pp. 50–2.

53 For an insight into London's Moroccan community, see Cherti, *Paradoxes of Social Capital*; and Cherti, *British Moroccans – Citizenship in Action*. Writing in 2009, for example, Cherti pointed out that London was home to a plethora of mosques, supplementary schools and community organisations that catered for the city's Moroccan community. See Cherti, *British Moroccans – Citizenship in Action*, p. 2.

54 See Ansari, '*The Infidel Within*', pp. 351–2; Ibrahim Sirkeci, Tuncay Bilecen, et al., *Little Turkey in Great Britain* (London: Transnational Press London, 2016), pp. 137–50; and Karan, *Economic Survival Strategies of Turkish Migrants in London*. For a list of Turkish places of worship in London, and in other British towns and cities, see Sirkeci, Bilecen, *et al.*, *Little Turkey in Great Britain*, p. 149.

55 For example, see Lewis, *Islamic Britain*; Kabir, *Young British Muslims*; Bowen, *Medina in Birmingham, Najaf in Brent*; and Bowen, *On British Islam*.

56 Jones, 'Islam and the rural landscape', 764.

57 See Eade, 'Nationalism, community, and the Islamization of space in London'; Ahmad and Sardar (eds), *Muslims in Britain*; and Phillips, 'Claiming spaces'.

58 Jones, 'Islam and the rural landscape', 763–4.

59 Jones found that these characteristics and experiences were also prevalent in West Wales. See Jones, 'Islam and the rural landscape'.

60 For an insight into active citizenship amongst Muslims in Britain, both in rural areas and beyond, see Jones, 'Negotiating absence and presence'; and Peucker and Akbarzadeh, *Muslim Active Citizenship in the West*.

61 The importance of location and place, and the heterogeneity of rurality and the 'rural migrant experience', have been recognised. See Neal, 'Rural landscapes, representations and racism'; and Robinson and Gardner, 'Unravelling a stereotype'.

62 Anser, 15 September 2016.

63 See Ray and Reed, 'Community, mobility and racism in a semi-rural area'; Jones, 'Islam and the rural landscape'; Jones, 'Negotiating absence and presence'; and Villis and Hebing, 'Islam and Englishness'.

64 For example, see Lewis, *Islamic Britain*; Richard Gale, 'Representing the city: mosques and the planning process in Birmingham', *Journal of Ethnic and*

Migration Studies, 31:6 (2005), 1161–79; Frank Eckardt and John Eade (eds), *The Ethnically Diverse City* (Berlin: Berliner Wissenschafts-Verlag, 2011); Bowen, *Medina in Birmingham, Najaf in Brent*; Charles Husband, Yunis Alam, Jörg Hüttermann and Joanna Fomina, *Lived Diversities: Space, Place and Identities in the Multi-Ethnic City* (Bristol: The Policy Press, 2016); and Les Back and Shamser Sinha, *Migrant City* (Abingdon: Routledge, 2018).

65 Philo, 'Neglected rural geographies', 200.
66 See Gale and Hopkins, 'Introduction: Muslims in Britain – race, place and the spatiality of identities', p. 15; and Hackett, *Foreigners, Minorities and Integration*.

Conclusion: Muslim integration, the rural dimension and research implications

Wiltshire is in many ways a quintessential English rural county. Known as a county of 'chalk and cheese', which refers to its rolling chalk downlands and pasture dairy land, its history is comprised of agriculture, farming, the wool trade and light industries. Its market towns and villages are framed by a wealth of ancient landmarks, hills, valleys, and stately homes, a rural landscape that Sarah Neal and Julian Agyeman have invoked as representing 'the sensuous appeal of the English countryside'.[1] Indeed, the county has gradually come to be associated with the traits and characteristics, but also the challenges and predicaments, that often afflict rural areas, including a large retired and ageing population, a low crime rate, poor infrastructure and transport networks, and pockets of poverty, isolation, marginalisation, vulnerability and limited access to services.[2] However, Wiltshire is also home to small and dispersed, yet well-established, Muslim minority communities whose histories are intertwined with their local rural surroundings despite not often featuring in the more popular images of the county's rural idyll. These include Bangladeshis, Indians, Moroccans, Pakistanis and Turks who have settled across the county throughout the post-1960s period, and whose everyday lives and ethnic and religious identities have played out against the county's rural landscape.

This book does not claim to have addressed all aspects of the Muslim migrant experience or local government approach in Wiltshire, nor to have assessed all of the various actors and dimensions relevant to the integration process. Previous chapters have already touched upon some of this study's key arguments and themes. For example, they have revealed that, in many ways, there has existed a local particularism and rural dimension to the integration of Muslim ethnic minority communities in Wiltshire. They have exposed how Wiltshire's local authority has approached immigration, integration and diversity across the post-1960s era. They have offered an insight into the role that ethnicity, gender, generation and Islam have played in Wiltshire's Muslim communities' migration and integration experiences. They have charted the extent to which there has existed a correlation between local policies and the county's Muslim populations' aims, ambitions and demands, showing that whilst the local authority has taken numerous and persistent steps to accommodate the county's Muslim communities, many aspects of their migratory experiences have been the consequences of their own sense of agency and self-determination. Yet simultaneously, this study's attempt to offer a comprehensive, long-term and multifaceted understanding of Muslim migrant integration has meant that it has engaged with concepts, ideas and theories from a wide range of disciplines in relation to a variety of local, national and international contexts. Thus, this study's findings and conclusions move beyond the novelty of the Wiltshire case study in a number of ways and have implications for various bodies of research, which can be framed around the five key points that were outlined in the introduction.

Firstly, this work complements research on migration and integration at a rural level. Whilst the last chapter placed the integration of Muslim migrant communities in post-1960s Wiltshire within the context of rural Britain in quite some detail, it is nevertheless worth reiterating that research on Islam and Muslim populations in Britain has overwhelmingly disregarded rural areas, whilst that on rural ethnic minorities' experiences has rarely focused on Muslim communities specifically. Although we know that, as per the 2011 Census, over three-quarters (76%) of Muslims reside in the urban areas of Greater London, the West Midlands, the North West, and Yorkshire and Humberside, with over 37% living in Greater London alone,[3] we are also beginning to understand that shifting the focus away from these major conurbations to more rural areas with smaller Muslim populations reveals a different set of ethnic and religious minority experiences.[4] Furthermore, with regard to the rural policy context, scholars have almost exclusively focused on local efforts to address rural racism, or the lack thereof, in contemporary settings, thus neglecting other aspects of local authority migration, integration and diversity policy across the post-1960s period.[5] Thus, regarding policy, Wiltshire's local authority has long been far more active and conscientious than rural Britain more generally has been given credit for. Furthermore, the assessment of integration from the viewpoints of both local government and Muslim migrants has revealed that rurality has played a clear role in the integration process on both sides. In doing so, this study supports and develops the small body of international scholarship that has argued that the migration and integration processes play out differently in rural areas compared to cities, whether in Germany, Greece, Ireland, Spain or the United States.[6]

Secondly, this study has revealed how Britain's national-level migration and integration policies have filtered down to, and shaped local policies in, a more rural area across the post-1960s period. Whilst this national-level policy has received extensive academic scrutiny,[7] research addressing the local level has been sparse by comparison, has overwhelmingly focused on cities and has lacked a historical perspective. The politics of migration and race have long been portrayed as a concern for urban political systems which, often home to significant ethnic minority populations, have found themselves responsible for migration politics, with many key issues such as education, housing and race relations falling firmly within their remit, and attempting to implement top-down policy.[8] Yet this study has shown that British policies and practices extended far beyond urban authorities with sizeable migrant communities. Wiltshire's local authority, despite its rural identity, also largely followed national mandate, whether with regard to race relations legislation, the implementation of assimilationist and multicultural policies, or a range of measures and strategies in the areas of anti-racism, community cohesion, equal opportunities, housing and religious identity. This is important because it reveals that there is a clear local rural dimension with regard to the development and implementation of migration, integration and diversity policies and strategies, a dimension that has not been thoroughly investigated across the post-1960s period despite the local political context and local authorities frequently playing such a crucial role in policy responses regarding ethnic minority communities and race relations.[9]

Thirdly, looking beyond Britain, this work supports the shift in focus from the traditional 'national models of integration' to the local aspect of migrant integration that has taken place since the 2000s especially. In doing so, it develops the ever-growing body of work that acknowledges the local dimension of migrant policies, experiences and integration, and focuses on the relationship between migrant communities and their local surroundings. Indeed, with regard to the governance of migration in Britain, Europe and the Western world as a whole, it is increasingly being recognised that city-level governments play a crucial role in devising and implementing their own migration, integration and diversity policies. Scholars have highlighted, for example, how Greater London Council implemented a series of radical policies in an attempt to promote racial equality and equal opportunity; how Berlin's local policies have shaped the integration of Turkish migrant women at the neighbourhood level in the city; how Rotterdam's local policies have deviated from the national level when addressing the integration of their migrant populations; the establishment of mosques *vis-à-vis* municipalities and the process of institutionalisation in the Canadian cities of Montreal and Laval; and how local-level migrant integration policies in New York and San Francisco have been influenced by the urban, rather than national, context.[10] However, whilst the importance placed on the local dimension of the governance of migration, integration and diversity has progressively intensified, little has been done to explore this so-called 'local turn' beyond the urban context.[11] Likewise, those works that have addressed immigrant and integration policies from a multi-level governance perspective, and offered an insight into the extent to which national influences have filtered down to impact policies at the local level, have also overwhelmingly drawn upon city case studies.[12]

Similarly, with regard to the lived experiences of ethnic minority communities, studies have increasingly argued that more needs to be done to expose the relationship that migrants have with their local surroundings, and to recognise them as active residents and actors within them.[13] Whether discussing British cities like Birmingham and London, European cities like Amsterdam and Paris, or American cities like Miami and New York, scholars have repeatedly reminded us that migrants' experiences, fates, challenges and opportunities are firmly rooted within, and shaped by, their various urban contexts, from those regarding education, entrepreneurship and housing to political participation, and racial and religious discrimination and inequalities.[14] Whilst it is clear that, as Ayşe Çağlar and Nina Glick Schiller argue, 'locality matters',[15] rural areas remain overwhelmingly neglected despite the ever-greater emphasis placed on studying migration at the local level. Indeed, cities may well constitute what Peter Scholten has called 'the hotspots of migration and diversity… where most migrants arrive, where they settle, go to school, find jobs, interact with others',[16] but by no means do they have a monopoly on the local dimension of the migrant experience.

Migration has for too long been seen as an urban phenomenon, with the local dimension being reduced to the study of cities, and global or gateway cities in particular.[17] Whilst this is gradually changing, with a shift in focus to smaller cities that have also been marked by migration taking place, it remains the case that the study of locality in migration studies equates to the study of urban settings. Thus, this study champions Ayşe Çağlar and Nina Glick Schiller's support for 'further explorations of the relationships between migration and localities that are not "gateway cities" including towns and rural areas'.[18] In fact, the Wiltshire case study has shown how a historical insight into a more rural locality can enhance and extend our understanding of the local dimension of migration, from the perspective of both local government and the migrant communities themselves. For example, it reveals how a local authority in a rural area has, like its urban counterparts, long devised and implemented migration and integration policies that, whilst consistently influenced by national-level mandate, also displayed aspects of local, and in this case rural, particularism. It also highlights that this not only occurred at the county level, but also at local government tiers below this, including district, town and parish. Furthermore, just like migrant populations in cities, Wiltshire's Muslim communities' lived experiences have also been shaped by their local contexts, resulting in a range of varying encounters with racism, intolerance and prejudice, a strong sense of agency, self-determination and active citizenship, and a number of challenges and compromises with regard to religious practice to list but a few. Thus, these findings offer an additional rural dimension to the study of migration at the local level as it is not just in cities that locality matters.

Fourthly, this book has exposed the importance of both studying Muslim migrant communities at a grassroots level and adopting a more interdisciplinary and cross-sector approach to migration history. It has moved beyond what has become the more dominant framing of debates on British Islam and Muslim populations within a post-*Satanic Verses*, and increasingly a post-2001, chronology. Often mapped out against what are seen to be key moments or turning points in the relationship between both Britain and the West and their respective Muslim populations, including the Rushdie Affair, the 2001 riots, 9/11, 7/7 and the War on Terror, deliberations on Muslims in Britain have been heavily shaped by the perceived conflicts and tensions between Islam and the West, and have frequently addressed and debated the clash of civilisations rhetoric, the prevalence of parallel lives and segregated communities, 'homegrown' Islamic extremism, underclass formation, and communities that are seen to pose a challenge to multiculturalism and social cohesion.[19] To the contrary, this study has purposefully shifted the attention away from these high-profile, and often global-reaching, events and developments, drawing upon a range of local government documentation and Muslim voices in order to expose the approaches and strategies regarding migration and integration adopted by both a local authority and small Muslim communities in a rural English county over time. Thereby, it has revealed the importance of recognising geography, locality, rurality, scale and the inherent diversity of British Muslims in the study of the integration process.[20]

Furthermore, whilst this study has adopted a historical perspective, it has also drawn upon academic research from a wide range of other disciplines, from anthropology, criminology and geography to political science, religious studies and sociology, and has framed its findings and conclusions within these. In doing so, it recognises the importance of bringing these different bodies of literature together and complements the growing number of works that acknowledge the benefits of interdisciplinarity within the field of migration history.[21] As well as speaking to a range of different disciplines, this study's wide scope has bridged what are well-developed, yet often separate, historiographies. By drawing upon the perspectives of both Wiltshire's local authority and its Muslim communities, and by addressing a range of topics and themes, including education, entrepreneurship, housing, multiculturalism, religious identity and practice, racism, victimisation and Islamophobia, and social cohesion, it has exposed a previously unexplored rural dimension to local government policy and Muslim experiences across the post-1960s period that complements existing comprehensive historical accounts of Muslim communities in Britain that have largely adopted more of an overarching national-level approach.[22]

All of these arguments, theses and historiographical framings feed into the fifth and final point, and the central theme that has run throughout this study, which is that regarding the integration of Muslim migrant communities. Despite the aforementioned claims of hostilities and tensions, there are also those scholars who argue against the notion that there exists an inherent conflict between Muslim minority communities and their Western host societies, and it is this view that this study supports. Jonathan Laurence, for example, has traced the numerous efforts made by European governments to incorporate their Muslim communities and predicts that integration will continue to take place for the foreseeable future.[23] Whilst acknowledging that Islam is often at the centre of anxieties about migrant integration in Western Europe, Richard Alba and Nancy Foner have offered an insight into how religious tensions could potentially decrease as Western European countries become more familiar with Muslims and Islamic practices.[24] Adopting a historical approach, Leo Lucassen has challenged both the notion that migrant communities in Europe today are not achieving integration as quickly as their predecessors and the perception that Islam acts as an inherent barrier to integration.[25] John Bowen has argued that fears regarding Muslim integration in the West are greatly exaggerated and based on a series of myths and misunderstandings, and his research on *shari'a* councils has revealed the extent to which British Muslims have adapted to life in Britain and applied Islamic law and practice to a British context.[26] Furthermore, across both the national and local level in Britain, scholars have charted and assessed a number of consistent and visible ways in which Muslims have contributed to, and engaged constructively with, British society. They have, for example, cited their involvement and participation in the arts, entertainment, the mainstream media, sports, politics and civic initiatives, their entrepreneurial, housing and educational aspirations and accomplishments, and the manner in which they have succeeded in carving out political, religious and social spaces for themselves.[27]

This study has offered a unique historical insight into the integration of Muslim migrant communities in rural Britain. Its assessment of Wiltshire's local authority's policies, practices and strategies, and the county's Muslim migrant populations' grassroots migratory experiences, has revealed that integration has been both pursued and achieved across the post-1960s period as a result of action and commitment on both sides. Although Wiltshire's local government's measures and policies were at times ad hoc, sporadic, and lacking in scope, reach and resources, there appeared to exist a clear local political concern for the integration of its small, and often dispersed, Muslim communities. The county's Muslims' experiences by no means escaped incidents of discrimination, racism, constraint, Islamophobia and prejudice, yet a sense of agency and self-determination, a willingness to compromise and negotiate with regard to their interests and needs, and a capacity to perceive and use Islam as a conduit of integration, prevailed. Whilst the conclusions reached for Wiltshire can by no means claim to be fully applicable to rural Britain more broadly, they nevertheless reveal that there has long existed a rural dimension to the integration of Muslim migrant communities. Thereby, they join an ever-increasing number of studies relating to both Britain and beyond in advocating the need for further research into how the integration process unfolds in more peripheral non-metropolitan areas.[28]

This book has given a voice to both Muslim migrant communities and a local authority that have traditionally been written out of post-war British immigration history. In doing so, it has shown that despite compelling and persistent images of the rural idyll, Muslim settlement and integration have long been taking place in Wiltshire, and that therefore a more rural county with relatively small Muslim populations also has a role to play in wider debates on Britain's multicultural society. It has revealed how, on a local level, the challenges and opportunities presented by the migration process have been considered, and overcome and embraced, respectively. Thus, it champions the benefits of shifting academic attention away from the major conurbations of Muslim settlement, and the need to reassess the way in which we perceive and portray the more rural British landscape. Most importantly, it challenges us to rethink Muslim integration in Britain.

Notes

1 Sarah Neal and Julian Agyeman, 'Introduction', in Sarah Neal and Julian Agyeman (eds), *The New Countryside? Ethnicity, Nation and Exclusion in Contemporary Rural Britain* (Bristol: The Policy Press, 2006), p. 1. For an insight into Wiltshire's rural nature, see Joan Thirsk, *The Rural Economy of England* (London: The Hambledon Press, 1984); Michael Aston, *Interpreting the Landscape: Landscape Archaeology and Local History* (London: Batsford, 1985); and Joan Thirsk (ed.), *Rural England: An Illustrated History of the Landscape* (Oxford: Oxford University Press, 2000).

2 See Paul Milbourne, 'The local geographies of poverty: a rural case study', *Geoforum*, 35:5 (2004), 559–75; Wiltshire Community Foundation, *Wiltshire Uncovered Report 2014*; and Wiltshire Council, *Wiltshire Core Strategy* (January 2015).

3 See Muslim Council of Britain, *British Muslims in Numbers*, pp. 16, 25.

4 For an insight into the experiences of Muslims in Cambridge, East Kent and West Wales, see Ray and Reed, 'Community, mobility and racism in a semi-rural area'; Jones, 'Islam and the rural landscape'; Jones, 'Negotiating absence and presence'; and Villis and Hebing, 'Islam and Englishness'.

5   For example, see Derbyshire, *Not in Norfolk*; Dhalech, *Challenging Racism in the Rural Idyll*; Henderson and Kaur (eds), *Rural Racism in the UK*; Neal, 'Rural landscapes, representations and racism'; and Chakraborti and Garland (eds), *Rural Racism*.

6   See Birgit Jentsch and Myriam Simard (eds), *International Migration and Rural Areas: Cross-National Comparative Perspectives* (Abingdon: Routledge, 2009); and Stefan Kordel, Tobias Weidinger and Igor Jelen (eds), *Processes of Immigration in Rural Europe: The Status Quo, Implications and Development Strategies* (Newcastle upon Tyne: Cambridge Scholars Publishing, 2018).

7   See Paul, *Whitewashing Britain*; Joppke, *Immigration and the Nation-State*; Hansen, *Citizenship and Immigration in Post-war Britain*; and Hampshire, *Citizenship and Belonging*.

8   See Ball and Solomos (eds), *Race and Local Politics*; and Garbaye, *Getting into Local Power*.

9   See Ken Young and Naomi Connelly, *Policy and Practice in the Multi-racial City* (London: Policy Studies Institute, 1981); Herman Ouseley, 'Local authority race initiatives', in Martin Boddy and Colin Fudge (eds), *Local Socialism?: Labour Councils and New Left Alternatives* (Basingstoke: Macmillan, 1984), pp. 133–59; and Solomos, *Race and Racism in Britain*, pp. 95–116.

10 See Solomos, *Race and Racism in Britain*, pp. 97, 108; Caelesta Poppelaars and Peter Scholten, 'Two worlds apart: the divergence of national and local immigrant integration policies in the Netherlands', *Administration & Society*, 40:4 (2008), 335–57; Aude-Claire Fourot, 'Managing religious pluralism in Canadian cities: mosques in Montreal and Laval', in Tiziana Caponio and Maren Borkert (eds), *The Local Dimension of Migration Policymaking* (Amsterdam: Amsterdam University Press, 2010), pp. 135–59; Annika Marlen Hinze, *Turkish Berlin: Integration Policy & Urban Space* (Minneapolis, MN: University of Minnesota Press, 2013); and Els de Graauw and Floris Vermeulen, 'Cities and the politics of immigrant integration: a comparison of Berlin, Amsterdam, New York City, and San Francisco', *Journal of Ethnic and Migration Studies*, 42:6 (2016), 989–1012.

11 See Tiziana Caponio, Peter Scholten and Ricard Zapata-Barrero, 'Introduction: the governance of migration and diversity in cities', in Tiziana Caponio, Peter Scholten and Ricard Zapata-Barrero (eds), *The Routledge Handbook of the Governance of Migration and Diversity in Cities* (Abingdon: Routledge, 2019), p. 3.

12 For example, see Peter Scholten, 'Between national models and multi-level decoupling: the pursuit of multi-level governance in Dutch and UK policies towards migrant incorporation', *Journal of International Migration and Integration*, 17:4 (2016), 973–94; and Ricard Zapata-Barrero, Tiziana Caponio and Peter Scholten, 'Theorizing the "local turn" in a multi-level governance framework of analysis: a case study in immigrant policies', *International Review of Administrative Sciences*, 83:2 (2017), 241–6.

13 See Hopkins and Gale (eds), *Muslims in Britain*; and Glick Schiller and Çağlar (eds), *Locating Migration*.

14 See Nancy Foner, Jan Rath, Jan Willem Duyvendak and Rogier van Reekum (eds), *New York and Amsterdam: Immigration and the New Urban Landscape* (New York: New York University Press, 2014); Elizabeth Aranda, Sallie Hughes and Elena Sabogal, *Making a Life in Multiethnic Miami: Immigration and the Rise of a Global City* (Boulder, CO: Lynne Rienner, 2014); Jean Beaman, *Citizen Outsider: Children of North African Immigrants in France* (Oakland, CA: University of California Press, 2017); Back and Sinha, *Migrant City*; and Connell, *Black Handsworth*.

15 Ayşe Çağlar and Nina Glick Schiller, 'Introduction: migrants and cities', in Nina Glick Schiller and Ayşe Çağlar (eds), *Locating Migration: Rescaling Cities and Migrants* (Ithaca, NY: Cornell University Press, 2011), p. 1.

16 Peter Scholten, 'Part I – Migration, history and urban life. Introduction by Peter Scholten', in Tiziana Caponio, Peter Scholten and Ricard Zapata-Barrero (eds), *The Routledge Handbook of the Governance of Migration and Diversity in Cities* (Abingdon: Routledge, 2019), p. 9.

17 For one of the most important works in the global cities scholarship, see Saskia Sassen, *The Global City: New York, London, Tokyo* (Princeton, NJ: Princeton University Press, 1991). For a critique of restricting the study of migration to global cities, see Glick Schiller and Çağlar, 'Towards a comparative theory of locality in migration studies'.

18 Ayşe Çağlar and Nina Glick Schiller, 'A multiscalar perspective on cities and migration: a comment on the symposium', *Sociologica, Italian Journal of Sociology Online*, 2 (2015), 1. doi: 10.2383/81432. www.rivisteweb.it/download/article/10.2383/81432. See also Eduardo Barberis and Emmanuele Pavolini, 'Settling outside gateways. The state of the art, and the issues at stake', *Sociologica, Italian Journal of Sociology Online*, 2 (2015). doi:10.2383/81426. https://pdfs.semanticscholar.org/33f5/e74bfe1aca6dee638c3c0953010c493e daf7.pdf

19 See, for example, Yunas Samad, 'Book burning and race relations: political mobilisation of Bradford Muslims', *New Community*, 18:4 (1992), 507–19; John L. Esposito, *The Islamic Threat: Myth or Reality* (Oxford: Oxford University Press, 1999); Abbas (ed.), *Muslim Britain*; Zachary Shore, *Breeding Bin Ladens: America, Islam, and the Future of Europe* (Baltimore, MD: John Hopkins University Press, 2006); Bruce Bawer, *While Europe Slept: How Radical Islam is Destroying the West from Within* (New York: Doubleday, 2006); Tahir Abbas, 'Muslim minorities in Britain: integration, multiculturalism and radicalism in the post-7/7 period', *Journal of Intercultural Studies*, 28:3 (2007), 287–300; Husband and Alam, *Social Cohesion and Counter-terrorism: A Policy Contradiction?*; and Robert S. Leiken, *Europe's Angry Muslims: The Revolt of the Second Generation* (Oxford: Oxford University Press, 2012).

20 The importance of these factors is also recognised in Hopkins and Gale (eds), *Muslims in Britain*.

21 See Lucassen, *The Immigrant Threat*; and Jan Lucassen, Leo Lucassen and Patrick Manning (eds), *Migration History in World History: Multidisciplinary Approaches* (Leiden: Brill, 2010).

22   See Ansari, *'The Infidel Within'*; and Gilliat-Ray, *Muslims in Britain*.

23   Laurence, *The Emancipation of Europe's Muslims*.

24   Alba and Foner, *Strangers No More*.

25   Lucassen, *The Immigrant Threat*.

26   John Bowen, *Blaming Islam* (Cambridge, MA: MIT Press, 2012); and Bowen, *On British Islam*.

27   See Richard Phillips (ed.), *Muslim Spaces of Hope* (London: Zed Books, 2009); Gilliat-Ray, *Muslims in Britain*; Ahmad and Sardar (eds), *Muslims in Britain*; Hackett, *Foreigners, Minorities and Integration*; Carolina Ivanescu, 'Leicester Muslims: citizenship, race and civil religion', in Jørgen S. Nielsen (ed.), *Muslim Political Participation in Europe* (Edinburgh: Edinburgh University Press, 2013), pp. 277–96; Timothy Peace (ed.), *Muslims and Political Participation in Britain* (Abingdon: Routledge, 2015); and Peter Hopkins (ed.), *Scotland's Muslims: Society, Politics and Identity* (Edinburgh: Edinburgh University Press, 2017).

28   For example, see Douglas Massey (ed.), *New Faces in New Places: The Changing Geography of American Immigration* (New York: Russell Sage Foundation, 2008); Ricard Morén-Alegret, 'Ruralphilia and urbophobia versus urbophilia and ruralphobia? Lessons from immigrant integration processes in small towns and rural areas in Spain', *Population, Space and Place*, 14:6 (2008), 537–52; Anita Cvetkovic, 'The integration of immigrants in Northern Sweden: a case study of the municipality of Strömsund', *International Migration*, 47:1 (2009), 101–31; Jentsch and Simard (eds), *International Migration and Rural Areas*; and McAreavey, *New Immigration Destinations*.

Bibliography

Wiltshire and Swindon History Centre (WSHC), Chippenham

F1/100/39, Wiltshire County Council Development Committee Minutes, 1963–1969

F1/101/5/1, Wiltshire County Council Policy, later Policy and Resources, Committee Minutes, 1973–1986

F1/101/5/3, Wiltshire County Council Policy, later Policy and Resources, Committee Minutes, 1993–1995

F1/101/5/5, Wiltshire County Council Policy, later Policy and Resources, Committee Minutes, 1998–2001

F1/101/7/5, Wiltshire County Council Economic Development and Environment Committee and Subcommittees Minutes 1996–1998

F1/101/10/1, Wiltshire County Council Education Committee Minutes, 1973–1981

F1/101/10/2, Wiltshire County Council Education Committee Minutes, 1982–1990

F1/101/10/3, Wiltshire County Council Education Committee Minutes, 1991–1995

F1/102/1–4/7–8/11, Wiltshire County Council Miscellaneous Joint Committees, Minutes and Agenda Papers, 1977–1996

F1/201/5/1, Wiltshire County Council Policy and Resources Committee Agenda Papers, 1973–2002

F1/201/7/4, Wiltshire County Council Economic Development and Environment Committee Agenda Papers, 1996–1998

F1/201/10/1, Wiltshire County Council Education Committee Agenda Papers, 1973–2001

F1/201/10/2, Wiltshire County Council Finance and General Purposes Subcommittee of Education Committee Agenda Papers, 1973–1990

F1/201/10/3, Wiltshire County Council Schools Subcommittee of Education Committee Agenda Papers, 1973–1996

F1/201/14/1, Wiltshire County Council Social Services Committee Agenda Papers, 1973–2001

F1/201/20, Wiltshire County Council Cabinet Agenda Papers, 2001–date

F1/202/8, Wiltshire County Council Joint Consultative Forum on Economic Development Agenda Papers, 1987–1995

F1/360/9, Wiltshire County Council, The Wiltshire Compact – a strategy to improve working arrangements between Wiltshire County Council and the voluntary and community sector, 2005

F1/360/12, Wiltshire County Council, 'No Barriers Week' (1–5 December): Disability Equality Wiltshire, brochure, 2008–2011

F8/100/109, Wiltshire County Council Education Department, Schools Policy Correspondence, Curriculum Development – Religious Education, 1974–1979

F8/100/118, Wiltshire County Council Education Department, Schools Policy Correspondence, Religious Education Standing Advisory Council, 1978–1986

F8/100/124, Wiltshire County Council Education Department, Schools Policy Correspondence, Multicultural Advisory Group, 1983–1992

F8/194/33, Wiltshire County Council Education Department, Youth Employment Correspondence, Equal Opportunities – Racial Equality – Gender Disability, 1986–1992

F8/933/E.B.26, Swindon Borough Education Committee, Elementary Education Correspondence Files, Basic Subjects – Immigrant Pupils, 1953–1973

F8/933/E.B.26a, Swindon Borough Education Committee, Elementary Education Correspondence Files, Basic Subjects – General, 1965–1974

F8/933/E.B.26b, Swindon Borough Education Committee, Elementary Education Correspondence Files, Basic Subjects – Immigrant Pupils, 1973–1974

F8/933/H.Y.88(a), Swindon Borough Education Committee, Correspondence Higher Education, Immigrants and Youth Service, 1967–1973

F8/933/H.Y.88(b), Swindon Borough Education Committee, Correspondence Higher Education, Swindon Council for Community Relations, 1968–1976

G6/132/105, Highworth Rural District Council, Clerk's Correspondence, Resettlement of Ugandan Asians, 1972–1973

G15/100/61, Trowbridge Urban District Council, Printed Council and Committee Minutes, 1972–1973

G23/132/89, Salisbury City Council, Clerk's Correspondence, Resettlement of Ugandan Asians, 1972

G24/132/1095, Swindon Borough Council, Finance and Law Committee Correspondence Files, Swindon Council for Community Relations, 1968–1972

G28/1/1/2/5, North Wiltshire District Council – Executive Committee Volume 5, Minutes and Agenda Papers, February–March 2001

G28/1/1/2/8, North Wiltshire District Council – Executive Committee Volume 8, Minutes and Agenda Papers, September–December 2001

G28/1/1/2/15, North Wiltshire District Council – Executive Committee Volume 15, Minutes and Agenda Papers, September–November 2003

G28/1/1/3/2, North Wiltshire District Council – Cabinet Committee Volume 2, Minutes and Agenda Papers, September 1999–January 2000

G28/1/1/5/5, North Wiltshire District Council – Community Services Committee Volume 5, Minutes and Agenda Papers, May 1987–March 1988

G28/1/1/5/8, North Wiltshire District Council – Community Services Committee Volume 8, Minutes and Agenda Papers, May 1990–April 1991

G28/1/1/23/1, North Wiltshire District Council – Policy and Resources Committee Volume 1, Minutes and Agenda Papers, July 1974–April 1979

G28/1/1/69/2, North Wiltshire District Council – Local Joint Consultative Committee Volume 2, Minutes and Agenda Papers, October 2004–December 2005

G29/1/1/1/4, Salisbury District Council, Cabinet Minutes and Agenda Papers, September 2002–November 2002

G29/1/1/8/4, Salisbury District Council, Housing Committee Minutes and Agenda Papers, May 2000–September 2001

G29/1/1/15/1, Salisbury District Council, Finance Committee Agendas, June 1975–September 1980

G30/Box807, Swindon Borough Council, Community Development Committee Agenda Papers, 1974–1984

G30/Box811, Swindon Borough Council, Community Development: Race Relations, Agenda Papers, 1980–1996

G30/Box922, Swindon Borough Council, Annual Reports, Standing Orders and Bye-Laws

G30/Box924, Swindon Borough Council, Publications and Reports

G31/1/1/2/8, West Wiltshire District Council, Housing and Sub-Committee Agendas, January–December 1980

G31/1/1/2/9, West Wiltshire District Council, Housing and Sub-Committee Agendas, January–December 1981

G31/1/1/2/14, West Wiltshire District Council, Housing and Sub-Committee Agendas, February–December 1986

G31/1/1/2/19, West Wiltshire District Council, Housing and Sub-committee Agendas, January–November 1991

G31/1/1/8/2, West Wiltshire District Council, Cabinet Agendas, January–December 2002

G31/1/1/8/3, West Wiltshire District Council, Cabinet Agendas, January–December 2003

G31/1/1/8/4, West Wiltshire District Council, Cabinet Agendas, January–December 2004

G31/1/1/8/8, West Wiltshire District Council, Cabinet Agendas, January–November 2008

G31/1/1/9/4, West Wiltshire District Council, Environment Sub-Committees Agendas, January–November 1977

G31/1/1/9/12, West Wiltshire District Council, Environment Sub-Committees Agendas, February–December 1985

G31/1/1/9/13, West Wiltshire District Council, Environment Sub-Committees Agendas, February–December 1986

G31/1/1/53/20, West Wiltshire District Council, Local Joint Consultative Committee and Sub-Committees, Minutes and Agenda Papers, February–September 1992

G31/1/2/7, West Wiltshire District Council Signed Minutes, January–December 1977

G31/1/2/9, West Wiltshire District Council Signed Minutes, November 1977–November 1978

G31/1/2/23, West Wiltshire District Council Signed Minutes, January–December 1985

G31/1/2/25, West Wiltshire District Council Signed Minutes October 1985–December 1986

G31/1/2/27, West Wiltshire District Council Signed Minutes, January 1987–December 1987

G31/1/2/34, West Wiltshire District Council Signed Minutes, January–December 1991

G31/1/2/36, West Wiltshire District Council Signed Minutes, January–December 1993

G31/1/100/132, West Wiltshire District Council, Local Joint Consultative Committee and Subcommittees, Signed Minutes, February–November 2000

1802/115/2, Community Council for Wiltshire, Correspondence: Community Care and Social Services, Newcomers to Devizes Leaflet, 1968–1974

3231/1, Wiltshire Racial Equality Council, Reports of Meetings Relating to the Formation of the Council and Annual General Meeting Minutes, 1976–1991

3231/2, Wiltshire Racial Equality Council, Council Minutes, 1988–1991

3231/3, Wiltshire Racial Equality Council, Council Minutes, 1991–1997

3231/7, Wiltshire Racial Equality Council, Council Agenda Papers, 1988–1997

3231/8: Wiltshire Racial Equality Council, Education Action Group Minutes and Correspondence, 1998–1999

3231/10, Wiltshire Racial Equality Council, Annual Reports with Annual General Meeting Minutes for the North and West Wiltshire Council for Racial Equality, 1983–1991

3231/11, Wiltshire Racial Equality Council, Annual Reports with Annual General Meeting Minutes, 1991–2000

3231/24, Wiltshire Racial Equality Council, Papers of Anti-Discriminatory Working Group, Later the Wiltshire Anti-Racial Network, 1994–1995

3299/42, Swindon: Manchester Road, Correspondence about the use of rooms by the Moslem community, 1992–1996

3332/29, Devizes Town Council, Council Minutes with Agenda Papers, 2007–2008

3371/121, Voluntary Action Swindon, Management Information, Reports on day care provision for elderly mentally dependent people and the Community Care Plans, growth provision and Bangladeshi women, 1979–1993

Local councils, uncatalogued material

Swindon Borough Council Unsigned Minutes, 1999–2000

Trowbridge Town Council meeting, 20 September 2005

Trowbridge Town Council meeting, 15 November 2005

Trowbridge Town Council, Town Clerk's Report to Policy and Resources Committee, 9 January 2007

Trowbridge Town Council meeting, 17 March 2009

Trowbridge Town Council, Town Clerk's Report to Policy and Resources Committee, 1 March 2011

Wiltshire Council, Trowbridge Area Board, 15 March 2012

Roundway Parish Council minutes, 20 October 2014
Wiltshire Council, Trowbridge Area Board, 16 July 2015
Wiltshire Council, Wiltshire Police and Crime Panel, 4 February 2016
Melksham Town Council, Policy and Resources Committee, 16 January 2017
Wiltshire Council, Melksham Area Board, 6 September 2017
Highworth Town Council minutes, 19 June 2018
Wiltshire Council, planning number 18/00239/FUL, planning application and
    supporting documents for cemetery in Salisbury, 2018

Oral history interviews (name, gender, ethnic background,
date(s) of interview)

Wali, male, Indian, 28 April 2016 and 18 May 2016
Kamel, male, Tunisian, 6 May 2016
Muhammad, male, Pakistani, 16 May 2016
Anonymous, female, Bangladeshi, 18 May 2016
Junab, male, Bangladeshi, 27 May 2016
Khan, male, Pakistani, 28 May 2016
Mahmood, male, Pakistani, 28 May 2016
Anonymous, female, Pakistani, 28 May 2016
Touria, female, Moroccan, 3 June 2016
Farzana, female, Pakistani, 13 June 2016
Mehmet, male, Turkish, 16 June 2016
Anonymous, female, Bangladeshi, 26 June 2016
Anser, male, Pakistani, 15 September 2016
Shahid, male, Pakistani, 15 September 2016
Anonymous female, Bangladeshi, 26 September 2016
Omar, male, Saudi, 28 September 2016
Anonymous, male, Bangladeshi, 28 September 2016
Onder, male, Turkish, 7 November 2016
Abdel, male, Moroccan, 17 November 2016
Anonymous, female, Bangladeshi, 18 November 2016
Azad, male, Bangladeshi, 28 November 2016
Anonymous, female, Bangladeshi, 28 November 2016
Anonymous, Moroccan couple, 1 December 2016
Anonymous, female, Moroccan, 1 December 2016
Shazuli, male, Sri Lankan, 1 December 2016
Hajra and Awais, Pakistani, 4 December 2016
Atiff, male, Pakistani, 5 December 2016
Zoubida, female, Moroccan, 8 December 2016
Anonymous, female, Moroccan, 8 December 2016
Atiqul, male, Bangladeshi, 9 December 2016
Kantha, female, Bangladeshi, 9 December 2016
Ozay, male, Turkish, 29 January 2017

Selvi, female, Turkish, 29 January 2017
Jilali, male, Moroccan, 30 January 2017
Ala, male, Bangladeshi, 26 March 2017
Radia, female, Bangladeshi, 30 March 2017
Anonymous, male, Bangladeshi, 28 June 2017
Sohidul, male, Bangladeshi, 30 October 2017

Media

'A Touch of the Taj Mahals', *Wiltshire Times and News* (17 January 1964)
'£40 Fine for Assault on Pakistani', *Wiltshire Times and News* (24 November 1967)
Anne Tomkinson, 'Swindon's Town Hall Becomes Community's "Mosque"', *Evening Advertiser* (5 February 1970)
'Muslims' Ritual Slaughter Raises Outcry', *Wiltshire Times and News* (28 January 1977)
'Investigation of Colour Bar Claim at Bradford', *Wiltshire Times* (6 May 1977)
Paul Wilenius, 'Club Sparks Racist Row', *Evening Advertiser* (14 September 1977)
'Bid to Beat Racism', *Evening Advertiser* (15 October 1983)
Robert Buckland, 'Anger at Mosque Go-ahead', *Evening Advertiser* (8 October 1993)
David Vallis, 'Meeting Room Battle is Over', *Salisbury Times* (2 March 1999)
Jay Rayner, 'The Hidden Truths Behind Race Crimes in Britain', *Observer* (18 February 2001)
Ben Fitzgerald, 'So Proud to be Swindonian!', *Evening Advertiser* (1 October 2001)
'VIP in Visit to Mosque', *Gazette & Herald* (28 January 2005)
Morwenna Blake, 'Moroccan Town Link Bid Takes Big Step Forward', *Wiltshire Times* (22 March 2006)
'Market Town Twins with Arab City', *BBC News* (3 October 2006)
Benjamin Parkes, 'Moroccan Centre Plan Falls Flat', *Wiltshire Times* (20 September 2007)
'Trowbridge in Wiltshire First in Britain to be Twinned with Muslim Arab Town', *Telegraph* (27 March 2009)
Stina Backer, 'Pork Pies Help Build Civic Links with Muslim Town', *Independent* (28 March 2009)
Christopher Hope, 'Islamic March through Wootton Bassett Should not be Banned, Says Sir Hugh Orde', *Telegraph* (5 January 2010)
Nicola Curtis, 'Anger in Trowbridge at Islamic March', *Wiltshire Times* (8 January 2010)
'Mosque Bid Withdrawn After Devizes Residents Object to London Road Location', *Gazette & Herald* (18 December 2014)
Tanya Yilmaz, 'Trowbridge Family to Serve up Moroccan Flavours on BBC Food Show', *Wiltshire Times* (27 June 2015)
Nigel Slater: Eating Together, Sharing Plates, BBC One (29 June 2015)
Andrew Lawton, 'Cafe India Celebrates Decade of Business in Chippenham', *Gazette & Herald* (19 January 2016)

Tanya Yilmaz, 'Trowbridge Mosque Opens its Doors to Address Misconceptions of Religion', *Wiltshire Times* (3 August 2016)

'Muslim Community Welcomes Cemetery Decision', *Wiltshire Times* (14 September 2017)

Rebecca Hudson, 'New Cemetery Planned for City as Existing Graveyards Reach Capacity', *Salisbury Journal* (5 February 2018)

Harriet Sherwood, 'First Mosque Opens on Outer Hebrides in Time for Ramadan', *Guardian* (11 May 2018)

Tom Rowley, 'The B-Road to Mecca: Britain's Rural Muslims are a Minority within a Minority', *The Economist* (17 May 2018)

'Mayors Celebrate Ramadan at Swindon Mosque', *Swindon Advertiser* (7 June 2018)

Speeches

Trevor Phillips, 'After 7/7: Sleepwalking to Segregation', Speech to the Manchester Council for Community Relations (22 September 2005)

PM David Cameron's Speech at Munich Security Conference (5 February 2011)

Legislation

Race Relations (Amendment) Act 2000; www.legislation.gov.uk/ukpga/2000/34/contents (accessed 21 January 2019)

Secondary sources and official reports

Abbas, Tahir (ed.), *Muslim Britain: Communities under Pressure* (London: Zed Books, 2005)

Abbas, Tahir, 'Muslim minorities in Britain: integration, multiculturalism and radicalism in the post-7/7 period', *Journal of Intercultural Studies*, 28:3 (2007), 287–300

—— 'Sparkbrook, housing classes & the market situation: forty years on', in Tahir Abbas and Frank Reeves (eds), *Immigration and Race Relations: Sociological Theory and John Rex* (London: I.B. Tauris, 2007), pp. 121–34

—— *Islamic Radicalism and Multicultural Politics: The British Experience* (Abingdon: Routledge, 2011)

Abbas, Tahir and Anwar, Muhammad, 'An analysis of race equality policy and practice in the city of Birmingham, UK', *Local Government Studies*, 31:1 (2005), 53–68

Afridi, Asif, *From Benign Neglect to Citizen Khan: 30 Years of Equalities Practice in Birmingham* (Birmingham: BRAP, 2015)

Ager, Alastair and Strang, Alison, 'Understanding integration: a conceptual framework', *Journal of Refugee Studies*, 21:2 (2008), 166–91

Agyeman, Julian and Spooner, Rachel, 'Ethnicity and the rural environment', in Paul Cloke and Jo Little (eds), *Contested Countryside Cultures: Otherness, Marginalisation and Rurality* (London: Routledge, 1997), pp. 197–217

Ahmad, Waqar, ' "Creating a society of sheep"? British Muslim elite on mosques and imams', in Waqar Ahmad and Ziauddin Sardar (eds), *Muslims in Britain: Making Social and Political Space* (Abingdon: Routledge, 2012), pp. 171–92

Ahmad, Waqar and Sardar, Ziauddin (eds), *Muslims in Britain: Making Social and Political Space* (Abingdon: Routledge, 2012)

Ahmed, Nazneen, 'Marking a good death: Muslim burial sites and practices in Britain from 1800 to the present', in Jane Garnett and Alana Harris (eds), *Rescripting Religion in the City: Migration and Religious Identity in the Modern Metropolis* (Abingdon: Routledge, 2013), pp. 103–14

Akhtar, Parveen, *British Muslim Politics: Examining Pakistani Biraderi Networks* (Basingstoke: Palgrave Macmillan, 2013)

Aksoy, Asu, 'Transnational virtues and cool loyalties: responses of Turkish-speaking migrants in London to September 11', *Journal of Ethnic and Migration Studies*, 32:6 (2006), 923–46

Alba, Richard and Foner, Nancy, *Strangers No More: Immigration and the Challenges of Integration in North America and Western Europe* (Princeton, NJ: Princeton University Press, 2015)

Alexander, Michael, *Cities and Labour Immigration: Comparing Policy Responses in Amsterdam, Paris, Rome and Tel Aviv* (Aldershot: Ashgate, 2007)

Ali, Amir, *South Asian Islam and British Multiculturalism* (Abingdon: Routledge, 2016)

Ali, N., Kalra, V.S. and Sayyid, S. (eds), *A Postcolonial People: South Asians in Britain* (London: Hurst, 2006)

Ali, Rahielah and Hopkins, Peter, 'Everyday making and civic engagement among Muslim women in Scotland', in Waqar Ahmad and Ziauddin Sardar (eds), *Muslims in Britain: Making Social and Political Space* (Abingdon: Routledge, 2012), pp. 141–55

Alibhai-Brown, Yasmin, *After Multiculturalism* (London: Foreign Policy Centre, 2000)

Allen, Chris, *Islamophobia* (Farnham: Ashgate, 2010)

—— 'Still a challenge for us all? The Runnymede Trust, Islamophobia and policy', in Dawn Llewellyn and Sonya Sharma (eds), *Religion, Equalities, and Inequalities* (Abingdon: Routledge, 2016), pp. 113–24

Al-Rasheed, Madawi, 'The other-others: hidden Arabs?', in Ceri Peach (ed.), *Ethnicity in the 1991 Census, Volume 2: The Ethnic Minority Populations of Great Britain* (London: HMSO, 1996), pp. 206–20

Altinay, Levent and Altinay, Eser, 'Factors influencing business growth: the rise of Turkish entrepreneurship in the UK', *International Journal of Entrepreneurial Behavior & Research*, 14:1 (2008), 24–46

Ansari, Humayun, *Muslims in Britain* (London: Minority Rights Group International, 2002)

——— *'The Infidel Within': Muslims in Britain since 1800* (London: Hurst, 2004)

Ansari, Humayun (ed.), *The Making of the East London Mosque, 1910–1951: Minutes of the London Mosque Fund and East London Mosque Trust Ltd* (Cambridge: Cambridge University Press, 2011)

Anwar, Muhammad, Roach, Patrick and Sondhi, Ranjit, 'Introduction' in Muhammad Anwar, Patrick Roach and Ranjit Sondhi (eds), *From Legislation to Integration? Race Relations in Britain* (Basingstoke: Macmillan Press, 2000), pp. 1–23

Aranda, Elizabeth, Hughes, Sallie and Sabogal, Elena, *Making a Life in Multiethnic Miami: Immigration and the Rise of a Global City* (Boulder, CO: Lynne Rienner, 2014)

Askins, Kye, 'Crossing divides: ethnicity and rurality', *Journal of Rural Studies*, 25:4 (2009), 365–75

Aston, Michael, *Interpreting the Landscape: Landscape Archaeology and Local History* (London: Batsford, 1985)

Atay, Tayfun, '"Ethnicity within ethnicity" among the Turkish-speaking immigrants in London', *Insight Turkey*, 12:1 (2010), 123–38

Back, Les and Sinha, Shamser, *Migrant City* (Abingdon: Routledge, 2018)

Bagley, Christopher, 'Immigrant children: a review of problems and policy in education', *Journal of Social Policy*, 2:4 (1973), 303–15

Ball, Wendy, Gulam, William and Troyna, Barry, 'Pragmatism or retreat? Funding policy, local government and the marginalisation of anti-racist education', in Wendy Ball and John Solomos (eds), *Race and Local Politics* (Basingstoke: Macmillan, 1990), pp. 78–94

Ball, Wendy and Solomos, John (eds), *Race and Local Politics* (Basingstoke: Macmillan, 1990)

Ballard, Roger (ed.), *Desh Pardesh: The South Asian Presence in Britain* (London: Hurst, 1994)

Ballard, Roger, 'Negotiating race and ethnicity: exploring the implications of the 1991 Census', *Patterns of Prejudice*, 30:3 (1996), 3–33

Bano, Samia, *Muslim Women and Shari'ah Councils: Transcending the Boundaries of Community and Law* (Basingstoke: Palgrave Macmillan, 2012)

Barberis, Eduardo and Pavolini, Emmanuele, 'Settling outside gateways. The state of the art, and the issues at stake', *Sociologica, Italian Journal of Sociology Online*, 2 (2015). doi:10.2383/81426. https://pdfs.semanticscholar.org/33f5/e74bfe1aca 6dee638c3c0953010c493edaf7.pdf (accessed 20 January 2020)

Barrett, Giles A., Jones, Trevor P. and McEvoy, David, 'Socio-economic and policy dimensions of the mixed embeddedness of ethnic minority business in Britain', *Journal of Ethnic and Migration Studies*, 27:2 (2001), 241–58

Barton, Stephen, *The Bengali Muslims of Bradford: A Study of Their Observance of Islam with Special Reference to the Function of the Mosque and the Work of the Imam* (Leeds: University of Leeds, 1986)

Bashi, Vilna Francine, *Survival of the Knitted: Immigrant Social Networks in a Stratified World* (Stanford, CA: Stanford University Press, 2007)

Basu, Anuradha, 'An exploration of entrepreneurial activity among Asian small businesses in Britain', *Small Business Economics*, 10:4 (1998), 313–26

Basu, Anuradha and Altinay, Eser, 'The interaction between culture and entrepreneurship in London's immigrant businesses', *International Small Business Journal*, 20:4 (2002), 371–93

—— and Altinay, Eser, *Family and Work in Minority Ethnic Businesses* (Bristol: The Policy Press, 2003)

Bavin, W.D., *Swindon's War Record* (Swindon: John Drew Ltd, 1922)

Bawer, Bruce, *While Europe Slept: How Radical Islam is Destroying the West from Within* (New York: Doubleday, 2006)

Beaman, Jean, *Citizen Outsider: Children of North African Immigrants in France* (Oakland, CA: University of California Press, 2017)

Beckinsale, R.P., *The Trowbridge Woollen Industry as Illustrated by the Stock Books of John and Thomas Clark 1804–1824* (Devizes: Wiltshire Archaeological and Natural History Society, 1951)

Benmayor, Rina and Skotnes, Andor (eds), *Migration & Identity* (Oxford: Oxford University Press, 1994)

Ben-Tovim, Gideon, Gabriel, John, Law, Ian and Stredder, Kathleen, 'A political analysis of local struggles for racial equality', in John Rex and David Mason (eds), *Theories of Race and Ethnic Relations* (Cambridge: Cambridge University Press, 1986), pp. 131–52

Blackstone, Tessa, Parekh, Bhikhu and Sanders, Peter (eds), *Race Relations in Britain: A Developing Agenda* (Abingdon: Routledge, 1998)

Bleich, Erik, *Race Politics in Britain and France: Ideas and Policymaking since the 1960s* (Cambridge: Cambridge University Press, 2003)

Borkert, Maren and Caponio, Tiziana, 'Introduction: the local dimension of migration policymaking', in Tiziana Caponio and Maren Borkert (eds), *The Local Dimension of Migration Policymaking* (Amsterdam: Amsterdam University Press, 2010), pp. 9–32

Bowen, Innes, *Medina in Birmingham, Najaf in Brent: Inside British Islam* (London: Hurst & Co, 2014)

Bowen, John, *Blaming Islam* (Cambridge, MA: MIT Press, 2012)

—— *On British Islam: Religion, Law, and Everyday Practice in Shari'a Councils* (Princeton, NJ: Princeton University Press, 2016)

Brah, Avtar, *Cartographies of Diaspora: Contesting Identities* (London: Routledge, 1996)

Bressey, Caroline, 'Cultural archaeology and historical geographies of the black presence in rural England', *Journal of Rural Studies*, 25:4 (2009), 386–95

Bristol City Council, *Equality and Inclusion Policy and Strategy 2018–2023* (2018)

Brown, Cynthia, 'Moving on: reflections on oral history and migrant communities in Britain', *Oral History*, 34:1 (2006), 69–80

Buettner, Elizabeth, ' "Going for an Indian": South Asian restaurants and the limits of multiculturalism in Britain', *The Journal of Modern History*, 80:4 (2008), 865–901

Bugg, Laura, 'Religion on the fringe: the representation of space and minority religious facilities in the rural–urban fringe of metropolitan Sydney, Australia', *Australian Geographer*, 43:3 (2012), 273–89

Bulpitt, Jim, 'Continuity, autonomy and peripheralisation: the anatomy of the centre's race statecraft in England', in Zig Layton-Henry and Paul B. Rich (eds), *Race, Government and Politics in Britain* (Basingstoke: Macmillan, 1986), pp. 17–44

Burchardt, Jeremy, *Paradise Lost: Rural Idyll and Social Change since 1800* (London: I.B. Tauris, 2002)

Burdsey, Daniel, ' "The foreignness is still quite visible in this town": multiculture, marginality and prejudice at the English seaside', *Patterns of Prejudice*, 47:2 (2013), 95–116

Burrell, Kathy, *Moving Lives: Narratives of Nation and Migration among Europeans in Post-war Britain* (Aldershot: Ashgate, 2006)

Burrell, Kathy and Panayi, Panikos (eds), *Histories and Memories: Migrants and Their History in Britain* (London: I.B. Tauris, 2006)

Butler, Tim and Hamnett, Chris, *Ethnicity, Class and Aspiration: Understanding London's New East End* (Bristol: The Policy Press, 2011)

Çağlar, Ayşe and Glick Schiller, Nina, 'Introduction: migrants and cities', in Nina Glick Schiller and Ayşe Çağlar (eds), *Locating Migration: Rescaling Cities and Migrants* (Ithaca, NY: Cornell University Press, 2011), pp. 1–19

Çağlar, Ayşe and Glick Schiller, Nina, 'A multiscalar perspective on cities and migration: a comment on the symposium', *Sociologica, Italian Journal of Sociology Online*, 2 (2015). doi: 10.2383/81432. www.rivisteweb.it/download/article/10.2383/81432 (accessed 20 January 2020)

Candappa, Mano and Joly, Danièle, *Local Authorities, Ethnic Minorities and 'Pluralist Integration': A Study in Five Local Authority Areas* (University of Warwick: Monograph Series in Ethnic Relations No. 7, 1994)

Cantle, Ted, *Community Cohesion: A New Framework for Race and Diversity* (Basingstoke: Palgrave Macmillan, 2005)

Caponio, Tiziana and Borkert, Maren (eds), *The Local Dimension of Migration Policymaking* (Amsterdam: Amsterdam University Press, 2010)

Caponio, Tiziana, Scholten, Peter and Zapata-Barrero, Ricard, 'Introduction: the governance of migration and diversity in cities', in Tiziana Caponio, Peter Scholten and Ricard Zapata-Barrero (eds), *The Routledge Handbook of the Governance of Migration and Diversity in Cities* (Abingdon: Routledge, 2019), pp. 1–7.

——, Scholten, Peter and Zapata-Barrero, Ricard (eds), *The Routledge Handbook of the Governance of Migration and Diversity in Cities* (Abingdon: Routledge, 2019)

Casey, Louise, *The Casey Review: A Review into Opportunity and Integration* (London: Department for Communities and Local Government, 2016)

Chakraborti, Neil, 'Beyond "passive apartheid"? Developing policy and research agendas on rural racism in Britain', *Journal of Ethnic and Migration Studies*, 36:3 (2010), 501–17

Chakraborti, Neil and Garland, Jon, 'An "invisible" problem? Uncovering the nature of racist victimisation in rural Suffolk', *International Review of Victimology*, 10:1 (2003), 1–17

—— and Garland, Jon, 'England's green and pleasant land? Examining racist prejudice in a rural context', *Patterns of Prejudice*, 38:4 (2004), 383–98

—— and Garland, Jon, 'Introduction: justifying the study of racism in the rural', in Neil Chakraborti and Jon Garland (eds), *Rural Racism* (Abingdon: Routledge, 2011), pp. 1–13

—— and Garland, Jon (eds), *Rural Racism* (Abingdon: Routledge, 2011)

Chamberlain, Mary, *Family Love in the Diaspora: Migration and the Anglo-Caribbean Experience* (New Brunswick, NJ: Transaction Publishers, 2006)

Cherti, Myriam, 'Reconstructing the history of Moroccan migration to the UK: an oral history approach', *Beihefte der Francia*, 62 (2006), 169–78

—— *Paradoxes of Social Capital: A Multi-Generational Study of Moroccans in London* (Amsterdam: Amsterdam University Press, 2008)

—— *British Moroccans – Citizenship in Action* (London: Runnymede Trust, 2009)

Chivers, T.S., *Race and Culture in Education: Issues Arising from the Swann Committee Report* (Windsor: NFER-Nelson, 1987)

Choudhury, Tufyal, *Muslims in the UK: Policies for Engaged Citizens* (New York and Budapest: Open Society Institute, 2005)

Clark, Ken and Drinkwater, Stephen, 'Recent trends in minority ethnic entrepreneurship in Britain', *International Small Business Journal*, 28:2 (2010), 136–46

Clark, Ken, Drinkwater, Stephen and Robinson, Catherine, 'Self-employment amongst migrant groups: new evidence from England and Wales', *Small Business Economics*, 48:4 (2017), 1047–69

Cloke, Paul, 'Knowing ruralities?', in Paul Cloke (ed.), *Country Visions* (Harlow: Pearson Education Limited, 2003), pp. 1–13

Cloke, Paul and Little, Jo (eds), *Contested Countryside Cultures: Otherness, Marginalisation and Rurality* (London: Routledge, 1997)

Cloke, Paul, Milbourne, Paul and Widdowfield, Rebekah, *Rural Homelessness: Issues, Experiences and Policy Responses* (Bristol: The Policy Press, 2002)

Coard, Bernard, *How the West Indian Child is Made Educationally Subnormal in the British School System: The Scandal of the Black Child in Schools in Britain* (London: New Beacon for the Caribbean Education and Community Workers' Association, 1971)

Commission for Racial Equality (CRE), *Youth in Multi-racial Society: The Urgent Need for New Policies; the Fire Next Time* (London, 1980)

—— (CRE), *Race and Council Housing in Hackney: Report of a Formal Investigation* (London, 1984)

—— (CRE), *Code of Practice in Rented Housing: For the Elimination of Racial Discrimination and the Promotion of Equal Opportunities* (London, 1991)

Commission on Integration and Cohesion, *Our Shared Future* (Wetherby, 2007)

Commission on the Future of Multi-Ethnic Britain, *The Future of Multi-Ethnic Britain (The Parekh Report)* (London: Profile Books, 2000)

Communities and Local Government, *The Moroccan Muslim Community in England: Understanding Muslim Ethnic Communities* (London, 2009)

—— *The Turkish and Turkish Cypriot Muslim Community in England: Understanding Muslim Ethnic Communities* (London, 2009)

—— *Creating the Conditions for Integration* (London, 2012)

Communities and Local Government Committee, *Preventing Violent Extremism: Sixth Report of Session 2009–10* (London: House of Commons, 2010)

Community Cohesion Independent Review Team, *Community Cohesion: A Report of the Independent Review Team, Chaired by Ted Cantle (Cantle Report)* (London: Home Office, 2001)

Connell, Kieran, *Black Handsworth: Race in 1980s Britain* (Oakland, CA: University of California Press, 2019)

Connolly, Paul, "'It goes without saying (well, sometimes)": racism, Whiteness and identity in Northern Ireland', in Sarah Neal and Julian Agyeman (eds), *The New Countryside?: Ethnicity, Nation and Exclusion in Contemporary Rural Britain* (Bristol: The Policy Press, 2006), pp. 21–46

Crawford, T.S., *Wiltshire and the Great War: Training the Empire's Soldiers* (Ramsbury: The Crowood Press Ltd, 2012)

Crittall, Elizabeth (ed.), 'Economic History', in *A History of the County of Wiltshire: Volume 4* (London, 1959). *British History Online* www.british-history. ac.uk/vch/wilts/vol4/pp1-6 (accessed 18 July 2017)

—— (ed.), 'Other Industries', in *A History of the County of Wiltshire: Volume 4* (London, 1959) *British History Online* www.british-history.ac.uk/vch/wilts/ vol4/pp220-253 (accessed 18 July 2017)

Cvetkovic, Anita, 'The integration of immigrants in Northern Sweden: a case study of the municipality of Strömsund', *International Migration*, 47:1 (2009), 101–31

Dahya, Badr, 'Pakistanis in Britain: transients or settlers?', *Race*, 14:3 (1973), 241–77

—— 'The nature of Pakistani ethnicity in industrial cities in Britain', in Abner Cohen (ed.), *Urban Ethnicity* (London: Tavistock, 1974), pp. 77–118

Daniels, Stephen, *Fields of Vision: Landscape Imagery and National Identity in England and the United States* (Cambridge: Polity Press, 1993)

de Graauw, Els and Vermeulen, Floris, 'Cities and the politics of immigrant integration: a comparison of Berlin, Amsterdam, New York City, and San Francisco', *Journal of Ethnic and Migration Studies*, 42:6 (2016), 989–1012

de Haas, Hein, Bakewell, Oliver and Kubal, Agnieszka, *The Evolution of Moroccan Migration to the UK* (THEMIS Scoping Study Report, International Migration Institute, University of Oxford, January 2011)

de Lima, Philomena, *Needs Not Numbers: An Exploration of Minority Ethnic Communities in Rural Scotland* (London: Commission for Racial Equality/ Community Development Foundation, 2001)

—— 'John O'Groats to Land's End: racial equality in rural Britain?', in Neil Chakraborti and Jon Garland (eds), *Rural Racism* (Cullompton: Willan Publishing, 2004), pp. 36–60

—— "'Let's keep our heads down and maybe the problem will go away": experiences of rural minority ethnic households in Scotland', in Sarah Neal and Julian Agyeman (eds), *The New Countryside? Ethnicity, Nation and Exclusion in Contemporary Rural Britain* (Bristol: The Policy Press, 2006), pp. 73–97

Defoe, Daniel, *A Tour through the Whole Island of Great Britain* (London: Penguin Books, 1986)

Dekker, Rianne, Emilsson, Henrik, Krieger, Bernhard and Scholten, Peter, 'A local dimension of integration policies? A comparative study of Berlin, Malmö, and Rotterdam', *International Migration Review*, 49:3 (2015), 633–58

Delcroix, Catherine, 'Two generations of Muslim women in France: creative parenting, identity and recognition', *Oral History*, 37:2 (2009), 87–94

Department for Communities and Local Government, *Strong and Prosperous Communities: The Local Government White Paper* (London: The Stationery Office [TSO], 2006)

Department of Education and Science, *West Indian Children in Our Schools: A Report from the Committee of Enquiry into the Education of Children from Ethnic Minorities (The Rampton Report)* (London: HMSO, 1981)

—— *Education for All: Report of the Committee of Enquiry into the Education of Children from Minority Groups (The Swann Report)* (London: HMSO, 1985)

Department of Trade and Industry, *Fairness for All: A New Commission for Equality and Human Rights* (London: The Stationery Office, 2004)

Derbyshire, Helen, *Not in Norfolk: Tackling the Invisibility of Racism* (Norwich: Norwich and Norfolk Racial Equality Council, 1994)

Devon County Council, *Devon County Council Race Equality Scheme*, May 2002–5

Dhalech, Mohammed, *Challenging Racism in the Rural Idyll* (Exeter: National Association of Citizens Advice Bureaux, 1999)

Dhillon, Perminder, 'Rethinking rural race equality: early interventions, continuities and changes', in Sarah Neal and Julian Agyeman (eds), *The New Countryside? Ethnicity, Nation and Exclusion in Contemporary Rural Britain* (Bristol: The Policy Press, 2006), pp. 217–38

Doran, Rose and Keating, Michael, 'Social cohesion in the local delivery context: understanding equality and the importance of local knowledge', in Peter Ratcliffe and Ines Newman (eds), *Promoting Social Cohesion: Implications for Policy and Evaluation* (Bristol: The Policy Press, 2011), pp. 141–59

Eade, John, 'Identity, nation and religion: educated young Bangladeshi Muslims in London's "East End"', *International Sociology*, 9:3 (1994), 377–94

—— 'Nationalism, community, and the Islamization of space in London', in Barbara Daly Metcalf (ed.), *Making Muslim Space in North America and Europe* (London: University of California Press, 1996), pp. 217–33

Eade, John and Garbin, David, 'Competing visions of identity and space: Bangladeshi Muslims in Britain', *Contemporary South Asia*, 15:2 (2006), 181–93

Eckardt, Frank and Eade, John (eds), *The Ethnically Diverse City* (Berlin: Berliner Wissenschafts-Verlag, 2011)

El-Solh, Camillia Fawzi, 'Arab communities in Britain: cleavages and commonalities', *Islam and Christian-Muslim Relations*, 3:2 (1992), 236–58

Ennaji, Moha, *Muslim Moroccan Migrants in Europe: Transnational Migration in its Multiplicity* (New York: Palgrave Macmillan, 2014)

Esposito, John L., *The Islamic Threat: Myth or Reality* (Oxford: Oxford University Press, 1999)

Esposito, John L. and Kalin, Ibrahim (eds), *Islamophobia: The Challenge of Pluralism in the 21st Century* (Oxford: Oxford University Press, 2011)

Falkenhayner, Nicole, *Making the British Muslim: Representations of the Rushdie Affair and Figures of the War-on-Terror Decade* (Basingstoke: Palgrave Macmillan, 2014)

Favell, Adrian, *Philosophies of Integration: Immigration and the Idea of Citizenship in France and Britain* (Basingstoke: Macmillan Press, 1998)

Fazakarley, Jed, *Muslim Communities in England 1962–90: Multiculturalism and Political Identity* (Cham: Palgrave Macmillan, 2017)

Fetzer, Joel S. and Soper, J. Christopher, *Muslims and the State in Britain, France, and Germany* (Cambridge: Cambridge University Press, 2005)

Findlay, Allan and McCollum, David, 'Recruitment and employment regimes: migrant labour channels in the UK's rural agribusiness sector, from accession to recession', *Journal of Rural Studies*, 30 (2013), 10–19

Finney, Nissa and Simpson, Ludi, *'Sleepwalking to Segregation'? Challenging Myths about Race and Migration* (Bristol: The Policy Press, 2009)

Foner, Nancy, Rath, Jan, Duyvendak, Jan Willem and van Reekum, Rogier (eds), *New York and Amsterdam: Immigration and the New Urban Landscape* (New York: New York University Press, 2014)

Fourot, Aude-Claire, 'Managing religious pluralism in Canadian cities: mosques in Montreal and Laval', in Tiziana Caponio and Maren Borkert (eds), *The Local Dimension of Migration Policymaking* (Amsterdam: Amsterdam University Press, 2010), pp. 135–59

Franceschelli, Michela, *Identity and Upbringing in South Asian Muslim Families: Insights from Young People and their Parents in Britain* (London: Palgrave Macmillan, 2016)

Gale, Richard, 'The multicultural city and the politics of religious architecture: urban planning, mosques and meaning-making in Birmingham, UK', *Built Environment*, 30:1 (2004), 30–44

—— 'Representing the city: mosques and the planning process in Birmingham', *Journal of Ethnic and Migration Studies*, 31:6 (2005), 1161–79

Gale, Richard and Hopkins, Peter, 'Introduction: Muslims in Britain – race, place and the spatiality of identities', in Peter Hopkins and Richard Gale (eds), *Muslims in Britain: Race, Place and Identities* (Edinburgh: Edinburgh University Press, 2009), pp. 1–20

—— and Naylor, Simon, 'Religion, planning and the city: the spatial politics of ethnic minority expression in British cities and towns', *Ethnicities*, 2:3 (2002), 387–409

Gallent, Nick, Hamiduddin, Iqbal, Juntti, Meri, Kidd, Sue and Shaw, Dave, *Introduction to Rural Planning: Economies, Communities and Landscapes* (Abingdon: Routledge, 2015)

Garbaye, Romain, 'British cities and ethnic minorities in the post-war era: from xenophobic agitation to multi-ethnic government', in Ahmed Al-Shahi and Richard Lawless (eds), *Middle East and North African Immigrants in Europe* (Abingdon: Routledge, 2005), pp. 200–17

—— *Getting into Local Power: The Politics of Ethnic Minorities in British and French Cities* (Oxford: Blackwell Publishing, 2005)

Garcés-Mascareñas, Blanca and Penninx, Rinus (eds), *Integration Processes and Policies in Europe: Contexts, Levels and Actors* (Dordrecht: Springer, 2016)

Gardner, Katy, 'Narrating location: space, age and gender among Bengali elders in East London', *Oral History*, 27:1 (1999), 65–74

—— *Age, Narrative and Migration: The Life Course and Life Histories of Bengali Elders in London* (Oxford: Berg, 2002)

—— 'Keeping connected: security, place, and social capital in a "Londoni" village in Sylhet', *The Journal of the Royal Anthropological Institute*, 14:3 (2008), 477–95

Garland, Jon and Chakraborti, Neil, 'Racist victimisation, community safety and the rural: issues and challenges', *British Journal of Community Justice*, 2:3 (2004), 21–32

—— and Chakraborti, Neil, '"Race", space and place: examining identity and cultures of exclusion in rural England', *Ethnicities*, 6:2 (2006), 159–77

Geddes, Andrew, *The Politics of Migration and Immigration in Europe* (London: SAGE, 2003)

Gillborn, David, 'Anti-racism: from policy to praxis', in Ben-Miriam Peretz, Sally Brown and Bob Moon (eds), *Routledge International Companion to Education* (London: Routledge, 2000), pp. 476–88

—— *Racism and Education: Coincidence or Conspiracy?* (Abingdon: Routledge, 2008)

Gilliat-Ray, Sophie, *Muslims in Britain: An Introduction* (Cambridge: Cambridge University Press, 2010)

Glick Schiller, Nina and Çağlar, Ayşe, 'Towards a comparative theory of locality in migration studies: migrant incorporation and city scale', *Journal of Ethnic and Migration Studies*, 35:2 (2009), 177–202

—— and Çağlar, Ayşe (eds), *Locating Migration: Rescaling Cities and Migrants* (Ithaca, NY: Cornell University Press, 2011)

Glynn, Sarah, *Class, Ethnicity and Religion in the Bengali East End: A Political History* (Manchester: Manchester University Press, 2014)

Gould, William, 'Diasporic cities in Britain: Bradford, Manchester, Leicester, London', in Joya Chatterji and David Washbrook (eds), *Routledge Handbook of the South Asian Diaspora* (Abingdon: Routledge, 2013), pp. 339–49

Grosvenor, Ian, *Assimilating Identities: Racism and Educational Policy in Post 1945 Britain* (London: Lawrence & Wishart, 1997)

Hackett, Sarah, *Foreigners, Minorities and Integration: The Muslim Immigrant Experience in Britain and Germany* (Manchester: Manchester University Press, 2013)

—— 'Turkish Muslims in a German city: entrepreneurial and residential self-determination', *Migration Letters*, 12:1 (2015), 1–12

—— 'The "local turn" in historical perspective: two city case studies in Britain and Germany', *International Review of Administrative Sciences*, 83:2 (2017), 340–57

Hainsworth, Paul (ed.), *Divided Society: Ethnic Minorities and Racism in Northern Ireland* (London: Pluto Press, 1998)

Hammerton, A. James and Thomson, Alistair, '*Ten Pound Poms*': *Australia's Invisible Migrants* (Manchester: Manchester University Press, 2005)

Hampshire, James, *Citizenship and Belonging: Immigration and the Politics of Demographic Governance in Postwar Britain* (Basingstoke: Palgrave Macmillan, 2005)

Hansen, Randall, *Citizenship and Immigration in Post-war Britain: The Institutional Origins of a Multicultural Nation* (Oxford: Oxford University Press, 2000)

Haq, Muhibul, 'South Asian ethnic minority small and medium enterprises in the UK: a review and research agenda', *International Journal of Entrepreneurship and Small Business*, 25:4 (2015), 494–516

Harloe, Michael, *Swindon: A Town in Transition. A Study in Urban Development and Overspill Policy* (London: Heinemann, 1975)

Harrison, Grace and Clifford, Ben, '"The field of grain is gone; it's now a Tesco superstore": representations of "urban" and "rural" within historical and contemporary discourses opposing urban expansion in England', *Planning Perspectives*, 31:4 (2016), 585–609

Heath, Anthony and Demireva, Neli, 'Has multiculturalism failed in Britain?', *Ethnic and Racial Studies*, 37:1 (2014), 161–80

Heath, Anthony, Fisher, Stephen, Rosenblatt, Gemma, Sanders, David and Sobolewska, Maria, *The Political Integration of Ethnic Minorities in Britain* (Oxford: Oxford University Press, 2013)

Henderson, Paul and Kaur, Ranjit (eds), *Rural Racism in the UK: Examples of Community-based Responses* (London: Community Development Foundation, 1999)

Herbert, Joanna, 'Migration, memory and metaphor: life stories of South Asians in Leicester', in Kathy Burrell and Panikos Panayi (eds), *Histories and Memories: Migrants and Their History in Britain* (London: I.B. Tauris, 2006), pp. 133–48

—— *Negotiating Boundaries in the City: Migration, Ethnicity, and Gender in Britain* (Aldershot: Ashgate, 2008)

—— 'Oral histories of Ugandan Asians in Britain: gendered identities in the diaspora', *Contemporary South Asia*, 17:1 (2009), 21–32

—— 'Negotiating boundaries and the cross-cultural oral history interview', in Richard Rodger and Joanna Herbert (eds), *Testimonies of the City: Identity, Community and Change in a Contemporary Urban World* (Abingdon: Routledge, 2016), pp. 251–67

Hewitt, Roger, *White Backlash and the Politics of Multiculturalism* (Cambridge: Cambridge University Press, 2005)

Hinze, Annika Marlen, *Turkish Berlin: Integration Policy & Urban Space* (Minneapolis, MN: University of Minnesota Press, 2013)

Holmes, Colin, *John Bull's Island: Immigration and British Society, 1871–1971* (Basingstoke: Macmillan, 1988)

Home Office, *Improving Opportunity, Strengthening Society. The Government's Strategy to Increase Race Equality and Community Cohesion* (London, 2005)

Home Office and Vantagepoint, *Community Cohesion Pathfinder Programme: The First Six Months* (London: Vantagepoint/Home Office, 2003)

Hopkins, Peter, 'Muslims in the West: deconstructing geographical binaries', in Richard Phillips (ed.), *Muslim Spaces of Hope: Geographies of Possibility in Britain and the West* (London: Zed, 2009), pp. 27–40

Hopkins, Peter (ed.), *Scotland's Muslims: Society, Politics and Identity* (Edinburgh: Edinburgh University Press, 2017)

—— and Gale, Richard (eds), *Muslims in Britain: Race, Place and Identities* (Edinburgh: Edinburgh University Press, 2009)

Horton, John, 'Producing Postman Pat: the popular cultural construction of idyllic rurality', *Journal of Rural Studies*, 24:4 (2008), 389–98

Hubbard, Phil, '"Inappropriate and incongruous": opposition to asylum centres in the English countryside', *Journal of Rural Studies*, 21:1 (2005), 3–17

Hudson, Kenneth, *An Awkward Size for a Town: A Study of Swindon at the 100,000 Mark* (Newton Abbot: David & Charles, 1967)

Husband, Charles and Alam, Yunis, *Social Cohesion and Counter-terrorism: A Policy Contradiction?* (Bristol: The Policy Press, 2011)

Husband, Charles, Alam, Yunis, Hüttermann, Jörg and Fomina, Joanna, *Lived Diversities: Space, Place and Identities in the Multi-Ethnic City* (Bristol: The Policy Press, 2016)

Hussain, Asifa and Ishaq, Mohammed, 'Managing race equality in Scottish local councils in the aftermath of the Race Relations (Amendment) Act 2000', *International Journal of Public Sector Management*, 21:6 (2008), 586–610

Hussain, Serena, *Muslims on the Map: A National Survey of Social Trends in Britain* (London: I.B. Tauris, 2008)

Ireland, Patrick, *Becoming Europe: Immigration, Integration, and the Welfare State* (Pittsburgh, PA: University of Pittsburgh Press, 2004)

Ivanescu, Carolina, 'Leicester Muslims: citizenship, race and civil religion', in Jørgen S. Nielsen (ed.), *Muslim Political Participation in Europe* (Edinburgh: Edinburgh University Press, 2013), pp. 277–96

Jacobson, Jessica, *Islam in Transition: Religion and Identity among British Pakistani Youth* (London: Routledge, 1998)

Jay, Eric, *'Keep Them in Birmingham': Challenging Racism in South-West England* (London: Commission for Racial Equality, 1992)

Jenkins, Stanley C. and Long, Angela, *Marlborough & Around through Time* (Stroud: Amberley Publishing, 2015)

Jentsch, Birgit and Simard, Myriam (eds), *International Migration and Rural Areas: Cross-National Comparative Perspectives* (Abingdon: Routledge, 2009)

Joly, Danièle, *Making a Place for Islam in British Society: Muslims in Birmingham*, Research Papers in Ethnic Relations No. 4 (University of Warwick: Centre for Research in Ethnic Relations, 1987)

Joly, Danièle, *Britannia's Crescent: Making a Place for Muslims in British Society* (Aldershot: Avebury, 1995)

Jones, Hannah, '"The best borough in the country for cohesion!": managing place and multiculture in local government', *Ethnic and Racial Studies*, 37:4 (2014), 605–20

Jones, Rhys Dafydd, 'Islam and the rural landscape: discourses of absence in West Wales', *Social & Cultural Geography*, 11:8 (2010), 751–68

—— 'Negotiating absence and presence: rural Muslims and "subterranean" sacred spaces', *Space and Polity*, 16:3 (2012), 335–50

Jones, Trevor, Ram, Monder and Edwards, Paul, 'Ethnic minority business and the employment of illegal immigrants', *Entrepreneurship & Regional Development*, 18:2 (2006), 133–50

Joppke, Christian, *Immigration and the Nation-State: The United States, Germany, and Great Britain* (Oxford: Oxford University Press, 1999)

—— *Is Multiculturalism Dead? Crisis and Persistence in the Constitutional State* (Cambridge: Polity Press, 2017)

Joppke, Christian and Seidle, F. Leslie (eds), *Immigrant Integration in Federal Countries* (Montreal: McGill-Queen's University Press, 2012)

Julios, Christina, *Contemporary British Identity: English Language, Migrants and Public Discourse* (Aldershot: Ashgate, 2008)

Kabir, Nahid Afrose, *Young British Muslims: Identity, Culture, Politics and the Media* (Edinburgh: Edinburgh University Press, 2010)

Kalka, Iris, 'Striking a bargain: political radicalism in a middle-class London borough', in Pnina Werbner and Muhammad Anwar (eds), *Black and Ethnic Leaderships: The Cultural Dimensions of Political Action* (London: Routledge, 1991), pp. 139–53

Karan, Olgu, *Economic Survival Strategies of Turkish Migrants in London* (London: Transnational Press, 2017)

Karn, Valerie, Dale, Angela and Ratcliffe, Peter, 'Introduction: using the 1991 Census to study ethnicity', in Valerie Karn (ed.), *Ethnicity in the 1991 Census. Volume Four: Employment, Education and Housing among the Ethnic Minority Populations of Britain* (London: The Stationery Office, 1997), pp. xi–xxix

Karn, Valerie and Phillips, Deborah, 'Race and ethnicity in housing: a diversity of experience', in Tessa Blackstone, Bhikhu Parekh and Peter Sanders (eds), *Race Relations in Britain: A Developing Agenda* (London: Routledge, 1998), pp. 128–57

Kaye, Ronald, 'The politics of religious slaughter of animals: strategies for ethno-religious political action', *New Community*, 19:2 (1993), 235–50

King, Russell, Thomson, Mark, Mai, Nicola and Keles, Yilmaz, '"Turks" in London: shades of invisibility and the shifting relevance of policy in the migration process', Sussex Centre for Migration Research, Working Paper No. 51 (September 2008)

Kirp, David L., 'The vagaries of discrimination: busing, policy, and law in Britain', *The School Review*, 87:3 (1979), 269–94

Kitching, John, Smallbone, David and Athayde, Rosemary, 'Ethnic diasporas and business competitiveness: minority-owned enterprises in London', *Journal of Ethnic and Migration Studies*, 35:4 (2009), 689–705

Kordel, Stefan, Weidinger, Tobias and Jelen, Igor (eds), *Processes of Immigration in Rural Europe: The Status Quo, Implications and Development Strategies* (Newcastle upon Tyne: Cambridge Scholars Publishing, 2018)

Kushner, Tony and Knox, Katharine, *Refugees in an Age of Genocide: Global, National and Local Perspectives during the Twentieth Century* (London: Frank Cass, 1999)

Lancashire County Council, *Equality, Cohesion and Integration Strategy 2014–2017* (Preston, 2014)

Laurence, Jonathan, *The Emancipation of Europe's Muslims: The State's Role in Minority Integration* (Princeton, NJ: Princeton University Press, 2012)

Laurence, Jonathan and Vaisse, Justin, *Integrating Islam: Political and Religious Challenges in Contemporary France* (Washington, D.C.: Brookings Institution Press, 2006)

Leiken, Robert S., *Europe's Angry Muslims: The Revolt of the Second Generation* (Oxford: Oxford University Press, 2012)

Lewis, Philip, *Islamic Britain: Religion, Politics and Identity among British Muslims* (London: I.B. Tauris, 1994)

—— 'The Bradford Council for Mosques and the search for Muslim unity', in Steven Vertovec and Ceri Peach (eds), *Islam in Europe: The Politics of Religion and Community* (Basingstoke: Macmillan, 1997), pp. 103–28

Lewis, Philip and Hamid, Sadek, *British Muslims: New Directions in Islamic Thought, Creativity and Activism* (Edinburgh: Edinburgh University Press, 2018)

Little, Jo, 'Gender relations in rural areas: the importance of women's domestic role', *Journal of Rural Studies*, 3:4 (1987), 335–42

Local Government Association, *Guidance on Community Cohesion* (London, 2002)

Lucassen, Leo, *The Immigrant Threat: The Integration of Old and New Migrants in Western Europe since 1850* (Urbana, IL: University of Illinois Press, 2005)

Lucassen, Leo, Feldman, David and Oltmer, Jochen (eds), *Paths of Integration: Migrants in Western Europe (1880–2004)* (Amsterdam: Amsterdam University Press, 2006)

Lucassen, Jan, Lucassen, Leo and Manning, Patrick (eds), *Migration History in World History: Multidisciplinary Approaches* (Leiden: Brill, 2010)

Macpherson, William, *The Stephen Lawrence Inquiry: Report of an Inquiry by Sir William Macpherson of Cluny* (London: Home Office, 1999)

McAndrew, Siobhan and Voas, David, 'Immigrant generation, religiosity and civic engagement in Britain', *Ethnic and Racial Studies*, 37:1 (2014), 99–119

McAreavey, Ruth, *New Immigration Destinations: Migrating to Rural and Peripheral Areas* (Abingdon: Routledge, 2017)

McDowell, Linda, *Migrant Women's Voices: Talking About Life and Work in the UK since 1945* (London: Bloomsbury, 2016)

McGhee, Derek, 'Moving to "our" common ground – a critical examination of community cohesion discourse in twenty-first century Britain', *The Sociological Review*, 51:3 (2003), 376–404

—— *The End of Multiculturalism? Terrorism, Integration and Human Rights* (Maidenhead: Open University Press, 2008)

McKenzie, Janet, *Changing Education: A Sociology of Education since 1944* (Abingdon: Routledge, 2014)

McKibben, Carol Lynn, *Beyond Cannery Row: Sicilian Women, Immigration, and Community in Monterey, California, 1915–99* (Urbana, IL: University of Illinois Press, 2006)

McKirdy, Carol, *Practicing Oral History with Immigrant Narrators* (Abingdon: Routledge, 2016)

McLoughlin, Seán, 'Mosques and the public space: conflict and cooperation in Bradford', *Journal of Ethnic and Migration Studies*, 31:6 (2005), 1045–66

McLoughlin, Seán, 'Discrepant representations of multi-Asian Leicester: institutional discourse and everyday life in the "model" multicultural city', in Seán McLoughlin, William Gould, Ananya Jahanara Kabir and Emma Tomalin (eds), *Writing the City in British Asian Diasporas* (Abingdon: Routledge, 2014), pp. 89–113

McLoughlin, Seán, Gould, William, Kabir, Ananya Jahanara and Tomalin, Emma (eds), *Writing the City in British Asian Diasporas* (Abingdon: Routledge, 2014)

Massey, Douglas (ed.), *New Faces in New Places: The Changing Geography of American Immigration* (New York: Russell Sage Foundation, 2008)

Matthews, Hugh, Taylor, Mark, Sherwood, Kenneth, Tucker, Faith and Limb, Melanie, 'Growing-up in the countryside: children and the rural idyll', *Journal of Rural Studies*, 16:2 (2000), 141–53

Maxwell, Rahsaan, *Ethnic Minority Migrants in Britain and France: Integration Trade-Offs* (Cambridge: Cambridge University Press, 2012)

Meek, Rosie, 'Young people, social exclusion and inter-generational tension in a rural Somerset town', *Children & Society*, 22:2 (2008), 124–35

Meer, Nasar, *Citizenship, Identity and the Politics of Multiculturalism: The Rise of Muslim Consciousness* (Basingstoke: Palgrave Macmillan, 2010)

Meer, Nasar and Modood, Tariq, 'Refutations of racism in the "Muslim question"', *Patterns of Prejudice*, 43:3–4 (2009), 335–54

Mellor, Jody and Gilliat-Ray, Sophie, 'The early history of migration and settlement of Yemenis in Cardiff, 1939–1970: religion and ethnicity as social capital', *Ethnic and Racial Studies*, 38:1 (2015), 176–91

Merton Council, *The Stephen Lawrence Inquiry – Merton Council's Response to the Macpherson Report* (October 2000)

Messina, Anthony M., *Race and Party Competition in Britain* (Oxford: Clarendon, 1989)

Milbourne, Paul, 'The local geographies of poverty: a rural case-study', *Geoforum*, 35:5 (2004), 559–75

Modood, Tariq, 'British Asian Muslims and the Rushdie Affair', *The Political Quarterly*, 61:2 (1990), pp. 143–60

—— *Multicultural Politics: Racism, Ethnicity and Muslims in Britain* (Edinburgh: Edinburgh University Press, 2005)

—— 'British Muslims and the politics of multiculturalism', in Tariq Modood, Anna Triandafyllidou and Ricard Zapata-Barrero (eds), *Multiculturalism, Muslims and Citizenship: A European Approach* (Abingdon: Routledge, 2006), pp. 37–56

—— *Multiculturalism: A Civic Idea* (Cambridge: Polity, 2007)

Moore, Helen, 'Shades of whiteness? English villagers, Eastern European migrants and the intersection of race and class in rural England', *Critical Race and Whiteness Studies*, 9:1 (2013), 1–19

Morén-Alegret, Ricard, 'Ruralphilia and urbophobia versus urbophilia and ruralphobia? Lessons from immigrant integration processes in small towns and rural areas in Spain', *Population, Space and Place*, 14:6 (2008), 537–52

Mukadam, Anjoom and Mawani, Sharmina, 'Excess baggage or precious gems? The migration of cultural commodities', in Peter Hopkins and Richard Gale (eds), *Muslims in Britain: Race, Place and Identities* (Edinburgh: Edinburgh University Press, 2009), pp. 150–68

Muslim Council of Britain, *British Muslims in Numbers: A Demographic, Socio-economic and Health Profile of Muslims in Britain Drawing on the 2011 Census* (London, 2015)

Myers, Kevin and Grosvenor, Ian, 'Policy, equality and inequality: from the past to the future', in Dave Hill and Mike Cole (eds), *Schooling and Equality: Fact, Concept and Policy* (Abingdon: Routledge, 2004), pp. 249–64

Nagel, Caroline, 'Constructing difference and sameness: the politics of assimilation in London's Arab communities', *Ethnic and Racial Studies*, 25:2 (2002), 258–87

Nasser, Noha, 'Expressions of Muslim identity in architecture and urbanism in Birmingham, UK', *Islam and Christian-Muslim Relations*, 16:1 (2005), 61–78

Nayak, Anoop, 'Race, affect, and emotion: young people, racism, and graffiti in the postcolonial English suburbs', *Environment and Planning A: Economy and Space*, 42:10 (2010), 2370–92

Neal, Sarah, 'Rural landscapes, representations and racism: examining multicultural citizenship and policy-making in the English countryside', *Ethnic and Racial Studies*, 25:3 (2002), 442–61

Neal, Sarah and Agyeman, Julian, 'Introduction', in Sarah Neal and Julian Agyeman (eds), *The New Countryside? Ethnicity, Nation and Exclusion in Contemporary Rural Britain* (Bristol: The Policy Press, 2006), pp. 1–17

—— and Agyeman, Julian (eds), *The New Countryside? Ethnicity, Nation and Exclusion in Contemporary Rural Britain* (Bristol: The Policy Press, 2006)

—— and Walters, Sue, 'Strangers asking strange questions? A methodological narrative of researching belonging and identity in English rural communities', *Journal of Rural Studies*, 22:2 (2006), 177–89

Nielsen, Jørgen S. and Otterbeck, Jonas, *Muslims in Western Europe* (Edinburgh: Edinburgh University Press, 2016)

Nizhar, Parveen, *No Problem? Race Issues in Shropshire* (Telford: Race Equality Forum for Telford and Shropshire, 1995)

North East Derbyshire District Council Single Equality Scheme (2016–2019)

North Lincolnshire Council, *The Promotion of Race Equality Guidance for Schools* (2004)

OECD Proceedings, *Immigrants, Integration and Cities: Exploring the Links* (Paris, OECD: 1998)

Office for National Statistics, *Religion in England and Wales* (11 December 2012)

Ouseley, Herman, 'Local authority race initiatives', in Martin Boddy and Colin Fudge (eds), *Local Socialism?: Labour Councils and New Left Alternatives* (Basingstoke: Macmillan, 1984), pp. 133–59

Owen, David, 'The demographic characteristics of people from minority ethnic groups in Britain', in David Mason (ed.), *Explaining Ethnic Differences: Changing Patterns of Disadvantage in Britain* (Bristol: The Policy Press, 2003), pp. 21–52

Palmer, David, '"Every morning before you open the door you have to watch for that brown envelope": complexities and challenges of undertaking oral history with Ethiopian forced migrants in London, U.K.', *The Oral History Review*, 37:1 (2010), 35–53

Panayi, Panikos, *Spicing Up Britain: The Multicultural History of British Food* (London: Reaktion Books, 2008)

—— *An Immigration History of Britain: Multicultural Racism since 1800* (Harlow: Longman, 2010)

Parekh, Bhikhu, *Rethinking Multiculturalism: Cultural Diversity and Political Theory* (Basingstoke: Macmillan, 2000)

Paul, Kathleen, *Whitewashing Britain: Race and Citizenship in the Postwar Era* (Ithaca, NY: Cornell University Press, 1997)

Peace, Timothy, 'British Muslims and the anti-war movement', in Timothy Peace (ed.), *Muslims and Political Participation in Britain* (Abingdon: Routledge, 2015), pp. 124–37

Peach, Ceri, 'The Muslim population of Great Britain', *Ethnic and Racial Studies*, 13:3 (1990), 414–19

—— 'South Asian and Caribbean ethnic minority housing choice in Britain', *Urban Studies*, 35:10 (1998), 1657–80

—— 'Muslims in the 2001 Census of England and Wales: gender and economic disadvantage', *Ethnic and Racial Studies*, 29:4 (2006), 629–55

—— 'South Asian migration and settlement in Great Britain, 1951–2001', *Contemporary South Asia*, 15:2 (2006), 133–46

Penninx, Rinus, Kraal, Karen, Martiniello, Marco and Vertovec, Steven (eds), *Citizenship in European Cities: Immigrants, Local Politics and Integration Policies* (Aldershot: Ashgate, 2004)

Peucker, Mario and Akbarzadeh, Shahram, *Muslim Active Citizenship in the West* (Abingdon: Routledge, 2014)

Phalet, Karen, Maliepaard, Mieke, Fleischmann, Fenella and Güngör, Derya, 'The making and unmaking of religious boundaries: comparing Turkish and Moroccan Muslim minorities in European cities', *Comparative Migration Studies*, 1:1 (2013), 123–45

Phillips, Deborah, 'Black minority ethnic concentration, segregation and dispersal in Britain', *Urban Studies*, 35:10 (1998), 1681–702

—— 'Parallel lives? Challenging discourses of British Muslim self-segregation', *Environment and Planning D: Society and Space*, 24:1 (2006), 25–40

—— 'Claiming spaces: British Muslim negotiations of urban citizenship in an era of new migration', *Transactions of the Institute of British Geographers*, 40:1 (2015), 62–74

Phillips, Deborah, Davis, Cathy and Ratcliffe, Peter, 'British Asian narratives of urban space', *Transactions of the Institute of British Geographers*, 32:2 (2007), 217–34

——, Simpson, Ludi and Ahmed, Sameera, 'Shifting geographies of minority ethnic settlement: remaking communities in Oldham and Rochdale', in John Flint and David Robinson (eds), *Community Cohesion in Crisis? New Dimensions of Diversity and Difference* (Bristol: The Policy Press, 2008), pp. 81–97

Phillips, Deborah and Unsworth, Rachael, 'Widening locational choices for minority ethnic groups in the social rented sector', in Peter Somerville and Andy Steele (eds), *'Race', Housing & Social Exclusion* (London: Jessica Kingsley Publishers, 2002), pp. 77–93

Phillips, Richard (ed.), *Muslim Spaces of Hope* (London: Zed Books, 2009)

Philo, Chris, 'Neglected rural geographies: a review', *Journal of Rural Studies*, 8:2 (1992), 193–207

Poole, Elizabeth, *Reporting Islam: Media Representations of British Muslims* (London: I.B. Tauris, 2002)

Poppelaars, Caelesta and Scholten, Peter, 'Two worlds apart: the divergence of national and local immigrant integration policies in the Netherlands', *Administration & Society*, 40:4 (2008), 335–57

Portelli, Alessandro, 'What makes oral history different', in Robert Perks and Alistair Thomson (eds), *The Oral History Reader* (Abingdon: Routledge, 2016), pp. 48–58

Race, Richard, *Multiculturalism and Education* (London: Continuum, 2011)

Rahman, Md Zillur, Ullah, Farid and Thompson, Piers, 'Challenges and issues facing ethnic minority small business owners: the Scottish experience', *The International Journal of Entrepreneurship and Innovation*, 19:3 (2018), 177–93

Ram, Monder, Jones, Trevor, Abbas, Tahir and Sanghera, Balihar, 'Ethnic minority enterprise in its urban context: South Asian restaurants in Birmingham', *International Journal of Urban and Regional Research*, 26:1 (2002), 24–40

——, Sanghera, Balihar, Abbas, Tahir, Barlow, Gerald and Jones, Trevor, 'Ethnic minority business in comparative perspective: the case of the independent restaurant sector', *Journal of Ethnic and Migration Studies*, 26:3 (2000), 495–510

Ram, Monder and Smallbone, David, *Ethnic Minority Enterprise: Policy in Practice* (Small Business Service Report, 2001)

Ratcliffe, Peter, 'From community to social cohesion: interrogating a policy paradigm', in Peter Ratcliffe and Ines Newman (eds), *Promoting Social Cohesion: Implications for Policy and Evaluation* (Bristol: The Policy Press, 2011), pp. 15–39

Ray, Larry and Reed, Kate, 'Community, mobility and racism in a semi-rural area: comparing minority experience in East Kent', *Ethnic and Racial Studies*, 28:2 (2005), 212–34

Rex, John and Moore, Robert, *Race, Community and Conflict: A Study of Sparkbrook* (London: Oxford University Press, 1967)

—— and Tomlinson, Sally, *Colonial Immigrants in a British City: A Class Analysis* (London: Routledge and Kegan Paul, 1979)

Robertson, Emma, "'Green for come": moving to York as a Ugandan Asian refugee', in Panikos Panayi and Pippa Virdee (eds), *Refugees and the End of Empire: Imperial Collapse and Forced Migration in the Twentieth Century* (Basingstoke: Palgrave Macmillan, 2011), pp. 245–67

Robinson, Vaughan, *Transients, Settlers, and Refugees: Asians in Britain* (Oxford: Clarendon, 1986)

—— 'Dispersal policies in the UK', in Vaughan Robinson, Roger Andersson and Sako Musterd (eds), *Spreading the 'Burden'? A Review of Policies to Disperse Asylum Seekers and Refugees* (Bristol: The Policy Press, 2003), pp. 103–48

Robinson, Vaughan and Gardner, Hannah, 'Unravelling a stereotype: the lived experience of black and minority ethnic people in rural Wales', in Neil Chakraborti and Jon Garland (eds), *Rural Racism* (Cullompton: Willan Publishing, 2004), pp. 85–107

Rutter, Jill, *Moving Up and Getting On: Migration, Integration and Social Cohesion in the UK* (Bristol: The Policy Press, 2015)

Saleem, Shahed, *The British Mosque: An Architectural and Social History* (Swindon: Historic England, 2018)

Samad, Yunas, 'Book burning and race relations: political mobilisation of Bradford Muslims', *New Community*, 18:4 (1992), 507–19

Sassen, Saskia, *The Global City: New York, London, Tokyo* (Princeton, NJ: Princeton University Press, 1991)

Schain, Martin, *The Politics of Immigration in France, Britain, and the United States: A Comparative Study* (Basingstoke: Palgrave Macmillan, 2008)

Schiller, Maria, *European Cities, Municipal Organizations and Diversity: The New Politics of Difference* (Basingstoke: Palgrave Macmillan, 2016)

Schofield, Camilla, *Enoch Powell and the Making of Postcolonial Britain* (Cambridge: Cambridge University Press, 2013)

Scholten, Peter, 'The multilevel dynamics of migrant integration policies in unitary states: the Netherlands and the United Kingdom', in Eve Hepburn and Ricard Zapata-Barrero (eds), *The Politics of Immigration in Multi-level States: Governance and Political Parties* (Basingstoke: Palgrave Macmillan, 2014), pp. 150–74

—— 'Between national models and multi-level decoupling: the pursuit of multi-level governance in Dutch and UK policies towards migrant incorporation', *Journal of International Migration and Integration*, 17:4 (2016), 973–94

—— 'Part I – Migration, history and urban life. Introduction by Peter Scholten', in Tiziana Caponio, Peter Scholten and Ricard Zapata-Barrero (eds), *The Routledge Handbook of the Governance of Migration and Diversity in Cities* (Abingdon: Routledge, 2019), pp. 9–11

Scholten, Peter and Penninx, Rinus, 'The multilevel governance of migration and integration', in Blanca Garcés-Mascareñas and Rinus Penninx (eds), *Integration Processes and Policies in Europe: Contexts, Levels and Actors* (Dordrecht: Springer, 2016), pp. 91–108

Schönwälder, Karen, 'Beyond the race relations model: old patterns and new trends in Britain', in Dietrich Thränhardt and Michael Bommes (eds), *National Paradigms of Migration Research* (Göttingen: V&R Unipress, 2010), pp. 109–25

Schrover, Marlou and Schinkel, Willem (eds), *The Language of Inclusion and Exclusion in Immigration and Integration* (Abingdon: Routledge, 2014)

Scourfield, Jonathan, Gilliat-Ray, Sophie, Khan, Asma and Otri, Sameh, *Muslim Childhood: Religious Nurture in a European Context* (Oxford: Oxford University Press, 2013)

Shaw, Alison, 'The Pakistani community in Oxford', in Roger Ballard (ed.), *Desh Pardesh: The South Asian Presence in Britain* (London: Hurst, 1994), pp. 35–57

—— *Kinship and Continuity: Pakistani Families in Britain* (Amsterdam: Harwood Academic, 2000)

Shore, Zachary, *Breeding Bin Ladens: America, Islam, and the Future of Europe* (Baltimore, MD: John Hopkins University Press, 2006)

Short, Brian, 'Idyllic ruralities', in Paul Cloke, Terry Marsden and Patrick Mooney (eds), *The Handbook of Rural Studies* (London: SAGE, 2006), pp. 133–48

Shucksmith, Mark, 'Re-imagining the rural: from rural idyll to Good Countryside', *Journal of Rural Studies*, 59 (2018), 163–72

Singh, Gurharpal, 'Multiculturalism in contemporary Britain: reflections on the "Leicester model"', *International Journal on Multicultural Societies*, 5:1 (2003), 40–54

Sirkeci, Ibrahim, 'Transnational döner kebab taking over the UK', *Transnational Marketing Journal*, 4:2 (2016), 143–58

Sirkeci, Ibrahim, Bilecen, Tuncay, *et al.*, *Little Turkey in Great Britain* (London: Transnational Press London, 2016)

—— , Şeker, Betül Dilara and Çağlar, Ali (eds), *Turkish Migration, Identity and Integration* (London: Transnational Press, 2015)

Skellington, Richard, *'Race' in Britain Today* (London: SAGE, 1996)

Slyomovics, Susan, 'The Muslim World Day parade and "storefront" mosques of New York City', in Barbara Daly Metcalf (ed.), *Making Muslim Space in North America and Europe* (Berkeley, CA: University of California Press, 1996), pp. 204–16

Solomos, John, *Race and Racism in Contemporary Britain* (Basingstoke: Macmillan, 1989)

—— *Race and Racism in Britain* (Basingstoke: Palgrave Macmillan, 2003)

Solomos, John and Singh, Gurharpal, 'Racial equality, housing and the local state', in Wendy Ball and John Solomos (eds), *Race and Local Politics* (Basingstoke: Macmillan, 1990), pp. 95–114

South West Trades Union Congress, *Who Makes Up the South West? The Facts Around the Region's Population and Migration* (Bristol, undated report)

Soysal, Yasemin Nuhoğlu, *Limits of Citizenship: Migrants and Postnational Membership in Europe* (Chicago: University of Chicago Press, 1994)

Spencer, Ian R.G., *British Immigration Policy since 1939: The Making of Multi-Racial Britain* (London: Routledge, 1997)

Strüder, Inge, 'Self-employed Turkish-speaking women in London: opportunities and constraints within and beyond the ethnic economy', *The International Journal of Entrepreneurship and Innovation*, 4:3 (2003), 185–95

Swindon Borough Council, *Swindon Population by Equality Groups* (undated)

—— *Equality Policy* (Cabinet, 14 April 2010)

—— *Swindon Local Transport Plan 3: 2011–2026* (April 2011)

—— *Equality Duty Publication Report* (January 2015)

Swindon Joint Strategic Needs Assessment, *Census 2011 Profile Number One. Population Overview of Swindon* (July 2014)

Swindon Wiltshire Local Enterprise Partnership, *Swindon and Wiltshire Economic Assessment 2016. Chapter 1: Executive Summary* (May 2016)

Tatari, Eren, *Muslims in British Local Government: Representing Minority Interests in Hackney, Newham, and Tower Hamlets* (Leiden: Brill, 2014)

Thamesdown and District Community Relations Council, *Mortgage Bar in Swindon* (March 1978)

—— *Black Apprentices in Thamesdown* (April 1978)

—— *Equal Opportunity – A Survey of Local Firms* (May 1978)

Thamesdown and District Council for Racial Equality, *Annual Report: 1982–83* (Swindon, 1983)

The Equalities Review, *Fairness and Freedom: The Final Report of the Equalities Review* (London: Equalities Review, 2007)

Thirsk, Joan, *The Rural Economy of England* (London: The Hambledon Press, 1984)

Thirsk, Joan (ed.), *Rural England: An Illustrated History of the Landscape* (Oxford: Oxford University Press, 2000)

Thomas, Paul, *Youth, Multiculturalism and Community Cohesion* (Basingstoke: Palgrave Macmillan, 2011)

—— *Responding to the Threat of Violent Extremism: Failing to Prevent* (London: Bloomsbury, 2012)

Thompson, Paul with Bornat, Joanna, *The Voice of the Past: Oral History* (Oxford: Oxford University Press, 2017)

Thomson, Alistair, 'Moving stories: oral history and migration studies', *Oral History*, 27:1 (1999), 24–37

—— 'Moving stories, women's lives: sharing authority in oral history', *Oral History*, 39:2 (2011), 73–82

Tierney, John (ed.), *Race, Migration and Schooling* (Eastbourne: Holt, Rinehart & Winston Ltd, 1982)

Tomlinson, Sally, *Ethnic Minorities in British Schools: A Review of the Literature, 1960–82* (London: Heinemann, 1983)

—— 'Race, ethnicity and education under New Labour', *Oxford Review of Education*, 31:1 (2005), 153–71

—— *Race and Education: Policy and Politics in Britain* (Maidenhead: McGraw-Hill Open University Press, 2008)

Tower Hamlets Overview and Scrutiny Committee, *A More Cohesive Borough: A Scrutiny Challenge Report* (June 2017)

Troyna, Barry and Williams, Jenny, *Racism, Education and the State* (Abingdon: Routledge, 1986)

Tyler, Katharine, 'Debating the rural and the urban: majority white racialized discourses on the countryside and the city', in Bo Petersson and Katharine Tyler (eds), *Majority Cultures and the Everyday Politics of Ethnic Difference: Whose House is This?* (Basingstoke: Palgrave Macmillan, 2008), pp. 75–93

—— 'The English village, whiteness, coloniality and social class', *Ethnicities*, 12:4 (2012), 427–44

Uberoi, Varun and Modood, Tariq, 'Has multiculturalism in Britain retreated?', *Soundings*, 53 (2013), 129–42

Valentine, Gill, 'A safe place to grow up? Parenting, perceptions of children's safety and the rural idyll', *Journal of Rural Studies*, 13:2 (1997), 137–48

Verma, Gajendra (ed.), *Education for All: A Landmark in Pluralism* (London: The Falmer Press, 1989)

Verma, Gajendra, 'Cultural diversity in primary schools: its nature, extent and cross-curricular implications', in Gajendra Verma and Peter Pumfrey (eds), *Cross Curricular Contexts, Themes and Dimensions in Primary Schools* (London: The Falmer Press, 1994), pp. 3–17

Verma, Gajendra, Zec, Paul and Skinner, George, *The Ethnic Crucible: Harmony and Hostility in Multi-Ethnic Schools* (Abingdon: Routledge, 2012)

Vertovec, Steven, 'Multiculturalism, culturalism and public incorporation', *Ethnic and Racial Studies*, 19:1 (1996), 49–69

—— 'Towards post-multiculturalism? Changing communities, conditions and contexts of diversity', *International Social Science Journal*, 61:199 (2010), 83–95

Vertovec, Steven and Wessendorf, Susanne (eds), *The Multiculturalism Backlash: European Discourses, Policies and Practices* (London: Routledge, 2010)

Villis, Tom and Hebing, Mireille, 'Islam and Englishness: issues of culture and identity in the debates over mosque building in Cambridge', *Nationalism and Ethnic Politics*, 20:4 (2014), 415–37

Virdee, Satnam, 'Racial harassment', in Tariq Modood, Richard Berthoud, Jane Lakey, James Nazroo, Patten Smith, Satnam Virdee and Sharon Beishon (eds), *Ethnic Minorities in Britain: Diversity and Disadvantage* (London: Policy Studies Institute, 1997), pp. 259–89

Visram, Rozina, *Asians in Britain: 400 Years of History* (London: Pluto Press, 2002)

Wallis, Steve, *Wiltshire through Time* (Stroud: Amberley Publishing, 2013)

Wallwork, Jodi and Dixon, John A., 'Foxes, green fields and Britishness: on the rhetorical construction of place and national identity', *British Journal of Social Psychology*, 43:1 (2004), 21–39

Warmington, Paul, Gillborn, David, Rollock, Nicola and Demack, Sean, '"They can't handle the race agenda": stakeholders' reflections on race and education policy, 1993–2013', *Educational Review*, 70:4 (2018), 409–26

Werbner, Pnina, 'From rags to riches: Manchester Pakistanis in the textile trade', *New Community*, 8:1–2 (1980), 84–95

—— 'Renewing an industrial past: British Pakistani entrepreneurship in Manchester', in Judith M. Brown and Rosemary Foot (eds), *Migration: The Asian Experience* (Basingstoke: Palgrave Macmillan, 1994), pp. 104–30

—— 'Fun spaces: on identity and social empowerment among British Pakistanis', *Theory, Culture & Society*, 13:4 (1996), 53–79

—— *Imagined Diasporas among Manchester Muslims: The Public Performance of Pakistani Transnational Identity Politics* (Oxford: James Currey, 2002)

Wetherell, Margaret, Laflèche, Michelynn and Berkeley, Robert (eds), *Identity, Ethnic Diversity and Community Cohesion* (London: SAGE, 2007)

Williams, Charlotte, 'Revisiting the rural/race debates: a view from the Welsh countryside', *Ethnic and Racial Studies*, 30:5 (2007), 741–65

Williams, Charlotte and Johnson, Mark R.D., *Race and Ethnicity in a Welfare Society* (Maidenhead: Open University Press, 2010)

Williams, Raymond, *The Country and the City* (Oxford: Oxford University Press, 1975)

Wiltshire and Swindon Users' Network, *Diverse Communities: A Study of Diverse Communities Living in Wiltshire and their Experiences with Health, Public and Social Care Services* (2013)

Wiltshire Assembly, *People, Places and Promises: The Wiltshire Community Plan 2011–2026* (2011)

Wiltshire Community Foundation, *Wiltshire Uncovered Report 2014* (Devizes, 2014)

Wiltshire Council, *Wiltshire's Diverse Communities: Results from the 2011 Census* (undated report)

—— *Qualitative Consultation with Wiltshire's Minority Ethnic Residents* (2008)

—— *Wiltshire Sustainability Appraisal Scoping Report. Topic Paper Ten: Inclusive Communities* (April 2010)

—— *Equality Matters (for Schools)* (June 2010: No. 3)

—— *Religion and Belief in the Workplace Policy and Procedure* (2011)

—— *Equalities Information and Objectives* (2015)

—— *Wiltshire Core Strategy* (January 2015)

—— 'Wiltshire Part of Pilot Scheme to Help Support Refugees' (22 July 2016)

—— *The Corporate Equality Plan* (January 2017)

Wiltshire Council, Wiltshire Standing Advisory Council on Religious Education (SACRE) Annual Report (September 2016–August 2017)

Wiltshire County Council, *A Summary of the 2001 Census for the County of Wiltshire* (Economic Research and Intelligence Unit, 2006)

Wiltshire County Council and Wiltshire Racial Equality Council, *Hidden Voices: A Study of Wiltshire's Minority Ethnic Residents* (April 2002)

Wiltshire Public Services Board, *Joint Strategic Assessment for Malmesbury Community Area* (2011)

—— *Joint Strategic Assessment for Westbury Community Area* (2011)

Wiltshire Racial Equality Council, *Placement Report in Human Rights* (2012)

Winstone, Paul, 'Managing a multi-ethnic and multicultural city in Europe: Leicester', *International Social Science Journal*, 48:147 (1996), 33–41

Witte, Rob, *Racist Violence and the State: A Comparative Analysis of Britain, France, and the Netherlands* (Abingdon: Routledge, 2014)

Worley, Claire, '"It's not about race. It's about the community": New Labour and "community cohesion"', *Critical Social Policy*, 25:4 (2005), 483–96

Young, Ken, 'The space between words: local authorities and the concept of equal opportunities', in Richard Jenkins and John Solomos (eds), *Racism and Equal*

Opportunity Policies in the 1980s (Cambridge: Cambridge University Press, 1989), pp. 93–109

Young, Ken and Connelly, Naomi, *Policy and Practice in the Multi-racial City* (London: Policy Studies Institute, 1981)

—— and Connelly, Naomi, 'After the Act: local authority policy reviews under the Race Relations Act, 1976', *Local Government Studies*, 10:1 (1984), 13–25

Zapata-Barrero, Ricard, 'Intercultural policy and multi-level governance in Barcelona: mainstreaming comprehensive approach', *International Review of Administrative Sciences*, 83:2 (2017), 247–66

Zapata-Barrero, Ricard, Caponio, Tiziana and Scholten, Peter, 'Theorizing the "local turn" in a multi-level governance framework of analysis: a case study in immigrant policies', *International Review of Administrative Sciences*, 83:2 (2017), 241–6

Index

EU authorised representative for GPSR:
Easy Access System Europe, Mustamäe tee 50,
10621 Tallinn, Estonia
gpsr.requests@easproject.com

www.ingramcontent.com/pod-product-compliance
Lightning Source LLC
Chambersburg PA
CBHW052000270326
41929CB00015B/2724